IMPLEMENTING
VIRTUAL
PRIVATE NETWORKS

Implementing Virtual Private Networks

Steven Brown

McGraw-Hill
New York San Francisco Washington, D.C.
Auckland Bogotá Caracas Lisbon London Madrid
Mexico City Milan Montreal New Delhi San Juan
Singapore Sydney Tokyo Toronto

Library of Congress Cataloging-in-Publication Data
Brown, Steven.
    Implementing virtual private networks / Steven Brown.
        p.   cm.
    ISBN 0-07-135185-X
    1. Extranets (Computer networks)   I. Title.
TK5105.875.E87B76   1999
004.6¢8—dc21   99-14543
                                                        CIP

McGraw-Hill

A Division of The **McGraw·Hill** Companies

    3 4 5 6 7 8 9 0   AGM/AGM   9 0 4 3 2 1 0 9

ISBN 0-07-135185-X

Throughout this book, trademarked names are used. Rather than put a trademark symbol after every occurrence of a trademarked name, we used the names in an editorial fashion only, and to the benefit of the trademark owner, with no intention of infringement of the trademark. Where such designations appear in this book, they have been printed with initial caps.

The sponsoring editor for this book was Simon Yates, the editing supervisor was Scott Amerman, and the production supervisor was Clare Stanley. It was set in New Century Schoolbook by Priscilla Beer of McGraw-Hill's Professional Book Group composition unit in cooperation with Spring Point Publishing Services.

Printed and bound by Quebecor/Martinsburg.

 This book is printed on recycled, acid-free paper containing a minimum of 50% recycled, de-inked fiber.

To my wife Dina,
for no other reason than I love her,
To Michael, for being a second father to me
and to God, for keeping me humble

CONTENTS

Contents

Contents

Contents   **xiii**

PREFACE

Virtual Private Networks (VPNs) are one of those technologies where you don't realize where they came from, but once they are established in a company's infrastructure, you wonder how you ever got any work done without them.

In his landmark work, *Diffusion of Innovations,* Everett M. Rogers, who is considered by many to be the Father of Diffusion Theory, lays out the foundation for the nature of innovation diffusion. Although there have been many great contributors to the field, this work is considered the standard text. In it, Dr. Rogers defines diffusion as follows:

> Diffusion is the process by which an innovation is communicated through certain channels, over time among the members of a social system.

A key word here is *innovation,* described by Rogers as

> an idea, practice, or object that is perceived as new by an individual or other unit of adoption.

It is this notion of being "perceived as new" that gives an innovation new life. An example of this theory can be seen in Phil Zimmermann's Pretty Good Privacy (PGP) encryption method. PGP was available, but thanks to Phil Zimmermann, a leader in encryption technology for many years, it has become widely accepted—even a sort of de facto standard.

Virtual Private Networks are in the same category as PGP. VPN technology is not a new technology, but it is perceived as new. If VPN technology has been around for some time, then why is this technology so hard to understand, design, and implement? The reason for that is the lack of clear information and clear resources to understand all the pieces that fit together that make Virtual Private Networks work.

The main thing to understand about VPN technology is that it is a framework, not an entity unto itself. PGP is the framework for RSA, IDEA, MD5, and random-number generators, as we will see later. VPN is the framework where encryption, authentication, and confidentiality can coexist and operate. Virtual Private Networks allow you to use the Internet as your own private network.

One of the main reasons why this technology is so hard to understand is that it is so diverse. It is difficult enough to understand encryption, let alone authentication services, key sizes, cryptography, and vulnerabilities. That is the main reason for writing this book: to share what's in the literature about VPN technology and, hopefully, to make it concise enough so that, after reading the book, you can look at a product and evaluate its solutions against the criteria you established for your company. With that in mind, I wrote this book to give you a model—an overview of where all the pieces of VPN technology fit together. Hopefully, by following steps I've laid out, by about the middle of the book, you will have a good understanding of how to install VPN technology and know where to look for answers if needed.

Since you will learn about the implementation of VPN technology around the middle of the book, why then is the book longer? Simple. Because of security issues. Security in VPNs is everything. This cannot be stated strongly enough. VPN technology changes the rules when it comes to thinking about your company's security. Security becomes a new model where conventional thinking is no longer valid. As a company, you've spent so much time and so many resources protecting your network from attackers, and you put up some kind of wall—a firewall, for example. With the firewall, it was hoped that your company was protected from attackers who could no longer penetrate your perimeter. With VPNs, you purposely transmit data out into the Internet and hope that no one can alter it. You also open up a hole into your network (e.g., mail traffic) and hope that no one else can enter in through that hole without some sort of proper authorization.

This is the reason the book is somewhat long. Implementing VPNs can be learned relatively quickly, given the fact that you understand basic concepts of networking in general, but understanding VPN security can take a lifetime. You just cannot sit still; you must stay on top of all the developments. That is the objective of Part 3 of this book, to give you a foundation for beginning to think in terms of VPN security. Throughout this book, I will constantly point out where security problems lie and how to increase the security of your VPN and your network in general.

When you finally understand Virtual Private Network technology and then can tackle the implementation and security aspects of it, I throw in a curve ball called the U.S. government. In fact, by the time you get to the end of the book, you may not be so worried by the hackers as by the U.S. government, and basically all governments in general. VPN technologies rely on something called encryption, and encryption, in the eyes of the U.S. and many governments, is considered munitions, or weapons, just like tanks and warplanes. Now governments regulate these munitions/encryption heavily and what that means is that your VPN technology, which relies on encryption for safety, is regulated by the government. Governments don't like people using encryption, since they are not able to read the data. So they outlaw heavy encryption, whereby they can break into it, but so could an attacker. We will examine some of these controversial topics as well.

Intended Audience

While technical in general, this book is written for several different audiences. One is that of the technical consultant and system administrator. For this audience this book will provide a thorough understanding of the different architectures of VPN technology, the different topologies that can be set up, and the actual installations of some very common marketplace products. During the writing of this book, I contacted several vendors who were kind enough to assist me in demonstrating how various VPN technologies are deployed.

The second audience is executives in charge who have to make the decisions of what kind of technology their company should use, considering cost versus benefits, and so forth. Don't be mistaken. VPN technology can cost money as well as save money, depending on what kind of infrastructure you desire. You may have heard of the enormous amounts of money that VPN technology can save. I will show you whether that is true. In a later chapter, I will demonstrate to you how you can easily come up with net savings and net cost of VPN technology.

Plan of the Book

This Virtual Private Network book is written in three parts. It is designed to take you from understanding what VPN technology is, to how to install the technology, to, finally, how to protect the technology. If you wanted to, you could start at any part. For instance, if you are just worried about securing an already existing VPN, you can jump ahead to Part 3, although you should skim the earlier chapters for security notes.

PART 1—The Foundation of VPNs

Part 1 presents the fundamentals of VPN technology: where it came from, where you use the technology, and, finally, what governments have to say about it.

1. *Introduction to VPN Technology.* Chapter 1 discusses where VPN technology came from and what kinds of applications VPN technologies are used in. We will look at the common components of VPN technology and the growth of this new technology.

2. *Network Security for VPNs.* This chapter sets the stage for network security, with regard to VPNs in general. Like all special machines and servers, VPN technology also has its own requirements, particularly concerning security. This is the starting point for talking about VPN security.

3. *Advantages and Disadvantages of VPN Technology.* This chapter highlights some of the benefits of using VPN technology, and some of the disadvantages as well. In addition, this chapter points out the cost savings and additional costs associated with VPN technology. At the end of this chapter, you are given a model to use in evaluating both of these factors.

4. *VPN Architecture.* VPNs come in all sort of colors, flavors, and designs, with all sorts of bells and whistles. As of this writing, several new VPN architectures have recently come to market. A concerted effort was made to include the most common architectures involved.

5. *Topologies of VPNs.* This chapter can be thought of as a continuation of Chapter 4. This chapter shows how, once you have the available architectures, you can place this architecture in a topology setting in your organization.

6. *Government Restrictions on VPN Technology.* This chapter finishes up Part 1 and details the government's involvement with VPN technology. This chapter begins to show why governments even bother regulating encryption and what happens to you if you don't abide by the laws.

PART 2—The VPN Implementation

Part 2 of the book is the next logical step in VPN technology. By this time, you will know the architectures and topologies available, along with some of the requirements. Now we begin to put the pieces together.

7. *The Basics.* This chapter starts off with the starting point of Internet access. The reason I wrote this chapter is that the firewall/VPN architecture is such a common topology, and many can-

not understand all the components involved. I show what you will need to get things rolling.

8. *Installing a VPN, Part I.*   This chapter is where we take what was learned in Chapter 7 and apply it to an actual installation of a very common type of installation, the firewall-based VPN.

9. *Installing a VPN, Part II.*   This chapter is a continuation of Chapter 8. While I am familiar with many VPN topologies, there are just so many implementations available, that any one person could not know them all. Therefore, I contacted several VPN vendors who were kind enough to supply me with information concerning their products.

10. *Troubleshooting VPNs.*   In this chapter, we look at some of the most common VPN problems today, and the ones I am frequently asked to help solve. This chapter will help you to begin to troubleshoot any kind of VPN technology.

11. *Maintaining a VPN.*   In any technology, VPN included, there are also maintenance requirements. Therefore, you need to understand what it is that keeps your VPN up and running.

PART 3—The Security of VPNs

This third part of the book discusses security with VPNs. It starts with what encryption is, how it works, and how it is used. It follows up by outlining what the weaknesses of encryption are, and finally, the other weaknesses that can impact your VPN.

12. *Cryptography.*   This is the starting point of how a plain message gets transformed into a message that is unreadable by the human eye. This chapter discusses the common techniques and algorithms to encode messages.

13. *Encryption.*   This chapter discusses how to use cryptography and encryption together to create a safe, secure environment with VPN technology. This chapter will examine both public- and private-key encryption algorithms.

14. *Secure Communication and Authentication.*   One major component of VPN technology is the ability to verify who is coming into your organization and how to restrict them to only certain resources. This chapter will discuss many of the available authentication services.

15. *VPN Operating System Vulnerabilities.* This chapter begins to move more into how and where an attack can occur. Many VPN products are simply installed on operating systems. Therefore, if the OS isn't secure, the VPN isn't secure. This chapter will look at some of the kinds of operating system vulnerabilities that will make your VPN unsafe.

16. *VPN Security Attacks.* A continuation of Chapter 15, this chapter shows how, once you've secured your internal network, you can protect your VPN data stream as it travels across the Internet. Specifically, the chapter deals with the major VPN protocols and the vulnerabilities in them.

17. *Security Toolbelt.* If an attack does occur, what do you do? This chapter gives you a list of places where you can go for help and find additional information. It also lists the appropriate law authorities where you can report security matters.

18. *Intrusion Detection and Security Logging.* Chapter 18 adds to the security toolbelt, described in Chapter 17, with systems and tools available that will help you to install a secure infrastructure. This chapter gives you more ideas to help with security.

19. *Emerging Technologies for VPNs.* This last chapter points to where VPN technology is heading. Chapter 19 will show you many of the interesting computer technologies on the horizon. It will also detail some of the newest attacks, including governmental attacks.

ACKNOWLEDGMENTS

I am deeply grateful to the Internet community at large. The Internet has allowed for currently developed and new information to be spread far and quickly, with access just a click away on a computer screen. It is the men and women who spread this information who are the real technical geniuses. There are however, some additional personal acknowledgments I would like to make.

First and foremost, I want to acknowledge and thank Simon Yates at McGraw-Hill for all the wonderful help with this book. Until I met Simon, writing this book was extremely time consuming and difficult. Mr. Yates took the time, patience, and guidance to help me develop a first-class manuscript. He allowed me to concentrate on the technical information, while he concentrated on the format and outline of the book. I would highly recommend Simon for any potential author with an idea for a project.

I would also like to acknowledge Todd Ziggefoose ("Rusty"). Rusty is a coworker of mine, who has extensive experience in security matters. He is an authority on firewalls, Virtual Private Networks, and network security. As a founding member and co-chair of the IOPS Network security group, and his involvement in IETF, he has worked extensively with his peers in the industry to develop a standard set of procedures to permit the various Tier 1 Internet Service Providers to work cooperatively in dealing with network security incidents. Rusty may be reached via email at *rusty@pobox.com*.

I would also like to thank Dr. Tom Powers. Tom was a marketing professor of mine at Nova University where I am pursuing my doctorate. It was Tom who showed me the proper way to outline, collect, and analyze information for professional publications and manuscripts. Dr. Powers is an extremely well-written and published author, with easily over 100 articles and books to his credit. It was in one of his lectures that he told us how it took him over four long years to publish one article, and that one reviewer had the audacity to imply he couldn't spell. Every time I wanted to quit writing this book, I thought of him and that reviewer, and kept going. Dr. Powers is a credit to both the teaching profession and Nova University.

IMPLEMENTING
VIRTUAL
PRIVATE NETWORKS

The Foundations of VPNs

CHAPTER 1

Introduction to VPN Technology

This introductory chapter on Virtual Private Networks (VPNs) will look at the definition of a VPN, both from a marketing and managerial point of view, and in terms that a technical person can understand. The remaining chapters of this book will assume that you can understand this definition. At the end of this first chapter, I would not expect you to be able to install a VPN, but hopefully you will understand the definition, along with some of the requirements associated with this technology. We will also look at the components that make up a VPN. *Components* simply refers to the aspects of the VPN technology that you will need to master to successfully install and maintain a VPN.

You may have heard that Virtual Private Networks is a new technology; we will examine if that is true. We will also look at the growth rate and who supports VPNs. The growth rate of VPNs is important in that VPNs will follow the Internet's speed of diffusion (this simply refers to the speed at which users have adopted the Internet). Your organization may not necessarily need a VPN; we will look at a couple of those examples as well. This should lead us into what kind of VPN service your organization needs, a national or international implementation; each one has its own rules to abide by.

This book is written with a bias toward the security of VPNs. As we go through this book, I will attempt to indicate where your organization can implement security measures to protect your VPN. You will see that there are many security issues affecting the safety of your VPN that are both inside and outside of your control.

What Is a VPN?

From a historical perspective the term Virtual Private Networks (VPNs) began making its way in early 1997, but there are those who disagree with this statement, causing some confusion as to the exact date of this technology. While it is true that the underlying technology used in Virtual Private Networks is the TCP/IP suite that was developed in the 1960s, some of the concepts developed date back a lot earlier. In order to explain VPNs, a couple of concepts need to be described: encryption and virtual. While this chapter does not deal with these concepts, if you don't understand what they are, you will not be able to understand the definition of a VPN. This definition is so important, it is the reason this chapter is titled "The Foundations of VPNs."

Encryption is nothing more than taking a message, such as "I'll be late," and converting it into some gibberish, say for example,

"2deR56Gtr2345^hj5Uie04." The other end of the process is called *decryption,* and it's the reverse of encryption, i.e., taking "2deR56Gtr2345^hj5Uie04" and converting it back to "I'll be late." The whole security aspect of Virtual Private Networks is that no one but the intended receiver will be able to accomplish the decryption part of the process. When you hear people mention things like the "security of VPNs" or the "safety of VPNs," this is what they are referring to.

Virtual refers to an "as if" situation. Say you are working on a desktop and call into a mainframe computer. The computer is expecting a certain type of terminal, such as a VT-100. How do you then communicate with the mainframe computer when you are using a desktop and it's expecting a VT-100 terminal? Your computer emulates a VT-100, meaning that your computer (via software) is acting "as if" it were a VT-100, and, therefore, the mainframe never has any idea your computer is not a real VT-100 terminal. Now expand on this and look at a simple telephone call. A person picks up the telephone and dials a number. Once the connection is made, a path is established over a pair of wires to a destination. That call is "locked" for the remainder of that session. If the person puts the telephone down but doesn't hang up, the circuit is still active and the path is still locked. This is referred to as a *virtual* telephone circuit. However, there is one major difference between the virtual circuit in this example and the virtual in VPNs. With the telephone example, no one else is allowed into the conversation, whereas in the case of VPNs it is more like a party line.

Now that we've looked at the concepts of virtual and encryption, we can begin to look at some of the definitions of Virtual Private Networks. Many people believe VPNs are their own private network over someone else's public network. Another commonly used definition is one or more WAN links over a shared public network, typically the Internet or the backbone of some network service provider. My definition of a VPN is as follows:

> An encrypted or encapsulated communication process that transfers data from one point to another point securely; the security of that data is assured by robust encryption technology, and the data that flows passes through an open, unsecured, routed network.

SECURITY NOTE   Keywords To Remember: Encryption / Encapsulation / Securely / Open / Routed

Looking at this definition reveals several things. First, a VPN is an encrypted or encapsulated communication process. All communication that takes place between nodes is encrypted, and it is the encryption process itself that guarantees the safety and integrity of that data. You will also note that the data passes through an open, unsecured, routed network. So, unlike the virtual circuit in the telephone call example, VPN data is passing through a party line, and the data itself can take many paths to its final destination.

Another way of looking at VPNs is that it is the simple process of sending encrypted data from one point to another, usually over the Internet. However, VPNs can also be used on leased lines, frame relay/ATM links, or Plain Old Telephone Network (POTN) services, such as Integrated Service Digital Network (ISDN) and Digital Subscribe Line (xDSL). Some VPN implementations, such as in frame relay topologies, are provided by some ISPs already. While it is a private network from an ISP's point of view, it is still a public network from a customer's point of view. By adding VPN technology to their frame segment, customers can get the additional benefits of VPN technology.

Now that we've looked at the definition of Virtual Private Networks and mentioned a couple of topologies where they are offered, let's look at a couple of simple examples in the placement of VPN services. Figures 1-1 and 1-2 present typical examples of VPN settings. Figure 1-1 shows

Figure 1-1
A corporate VPN.

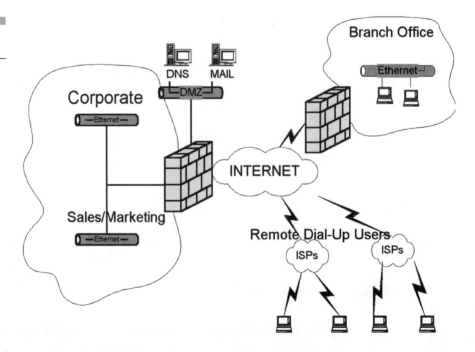

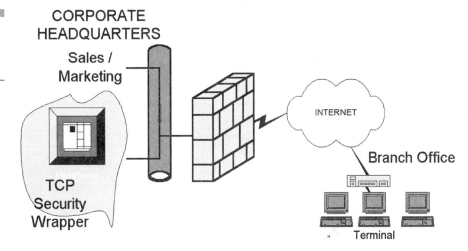

Figure 1-2
Corporate VPN with older legacy main-frame system.

the corporate network being connected to a public network for transport, a common placement used in VPN technology today. You will notice the Internet is being used as the transport carrier of VPN technology, but the Internet cloud could have been easily replaced by an ATM or frame relay cloud.

Figure 1-2 illustrates another corporate VPN configuration, but with a legacy system. There are lots of discussions about the Y2K problem, and mostly they relate to these older legacy systems. VPNs depend on encryption, and encryption software is not written for a majority of these legacy systems. Therefore, you will need some type of security wrapper around these legacy systems, in much the same way that TCP wrappers work in client/server applications today.

If you are going to allow VPN access to these older legacy systems, you need to make a decision. Do you really need to grant access to these systems, or just access to the data on these systems? If it is just data access, see if you can move the data to another machine. If you need to grant access to the legacy system itself, you will need special software written for these machines to implement the VPN encryption algorithms

A great feature of VPN technology is its scalability. As network providers increase the bandwidth on their backbones, VPNs can scale to take advantage of this additional bandwidth. Since VPNs are also platform-independent and rely on no particular operating system, almost any device in your company can function as either a VPN client or server. VPNs will also allow room for growth; most VPN devices will handle whatever services are placed upon them. They will allow you to create "tunnels," or end-to-end communications with encryption, on demand. You can create tunnels to others sites, such as "Corporate Headquarters to Major Sales Offices," and later create more tunnels for different offices.

You also need to decide if your organization needs to use encapsulation. *Encapsulation* is the process of taking a data packet and wrapping it inside an IP packet. If you want to use the IPX protocol to communicate to another site over the Internet, the IPX packet is wrapped inside another IP packet and sent. You can also encapsulate an IP packet inside of an IP packet; this configuration adds another layer of protection. Therefore, if you need to use the IPX protocol, you will need a device to encapsulate that IPX packet inside of an IP packet. Some VPN devices support this functionality; even gateways support this feature.

VPNs Come in Four Areas

I use the term *area,* since that is how VPNs are described in many current articles. Areas simply mean common VPN implementations. After you examine the next four areas, you will notice the commonality between terms used here and other terms used to describe Internet services. VPNs are not new, but they add a layer of encryption technology to the underlying Internet services.

Intranet An intranet VPN is created between the corporate headquarters and a remote sales office, or between headquarters and remote satellite offices. Figure 1-3 illustrates a typical intranet offering. The only difference here is that the intranet is accessed outside the network, meaning the access to it comes from the outside. Typically, it is only used inside a company's network and accessed by company employees. An intranet VPN is still accessed by the company employees, but the access is coming from outside rather than inside.

Remote Access A remote access VPN is created between corporate headquarters and remote mobile users. Figure 1-4 illustrates one of the most common approaches to VPNs. With encryption software loaded on a remote laptop, an individual will establish an encrypted tunnel to the VPN device at corporate headquarters.

Extranet An extranet VPN is created between a corporation and its customers or suppliers. In Figure 1.5, the extranet will allow access

Figure 1-3
An intranet VPN.

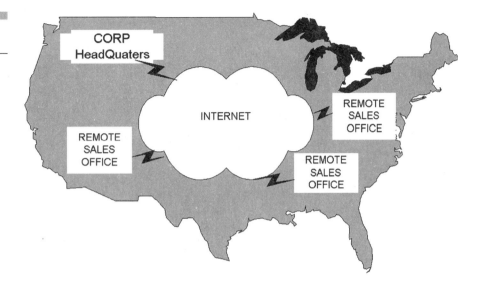

either by using the normal HTTP protocol used in Web browsers today, or it will allow the connection to be made using some other service and protocol agreed to by the parties involved. This is where electronic commerce will have its greatest impact. This setup will give a corporation the ability to deal effectively and securely with its major trading partners and revenue-generating customers.

Figure 1-4
A remote access VPN.

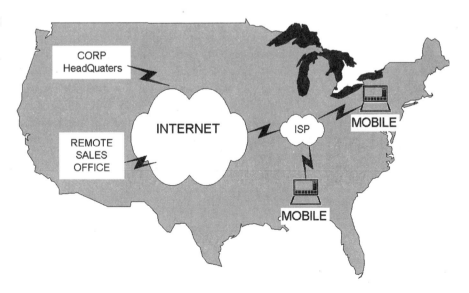

Figure 1-5
An extranet VPN.

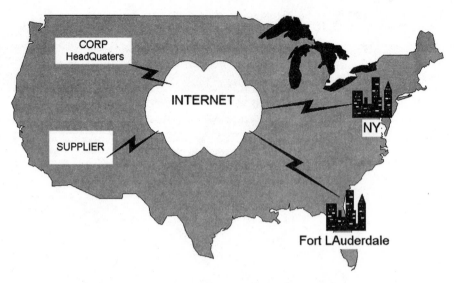

Intracompany VPN   A fourth area, not readily deployed by companies today, is an internal intracompany VPN. What reasons would cause a company to use an intracompany VPN? Some of the reasons are set forth by security surveys that report that attacks by internal employees are their number-one threat. The Computer Security Institute (CSI), with the participation of the FBI International Computer Crime Squad's San Francisco office, conducts an annual survey of U.S. corporations, government agencies, financial institutions, and universities. Below lists the results of the "1998 Computer Crime and Security Survey."* The fourth bulleted item is the most disturbing in terms of financial loss due to employees. Figure 1-6 lists the financial losses of these organizations.

- 64% of respondents report computer security breaches within the last twelve months. This figure represents dramatic increases of 16% over the "1997 CSI/FBI Computer Crime and Security Survey" results, in which 48% of respondents reported unauthorized use and a 22% increase over the initial 1996 survey, in which 42% acknowledged unauthorized use. (Note: If you include those reporting only incidents of computer virus or laptop theft, the number rises to 88% of all respondents.)

- Although 72% of respondents acknowledge suffering financial losses from such security breaches, only 46% were able to quantify their losses. The total financial losses for the 241 organizations that could put a dollar figure on them add up to $136,822,000. This figure represents a 36% increase in reported losses over the 1997 figure of $100,115,555 in losses.

*From CSI 1998 annual survey [http://www.gocsi.com/].

The Cost of Computer Crime

The following table shows the aggregate cost of computer crimes and security breaches over a 24-month period.

Note: 72% of our survey respondents suffered financial losses, but only 42% of respondents could quantify the losses.

How money was lost	Incidents w/ Quantified Losses			Lowest Reported		Highest Reported		Average Loss		Total Loss		
	1997	1998	97-98	1997	1998	1997	1998	1997	1998	1997	1998	97-98
Theft of proprietary info.	21	20	41	$1,000	$300	$10,000,000	$25,000,000	$954,666	$1,677,000	$20,048,00	$33,545,000	$53,593,000
Sabotage of data or networks	14	25	39	$150	$400	$1,000,000	$500,000	$164,840	$86,000	$4,285,850	$2,142,000	$6,427,850
Telecom eavesdropping	8	10	18	$1,000	$1,000	$100,000	$200,000	$45,423	$56,000	$1,181,000	$562,000	$1,743,000
System penetration by outsider	22	19	41	$200	$500	$1,500,000	$500,000	$132,250	$86,000	$2,911,700	$1,637,000	$4,548,700
Insider abuse of Net access	55	67	122	$100	$500	$100,000	$1,000,000	$18,304	$56,000	$1,006,750	$3,720,000	$4,726,750
Financial fraud	26	29	55	$5,000	$1,000	$2,000,000	$2,000,000	$957,384	$388,000	$24,892,000	$11,239,000	$36,131,000
Denial of service	n/a	36	36	n/a	$200	n/a	$1,000,000	n/a	$77,000	n/a	$2,787,000	$2,787,000
Spoofing	4	n/a	4	$1,000	n/a	$500,000	n/a	$128,000	n/a	$512,000	n/a	$512,000
Virus	165	143	308	$100	$50	$500,000	$2,000,000	$75,746	$55,000	$12,498,150	$7,874,000	$20,327,150
Unauthorized insider access	22	18	40	$100	$1,000	$1,200,000	$50,000,000	$181,437	$2,809,000	$3,991,605	$50,565,000	$54,556,605
Telecom fraud	35	32	67	$300	$500	$12,000,000	$15,000,000	$647,437	$539,000	$22,660,300	$17,256,000	$39,916,300
Active wiretapping	n/a	5	5	n/a	$30,000	n/a	$100,000	n/a	$49,000	n/a	$245,000	$245,000
Laptop theft	160	162	322	$1,000	$1,000	$1,000,000	$500,000	$38,326	$32,000	$6,132,200	$5,250,000	$11,382,200

Total $100,119,555 $136,822,000 $236,941,555

CSI/FBI 1998 Computer Crime Survey   Source: CSI

Figure 1-6   Computer crime statistics.

- Security breaches detected by respondents include a diverse array of serious attacks. For example, 44% reported unauthorized access by employees, 25% reported denial of service attacks, 24% reported system penetration from the outside, 18% reported theft of proprietary information, 15% reported incidents of financial fraud, and 14% reported sabotage of data or networks.

- The most serious financial losses occurred through unauthorized access by insiders (18 respondents reported a total of $50,565,000 in losses). Theft of proprietary information (20 respondents reported a total of $33,545,000 in losses), telecommunications fraud (32 respondents reported a total of $17,256,000 in losses) and financial fraud (29 respondents reported a total of $11,239,000 in losses).

- The number of organizations that cited their Internet connection as a frequent point of attack rose from 47% in 1997 to 54% in 1998. This represents a 17% increase over the initial 1996 figure of 37%. And significantly, the number of respondents citing their Internet connection as a frequent point of attack is now equal to the number of respondents citing internal systems as a frequent point of attack. (In the past, internal systems have been considered to be the greater of problems. It is not that the threat from inside the perimeter has diminished, it is simply that the

threat from outside, via Internet connections, has increased.) This trend
was reinforced by another piece of data. Of those who acknowledged
unauthorized use, 74% reported from one to five incidents originating
outside the organization, and 70% reported from one to five incidents
originating inside the organization.

SECURITY NOTE The most disturbing fact of the security surveys is
the fourth bulleted item. It is this item that will most definitely push for
this intracompany VPN setup in topology, as shown in Figure 1-7.

Figure 1-7
An intracompany
VPN.

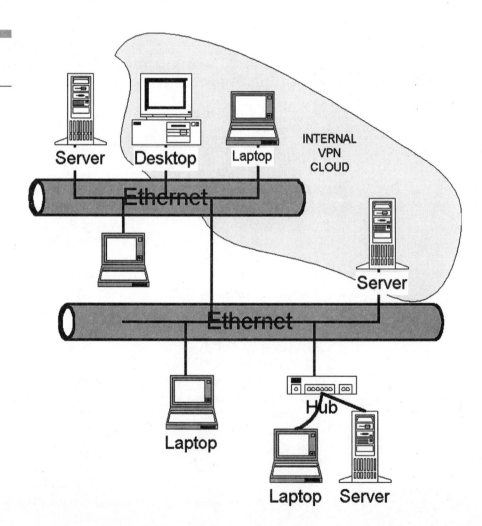

With this intracompany VPN, it will be possible that within the corporation boundaries a VPN tunnel could be created. All traffic that a company considers critical could be passed over the wire encrypted and safely stored without being tampered with. Financial records, executive meetings, and so on will pass safely from source to destination inside a company network.

Components That Make Up a VPN

VPNs consist of hardware and software, but they also require a set of components. These components are simply requirements ensuring your VPN is secure, available, and easy to maintain. The actual requirements fall into a range of attributes that an organization needs to consider when implementing or designing a VPN. These components are necessary whether an ISP provides you a VPN service or you decide to install one yourself.

Availability

Availability applies to both uptime and access time. It does a user no good if he or she has authorization to access the corporate servers 24 hours a day, 7 days a week but cannot get to them due to network problems. Unfortunately, many network problems may be out of your control and sometimes even your local ISP's control. If you use a frame relay or ATM VPN, you may get some guarantees from your ISP on availability, but not with the Internet.

Control

Some executives fear that if someone else maintains and controls their company's VPN, there's a greater possibility for security breaches. In reality, managed VPN services can be of great value to a company due to the training, expertise, careful monitoring, and alerting utilities that some managed service providers offer. An important consideration is that no matter how big your organization is, you will most likely have only one Virtual Private Network; you may have other access points, but still only one corporate VPN. How much are you then willing to invest in training, certification, and equipment to get your IT staff up to speed on VPN technology and security issues?

Compatibility

To use VPN technology—and the Internet as the transport medium—a company's internal network protocol architecture must be compatible to the Internet's native IP. In addition, it must be able to translate the company's networking protocols to layer 3 (the network layer) of the International Standards Organization (ISO) model. This implies that your company must be IP-aware and have the understanding that if you are running SNA or IPX protocols, you cannot connect directly to the Internet, unless you first convert SNA or IPX to IP. Many devices do this—a gateway, for example—but this adds another layer of complexity to your network. In addition, if you are going to use the Internet, you need to use the addressing convention that the Internet uses (based upon the Internet Protocol Addressing Structure). So if you are a Macintosh shop, you need to translate the addresses of your machines to "valid public" addresses that are used by the Internet.

■■■ ■■■ ■■■ ■■■ ■■■ ■■■ ■■■ ■■■ ■■■ ■■■ ■■■ ■■■ ■■■ ■■■ ■■■
GENERAL NOTE   Later I will talk about addressing, routing problems, and network address translation (NAT). If you haven't done so, please read RFC 1918.

Security

Security is everything with a VPN; this cannot be stated strongly enough. A VPN is *not* a company's private network; others can intercept, collect, and analyze the data. However, as we will see in later chapters, the threats and the security concerns can be dealt with. Security encompasses everything with a VPN, from the encryption process you implement and the authentication services you decide on to the digital signatures and certificate authorities you use. Security also encompasses the software that implements the encryption algorithms on the VPN device. If you are using an operating-system-based VPN, what are the vulnerabilities of that operating system? You should now begin to realize that security plays such an important part of VPNs, and why VPN security will be emphasized throughout this book.

Interoperability

Since VPN technology is relatively new from an implementation point of view, many compatibility issues arise from security, user, and encryption standards. There is a whole suite of vendors' products available that offer hardware, software, encryption, and authentication schemes for VPN technology; therefore, it is very difficult to choose one. One important consideration is where the VPN fits in your organization. Are you looking for end user–to–end user interoperability, or are you considering LAN-to-LAN VPN connectivity? This will help determine vendor manufacturers, software suppliers, and even consultation requirements.

Be sure to look for certification. The International Computer Security Association (ICSA), a security assurance firm established in 1989, certifies computer security products. Their goal is to improve the interoperability of security products and certifies them accordingly; vendors submit their products to ICSA for certification. The Internet Protocol Security (IPSec) standards, which will most likely be one of these security standards in the future, are certified by ICSA. Their mission as described by their Web page is as follows:

ICSA Mission

> ICSA is an independent organization that strives to improve security and confidence in global computing through awareness and the continuous certification of products, systems and people. ICSA services include security-related research, conferences publications, professional membership, vendor and user based consortia as well as certification. [http://www.icsa.net/services/product_cert/ipsec/]

Reliability

When a company decides to install an ISP's VPN product, they are really at the mercy of that ISP. One frustration many executives feel is that when their network goes down, they have no control to monitor or fix the situation. They are resigned to sit back and wait for someone else to correct the problem. Given the number of clients a typical ISP might have, it may be some time before resources are available to fix the problem. Even when the problems are resolved, some customers may not be notified immediately, thereby adding to the delays.

Data and User Authentication

VPN authentication consists of data and user authentication. *Data authentication* reaffirms that the message has been sent in its entirety and hasn't been altered in any shape. *User authentication* is the process of allowing user access into your network. It's important that in any VPN technology both are offered. You may want external users to be able to access your internal network. This requires secure authentication and user verification before external users enter your internal network. There must be a way to provide for proper verification to allow internal access and authorization to only allow those necessary services needed by the authenticated users.

Once a hole is established into your network, and I am referring to any security vulnerability in any piece of hardware of software, how then do you keep unauthorized users out? How do you spot the legitimate users from the nonlegitimate users? What can you do to protect yourself from such activity? As we will see in later chapters, cryptography, encryption, and hashing functions enable proper access and authentication.

Traffic Overhead

In all kinds of technologies there are trade-offs: speed versus performance, security versus flexibility. VPNs fall into the same category. When we begin to talk about packet sizes, encrypted packets, headers, and so forth, overhead comes into play. If a VPN device encrypts every single packet leaving its network adapters, you can imagine the kind of CPU processing power that is needed on that machine. If the VPN encapsulates every packet, you may be increasing packet size, thereby affecting your bandwidth utilization.

One of the modes in the IPSec security standard adds overhead to each packet for the sake of security. Now you will experience bottlenecks on your links; your ISP's connection to you will become overutilized and you may need a bigger pipe. To minimize this, you should be able to decide on what types of traffic need to be protected. General broadcasts, multicasts, and similar traffic doesn't need to be encrypted; however, it needs to be authenticated. VPN devices can add authentication to these packets without the overhead associated with the increased packet size, and the receiver can be sure that the data is unadulterated. A good VPN service, then, would give you the option of specifying what kind of data gets encrypted, what kind of data gets authenticated, and what kind of data can freely flow untouched.

IPv6

The next Internet protocol under development is IP version 6 (IPv6); with it will come new features and problems of its own. Considering the packet size of IPv6 will be larger than IPv4, how then will these encryption techniques, tunneling protocols, and encapsulation techniques affect the network devices that need to decrypt/encrypt the new larger packets? Will network performance be adversely affected by IPv6, or can the network devices scale? As far as security is concerned, IPSec has IPv6 already built into its standard, but presently vendors differ on the support of IPv4, IPv6, and IPSec. Hopefully, within the next year or two there will be a convergence on a common set of security protocols. This is another issue you must address when considering and implementing different technologies for your corporation's VPNs.

Maintenance

You will need to decide what kind of technology and what kind of support your company needs. Will you be using a managed ISP VPN service, or will you do it yourself with your company's resources? If you decide to implement the VPN yourself, do you have the security staff? Can your IT department get up to speed with security issues? Security updates should be thought of in the same way virus-checking software is thought of: that it is only as good as the last known virus.

In later chapters, I deal with different aspects of security, including how to identify and handle attacks. After reading these chapters, you should decide if it is worthwhile to implement security measures yourself or hire outside consultation.

Nonrepudiation

Nonrepudiation is the process of positively identifying the sender in such a way that the sender cannot deny it. This has broad implications for suppliers, retailers, vendors, and key trading partners. Electronic trade, legal documents, and financial trading all rely on knowing who placed the order. If there is even a hint of uncertainty, a company cannot guarantee who placed the order. In order for electronic commerce to become a viable option over the Internet, nonrepudiation must exist. The use of certificate authorities and digital signatures, which will be explained in later chapters, should ensure this.

Who Supports VPNs?

Many smaller ISPs are competing with the larger providers in offering VPN services. It should come as no surprise, given the projected growth rates for VPNs, that all ISPs would offer some type of VPN services. As VPN technologies differ, so do the ISP's implementation of them. Some big ISPs are solely looking at hardware encryption devices, while other ISPs are looking at software solutions. A common differentiation between the two is that supposedly hardware encryption devices can encrypt and secure packets faster than software devices. There are some statistics on software VPN performance that contradict this, so this should not be a deciding factor alone. If a company has to manage thousands of VPN connections, they may want to consider a hardware device, but you should check out software performance statistics first. You might be paying for a premium service you don't need.

ISPs are also testing the latest VPN tunneling and security protocols that will be used on the Internet in the future. The three main security protocols that exist today are Layer 2 Forwarding Protocol (L2F), Point-to-Point Tunneling Protocol (PPTP), and the Internet Security Protocol (IPSec). These standards will be discussed in later chapters and must be supported by any ISP. Most likely, though, one or two of these will prevail, or possibly a combination of them. In fact, at the time of this writing, Layer 2 Forwarding Protocol and Point-to-Point Tunneling Protocol are being combined into what is known as Layer 2 Tunneling Protocol (L2TP).

Other major concerns for customers are performance, latency, and security. While many ISPs are looking for ways to offer their customers Service Level Agreements (SLAs) and Quality of Services (QoS) contracts, they are relying on standards for the security issues.

Growth of VPNs

The Internet has grown beyond anyone's expectations, and some estimates state that there will be over 250 million users by the turn of the century. Surveys differ from one to another, but all agree that anywhere between 60 to over 100 million have Internet access now. The high growth rates of the Internet, the number of Internet users, and the amount of Web traffic and individual domain registrations have sparked the upward trends in this growth rate. The U.S. Department of Commerce estimates that there will be over a million corporations connected to the Internet by the year 2000. This clearly illustrates the impact that the Internet has and will have in the next century. Several studies have been done to suggest that by the turn of the century between 50 to over 80 percent of all businesses will use some kind of VPN service. They suggest that U.S. multinational corporations with just 200 remote users can save over $1.5 million in just 4 to 5 years by using the Internet rather than leased lines.

ISPs have tried to handle the growing requests for increased Internet access with more modem banks and larger bandwidth pipes. Unfortunately, even with this demand ISPs still lose money providing basic access service to the Internet. This is evident by the fact that many ISPs are beginning to turn away from offering monthly, unlimited Internet usage. With that being the case, ISPs must now go after business customers and corporate clients, and what these businesses demand, ISPs must offer.

Global accesses, marketing research, selling, data collecting, and supporting customers are but a few of the requests placed upon ISPs by their business customers. Businesses demand these services, so ISPs must offer them. However, these new services come at a price. One is performance; the additional traffic that these new services provide place a heavier burden upon the ISPs to upgrade their infrastructure. Another major area is security. Refer back to our previous definition of a VPN and how it is not a "private network." Anyone who is on the Internet can potentially look at the data that goes across it, access it, modify it, and potentially use that information for his or her own private gain. The question then will be, is security sufficiently implemented to make businesses trustworthy enough so that the Internet may be used as a medium to conduct business? Not many ISPs want to take the responsibility for guaranteeing the security of your data as it travels over their network. Will it then be up to the vendors, who sell Internet products such as firewalls and routers, to guarantee safety? Not necessarily so, but by understanding the security risks and the associated procedures to avert risks, and by using some common sense, you can protect your data.

VPNs play an important part in the process that allows companies to conduct business inexpensively. VPNs offer businesses a way to reduce costs, improve services, and maintain their customer base. Some of the reasons that so many businesses will use VPNs to conduct business are as follows:

- VPNs use the Internet as their backbone.
- The Internet is a very affordable medium for both commercial and private customers.
- The Internet spans the globe.
- Internet conductivity is extremely efficient in today's market, and most ISPs bear the burden of getting you connected.
- VPNs are flexible, dynamic, and scalable.
- VPNs (in some cases) can utilize a company's investment in hardware already.
- VPN's base technology is the Internet TCP/IP's suite of protocols, which makes it easier to understand and implement than a brandnew technology.

Identifying a Need for VPN

How can you be convinced that your company needs a VPN? Can it really help your business expand and grow? While you always hear of the potential benefits to an organization implementing VPN technology, there are only certain areas and applications where VPN technologies would be beneficial.

Areas in Which VPN Technology Would Be Beneficial to Your Organization

- Remote user access
- Extranet applications
- International sites
- Diverse geographical user base
- The need to support a diverse geographical customer base
- Inexpensive Marketplace Expansion
- Modest bandwidth requirements

- Need for low-cost global reach
- Dial access outsourcing
- Virtual leased lines

Along with the beneficial areas, there are also some areas in which VPN technology would not be suitable to your company. These apply to your internal company infrastructure and to your particular requirements.

Areas in Which VPN Technology May Not Be Beneficial

- Where performance is a premium
- Where latency is unacceptable
- Where nonstandard protocols that cannot be encapsulated with the Internet native IP protocol
- Mostly isochronous traffic, e.g., telephone

Business Need for VPNs

Information is a critical asset for any company, and the lack of obtaining that information could mean missed deals, delayed contracts, and so on. Therefore, implementing some type of VPN technology would be a good idea for all organizations. Vast majorities of companies use the Internet to send email; however, the vast majority don't consider that the mail is sent in plaintext mode, and anyone who has Internet access can read that mail. What would happen now if you needed to send data across the globe? Will you take the chance that someone could intercept it, read it, and possibly modify it? The very nature of competition makes the need for information dependent on the speed of getting that information. If Company A forgoes the use of VPN technology, they can be sure that Company B will use that technology. Considering that the workforce of the future will be mobile, a company could not possibly build or lease enough lines across the planet to ensure secure communications; the cost of that idea is just too prohibitive to even be considered.

When examining the growth of countries such as India, Russia, and China, and reading all the economic reports available from U.S. government agencies such as the Commerce Department, many predict that the future major increases in growth rates will be in these countries. The growth will not just be in population, but in gross domestic product (GDP), which is the growth rate that buys and sells with U.S. American manufacturers. If that is the case and it is accepted, how can a company then refuse to do business with this potentially huge marketplace?

When looking at IBM, a U.S. icon, little attention is given to the fact that IBM derives most of its revenues overseas. However, just looking at its last year's annual report will reveal this. Most companies do not have IBM's financial strength to set up shop in all countries, so in order to remain competitive, they will need some way to reach this market-place. This is where VPN technology will come in.

How to Choose VPN Services

A first step in choosing a VPN service is to ask a basic question: How will you get data from point A to point B? Then you need to ask yourself where point A and point B are. It is this decision that may cause some security problems.

In looking at Figure 1-8, point A is somewhere in Salt Lake City and point B is somewhere in Texas. As far as this diagram is concerned,

Figure 1-8
Domestic VPN
service.

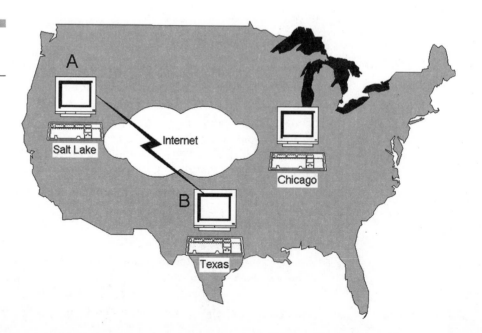

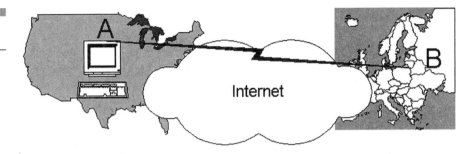

Figure 1-9
International VPN.

this is a pretty straightforward VPN configuration. The major impact here is deciding on what kind of hardware, software, and consultation services you will use. The rest of the configuration—installation, coordination, and maintenance—will be straightforward. The major consideration here is what things will be in your control, and you can decide how much or how little you will want to maintain this VPN yourself versus an ISP's managed service VPN offering. Now compare Figure 1-8 with Figure 1-9, a totally new scenario with its own problems and potential security implications.

Figure 1-9 shows an international case for VPN. All of the normal functions still apply, but what is added is the watchdog of the U.S. government. As stated earlier, VPN is encryption. Encryption is considered munitions, and the U.S. government regulates munitions. Now what is munitions and why does the U.S. regulate the use of it? The U.S. government and practically all governments have placed munitions under their defensive authority. Munitions for most countries are terms used for defense; warships, bombers, and tanks are all type of munitions.

You may still wonder how can encryption be considered munitions, but think back to the earlier definition of encryption, repeated here:

> Encryption is nothing more that taking a message, such as "I'll be late"
> and converting it into some gibberish, say for example,
> "2deR56Gtr2345^hj5Uie04." The other end of the process is called
> decryption, and it is the reverse of encryption, e.g., taking
> "2deR56Gtr2345^hj5Uie04" and converting it back to "I'll be late."

During wartime, governments try to pass secrets to their allies, or governments try to intercept the enemy's secret transmissions. These communications all used a basic form of encryption to send these messages. If it helps you, you can think of encryption as a type of Morse code (A=... B=. -. C=. —-, etc.).

How Does This Scenario Affect VPNs?

Encryption laws govern the use of encryption technologies (munitions), which are the underlying security mechanisms of VPNs. Certain types of strong encryption techniques are not allowed to be exported outside the U.S. borders. What this means to a company is that if you are using a VPN to do commerce with an international vendor or trading partner, you must be willing to accept a lower security standard. Unfortunately, by today's standards even the allowable exportable encryption techniques are very weak.

Currently several members of Congress have introduced congressional bills to ease the restrictions on the exportation of strong encryption, mainly because stronger encryption products are already available outside the U.S. This is unfortunately true: High-tech companies are not allowed to export strong encryption products, although the same products are already readily available outside the U.S. borders. Strangely, a U.S. manufacturer can't import the overseas encryption product then export it again, even though it originated overseas. This, of course, is not just a U.S. dilemma; almost every country has some sort of encryption policy.

From a business perspective, saying that implementing a VPN is not a good idea because of the lack of strong security features would be a mistake. Due to VPNs scalability features, you can implement VPN technology and then expand it to borders outside the U.S., once the encryption policies are eased. The U.S. government does realize that the encryption laws are old, and it is beginning to loosen its restrictions. As of this writing, President Clinton just announced the easing of the so-called 56-bit DES encryption technology. Unfortunately, the reason behind this may have to do with it just having been broken. In later chapters, we will discuss encryption algorithms and bit sizes, and how they affect the security of your VPN.

GENERAL NOTE As a side note, in 1991 a telecommunication carrier released a press statement saying they were the first company to offer an international VPN service with Europe with strong security measures. Therefore, from this it would seem that VPN service and security has been available for a long time. However, just how reliable, secure, and robust it is still needs to be decided. In the previous paragraph, I explained how the government's actions affect security, so you need to be careful when attesting to the claims of vendors regarding security.

Conclusion

This introductory chapter explored what articles in the marketplace describe as a Virtual Private Network. I use the term *marketplace,* since there is not much academic literature available on this topic and most of the material comes from vendors. We defined VPN and talked about the concepts of encryption and virtual and how they applied to VPN technology. You now should be able to understand the terminology used in VPNs, along with the components that make up a VPN and the areas in which VPNs may be beneficial to your organization.

An important thing to remember is that while the terminology is new, the technology is not. VPN technology dates back to the 1960s, and its underlying encryption process dates back to pre-World War II days. You can consider the encryption aspect of a VPN technology as Morse code. The U.S. sends a coded message to its naval base in the South Pacific. It is up to the enemies to try to decode that message. In order for that naval base to decrypt that message, they had to be given a special key. (This type of encryption, known as symmetric, will be discussed in later chapters.)

The best advice on VPN and security is to expect security breaches to happen. With technology changing every day, how can you guard against it? With common sense and a lot of hard work, you can at least protect yourself up to today's standards.

Even though VPNs can be a highly complex technology to understand and implement—even deciding if they are right for your organization can be a complicated matter—in most cases some sort of VPN implementation is right for every organization. Even if you don't have a need for any type of encrypted data, you always need a way to achieve cost savings, and VPN technology is one way to obtain them. In addition, your customers and suppliers will most likely be using a VPN in the next few years. Just think to yourself how many times you send email; chances are you are using the Internet.

In later chapters, we will look at VPNs, along with their different architectures, topologies, and offerings, and discuss how each one of them fits into an organization.

CHAPTER 2

Network Security
for VPNs

The term *network security* covers an incredible array of services, processes, and requirements for an organization. This is evident from the number of books and articles published on the subject. More specifically, network security is the security that is placed on the organization's network components, such as routers, gateways, servers, and so on. It can also be used to describe processes that are needed for the safe implementation and maintenance of an organization's network. In this chapter we will discuss network security in terms of a VPN implementation and where it should function to achieve the best-possible secured environment. We will also look at some things that make your organization vulnerable to an attack. Knowing your enemy is a first step; by knowing who your enemy is and other similar weaknesses you can concentrate security resources into those areas that guarantee the best security measures.

Security resources are like any other budgetary item in an organization and must compete for limited financial resources; therefore, the way you allocate these resources is critical. What if you are attacked? How would you spot it and how could you react to it? We will look at some very useful security measures for alerting you to intrusions. Once we have established a good sense of security practices, we will then see how they apply to VPNs and what you can do to make your VPN more secure. By knowing the different types of attacks and the forms they take, you can protect your company against them. VPN security attacks are no different than other kinds of security attacks.

What Is Network Security?

Network security should be considered a part of total overall security for an organization. In fact, the term *network security* covers so many aspects of an organization that a better term might be *information security,* since this term is more encompassing. Does it really matter to management whether the information resides on a server or database, and whether or not someone can access it through a firewall? Information security encompasses network security, computer security, access security, physical security, and so on. Of course, with all this security, who decides which information is critical and which is noncritical? This is not a question that can be as easily answered as you might think. Is every single piece of email, every document, and every single object in a database a critical business mission asset? Since capital resources for any organization are scarce, so too are the resources to implement security. In that case, upper management must decide what value is placed on what information and provide the needed resources to protect that information.

Saying that all data is confidential to an organization is implying that we must use some form of encryption on all data. In other words, since a lot of security breaches are done by internal employees and if all data is critical, then it follows that encryption is needed for all data. Of course, this is not the case: all data is not confidential and all data is not mission-critical business data. So now, instead of allocating so much of those scarce financial security resources to everything, you can implement stages of security and still implement a full range of security products together, with the needed resources on the critical data and a lesser security policy placed on the noncritical data.

When thinking about network security, especially when implementing VPNs, you should look at the Open Systems Interconnect (OSI) stack. This model has been used in virtually every single computer system to date. It describes how the individual layered components are in charge of a specific set of services and that each layer sits on top of the other. This allows manufacturers to build products and not have to worry about interoperability issues. Of course, what happens in the model world and the real world sometimes doesn't mesh.

The OSI stack has seven layers: application, presentation, session, transport, network, datalink, and physical. Each layer is responsible for its own set of individual functions, such as reliability, setup, correction, and so forth. But here in itself lies a major security problem. Common attacks that occur today, such as buffer overflows, CGI exploits, and other security attacks, happen throughout all these layers. Each layer can be attacked and compromised, so what will make a VPN secure? One obvious answer is to have the VPN as far down the OSI stack as possible. Figure 2-1 illustrates an optimal placement for VPN technology.

In Figure 2-1, the VPN technology is implemented as far down the OSI stack as possible. This creates a benefit and a potential problem. Having this technology placed as low in the stack as possible helps eliminate many of the attacks that could have taken place if it were higher up. In a later chapter we will discuss the different types of attacks. For now, though, the lower you can place the VPN technology in the OSI model, the fewer the number of attacks that can be placed against it.

However, keep in mind that this placement might also cause compatibility problems. By implementing the VPN software further down the OSI stack, the technology has the possibility of interacting more and more

Figure 2-1
VPN technology on
the OSI stack.

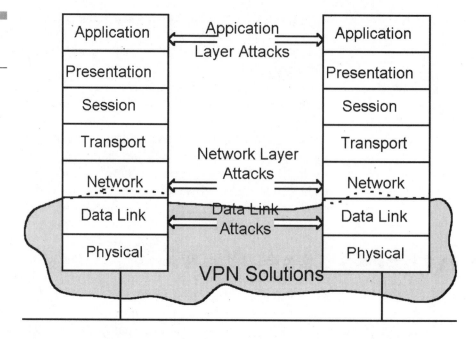

with the specific components that make up the operating system. Unfortunately, device drivers, optimizers, and loaded modules could have interoperability problems with the installed VPN technology. You just need to be aware of these kinds of problems when you talk to your vendors.

I would also expect this to be more of a problem with remote-user laptops and desktop machines. Vendors usually test their software on various servers that have been loaded and configured with a common set of software programs that are in use today, thereby giving them the opportunity to test the interoperability with these systems. Unfortunately, the same situation does not exist with desktop machines; there are just so many different applications and configuration setups that a vendor could not be expected to test them all. Therefore, when you decide to go with a particular vendor's solutions, make sure you have support for these problems.

What Can You Do to Protect Against Threats?

Is there anything you can do to stop someone from attempting to hack into your site or compromise some of your servers, whether he or she is an internal employee or someone external to the organization? The answer is obviously no, but it should begin to make you wonder why your organization was chosen. What is it about your company that makes it an attractive target to a potential security violation? To try and find this out ask yourself this question posed in the next section.

Whom Are You Protecting Your Company From?

The answer to this question may not be as apparent as you think; you may not have considered it or even thought of it. But ask yourself, who are your enemies? Who may have a grudge against you? Could it possibly be one of your competitors? Maybe a disgruntled employee or someone who just happened to stumble across your company data stream while on the Internet? Do you think, or can you even imagine, that it's an internal issue? Is it a remote possibility or is it a nonissue you need not worry about? A nonissue is still an answer. It may not be the kind you inform upper management about, but you may have decided that the cost of implementing security is just too expensive.

But look at it from a different perspective. Do you leave your front door open when you sleep at night? Probably not. You most likely close the door, but you might leave it unlocked. You may decide to close and lock it, and you may go even further by closing it, locking it, and installing a security system. Now you could decide to have that security system sound a piercing alarm when triggered or send a silent alarm to a central monitoring facility. Now, look back at the answer that implementing security is just too expensive. You should be able to see that security is a multifaceted item where items can be layered on top of one another, and you can increase your security as you go along.

Now that we see how security can be layered, let's look at what organizations typically do. Companies usually try to implement several different vendors' products for their different security needs. Many organizations use between three and eight different vendors to implement different security procedures, depending on their security concerns. Security should not be considered a standalone function; therefore, a standalone security product—the "one size fits all" model—would not work. Instead, an organization needs to think in terms of its specific security concerns and areas, and then allocate its different security outlays. Figure 2-2 shows how a security budget could be divided up for a client/server organization. The percentages would change in different environments. For instance, in a mostly mainframe environment, the

Figure 2-2

Sample outlay for
an organization's
computer security
budget.

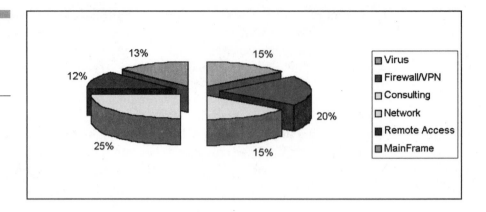

Figure 2-2
Sample outlay for an organization's computer security budget.

percentage of mainframe security would probably be higher.

Figure 2-2 illustrates a case example of allocating a security budget among various security areas. In this example, the security budget is divided into remote access, mainframe, network, virus, firewall, and consulting. This security budget would change depending on the company's needs, but it should get you thinking that security is layered and can be piecemealed. It takes management to say which kind of data is important and which data is not. When I refer to data as not being important, I do not mean to imply that the data itself is unimportant. I am referring to its sensitivity. For example, if a security violation occurred and that data was compromised, could it be used to hurt the organization? If not, then simple backups should be enough for this type of data.

Weaknesses

Most organizations will not admit their weaknesses. If you don't admit these weaknesses, then how can you protect yourself against them? Every network is vulnerable, every network is insecure, and every network can be compromised. Periodic audits do help, but understanding your network infrastructure also helps. By understanding and fully realizing the topology, you can identify the weaknesses. Do you have Internet access? If you do, then you should realize that you have a way for someone to get in.

Most people concentrate on securing the firewall and assume that the firewall is the perimeter protection device. But is it? In most topologies I have seen, there is a firewall, but there is also an external router connected to your ISP connection. Most people just forget about this device. Why can't someone just hack into your router? They can and they do. Take nothing for granted.

Do you have dial-in remote access? If so, then you know that anyone who has your internal number can try to dial in. Do you realize that remote access devices like modems aren't security devices? Some modems do not hang up when Data Terminal Ready, or DTR, drops. A setting used on modems, DTR is a configurable option that signals to the modem that the terminal is connected and turned on. If you set DTR to drop on terminal software disconnect but not on hardware disconnect, you are opening yourself up to another hole. If an authorized user who has dial-in access dials in, gets permission, and then for some reason drops the connection later, that connection to the remote access device may still be active. What this implies is, some other user can dial in and get an instant session, and it is very easy for a software program to keep trying different numbers before finding one that succeeds.

Do you have network jacks installed in your conference rooms, which means anyone with a laptop can plug into one of the jacks and snoop on your network? Some outside individual can enter and connect to the jack, and if your company has dynamic IP address allocation active on a server, obtaining an address is relatively easy. Once they are on the network, with some monitoring software they can easily capture traffic on the network and read passwords on a company LAN, since passwords are sent in clear-text mode. This can be done and has been done numerous times.

User Access Control

User access control mode only allows users permissions and rights needed for them to do their jobs. Access control is a mechanism where if User A only needs files in a certain directory, he or she will be granted that authorization. If, however, User B needs access in a different directory, he or she will be granted authorizations in that directory. User access control is extremely important when you are implementing VPN technology. First, you have to make sure that you are only granting access to authorized users. Then you must be sure that those authorized users are only being granted access to those servers that you deem necessary. When you start implementing extranet and intranet VPNs, you must make sure that your internal employees who are working from home have access to the internal intranet. Your customers, suppliers, and vendors will most likely connect to your company's extranet via the VPN you set up, and you must be sure that these accesses are restricted to the extranet only and not any internal hosts. In the topology chapter of this book (Chapter 5), I present some examples of where your organization should place your extranet.

Will your access control mechanism allow you to incorporate your Lightweight Directory Access Protocol (LDAP)? The LDAP, which will be discussed more in Chapter 14, is an Internet standard to allow cross-network access to directory services on different operating systems that support it. With your VPN you might want this feature implemented to be able to maintain security on what users are allowed what services. This will help in ease of maintenance and authorization of users to allowable directory services.

Trust No One

We've all seen this phrase more times than we care to remember. While it may not be the most civil way to run an organization, unfortunately, in today's corporate environment it is a good policy to implement. Anyone, and I mean anyone—employees, consultants, interns, telecom-wiring personnel—can hook up to your network and, with a laptop, use a packet monitoring application to capture data and analyze it. By examining that data, many security passwords, sensitive emails, and reports could be captured.

I prefer to believe in trusting people until they've proven untrustworthy, but that itself presents a problem. By the time they prove untrustworthy, they may have already done damage. So then what can an organization do? The best phrase that sums it up would be what former President Ronald Reagan said, "Trust, but verify." The organization must set up a procedure where everything is recorded, and that access is granted only for those individuals that need it. Contingency plans are also needed so that in times of necessity, the normal process can be sidestepped for the sake of efficiency. A simple example would be that of a new salesman who is out on a call with a customer and needs a report from a server. The normal process of having him submit his credentials to security to be given access in 24 hours is not the right answer. This is just one example; there are hundreds more. You must balance security concerns with the flexibility needs, or tension and aggravation will mount between the different departments in the organization and just lead to more chaos.

So What Can You Do?

Add more passwords? Add more encryption? In fact, if an organization wanted to, they could encrypt all data that passes through their networks, both internal and external. Monitoring software could be added that showed the source and destination addresses of every network device individuals visited and compare it to what they should be accessing during normal working hours. In addition, every server could be password-protected with passwords that change every week or every day, and each office and closet could have an access device that needs a security card.

What all these new security measures would probably lead up to is one of two things: either an organization will enjoy the tightest security process in the industry, or its employees will have a 4-day work week, since every week there will be something wrong with some security feature implemented, and they will not get any work done for that day anyway. To prove this, if you are a manager, just take a survey of internal employees and see how many times some security feature has hindered their job.

Security has to be attacked in stages and looked upon as buying insurance. There are some things you can do, there are some things you can't, and there are things you buy insurance for. There are a couple of phrases to remember with regard to security that come from management philosophies:

- Known unknowns
- Unknown unknowns

You can minimize the impact to your organization on the first bulleted item, but you need to recover on the second item. Let's take the first item and look at some examples.

Known Unknowns

Some examples of known unknowns are as follows:

- Your data can get stolen.
- Your hard drive can get corrupted.
- Someone could hack into your Web server.
- Someone could run a CGI script on your Web server.
- You could receive infected email.

The damage of these items can be minimized and possibly averted. You could set up antivirus software to check for infected email, and you could stop CGI scripts from running on your Web servers. You should understand the idea behind the known unknowns now: You could set up individual cases and take action to correct them, thereby reducing the impact to the organization. You will see that if you apply just a minimal amount of time to these actions, you will be able to come up with a list hundreds of times longer than the list I just gave as an example. Then after you come up with this list, you can prioritize them and set up security plans for each item. Now, concerning VPNs, as you progress through this book, you will read about issues and concerns affecting the security of VPN networks. When you read about these, create the same bulleted list and then apply the necessary security steps to minimize the damage that will affect your organization.

Unknown Unknowns

Following are some examples of unknown unknowns:

- The Y2K problem
- The Internet
- Virtual Private Networks

Are these really unknown unknowns? Let's take a look at these and consider the implications to the organization. We've known for some time about the Y2K problem. In fact, we knew about it when the original code was built. We built an assumption into the code that computers would never go past the year 2000. So now, every organization is spending massive amounts of financial resources to correct the problem, and even with this outlay of money, there are no guarantees. Already there are lawsuits, and they will continue to grow in number. And who pays out these legal bills? The organization's insurance carriers.

No one knew how or why the Internet would grow fast. The Internet has brought forth a great barrage of new products and services. Is your organization one of those offering these services? If you are not offering these services, is your organization taking advantage of them?

Virtual Private Networks are also growing at tremendous speeds similar to the Internet's rate of acceptance. VPNs can be extremely transparent to the end user; in fact, so much so that they have no idea they are actually using it. The underlying technology is old, reliable, and tested, so there is no learning curve. The only new item is encryption, which actually isn't new but is used in a new way. Considering today's "strong" encryption products, meaning greater than 56-bit DES, most hackers don't have the processing power to decode these encrypted messages. These kinds of unknown unknowns are hard to spot and must be dealt with efficiently and effectively when they arrive.

Security Is Like the Changing Wind

One thing about security is that it is always changing, and your implementation of security procedures has to be in line with this way of thinking. For a long time, simple passwords were fine for individual machines and other network devices, but now simple passwords have outlived their useful life. Before, passwords were moved to a centralized server for security. Now passwords are referred to in terms of 2- and 3-factor authentication (which will be discussed in Chapter 14).

Operating systems and the processes that run on them have lists of known vulnerabilities associated with them. New viruses are constantly appearing. With VPNs and firewalls, you are no longer just concerned with security internally. Now you must be concerned about security externally on a public network like the Internet. So keep in mind that having a very dynamic security policy is a very good idea. Training, mailing lists, and security advisement are a part of a good security policy. Also, you should have a good dialog with every vendor, and hopefully, they will keep you updated on security problems concerning their products.

Employee Sabotage

Unfortunately, many organizations live in a world where as soon as an employee leaves the company, whether the termination was instigated by the employee or the management, immediately his or her password is revoked. Organizations really do not have any other options; however, with regard to essential technical personnel, this issue can get even more complicated. Most disgruntled users might take or destroy reports or delete sensitive email, but without full access, they really can't do any extreme damage to a company's resources. In the case of important technical personnel, the rules are different; dealing with these individuals in a careful manner would be prudent. Not only is revoking their passwords critical, searching for any backdoors they may have built in is mandatory. But how do you find those backdoors? Most likely the systems they are comfortable with and use day in and day out are possibilities for backdoors.

Now added to the password worries are the digital certificates they have stored on the certificate authorities. With access to critical servers, these individuals still will be able to issue commands on company servers, since the server will ask the CA for permission and the CA will verify it. Therefore, in addition to revoked passwords, the CA has to know that this person is now an untrusted user and reject all his or her attempts for service requests. This notification has to now be made by others, since that user is no longer on staff. Therefore, a procedure has to be added to the regular password deletion chores.

Key Recovery

Key recovery is an interesting and hotly debated topic. Key recovery has been referred to as a backdoor and a trap door. There are three major sets of players in this area, each with their own viewpoints. One is the U.S. and certain foreign governments, who want all encryption products to have a key-recovery feature to allow them to decrypt a message. In Chapter 1, we touched on the encryption/decryption keys. The encryption key encrypted the message, whereas the decryption key decrypted the message. With key recovery enabled, however, there would be two decryption keys. Now you can no doubt see why this topic is hotly debated. Who would want the government to have access to that second decryption key? The second group is organizations and privacy groups opposed to government intervention and their eavesdropping on messages. The third group, businesses, have their own concerns. What happens if an employee quits or dies? What about the files and data that have been encrypted by that employee's private key? How can a company gain access to those files? This is the type of key recovery business wants. Of course, any business could just use a global private-public key combination only known to a certain set of individuals and achieve the same result.

Background Checks

Background checks are another common process in new-hire areas, especially the high-tech world. No longer is the typical profile of a potential security problem a middle-aged man who feels he gave all for his company and they left him to drift. It's now the 20- to 30-ish programmer who works 70 or 80 hours a week and is upset about making the

CEO rich. In today's organizations it seems, with layoffs, cutbacks, greed, and lack of motivation, security breaches will get worse in the coming years. Background checks can and do occasionally spot individuals who you would rather not have in your organization. With the legal system today, if something happens in your organization, you would probably be held liable. You should institute some type of security check on certain key high-profile individuals with access to customers' data on corporate servers, such as credit card number databases.

The Hidden Cost of Security

As mentioned in the last section, security comes at a cost. The more security your organization implements, the higher the cost incurred. In addition, not only will the maintenance requirements and the technical expertise needed to manage this increase in security be higher, but also the aggravation of the end user. Most people associate security with the additional capital outlay of hardware, software, and technical expertise. But very little is mentioned regarding the amount of frustration end users experience when security impedes their ability to work. If a particular machine or server has problems, it usually only takes a little while for the admin person to respond. With security issues, the end user will first contact the admin person for that department. After spending time with that user, that administrator may need to report the problem to the security staff of the organization and wait for them to respond.

In addition, security itself is secretive in nature. If a problem develops, there is not going to be a general alert so that everyone knows it is the security server causing a problem. It could be a long wait before someone even knows the problem lies with a security issue; therefore, if the admin person isn't trained on security issues, he or she cannot accurately identify them in a timely manner. It then becomes extremely frustrating to the end users when a network security server goes down, the firewall doesn't pass traffic, the authentication server goes down, or the Web servers will not accept your certificates.

These are the hidden costs involved in security, and unfortunately in this present day, there are no alternatives. You can't decide to take security matters lightly because of these hidden costs. Do you want to be the manager who says security costs too much and then someone breaks into one of your critical servers and steals your company's confidential information? The best way to look at this then is to use the analogy of your own personal insurance. Most people feel secure having automobile, house, life, disability, and other types of insurance. Even though you have all this insurance in case of problems, you still try to avoid having these problems in the first place. So maybe then if you think of security as a type of insurance, it is worth it. You don't want to use it, but you are glad if you have it if the need arises.

How to Identify Attacks

Audit and Logging

How do you identify attacks, how do you audit them, and how do you log them? A good security policy has audit and logging as staples in its process. No organization knows when it's coming under attack; if they did, they could stop it. What normally happens is that they are informed that they have been broken into or somebody has tried to break in and was unsuccessful. Now they need to backtrack and see if the log files can identify where the intruder came from, what IP address and, if possible, via what ISP. It is most likely that the attacks occur over a period. Like a thief casing out the next job, hackers watch the traffic and take note of patterns, especially repeated patterns that will allow them the ability to compromise that stream. This leads us to the next item, monitoring.

Monitoring

Audit and logging are fine and necessary tools to try to reveal the identity of a potential security violation. Monitoring, however, is the real-time viewing of packets as they pass the boundary between the internal corporation's network and a public infrastructure. This monitoring comes from a good rule-based policy the corporation has established—what type of traffic to allow in, the type of traffic to allow out, what services are allowed, and depending on the topology of the network border access point, where is the traffic directed to, either internally or off to a DMZ. Real-time monitoring is the only effective way to watch for deviations against the established rule-based policy the corporation has set forth. For example, if you have decided that only DNS traffic is allowed in to a specific host, but someone tries to Telnet to the host, a trigger should be alarmed to indicate possible intrusion. This is illustrated in Figure 2-3. The problem with real-time monitoring for a network security administrator is that it can set off hundreds of alerts. Most likely the adminis-

Figure 2-3
Alerting denied
traffic.

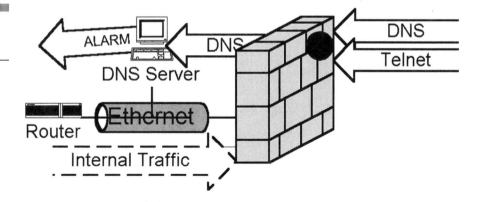

trator will get frustrated from all these alerts and shut off the monitoring on a station.

In Figure 2-3, Domain Name Service (DNS) traffic is normally allowed to pass between the Internet and the DNS server. The firewall that is in between this communication examines the packet and makes a decision based on the type of traffic and the destination address. If it is DNS traffic destined for the DNS server, it will be allowed to pass. Potential hackers could attempt to Telnet to this DNS server; they could have easily found the IP address numerous ways. However, the firewall should examine its rules-based policy and then deny the request and issue an alert to a monitoring station.

Hard Disk Encryption

Although not often considered with regard to security procedures, hard disk encryption could open up a new set of requirements for your organization for two potential reasons. One is key recovery. Most encryption software places your public and private keys on your hard disk. What happens if your hard disk crashes? You have lost the key and cannot revoke that key (making it useless) or duplicate it. In this case, you need to create a new set of public/private key combinations. What happens if you take the hard disk to be repaired? Another person can copy the data on that drive before returning it to you, and therefore have access to your private key. With some networking services, it is very easy to allow others access to your computer without even knowing you allowed that access. Also, if your laptop is stolen, your key is gone and in someone else's hands. You may want to use encryption technologies on that drive or selected directories of that drive to protect yourself.

What Are Some Security Requirements of VPNs?

VPNs differ in the amounts and types of security that are applicable to them. All the normal security procedures apply to VPNs as they would to any other network device. In addition to these normal security procedures, security processes are needed due to the uniqueness of VPN technology. But to recognize why all this security is needed, just start by looking at a summary of statistics on computer incident reports. The CERT Coordination Center is an organization dedicated to helping businesses keep abreast of the latest security violations and offers technical assistance to companies. They keep a running total of the incident reports mailed to them and make this information available to organizations to help them examine their security policies. In 1997 alone there were over 39,000 incident reports affecting more than 146,000 sites, and of these the most serious types of attacks were as follows*:

- IMAP attacks
- Denial-of-service attacks
- cgi-bin exploits
- News server attacks
- Root compromises
- Linux exploits
- IRIX buffer overflows
- IRC in root compromises

As of the second quarter of 1998 they have received over 17,000 incident reports, and with the growth of VPN technology and the use of the Internet as a transport for commerce, that number should increase in time. Therefore, the security of VPNs is extremely important for any company conducting business via the Internet or any public network. These security requirements include encryption, VPN devices, authenti-

---

*Special permission to paraphrase and reference "CERT®/CC Statistics" from the "1997 CERT®/CC Annual Report," © 1998 by Carnegie Mellon University, is granted by the Software Engineering Institute.
CERT®/CC is registered in the U.S. Patent and Trademark Office.
CERT®/CC statistics are available on the Internet (*http://www.cert.com.org*). Readers may learn about the latest updates to these statistics at this location.

cation, nonrepudiation, point-to-point encryption, centralized security management, and backup/restore procedures.

Encryption

As you now know, encryption is simply the process of converting some readable text into nonreadable text. The goal is to only allow that person for whom it is meant to return it back into readable text. This is important because there are different encryption techniques that work at different layers of the OSI model. There are data-link layer encryption algorithms and network layer encryption algorithms. In later chapters we will discuss different encryption technologies. But what's important to remember now is that, depending on your organization's hardware infrastructure, you may have to rely on certain types of encryption that are only suitable for that hardware and/or the IT experience you have on staff. From a security perspective, you need to know what kind of encryption technology your organization uses. Encryption strengths and products directly affect the security of your VPN; therefore, you must treat whatever encryption technology you implement just as any other network entity that needs careful monitoring and maintenance.

VPN Devices

Today VPNs are implemented on firewalls deployed at an organization's boundary to the Internet. In addition to firewalls, VPNs can be implemented in operating-system platforms such as UNIX and Windows NT, black boxes, and routers. With the operating-system VPN platforms, your IT staff may be very comfortable in installing, maintaining, and troubleshooting VPN. Operating-system platforms contain holes, and the term *hole* just means any vulnerability in the operating system. Your IT will have to be responsible for plugging such holes. With black-box implementations your IT staff may be uncomfortable; however, the black-box vendors take care of that responsibility themselves, and they are making their product offerings as easy as possible to deploy.

Authentication

In any major organization there will be several password-protected servers and applications. Users may have multiple passwords, different ones for different servers. They are always told never to write their passwords down or tell anyone else their password. So if they are like the rest of the human population they will either choose one of two options. They will:

1. Write it down anyway; or

2. Choose a password that is very easy to recall.

This is the problem with password protection and one of the reasons they are easily guessed. In fact, one such security attack is a "dictionary attack," a simple guessing type of attack, and if you search the Internet for data on these types of attacks, you will see they are still very successful. Later I'll discuss user authentication scenarios and potential corrections to these types of problems in terms of a so-called 2-factor authentication, which eliminates this type of guessing attack. (There is also 3-factor authentication, which is implemented in highly secure environments such as intelligence agencies.)

Nonrepudiation

There has to be a way for one party to be absolutely sure that the other party has indeed sent the message. Without such a guarantee, financial house, banking, and sales transactions could not occur. For example, say a brokerage house offers online trading and uses digital certificates as a mean of authentication so a user can place a buy or sell order. If, due to market forces, their stock instrument moved in the opposite direction than they intended, what's to stop them from denying they ever sent the order? In a contract signing, how many times are contracts now faxed from one party to the next with the assumption that the other party signed the contract? Again, what is to stop someone who makes a mistake saying they never signed the contract if the signing was done electronically over the network? Today's answer to these types of problems is digital signatures.

Point-to-Point Encryption

VPN-encrypted tunnels safeguard the data as it passes through a public network. A couple of terms are often used with VPN technology: encryption and encapsulation. When we look at specific examples in later chapters we will examine these two concepts more closely. For now, the main difference is that encryption just encrypts the data, whereas encapsulation takes the data packet of the original packet, wraps it in its own packet and then encrypts that whole packet. You usually have devices that either do one or the other. Depending on what kind of technology you use, it can remain encrypted until its final destination (i.e., the actual encrypting/decrypting device can be the end host). Now once the packet is on the inside of that network device, it can become decrypted and stored on a server. Since many security surveys show that internal security breaches are a major concern, what's to stop a person from the inside hacking into that server and reading email and databases or retrieving files? So where do we stop with security—the server, the workstation, or just the LAN segments of the Internet border connection point? That's up to the organization to decide, after considering all the advantages and disadvantages.

Centralized Security Management

At any time in client/server architecture there are different applications running on different servers supporting different clients on different networks. Just think what it takes for an IT department to support this topology. Adding security into the process will now involve different staff members doing different security procedures and implementing different security protocols on different servers on the different networks. Considering how it is sometimes very difficult to get one's job done when there is a security problem, can you imagine if there are several different security problems? It happens now when one application is upgraded; sometimes other applications don't work. If a security application is upgraded or modified, it may affect the whole organization, and it may be days before people even know what happened.

Backup/Restore Procedures

Backup and restore procedures are usually designed for servers and user home directories, but what about the company's VPN? The keys of a VPN device are what make the VPN technology safe. If your VPN devices experience problems, how would you reinstall the device? The keys in your VPN device are known by other parties with whom you have set up VPN service. If you can't restore the keys, you will not be able to reestablish communication with the other parties. Therefore, your backup and restore policy should take into consideration the operating systems, patch levels, implemented rules policy, and the keys associated with your particular VPN solution.

Why Is Security So Important When Implementing VPNs?

In order for VPNs to be an effective means for electronic commerce, extranet applications and Internet financial transactions; secure, current state-of-the-art sophisticated authentication; cryptography; and encryption technologies must be utilized at each end of the VPN tunnel. What measures then make up the criteria of security for VPNs? That is, what kinds of guarantees does an organization need to be trustful of using VPN technology in their transactions? Following are some imperatives for any security setup:

Only Authorized Parties Are Allowed Access to Corporate Applications and Servers This is such an important aspect of VPN technology; you are allowing persons coming in off the Internet or other public network and giving them access to your servers. Say for example that you decide to collaborate with a competitor on a new product and decide to use VPN technology for transactions. This and similar other cases illustrate the need to be very selective in whom you give access to and what services you give them access to.

Anyone Who Comes Across Your VPN-Encrypted Stream of Data Must not Be Able to Decrypt that Message Your VPN data will be traveling across a public network, and anyone has the ability to intercept that data. The safeguarding of that data relies on encryption, including the strength of it and a vendor's particular implementation of it. A new technology called steganography, which will be discussed in Chapter 19 on emerging technology, will add another layer of protection to encryption. An organization has to be sure that the data is safe and cannot be read by others, but they also should expect it to happen.

The Data Must Remain 100 Percent Untouched Other individuals will undoubtedly see the encrypted traffic and try to read it. However, another concern is if they try to modify it and send it on its way to the original destination. Integrity is a different issue when it comes to VPN technology. There are encryption standards that provide for authentication, encryption, and data integrity; data must not be modified and must remain in its full untouched, original form. If the data can be modified, how can you tell that the data actually came from the sender untouched? As explained in later chapters, there are encryption techniques that will help to ensure that the data has not been modified.

Users Must Have Different Levels of Access   Individual users must also have the ability to have different levels of access when they enter your site from noninternal networks. Say, for example, that you have several types of users you want to give access to—internal employees, salespeople, and corporate management, along with customers, suppliers, and vendors. You have to distinguish between their access levels when entering your organization. Not only is the authorization to particular servers needed, but also to the individual subnets they are allowed to access. With some VPN devices, you need to allow specific subnets per tunnel for users; this has the benefit of restricting outsiders to individual networks. It also adds a burden when you want to give internal employees unrestricted access, since you will need to allow them on all tunnels.

Interoperability Issues Must Be Addressed   Interoperability is an issue with different platforms and different systems working together toward a common goal. How then does that relate to security, especially security concerned with VPNs. VPNs need to work across all platforms, e.g., if you have Macintoshes in your organization and you need them to be able to use the VPN, you may need to add some software to their systems. Consider how many platforms and operating systems you have in your organization, how many different types of transports, how many different types of topologies, and so on. Then determine how many of these systems need VPN access and how this can be accomplished. Remember, when you add something new, you increase the risk that other unfortunate consequences occur. Now multiply that by the number of systems you have, and you will get an idea of potential problems.

Ease of Administration Should Be Provided   The VPN device should provide ease of administration, the setup should be straightforward, and maintainability and upgradability of the VPN must be assured. One such ease of administration should be user access ability. In any organization, most likely there will be people leaving, people being hired, people needing Internet access, people no longer needing Internet access, and so forth. So there must be an easy way to add/delete users without tying up your network administrator or telling people it will take a day or so to give them access.

Legal Ramifications Must Be Considered   Much has been said about the Y2K problem and the potential legal and financial responsibilities that corporations will be held accountable for in the year 2000. What about the security issues? If you decide to conduct business on a public network, knowing full well that it is public and the potential for security violations exist, you may be held liable if internal documents sent to you by vendors and other customers become compromised. If a third party sends you confidential information via the Internet, they will expect you to hold that information securely. What happens if someone breaches your security due to your security policy that is in place? The Y2K legal liability will center on how much you did compared to others in implementing Y2K corrections. Most likely security liability will center on those same types of questions.

Implementing a Good Security Policy

Different organizations think differently on how to implement a good security policy. Some organizations want to monitor all internal traffic going out to the Internet, some only want to monitor incoming traffic, and some want a combination of both. Some organizations have more trust in the majority of their employees to conduct themselves in a professional manner, and other organizations trust their employees but are afraid of that one employee who could expose the corporation to a potential lawsuit. Still other organizations just don't trust their employees and authenticate everybody. Whatever your organization dictates should be the established norm. With that there are two schools of thought that all organizations follow:

1. That which is not expressly prohibited is permitted.
2. That which is not expressly permitted is prohibited.

Many organizations implement their rule-based policy on their firewalls according to the second item. The first item, while being very flexible, can be a security risk to implement. The second item is a very secure way to implement a rule policy that continues to allow users access to the Internet. There are only a standard set of network services any internal user would need to conduct their work: SMTP, HTTP, HTTPS, NNTP, and DNS. These five services cover 90 to 95 percent of necessary user access; any other necessary services could be added for an individual and restricted to his or her workstation. Additional services such as IRC, TELNET, and FTP can be added on an as-needed basis and restricted to certain individuals who need them.

The firewall or other network boundary device is designed to block all incoming traffic. By poking holes in it (allowing incoming services), you are circumventing its main design; however, if you don't poke holes in this device, your users will not be able to do simple tasks such as email. Therefore, creating holes in this device is a necessity, but it is a necessity that should be minimized. This approach can even be further refined to allow services through the device, and only allow those services to be directed to a DMZ zone, which in turn directs traffic internally. Figure 2-4 demonstrates directing traffic to a DMZ.

Figure 2-4 illustrates a good policy to implement in your organization. Any traffic that is coming in from the Internet is first routed to a DMZ zone. This accomplishes two things. First, it allows an organization to direct traffic to the DMZ, and only that traffic that is necessary will then be redirected to the internal networks. Second, it allows all incoming traffic to be examined first, by placing antivirus software on the servers on the DMZ; the packets could be examined first and cleaned if

Figure 2-4
Directing all traffic via the DMZ.

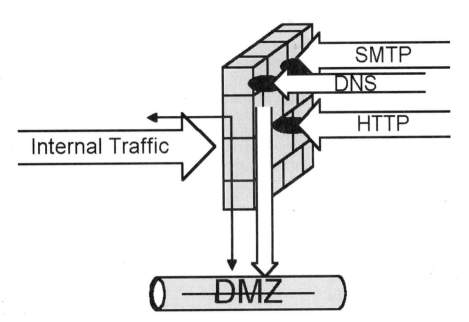

necessary. Some vendors supply software that will run on the VPN device that will accomplish this, but because of the processing power required for antivirus software, you may choose to have a separate server for this function.

Is Your Organization Vulnerable to Attacks?

Every day, different attacks are announced in newspapers, security organizations, and federal agencies. As mentioned earlier in the chapter, the CERT site itself logged over 39,000 incident reports affecting more than 146,000 sites. So if you ask yourself: Is my organization vulnerable to attack? The answer is *yes*.

Every organization is vulnerable to attack; we don't live in an ideal world. A few months ago, a group of hackers presented themselves before Congress and stated they can take the Internet down in 20 minutes. I don't doubt their statement; the way the Internet has been designed, it can be taken down. At any moment one person could stop an organization's Internet access, so with a group simultaneously attacking several strategic points, it could happen. However, it could also be minimized. Just as a credit card company watches your credit card account for suspicious activity, ISPs can monitor their Internet links for suspicious traffic. This is not to say it is easy; it is a difficult, time-consuming, and resource-hungry process. Most likely, with ISPs beginning to offer quality of service and service-level agreements, they may begin to monitor their traffic.

Processes and procedures have been developed that aid in minimizing the impact due to attacks. They provide a framework in which a corporation could examine itself and apply metrics to individual items. Then they will be able to get a feel for where the vulnerabilities lie and apply security measures against those vulnerabilities.

Risk Analysis

How many companies actually perform a risk analysis not solely on paper? How many companies will actually take a server down or remove some critical data and see what happens the next day? Not too many I would imagine. Yet how often does a server go down, a link go down, or a bottleneck appear somewhere, preventing employees from doing their work? These very situations provide the opportunity to gather data and examine how vulnerable you are. Countless books on risk analysis are available, and many companies specialize in risk analysis. Many companies do daily backups as part of their risk-prevention procedural guidelines. Now most problems and inconvenience are corrected in an hour or a day. But what about when the data is traveling across the Internet and something happens? You can't just back up from the tape. While you may not have lost that information, it may be floating somewhere "out there."

Now what would a risk analysis procedure tell you to do? Send the information again, mail the information, or try sending it via a different route than one previously? Taking the worst-case scenario that your competition has the information, it may have been better to send it in several sections rather than one whole piece and possibly over different links and routes. While there is only one Internet, there are many routes frome point A to point B, and by having dual connections to the Internet and an installed routing policy that permits different paths, you minimize the impact.

Information Risk Management

Information Risk Management (IRM) is a framework in which security is handled from the inside. It tries to balance the needs for security and the needs for individuals to work effectively. It encompasses a broad range of policies and procedures, given the limited resources of security budgets in corporations today. IRM covers the ability to monitor, detect, and respond to threats, vulnerabilities, and security breaches. It uses metrics to determine how well you are prepared for a security violation. Some of the processes included are as follows:

- Defining the network security problem domain
- Event detection and response
- Security configuration management
- Policy verification
- Policy management
- Real-time monitoring
- Response

Adaptive Security

As mentioned before, security needs are constantly changing; therefore, a dynamic changing security policy is needed to protect a corporation's internal network. This means a flexible VPN product that can adapt and change to security needs should be made. It also means continually training your IT staff to keep current with the latest security breaches, patches, and corrections. You cannot install a firewall, a router, or a black box at your company's border access point and just forget about it; you would be opening yourself up to potential security and legal liabilities.

What Are Some Types of Attacks?

There are many different types of attacks. Some attack hardware and some attack software. Some are directed in nature trying to achieve a specific purpose. In later chapters, we'll go through each of these different types of attacks so you can understand them, but for now several of the attacks are as follows:

- Timing attacks
- Brute force attacks
- Dictionary attacks
- Guessing attacks
- Remote attacks
- Telnet-based attacks
- Denial of service attacks
- Smurf attacks

These attacks can occur on routers, operating systems, and applications that run services, such as Web servers. Attacks also occur on cryptosystems and encryption schemes that are the security of VPNs and other public and private networks. Each device is vulnerable to some kind of attack, but knowing what you are using in your organization and the type of attack it may encounter will help you develop a good security policy to stop it, or at lease prepare for and minimize the impact.

Conclusion

As seen in this chapter, VPN security should be an extension of the organization's overall security policy, and a well-thought-out security policy/strategy should be designed and implemented. The policy should cover such things as: who is responsible for what function in a security setting, how do you measure yourself against metrics, what is the budget for security, and what is the escalation procedures when something does happen? These attributes of a good security policy should be well planned out beforehand. In addition, active security monitoring is an area of development that is actively pursued by many vendors. For example, just as a SNMP management station would receive traps from nodes throughout the network, so too could a help desk receive alerts from a security monitoring station. A device situated near a network border access point would receive alerts from the monitoring agent on that device. Then, acting upon the data it receives, it would begin the process of logging alerts and event correlation and, depending upon the threshold point set, send an alert to a trouble help desk (shown back in Figure 2-3) for resolution or escalation.

In any organization, information—not just data, but reliable, accurate business-critical information—is a critical business asset. While technology is making it easier to obtain this valuable information in minutes rather than the hours or days, which was the case not too long ago, the trade-off is security. For someone working from home, a remote office, or halfway across the globe, getting that data in minutes means work completed, presentations finished, and contracts signed, but it also means opening up the risks that are associated with the benefits. Data tampering, unreliable transport, latency problems, and identification problems are just a few of the risks. Just look at cellular phones. Five years ago only selected executives may have had phones, but now they are in the reach of everyone. Look what happens, though, when a satellite malfunctions or during a switching-station malfunction—no cellular phone services until the problem is revolved. However, in the case of VPN security breaches, someone or some organization can know your company's secrets.

3

The Advantages and Disadvantages of VPN Technology

In every article that you could read about VPN technology, it would appear as if VPN technology is synonymous with substantial cost savings and ease of use. While this might be the case, there is another side of VPN technology. VPNs do come with additional costs, additional organizational requirements, and additional burdens placed upon the IT staff of that organization. VPNs do permit an organization to obtain cost savings by using a public network instead of a leased line setup, and their greatest strength lies in their flexibility to use that public network to conduct business.

In this chapter we will look at some of the cost savings of VPN technology, then we will look at the additional costs incurred. There are always costs involved when implementing anything new in an organization, and there are always trade-offs. We will look at those items that a company can eliminate to achieve these cost savings, then we will look at what additional requirements a company needs that offset cost savings.

We will also look at the feasibility of VPN technology. Much has been written about why VPN technology is good for an organization, but there are a couple of situations where VPNs would be of no use to a particular company. We will look at these, and hopefully by the end of this chapter, you will understand the advantages and disadvantages that VPN technology offers.

VPN Benefits

VPN benefits is just a general term that is used to describe all the potential benefits when implementing VPN technology. It is divided up into separate areas, with benefits that are applicable to each area of the organization. Some of the benefits that have been written about are as follows:

- Telecommunication charges
- Leased lines
- 800 numbers
- Administration
- Dial-up remote access equipment
- Ease of maintenance
- Simplified network management designs

It is in these areas that potential benefits can be achieved. It would seem then, with all these benefits to an organization, every organization would immediately implement this new technology. While it is true that VPNs have the potential to save a lot of money, they also have the potential to cost money, and as with everything else, there are advantages and disadvantages. This is not to imply that there are disadvantages in the VPN technology itself, but more in the way they are designed and implemented. You can install a very inexpensive VPN in your organization; in fact, there are shareware packages today that will allow you to create a VPN-encrypted tunnel. Your staff could probably put one in for free. On the other end of the spectrum, you could implement the most expensive VPN solution, but what does that buy you?

In the first couple of chapters in this book, several questions were posed that you should have asked yourself before installing a VPN. Along with these questions, this chapter should help you establish a need for VPN technology. Once you have established the need, decided to implement VPN technology, and understand the requirements, with the help of the next couple of chapters, you can determine the architecture of your VPN technology.

Cost Savings of VPNs

Articles today always present some kind of financial statistics on the enormous potential cost savings to an organization when implementing VPN technology. They state that by eliminating many of the devices that are associated with the leased-line telecommunication infrastructure, you reduce the costs that are incurred with long-distance telephone service. By eliminating devices such as leased lines and expensive remote access equipment, they also reduce a corporation's IT staff time on administration and maintenance of these devices, thereby producing savings in the range of 60 to 80 percent.

To arrive at that number, studies simply eliminate the number of access lines a typical corporation has, along with an estimated number of lease lines, and then multiply that by number of users who will be remotely accessing the equipment. Therefore, maintenance and support of these devices is not needed, so you can estimate the number of hours eliminated that were needed to support this type of equipment and calculate a cost saving. So this financial statistic you read about includes the actual equipment, telecommunication lines, and the support structure. Therefore, the major impact in cost savings for VPN technology comes from the elimination of charges incurred during normal working conditions using a regular lease-line scenario. Other considerations for elimination are as follows:

- Leased lines
- Dial-up lines
- Dial-up access equipment
- Staff time to configure end-user equipment
- Staff time to maintain end-user equipment
- Maintenance equipment contracts
- PBX equipment (customer owned)
- Dial-up authentication server
- UPS systems for dial-up equipment
- 800 numbers
- Costly frame or ATM links
- ISDN connections
- Support for IP, DNS, and routing issues

So it would seem that VPN technology could yield potentially huge cost savings for any organization. In later sections, we will then look at the additional costs attributed to implementing VPN technology. With both of these sections you then can get an accurate prediction of total VPN savings or VPN costs. Some organizations will have many savings, some will have more costs, but each will have some of both. Many, if not all, organizations will have a hybrid of savings and costs.

Benefits of Network Design

Network design is an area where VPN technology can really pay off in terms of architectural design, flexibility, and maintenance. The need for complex WAN design, link performance calculations, bandwidth pipes sizing, and redundancy is no longer an organization's concern. Your main concern here is with the connection to the Internet via your local ISP provider, who will handle all the issues associated with your connection.

Figure 3-1
Design of a WAN.

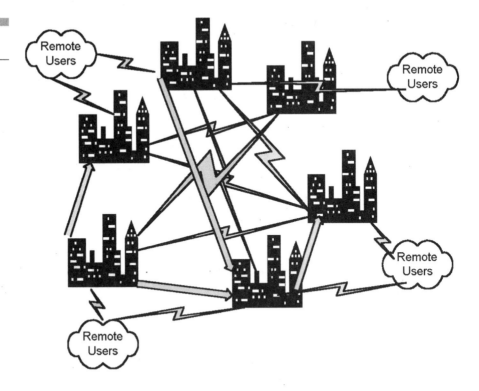

Before the Internet, an organization had the hassle of designing and installing a set of leased lines to certain locations. They needed to take into consideration downtime, redundant links, and scalability and performance issues. The leased line type of architecture unfortunately did not scale well and is extremely expensive. Figure 3-1 illustrates what a typical network administrator had to deal with when designing a WAN over leased lines. The network administrator had to be concerned with traffic flow between geographically diverse departments, buildings, and cities, and create the right pipe size for this traffic. Then they had to deal with remote-user dial-in access accounts and the additional burden of installing redundant links in case of failure of their primary communication link.

Figure 3-1 clearly shows the complexity of the design that was placed upon the designer. What's important to note is the number of links that were need in this topology setting. This forced the organization management team to decide which cities were considered the most important, since the expense of redundant links dictated that each city could not

Figure 3-2
Connecting to an ISP
for WAN connectivity.

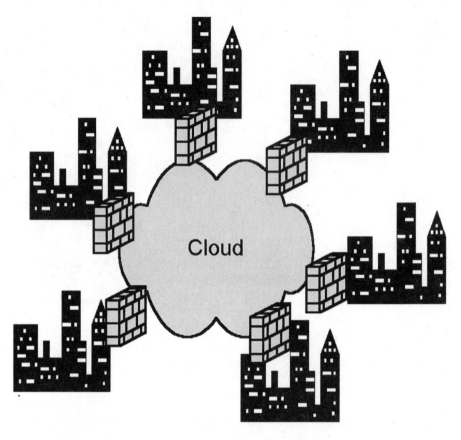

have dual lines connecting them. Therefore, usually only a couple of cities got dual lines, with the other cities having one leased line and one dial-up line for backup situations.

With VPN architecture, all that work has been reduced. As shown in Figure 3-2, all that is needed is an Internet connection, and the ISP takes care of the transport. Now the WAN network can be scaleable, redundant, and standard based (TCP/IP), and support distributed management capabilities.

In addition, all the issues that were associated with redundancy and fault-tolerant attributes have been off-loaded to the ISP. The main concern here is choosing the right bandwidth pipe to the ISP. You will need to examine the traffic patterns on your networks and estimate a percentage of this traffic that will need Internet access. You can also conduct a trend analysis to estimate the amount needed in the future. With this data you may decide to go with an upgraded bandwidth pipe.

Centralized Management

Some vendors support the feature of centralized management for their VPN products. This is a both a strong security feature and a great troubleshooting mechanism. Suppose you have eight different sites all connected to the Internet and all protected by a firewall/VPN combination or some other VPN device, as illustrated in Figure 3-3. Now assume you are working on a problem connecting an application from a client machine in one department to a server in another department through the VPN. Difficulties arise when trying to get multiple IT staffs involved and coordinating some kind of troubleshooting process to resolve the problem in a timely manner.

Figure 3-3
Centralized management station.

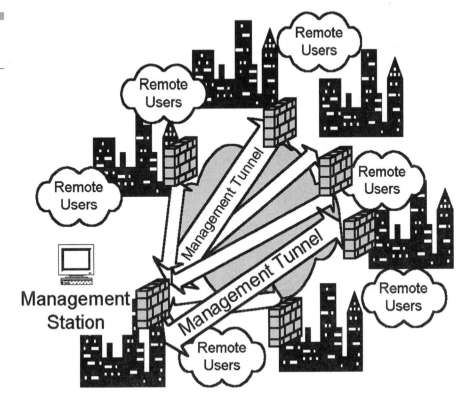

While your solution may work on paper, it usually doesn't work in the real world. What happens is you try one thing. It doesn't work, so you try something else. Then you decide you should call the vendor, so you set up a meeting with the vendor and all the original IT staff who were working on the original problem. This process goes on and on, and each time you need to set up meetings with several people to try to correct one problem. You are trying to troubleshoot over the telephone, which can cause more confusion and time delays due to miscommunication or misinterpretation of the original problem. By having a centralized management process, you eliminate all the above-mentioned coordination problems. All you need is to have the end user and the VPN technician online, and by monitoring both VPN ends, you can easily begin to isolate the problem.

Having this centralized management feature greatly simplifies the maintenance and troubleshooting processes of your VPN infrastructure. It eliminates the need for multiple diverse IT staffs and lessens their administration burdens. Remember that if you do not install a VPN infrastructure that has remote management capabilities, you will need to figure out another way to manage these devices. One such way is to put a modem on every VPN device's console port that you have in your organization. If you decide to go this route, make sure you use modems that have encryption software installed. You do not want someone accidentally to dial in to that number and get access; encryption software modems will only communicate with other encryption modems.

End-User Benefits of VPNs

Today's business must go to where the customer is, whether it is next door or across the globe. This places a burden on the organization in that it demands a geographically diverse and mobile workforce. This means day-or-night access is required to study customer profiles reports, develop presentations, and research potential customers; whether it is 2:00 p.m. in New York or 5:00 a.m. in Tokyo, the network access must be there. With ISP access and VPN technology there is the opportunity to close deals, verify contracts, and so on. Since compatibility is a major issue with different network protocols, there had to be a way to overcome this. The Internet has solved this problem. It is technically *one* network using *one* protocol that was invented over 30 years ago and has withstood the scrutiny of scientific analysis, which makes it reliable for business needs.

Pay As You Go

In addition to the expensive long-distance telephone charges incurred, there are also the costs for branch offices and remote satellites. With a leased line, frame relay, or other infrastructure, you have to pay for idle time. Even if you are not using the pipe, you are being charged. In the case of the Internet, you only pay for online time, which is usually a local call plus a monthly fee. This could add up to drastic cost savings for a small remote office that has to pay for its own telecommunication costs.

Data Access

In a normal scenario, a salesperson needs a special proposal, contract, or other document to give as a presentation to a customer. Currently they have to dial up into the corporate network and access some intranet. With the VPN in place they can make a connection right to the server in question and download the appropriate material, thereby eliminating the need to ask the potential customer if they have an outside line they could use to make the dial-up connection. VPNs also give the remote user different types of access into the organization, via different applications. Say, for example, you are running a special client application that needs to make a connection to an internal server via some port other than the service HTTP (Port 80); maybe you are using a database front-end GUI. With VPN software running on your laptop, you can use the Internet as if it were your local network and connect to your server via whatever service you desire.

Prioritization of Traffic

Several vendors offer prioritization of traffic through their VPN product. This adds great flexibility to a company's utilization of traffic across their Internet link. Since the VPN allows access to an organization's extranet, intranet, or internal servers, it might be decided that in order to conserve bandwidth only certain types of traffic are allowed to pass freely, while other traffic is queued according to its relevant importance. In certain topology setups you can direct all VPN traffic via one link and all non-VPN traffic via another link. Just having this type of flexibility is a great feature, considering how much CPU processing power is needed to examine each packet.

Benefits of a Global Reach

With the Internet comes global access that will allow any user on the planet to connect to his or her company's LAN, so long as there is an ISP provider in that area. This allows an organization to expand its presence across the globe and sell products to anyone who may want them. This gives small organizations a tremendous opportunity for growth and big organizations an even bigger reach. With the budget of many small organizations' marketing departments fixed, the Internet gives these companies a potential marketplace of over 5 billion people. What's more exciting is that the Internet is still an American Internet, not that the U.S. controls it, but by far the U.S. makes the most use of it. With the growth of other countries in Europe, Asia, and the Americas, the Internet will be extremely important in the twenty-first century.

Teleconferencing

While this technology is in demand today, it is not utilized as much as it could be over the Internet. This is due primarily to performance issues. Teleconferencing will continue to grow, and increased demand will be placed upon ISPs for it. While you wouldn't be able to enjoy teleconferencing from every small office across the planet, you will have the ability to teleconference to strategic points across the globe, saving time and money. This is where strategic partnerships will come in, between organizations and ISPs that have a global reach and can offer some kind of quality of service. When an ISP can offer guarantees to an organization of some type of quality of service between major cities in the world, that ISP will become a partner. Since the organization will depend on that ISP to deliver the network infrastructure that teleconferencing demands, it will not take a chance on having that traffic off-loaded to another ISP en route to its destination.

IP Telephony

While IP Telephony is not as much in demand as teleconferencing is today, it is a very fast-growing service that will demand the same type of quality guarantee that teleconferencing demands. The potential growth curve of IP Telephony will probably outstrip that of teleconferencing due to the cost savings that can be achieved using the Internet as a communication medium in everyday calls. If you have read the magazines over the last year or so, you have noticed how the big telephone companies tried to persuade Congress to pass laws protecting their monopoly. When Congress rejected those approaches, the big telephone companies started buying ISPs; they knew the potential growth of this service and the inexpensiveness of it when compared to regular long-distance calls via a telephone circuit.

Benefits to ISPs

ISPs can also enjoy benefits of VPN technology. They will be able to go after their business customers with all types of services that are demanded by businesses today. In the near future, telephone companies will charge by the packet and eliminate the free local toll calls. This is inevitable due to the deregulation laws being passed across the country and by Congress. ISPs will follow suit by charging business customers a per-packet-based toll charge. In addition, ISPs will offer firewall protection, end-user consultations, and custom design and management of their customers' networks. These services are offered today by the largest carriers, so smaller carriers will follow suit. More than 50 percent of network service providers today offer some kind of VPN service.

New Business

As the Internet becomes more of a transport for global commerce, an organization's Internet connection will become extremely important. Business partnerships between companies and their ISP providers will become common. Joint ventures will mostly likely happen between organizations that need global access and ISPs that can provide that access. In addition, as new Internet technologies become common and as the new Internet2 takes off, ISPs will begin to offer their customers new products and new services, just as the Bell companies offer additional services like Call Waiting and Caller ID to their customers.

Managed Services

As networks become more and more complicated, organizations will begin to farm out their network management. While some of them outsource today, the networking technologies that are being developed are changing too fast for any organization to keep up. With VPN deployment, security will become a critical issue, and many organizations will decide to leave that to the professionals. ISPs whose strengths are in security expertise and network experience and who have the network capabilities needed by companies will be in great demand for customers who want a single shop for all of their networking needs.

Competitive Advantage of VPNs

Yes, VPNs do offer a competitive advantage. Unfortunately, those advantages might disappear once all organizations begin using VPNs, which some predict will be early in the next century. This certainly is true for organizations that haven't spent a fortune on internal network design and now will use global Internet access, thereby saving on networking equipment, design, consultation, and maintenance contracts. As the Internet is a routed network, the redundancy factor is built into this network. Some VPN vendors support a policy of prioritizing traffic, so if you have a busy network, your organization can decide what traffic has priority and at what times to make this prioritization active. As more and more organizations connect to the Internet, competitive advantage will be delivered in terms of reliability, latency, and additional features offered by the VPN. And as more ISPs offer additional Internet technology features, more companies will demand these features, which will increase their competitive advantage.

The Internet As a Competitive Advantage

Do you think the Internet is a competitive advantage tool? You might say yes and be correct when asking that question of your own organization. You could also say no and, again, you could be right, given your company's needs. Has your business defined its "critical success factors," such as "vision," "objective," and "mission," and other charters of your company, as seen now on every company bulletin board? If your mission is to deliver the fastest and least expensive Internet service for a company between two points, then maybe the Internet and VPNs are competitive-advantage tools. In any sound management decisions, your company should strive to deliver a quality product in a reasonable amount of time.

Cost of VPN Technology

Many of the articles written today detail how much money VPNs can save. The amounts are staggering, but are they accurate? I believe in these cost-savings statistics like I believe in politics: There is truth out there somewhere; you just need to find it. Some of the additional costs not usually mentioned but incurred are as follows:

- ISP's network infrastructure
- VPN equipment
- Maintenance costs
- Licensing
- Y2K-compliant's legal aspect
- Encryption strengths costs
- Administration
- Security staff
- Help desk
- Additional telecommunication costs

As you can see by these few items, VPNs do incur additional outlays of financial resources to implement this technology, but they can also save a company a lot of money. Let's face it. There is no such thing as a sure thing, but there are benefits that can be had. VPN technology falls into this category: If everything goes right, the actual numbers are present, and certain assumptions are made, you are looking at cost savings in the neighborhood of 60 to 80 percent for your telecommunication charges. In the real world, however, cost savings of around 30 to 40 percent are more likely, which is still an incredible saving. The reason I say 30 to 40 while others say 60 to 80 is twofold. First, most of the savings statistics I read come from the same two or three surveys. The second reason is presented in the next few sections. By the time you reach the conclusion of this chapter, decide if the savings are in the 30-to-40 range or the 60-to-80 range, and remember that 30 to 40 percent is still great.

ISP's Network Infrastructure

Why would the ISP's network infrastructure add an additional cost to a company? Looking back at Figures 3-1 and 3-2, we off-loaded all net-

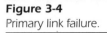
Figure 3-4
Primary link failure.

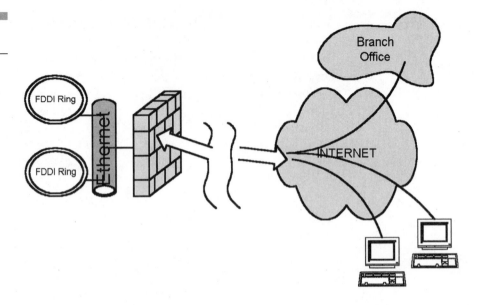

work infrastructure access points to the ISP that was providing us with Internet connectivity. Figure 3-4, however, reveals a potential problem. How many points of entry do you want to have into your organization? From a security standpoint, one is all you should have, but from a realistic work-related point of view, you can't really afford to have only one. Figure 3-4 shows only one way to get into your organization.

If your Internet link goes down, you are isolated. If a computer is off the network, no work will get done on that station; the user will need to move to another station. Many organizations that use the Internet for commerce experience this same type of problem. For example, say a consulting company is left waiting for a proposal that corporate headquarters attached in an email. That email is stuck on some internal mail server in your organization because it cannot get out to the Internet to be delivered. The example of the single computer being off the network will be like that of a corporation that just had its Internet connection stopped, either by the ISP or by a hardware problem somewhere. Corporations will find themselves floundering if their Internet connection is broken, so what really should a company do to protect itself?

Figure 3-5 illustrates what a company has to do in case of the primary failure of its Internet link. It will either have to have a secondary link or some type of remote access equipment to conduct business. This is an example of the known unknowns mentioned earlier. This situation can happen and you can protect yourself, but you have to make plans for it.

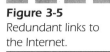

Figure 3-5
Redundant links to
the Internet.

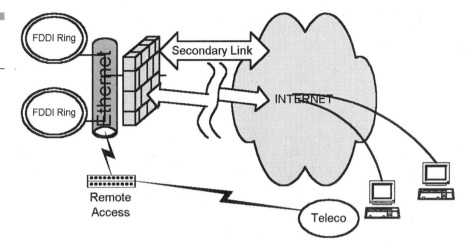

Now remember all the cost savings that were associated with VPNs. Those statistics don't take into consideration factors such as secondary links to ISPs and remote access equipment in cases of primary failure. Here is where we begin to see the additional costs; it is not the technology costing your company more money, but your company's requirement that it cannot afford any downtime.

Looking back at Figure 3-2, say that your organization has just off-loaded your WAN concerns to the ISP. Your company should be free of the hassle of WAN design, and therefore it should realize additional cost savings. But the key word here is *off-load,* not *eliminate.* You haven't eliminated the need for someone to do a costly design analysis plan and implementation; you merely pushed it off to your ISP, as shown in Figure 3-6.

Figure 3-6 clearly demonstrates all that has been accomplished is to push off the burden of WAN design to the ISP. This is an important consideration to take into account when designing your business needs, since these will determine why and how to connect to various ISPs. Even in this figure, it is not fully complete, since there are no redundant links to other ISPs. ISPs can experience problems, so does your organization want redundancy, which drives up the cost? Does it matter to you whether it is your router or your ISPs router that is down? You cannot get out, therefore, you cannot get work done.

VPN Equipment

Where does all this equipment come from and how much does it cost? You are adding some very sophisticated equipment to your corporation's

Figure 3-6
ISPs WAN
connections.

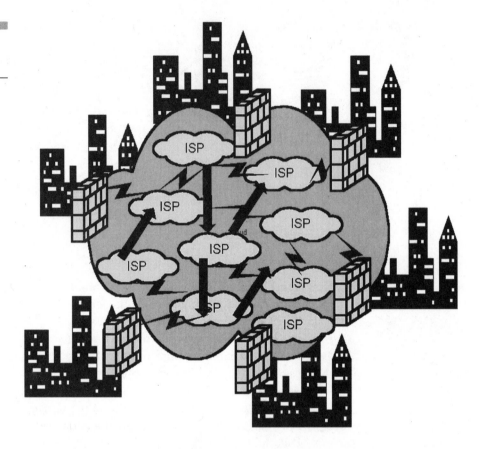

network. This can be in either a stand-alone configuration or in some combination using some other types of equipment, e.g., a VPN device with a RADIUS user authentication server. Are you going to be placing this equipment in a new subnet, or a new network? What about adding remote access equipment (RAS)? Your users will need some way to establish their authentication and be given authorizations. Will you be using a vendor's RAS or have some internal machine running some kind of user database? Is there another type of hardware and/or software equipment you will be adding, such as routers, hub, wiring, and CSU/DSUs? Now multiply this by the number of sites you have, and you can get a ballpark figure of the capital costs.

Maintenance Costs

Just like the other hardware equipment you have, you most likely will have maintenance contracts for this equipment. You can either choose hardware, software, or both. Does the maintenance contract come with upgrade features free of charge? We talked about interoperability features with the future IPSec, PPTP, and L2TP security standards for Internet VPNs. Does your maintenance contract covers these upgrades if and when available?

A major concern will be downtime. How long will it take your vendor to repair or replace the equipment and at whose expense? The expense portion would probably be negligible compared to the cost of being unable to conduct business. This brings up an important consideration though; every vendor has tiers of maintenance agreements, each varying in price. Normally they range from 4 hours to 24 hours and on weekends. Each of these types of contracts has a sliding scale of price ranges; therefore, this is another expense incurred with using this technology.

Licensing

Another area of the VPN issue is licensing; some vendors don't implement this feature, some vendors add this into their firewall products, and some VPN vendors add them on the fly. Licensing is not all the same on products; with some vendors, licensing means the number of simultaneous users passing through the network device. While some add a simple license fee to a router, which allows unlimited VPN connections, others base licensing fees on the number of tunnels you can create. If you know what your VPN is used for, you can predict the number of users, tunnels, and so forth that will be needed. At least make sure you get a licensing arrangement that is scalable. Don't buy a top-performing server when all you can get is a 1000-user license. You might want to examine this first. Also be careful about buying licenses 100 users at a time; it might be prohibitively expensive.

Y2K-Compliant Legal Aspect

While everyone is rushing to fix Y2K problems, think about connecting your internal network via a VPN and connecting to a non-Y2K system somewhere else in your organization. From your company's perspective, you avoided the bug; you will only have to redo that system, which is not a major liability. Now look at it from a supplier's or customer's point of view. You allow them access to your internal system via a VPN (your extranet) or some special application written for older legacy systems. Data is added, deleted, or obtained from a non-Y2K system. What happens now? You either gave access or were granted access to a system that have should been Y2K-compliant but wasn't, and something happened—incorrect data was sent back, financial data was wrong, or bills were not processed. Where does the legal responsibility lie? Now if you use a VPN for international access and are aware of the Y2K problems abroad, how liable are you? As a company you must make sure that all systems that are participating in the VPN domain are Y2K-compliant.

Encryption Strengths Costs

Ask yourself, what are the encryption strengths concerns of VPNs and why should it affect your company as an organization? Where are the additional costs that are incurred with these encryption strengths? When we talked about encryption earlier, we noted that governments regulate the encryption algorithms used; they consider it a type of munitions. Therefore, the actual encryption algorithm is not the cause of the additional cost; the processes you must install to overcome the potential security problems associated from governmental interference is. Figure 3-7 illustrates the problem with different encryption strengths.

Figure 3-7
Encryption strengths.

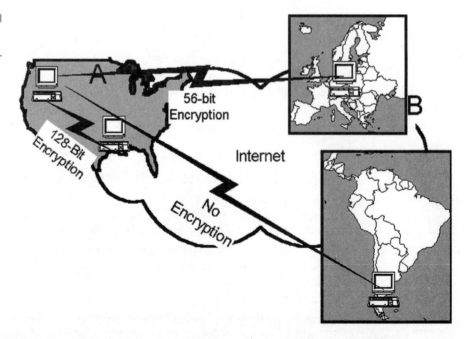

Figure 3-7 shows the encryption strengths to certain countries that are allowed under U.S. export control laws and the host countries' allowable incoming encryption strengths. Starting at the terminal in the upper northwestern United States, you can see you have to use different encryption strengths to each country. They are as follows:

- *128- or unlimited-bit encryption strengths in domestic communication.*   The U.S. government does not regulate the encryption strength used domestically.

- *56-bit DES encryption between the United States and the United Kingdom*   At the time of this writing, only 40-bit is actually allowed, but being just compromised, the U.S. eased its 56-bit DES policy, and the U.K. most likely will follow

- *No encryption to South Africa.*   At the time of this writing, encryption algorithms of any size are illegal to use in this country.

All three of these communication transfers originated from your corporation and travel over the same ISP, leaving your company to their final destination. So where is the weakness? Just as in the saying "a chain is as strong as its weakest link," so too is the security of the data as strong as its weakest encryption.

To protect against this type of problem, you have to install a VPN device that will handle encryption strengths based on destination. Unfortunately, this not the easiest setup to accomplish as far as ease or flexibility. Your VPN device has to have the ability to create a tunnel based upon destination IP address and apply encryption strength to that tunnel. As illustrated in Figure 3-8, the VPN device has to implement the following encryption algorithms based upon the destination device:

- *Address 1.1.1.1.*   Encrypt data to 56-bit DES encryption
- *Address 2.2.2.2.*   Perform no encryption on the data
- *Address 3.3.3.3.*   Encrypt data to 128-bit DES encryption

Unfortunately, I've not seen any VPN device that accomplishes this task. This would also be a difficult setup to implement, since you would need to know every possible destination IP address you wanted to reach to apply a specific tunnel characteristic. However, some VPN devices will downgrade their receiving end to accommodate different encryption algorithms. For example, if the VPN device is set to use 56-bit DES and the originating host is only using 40-bit DES, some VPN devices will answer to the 40-bit DES originating device.

Figure 3-8
Encryption algo-
rithms based upon
destination address.

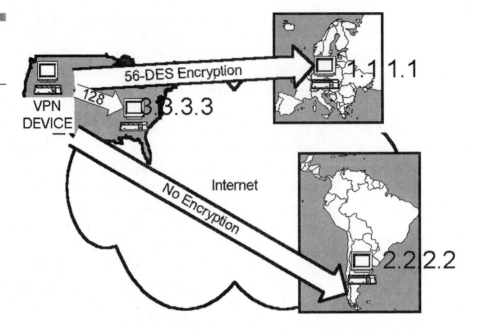

The additional cost incurred in these types of problems might cause a company to forgo communication to countries that do not allow encryption technology, thereby eliminating potential markets. An expensive option would be to set up a leased line to these countries to implement secure communications. You can also set up different VPN devices depending on destination, use the appropriate encryption strengths, or just take a chance and send the communication in clear text. These additional costs are something that you need to consider when implementing your VPN technology.

Administration

Someone will have to be responsible for monitoring and maintaining the VPN, whether you or your ISP. If the ISP supplies a managed service, then this is included in the fee for the service. Normal upgrades and patch updates can be handled over the phone in most cases if your VPN device is an operating system device such as UNIX or a router type. With hardware types there is usually a floppy disk that is loaded into the device, so that on power-up the hardware will install the new revision. In either case just some coordination is needed, since a reset of the device will probably be necessary.

If your internal staff is handling the administration duties, they must be equipped with administration procedures for this new hardware. If you are installing these devices across multiple locations, you will need to manage these devices remotely. The two types of access you will need are as follows:

- *In-band.* This is where you can create an encrypted management tunnel between the VPN devices, so you can remotely manage them over the Internet.

- *Out-of-band.* This configuration places an encryption modem on the console ports of the VPN devices at the different locations. You need to have this configuration in case you cannot get in-band to your VPN device. Say, for example, you are remotely installing this device, and inadvertently a setting gets placed denying in-band access. You've just lost connectivity to that device, so you need another way into that device. In addition, make sure you use encryption modems. They will only communicate with the encryption modems you set up, thereby blocking any incoming calls from other modems.

Security Staff

This additional cost will be one of your company's biggest outlays in terms of the financial and technical resources needed to implement and monitor VPN technology. The security aspect of VPN relies on the strength of the encryption algorithm underneath it. If you implement this technology yourself, are you sure you are implementing the strongest available encryption algorithms? What about the authenticity of the VPN users? How is this accomplished and by what mechanism? Are you going to be using a RADIUS server, digital signatures, or certificate authorities? If you decide on using certificate authorities for user authenticity, will you or a third party maintain the certificate authority server?

SECURITY NOTE If you decide to use a third party as your certificate authority, take a field trip to their headquarters to see the security you are putting your trust in. You will be surprised to find some of them house the certificates in buildings that will remind you of Fort Knox.

If your organization has decided to go with a managed VPN solution from an ISP provider, your security responsibilities have not changed, only minimized. Your ISP will not be your security consultant; their responsibility lies only in managing the infrastructure in place. Your organization decides on the corporate security policy, and your ISP will implement it. Granted, ISPs will assist you in defining that security policy and make recommendations, but they will not tell you what is right for your organization. Therefore, you will need some technical people who will have the responsibility of defining security policy for your company and keeping up with changes to that policy.

Help Desk

There are a lot of articles that conclude that the help desk functionality will be off-loaded to your ISP when you implement VPN technology. I do not agree with any of those statements. Think about it. Your ISPs only responsibility is to make sure the user can connect to the Internet, not to make sure your applications are running. Even if you are using a managed service, they are managing the VPN device, not the hundreds or even thousands of remote laptops your organization has. You or your ISP will install some VPN device from a specific vendor, and along with their product may come some software that runs on a laptop that gives you the functionality of creating a VPN to your company. Whose responsibility is it to troubleshoot that software: you, your ISP who sold you the managed service, or the vendor who sold the software?

GENERAL NOTE   One important thing about this software: you can expect interoperability problems at the beginning, but you will resolve them in time. The best advice I can give you is to start with a clean laptop with the bare minimum of software on it. That is, install your operating system only, then install the VPN software. Configure it and test it, then add other applications if necessary.

I touched on this issue in a previous chapter; the vendors are trying to resolve these problems, but they exist and you need to be made aware of them.

Now, what if your company is using some kind of special tunneling software or some kind of specific application to make use of a VPN you have installed? How can the ISP know how to troubleshoot it? No matter what you read otherwise, you are going to need a help desk of some type, even if its only your current staff and some sort of support process with your vendor. What kind of service contract do you have with the vendor? A 30-day, 90-day, or unlimited support structure? This is yet another cost that will be incurred by your company.

Additional Telecommunication Costs

We've just looked at some of the additional costs associated when you decide to implement VPN technology. These previous costs were associated with the infrastructure needed to support a VPN. The next costs are the direct costs that you incur with telephone service, which, ironically, you were led to believe that VPN technology would eliminate the need for.

Long-distance

Article after article you read about using the Internet for communications implies that you will eliminate the need for lease lines for your company and thereby realize substantial cost savings due to the users needing local calling only. This is a big misconception.

GENERAL NOTE   While there *may* be universal Internet access, there is not universal local calling Internet access.

   The current thinking is that users dial into a local ISP, and with a small monthly Internet connection fee, they can conduct all their business free of charge, since the telephone call is free. However, there is a big difference in rates between state-to-state long-distance calls and in-state long-distance calls. While ISPs try to establish a local connection in every area code, they cannot establish a local connection point in every exchange. For example, Figure 3-9 is a listing of less than half of the exchanges in area code (617).
   What this means is that if remote users have to dial into an ISP and make a connection, they could be incurring in-state long-distance charges. If their telephone carrier doesn't handle all the local exchanges, they will

Figure 3-9
Exchanges in area
code 617.

202	203	204	205	207	209	213	216	217	219
221	224	226	229	230	231	233	235	237	238
239	245	246	251	255	256	259	270	271	272
273	274	275	276	279	280	283	284	286	289
290	293	294	297	299	301	302	304	306	307
309	313	316	317	318	319	320	321	322	324
326	329	331	334	335	336	337	340	341	344
356	359	366	370	377	379	380	383	386	388
391	393	395	396	397	398	399	400	401	402

be incurring expensive per-minute long-distance charges in addition to the monthly Internet access charges they already are incurring.

800 Numbers

You cannot eliminate your entire 800 dial-up remote access modem bank. If, for example, your remote users are going cross-country to a customer's site, they still need a way to access your company's databases. Unless the customer can give them a network connection to use so they can create the VPN to your destination, they will need a dial-in solution. For a dial-in solution to work, they will either have one of two options:

1. *Global ISP.* Your company will need an ISP in every location so remote users can connect to the Internet and retrieve your company's data. This touches on two problems mentioned in the last section, in-state long-distance charges and the area code exchanges.

2. *800 numbers.* You will need to establish a bank of 800 numbers to allow for this communication, and along with this comes the responsibility of access lines, equipment needs, and support for this RAS equipment.

As you can see in this section, you haven't really eliminated the need for some type of remote access equipment, but merely minimized the requirement needs. Your company needs a back way in.

These additional telecommunication costs are in direct disagreement with most of the articles written about the savings of VPN technology when concerning telephone communication costs. It's up to you to decide if you really need these 800 numbers; otherwise you may have to incur in-state long-distance telephone charges.

Quality of Service Guarantees

Can service providers offer such things as quality of service (QoS) guarantees over the Internet? It may be a possibility for the big ISPs who have their own connection points in major cities. Referring back to Figure 3-6, how can an ISP guarantee response times from networks they don't control? Recently a major carrier that offered some kind of service guarantee on their controlled network had a switch malfunction, which wound up costing them money. If this can happen on a private network, how much more unlikely will ISPs offer quality of service over the Internet?

Quality of service is a process where switches and routers set up resources to move data quickly and reliably. Quality of service guarantees try to cover some of the following attributes:

■ Define delay

■ Jitter

■ Cell/packet loss ceilings

■ Security

■ Bandwidth on an application basis

■ Specify acceptable delay

■ Discard ratios

The easiest solution of course to the QoS problem is to add more bandwidth, but that option is expensive for many corporations, and not all applications need that much bandwidth. Quality of service helps in defining a prioritization scheme where bandwidth-hungry applications get the services they need and less intensive applications will still get their bandwidth needs satisfied.

Intensive high-bandwidth applications such as IPtelephony and VPNs have increased the need for QoS standards. One such standard is the Internet Engineering Task Force (IETF), Differentiated Services (Diff-Serv). The idea behind Diff-Serv is to allow ISPs to deploy different QoS levels on the Internet's backbone. Diff-Serv allows users to mark data packets so routers can forward them appropriately. You can view the latest differentiated service drafts at: *http://diffserv.lcs.mit.edu/*.

The previous attempt to implement some type of quality of service guarantees was the IETF's Resource Reservation Protocol (RSVP). RSVP relied on a type of signaling mechanism between devices on the Internet, specifically routers. This signaling setup was done on a per-connection basis, and it required that all routers on the Internet agree to a specific level of service. Diff-Serv has all but replaced RSVP as the working standard of choice due to RSVP's complex design and lack of scalability.

The future Internet protocol IPv6 packet header contains two fields that are concerned with quality of service. They are class (an 8-bit number) and flow-label (20 bits). The Class field distinguishes between the different priorities or classes of data packets, and the Flow-Label field is used by a source to identify packets that need some special handling requirements. Unfortunately, at this time implementation definitions for how to use these fields are still under development. The Internet's working task force responsible for QoS is still deciding how the flows of these packets at layers 2 and 3 communicate and how they both relate to the upper-layer applications.

Service Level Agreements

Service level agreements (SLAs) are contractual agreements between your organization and your Internet provider. Some of the aspects that are spelled out in the contracts are data rates, types of services, and performance statistics. The objective in establishing a SLA with your provider is to quantify specific objectives and metrics that will used as a benchmark to ensure adherence to the agreement.

SLAs are becoming a competitive tool for organizations. Before the Telecommunications Act of 1996, network availability was handled by the main telecommunication carriers and regulated by governmental authorities. Their main goal was just to provide a level of service for the entire industry. After the telecommunications act, the major Bell operating companies found themselves in the middle of competition. Customers now could choose a provider who could guarantee some level of service. In addition to the SLA between customer and provider, the act also specifies the SLA between providers.

In any service level agreement, the following three areas, which concern the actual data transport mechanism that your company is establishing with the service provider, should be addressed: network uptime, bandwidth, and latency. Your provider can give you some kind of guarantee for the first two, but the latency issue is still a major stumbling block in terms of any kind of performance guarantee.

Network Uptime

Network uptime is the actual time that the network is up and available to pass traffic. It is important to consider both *up* and *pass*. The network could be up but unable to pass traffic. If you are monitoring on the data link level, a device could report to you as being up, but the network layer of that device, the actual layer that forwards your traffic, could be down. In that case, as far as you are concerned, your network is down and no traffic will flow. This condition could happen on a router with a bad or incomplete routing table. If your provider's router, the one responsible for passing your traffic, has its routing table corrupted, your traffic may get redirected back into your organization or just dropped. This type of situation does not occur often, but it can occur. The point is that the router will still indicate to be up by any monitoring software, but your traffic will not get out.

In today's networking environment, the amount of time the ISP's network is up and available for use by the customer is very high. This number is extremely large due to the reliability of today's network equipment. When your ISP quotes you on this available network uptime, expect it to be in the range of 99 to 99.9 percent.

Bandwidth

Bandwidth can take different meanings. It could mean the bandwidth of your pipe to your provider, or it could be the available bandwidth over your ISP's backbone. This backbone number is usually quite large, usually in the terabits per second range (a terabit is 10^{12} or 1,000,000,000,000 bits per second). This incredible bandwidth availability has been made possible by Synchronous Optical Network (SONET) technology. SONET is an optical network using light rays as the carrier. By multiplexing the different wavelengths of light onto a single fiber the size of a human hair, tremendous bandwidth can be achieved. This single strand of fiber can carry over a half million simultaneous telephone conversations.

As more providers switch to SONET technology, the available bandwidth along the Internet's backbone will continue to improve the response times on the Internet. However, SONET technology is being applied to the Internet's backbone first, then it will spread out to other local areas. What this means is that even if you can go across the country in a matter of a second, it still might take you 3 or 4 seconds to finally reach your destination. This is because you are going off the SONET backbone to a slower link. In most service level agreements, bandwidth statistics can be easily written and verified by the provider. This brings us to the last issue, latency.

Latency

Latency is an issue that will not be resolved anytime soon. It is the concept that explains the time delay in setting up the initial communication link between points. Your network connections will traverse two, three, or multiple ISPs backbones. How then can an ISP give you a latency guarantee from these two end points? What you probably will get is a latency guarantee across your ISP's backbone only. For example, your agreement might say that once your data stream is placed on the East Coast's backbone, it would reach the West Coast in under 50 milliseconds. This is about the best kind of latency guarantee you can expect.

ISPs have tried to handle this latency issue, but there is no clear solution to the problem. One outcome might be that ISPs begin to work together and come up with agreements to help each other. The SLAs that were mandated by the telecommunications act should prod them in the direction of offering latency agreements to each other. What this will accomplish is that with these SLAs in place between the different providers, they can then go back and offer their customers latency guarantees, since they will have the latency guarantees of other providers.

One final note: whatever quality of service guarantees or service level agreements your provider quotes you will be on a sliding financial scale. The more guarantees you want, the more the financial costs you will incur. Now apply these last two sections of bandwidth and latency to VPN technology. If you need extremely fast VPN access times or additional bandwidth requirements, you again will have to incur an additional cost.

Conclusion

In this chapter I tried to cover as much as possible on the advantages and disadvantages of VPN technology. I hope that reading this chapter clears up some of the confusion about what the benefits are and how much they are going to save you. The price started low (your internal staff) and increased to a very expensive price (equipment, consulting, design, and maintenance). Remember that you get what you pay for.

VPN technology is a growing force, just as the Internet is growing. We looked at several of the cost savings of VPN technology. There were savings on telecommunication charges, as well as on leased lines and 800 numbers. There were savings on administration overhead and the elimination of some dial-up remote access equipment. Ease of maintenance and simplified network management designs were also on the plus side.

On the other hand, VPN technology required additional outlays of money to an organization. Some of these outlays involved concerns about the ISP's network infrastructure, cost of the VPN equipment, cost of maintenance, cost of licensing, and cost of the security protection to make sure your organization is Y2K-compliant. Handling the additional encryption strengths and maintaining the security and help desk staff are other expenses, as are the additional telecommunication charges that you thought you could totally avoid.

Now putting this all together, if you wanted to calculate the true cost savings of VPN technology, use the following formula:

$$\$VPN\ savings = [(elimination\ costs) - (additional\ costs) + (competitive\ advantage)]$$

where *elimination costs* is the elimination of services that realizes a net savings to your organization and *additional costs* are those costs incurred when you add features such as redundancy and fault tolerance. The following lists quantify the elimination costs and additional costs a little further:

Elimination Costs

- Leased lines
- Dial-up lines
- Dial-up access equipment
- Staff time to configure end-user equipment
- Staff time to maintain end-user equipment
- Maintenance equipment contracts
- PBX equipment (customer owned)
- Dial-up authentication server

- UPS systems for dial-up equipment
- 800 numbers
- Costly frame or ATM links
- ISDN connections
- Support for IP, DNS, and routing issues

Additional Costs

- VPN equipment
- Maintenance costs
- Licensing
- Y2K-compliant concern
- Encryption strengths concerns
- Administration
- In-band and out-of-band monitoring capabilities
- Security staff
- Help desk
- Long-distance
- 800 numbers
- Quality of service contracts

Hopefully you now have a feel for VPN technology, at least from the high-level view, along with some of its complements and its advantages and disadvantages. As this book goes along, we will get more into the technical aspect of VPNs and the major security concerns of VPNs.

As a final note, remember back in earlier sections I stated that most surveys predicted cost savings between 60 and 80 percent, whereas I thought the savings were more in the range of 30 to 40 percent? Now you can see why 30 to 40 percent may be a more accurate measure of true cost savings.

CHAPTER 4

VPN Architecture

As we move forward with our discussion of VPN technology, you now should have a sense of the terms that are used with VPN technology and how security deeply impacts the safety of your data as it passes a routable untrusted network. Now that you have some basics, let's move into the area of the VPN architecture itself. When you consider the number of VPN products in the marketplace, it can become quite staggering. There are so many types of VPN technology, with each having its own place and function, and each having its own associated advantages and disadvantages. In this chapter we'll examine some of the different architectures of VPN technology, including network service provider-supplied VPNs, firewall-based VPNs, black-box-based VPNs, router-based/remote access-based VPNs, application-aware VPNs, multiservice VPNs, and software-based VPNs. Just from this sampling of VPN products you can see that there is a VPN for any organization and any type of network infrastructure.

We will also discuss the attributes that you should consider if you decide to install your own VPN, the areas of expertise your company will need to implement and maintain the VPN, and the ongoing functionality. Then we will look at what you can expect from a VPN before you implement one. With architecture there is also ongoing change management and reporting capabilities for your VPN product. You should discuss change management up front with your VPN supplier; maintenance requirements appear after you have purchased and installed your VPN device, and if you don't discuss change management beforehand, you might end up purchasing a VPN device that doesn't meet your needs.

We will wrap up this chapter by discussing certification. Many vendors are now submitting their products to be tested against other products, with security protocols that will be the de-facto Internet security standard in the future.

Introduction to Architecture

There are countless options for installing VPNs, from stand-alone black-box VPNs and router-based VPNs to firewall-based and software-based VPNs. In addition to these architectures, there is a wide range of services and features that can be implemented on these devices. After reading some material on VPNs, it would seem that you could install almost any feature you wanted to, from user authentication and web filtering to antivirus software. Unfortunately, like everything else, there is a trade-off between the number of services available on that product, the processing requirements needed to run these services, and the final support of these services.

GENERAL NOTE Antivirus and encryption software are very CPU-intensive applications. Be careful about putting them on a single platform.

SECURITY NOTE Antivirus software is just an add-on application in many cases. Make sure it contains no holes.

You should separate your VPN service from other application services. Say, for example, that you are using an operating system-based firewall and decide to install a VPN product on top of the operating system. Then on top of this you want to add a vendor's antivirus software. This box must handle the process of checking the traffic that flows through it, which it was designed for, the added overhead of the encryption and decryption processes of the data, and any necessary key-management processes. Now you are adding antivirus software, a very intensive CPU application. There is a temptation to add services to an already-existing server for the sake of convenience, but if it can be avoided, do so, especially when it comes to your critical security servers.

In the appendix is a list of VPN vendors that will serve as a starting point. Each vendor's product could fill a niche for your company. By perusing this chapter and the vendors' Web sites, you can get a good sense of the VPN products available.

Which Is the Best VPN for You?

No one can answer this specifically for you. However, if you are unsure about what kind of VPN technology to use, there are some guidelines to help you decide. Following are a set of questions that you and your IT staff should ask before deciding on a VPN solution.

Do I Know What a VPN Is?

You can't install what you don't understand, whether you are doing this yourself or contracting it out. Will the VPN be implemented in-house, developed and maintained by a consultant firm, or supplied and managed by an ISP? In each case you lose some control but gain technical expertise. If you have hired a consulting firm or an ISP to develop and manage it, most likely they will install what is most comfortable to them. They will utilize a set of processes in maintaining your VPN that they have developed, resulting in an efficient installation. True, you may give up some control, but you certainly can request training on your VPN product and be given a list of criteria of why this VPN device is right for your organization. In addition, if you have gone through some of the chapters of this book, especially the first couple and Chapter 11, on maintenance, you will be able to subjectively to question their VPN offering, keeping in mind your organization's needs.

Do I Feel Comfortable Installing a VPN?

Consider the following mathematical concept below in terms of VPN technology:

$$VPN = f(security)$$

This statement, which says that VPN is a function of security, is the same mathematical formula you used in high school algebra, $Y = f(X)$. Y is a function of X, implying that by varying the values of X (security factors), you affect Y (VPN safety). VPN technology must be thought of in the same context. When you vary the value of (security), you impact the security of your company's VPN.

SECURITY NOTE   It is extremely important to keep up with security issues; there are factors that are beyond your control that affect the security of your data, e.g., 56-bit DES being compromised.

VPN security relies on your hardware device, it's underlying operating system, the strength of the encryption algorithm used in the VPN technology, and the key-management infrastructure you have installed. In addition to these items the certificate authority you have decided to trust as an authoritative source must be validated. The technical expertise of your internal IT staff must be examined, along with the technical expertise of the vendor with whom you are dealing, since you are making an assumption that they are the VPN/security experts.

Is the Only Purpose Cost Savings?

Seemingly every article written about VPNs gives some financial statistics and produces numbers on nice charts and graphs about the huge cost savings of VPN. In Chapter 3, I laid out a checklist of items to give you a good feel for the potential savings. One thing apparent in that chapter is that the things that supposedly can be eliminated are not really eliminated but honed down a bit. However, if cost is your only criteria, you may have a very flexible time in choosing a VPN provider. After sending out your Request for Proposals (RFPs), you could always just go with the lowest bidder. You can also download freely available encryption and make your own VPN tunnels. You have a lot of options; taking your time and carefully considering the alternatives will help you decide.

Will I Be Using VPN for Global Commerce?

If you decide that your VPN's main goal is for global commerce, then you need to remember that the security behind the strength of a VPN relies on both the U.S. government and the destination host government's encryption policies. Therefore, your actions would require you to add whatever steps are necessary to abide by the laws of each country to keep the data safe. You may decide that it is just too risky, but you could also decide to abide by whatever strengths are allowed and work within them. You could decide in these cases not to send the complete data stream at once, hoping that if someone was snooping on the network they are longer there. You also may decide to have multiple ISPs, and consequently you might have multiple routes to the same destination. I say "might" because there are only a few cables that connect country to country; these are the trunk lines. Your data may be funneled onto the same trunk line connecting these two countries.

You could also decide to do a nested encryption process. Say, for example, you are allowed 40-bit DES between the United States and England, and you and your recipient have your own encryption key pairs. You could encrypt that message, email, document, and so forth with the recipient's public key. Then when that data stream passes your VPN device, it would then get encrypted again. Your end destination would then need two keys to decrypt that data stream; the first one would be used by the VPN device itself, and the second one would be your recipient's private key. In addition, by adding the capabilities of a hashing function, you can add authentication and data integrity to that packet. Since many governments do not restrict the use of strong authentication algorithms, you could at least be sure that it arrived untouched, possibly over different routes, and has gone through the encryption process twice.

Will You Be Installing an Extranet?

When we talk about extranets, security, particularly Web server security, is paramount. There are a lot of security risks with extranets, not because of the extranet itself as a concept, but more towards the host of this concept. Probably like everything else, you are placing your extranet on a Web server of some type. Therefore, it will have an underlying operating system, some Web server software, and some type of application front end (let's say a database of some kind). Any one of these items could have security problems associated with them.

SECURITY NOTE   Your VPN extranet is a Web server, so all the security features that apply to Web servers apply to a VPN extranet.

Let's assume your extranet is doing financial transactions between you and your supplier, customers, and vendor. You want to make sure that the VPN tunnels you create to this server are the most secure of any type. If you cannot use the strongest encryption software available due to governmental regulations, then you use the strongest encryption software for U.S. domestic use and use some other encryption strength for international use. Say, for example, you have a Web server farm—national customers use one server, international customers use another Web server, and each VPN connects to their respective servers using the maximum allowable encryption under the law for that particular country.

Is Your Organization Technically Astute Enough to Install and Maintain a VPN?

This question, like "Do you know what a VPN is?," should indicate to you if you are going to need outside consulting or an ISP that offers a managed VPN solution. If you know what a VPN is, then ask yourself, can you support and maintain it? Most IT staffs are taxed anyway these days, and now you are going to tell your IT staff that, in addition to their normal duties, they have to be responsible for this new VPN technology. When you explain to them that they may responsible if a break-in occurs or that they may have to be on-call all hours of the night when you add your alerting software, how do you think they will take it? A funny situation occurred when a previous employer decided on a Friday night to install monitoring software for email. If a single person, out of thousands of users, couldn't send his or her email, this device would page you and you would have to come in at any hour or any night of the week. I thought about how many end users are always having trouble with their email, and Monday I had another job. The lesson here is that if there are too many alerts, your IT staff will leave.

Do You Want to Use a Frame Relay or ATM VPN?

As stated previously, VPNs come in all shapes, sizes, and colors. You may already have a frame relay provider and may want to install a VPN on that transport. I've not installed any ATM VPNs, but based on the readings they seem to be a viable option—except for one catch. In some of the readings the ISPs added the encryption to their devices, and that's how you receive the VPN benefit. A potential problem concerns the encryption algorithms used. In several of the cases I've read, it seemed as if they were proprietary, and anything proprietary alerts me to possible interoperability problems. If I don't understand the technology, I cannot vouch for its security. But you may have a very good relationship with your ISP and the staff to vouch for their VPN solution.

What Type of Security Will You Be Using?

Remember that VPN technology is still emerging. Some of the security protocols that will be standard are the Point-to-Point Tunneling Protocol (PPTP), the Layer 2 Tunneling Protocol (L2TP), and the Internet Security Protocol (IPSec). Do you know what standard you will be using? Can you guess what your VPN partners will be using? If the VPN technology is just to connect corporate offices, then you could establish corporate policy stating one standard will be used. If you are going to be connecting to potential customers and trading partners with your VPN technology, then you cannot set corporate policy. In a situation like this, you will want to wait or install the VPN technology that can be upgraded to whatever standard is accepted.

What Type of Hardware Infrastructure Does My Organization Support?

Understanding your organization's operating system infrastructure is an important consideration, since if you decide that you are going to tackle this project yourself, your IT staff must have the skills for the particular platform. Don't even consider installing and maintaining a VPN if you are an NT shop and all your requirements point to a UNIX-based solution. That would be suicide. The same goes for the reverse. The underlying operating systems and the patch revision levels are difficult enough to maintain. If, however, you still decide to do it yourself, then at least go with a black-box type of solution. They usually can be configured and maintained by just using a Web browser, which would make things easier for your IT staff.

How Many Users Do You Estimate to Be Using This VPN?

When looking at this issue, you will want to get a feel for the number of future users for your VPN technology, not just current users. If you are an end supplier and all your customers will be dealing with you over your VPN, you need to scale. If you are a sales firm or franchise and all your outlets will be using VPN technology, you will need to bandwidth. This will involve performance issues from your ISP. Can you be guaranteed any kind of service or any kind of quality of service agreements? In this case, since a good part of your revenue will be derived from VPN operations, you should discuss the bandwidth requirements with your ISP to size your pipe correctly. You may also consider separate pipes, separate ISPs, separate VPN devices, and so on. You will also need a way to authenticate all these users and set up a database accordingly. This kind of performance, no downtime, and authentication should be your main criteria.

There Are Many More Questions You Can Ask Yourself of Your Organization

Depending on how you answer these questions, your VPN should begin to take form and you should start limiting your choices on what kind of architecture you can support and maintain. You should have an estimation of the number of VPN tunnels you might need, as well as what type of encryption strengths does your organization need versus what kind can you use (Remember: There are encryption export laws that affect the strength of the encryption you use, but there are certain exceptions for certain types of organizations, such as banks). In the following sections we will discuss each type of VPN architecture.

VPN Supplied by Network Service Provider

This may be a very easy and efficient way to connect your organization to the Internet and to enjoy the benefits of a VPN. The network service provider will probably establish a device on your company's premises that will create the VPN tunnel for you. This, however, is not an absolute requirement; some ISPs can install a front-end PPTP switch on their premises that will automatically create VPN tunnels for your traffic. The end destination of the communications will decrypt the packets and deliver the data to your host.

A firewall is also a possibility to be added in this type of environment, usually right in front of a network device or between them. Similar to the older way of setting up a DMZ, the internal router connects to one port of the firewall, the other port of the firewall connects to the external router, and the external router's serial port connects to the ISP. They also should take care of issues such as IP addressing, routing, and mail. Figure 4-1 illustrates a typical network service provider VPN solution.

The ISP will either set up a device on your network or have a front-end VPN switch on their premises to create the VPN tunnel. If the device is on your premise, it will most likely be an operating system-based device, such as a UNIX server or black box, since this allows for the remote managing of that device. A criterion here is to define who takes care of what responsibilities. In Figure 4-1 the lines of responsibilities are clearly defined. The service provider takes care of the equip-

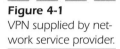

Figure 4-1
VPN supplied by net-
work service provider.

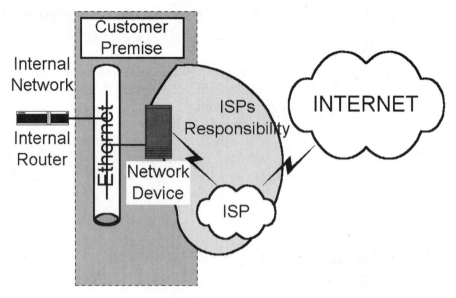

ment associated with the communications of that device. I use the term
communication here because the hardware device is, of course, the ISP's
responsibility. But what about the communications to that device?
Before you say they are the ISP's responsibility, take a close look at Figure 4-2. You should see a different scenario. You will see a blurring of

Figure 4-2
Exploded view of
NSP-provided VPN
solution.

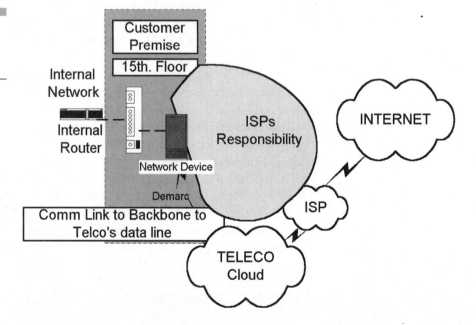

the lines of responsibilities. This should make you take better precautions responding to communication outages.

Here again is the ISP's VPN solution, but now the dividing lines of responsibility are not clearly defined. Who is responsible for the demarcation point, the telecom lines, or any hubs that may be in place? Some organizations have the same ISP and telecom, some don't. Some have wiring harnesses that travel a backbone to the basement and then to the telecom cloud and finally to the ISP. This means that for VPN technology, or, for that matter, any telecommunication service, you need to have a test in place for each isolation point. You need to be able to pinpoint the problem immediately. I have seen problems with VPN technology due to a bad intermittent circuit switch. So if you don't have a procedure in place, you could be arguing for days between your IT staff, your telecom provider, or your Internet provider. What about equipment failures? Your company does not own the equipment. You cannot simply swap in another device when one fails. You need to know how long it will take your ISP or telecom provider to diagnose and correct the problem. Just ask yourself how long you can afford to stay down. This is just one problem. Some of the other issues include security, change control, troubleshooting, features, authorization, network utilization, device utilization, client apps, and key management. (Note: These following problems apply to all implementations of VPN architecture. The only difference is whose responsibility it is, yours or your ISPs?)

Security

I doubt the network service provider would be responsible for security, even if they supplied the equipment. The security of VPNs will be based on standards that are accepted by the vast community of the Internet society. The ISPs are supplying Internet service first and VPN service second. Your actions could have caused the security problem. Say, for instance, you want a VPN tunnel to an older legacy system. The access is granted, and the user applies an older hack to gain administrator privileges on that device. Is it your fault, since you allowed the communication? Or is it your ISP's fault for not telling you shouldn't allow those particular types of services to that device? After all, they are supplying you a VPN solution; they should be experts. In this case, hire an outside security team to formulate a security policy and have the ISP implement that policy.

Change Control

You need to know who makes access policy control changes and how long it takes to implement these changes. Your provider may not be available or may be busy troubleshooting another customer's problem. It would be prudent for you to realize it takes a little time to go through a change control process. It has been my experience that sufficient time is needed, anywhere from 4 to 24 hours. This is for a couple of reasons. After your device is up and running, you usually will not bother with it. It may be months before you even decide to add another service. The changes you are requesting are for someone else who wants access to a particular service or destination, which, of course, the administrator cannot arbitrarily grant. Usually it takes days just to get the necessary permissions. Then to track the change control, you will normally fill out something to notify your managed service provider that something is about to change per your request. After all these steps 1 day hardly seems that long to wait. Then you need to determine how to monitor change control. If you requested a change to your existing architecture, you need to know how and when that request got implemented. You need feedback to verify that the change controls you wanted, either by email or phone call, and you will need some feedback on how the change was implemented. Remember, in adding new services you may need to go through some troubleshooting along the way, so you may eventually go through several change controls, and you'll need to keep track of each one of them and monitor them.

Troubleshooting

In any kind of VPN setting, when things go wrong or problems occur—or, even worse, when intermittent problems develop—who will help you? I find intermittent problems are the hardest types of problems to diagnose; they occur, disappear, and then occur again. You bring in your technical team and consultants, but if the problem doesn't manifest itself or they haven't seen a similar problem, it could be weeks before the problems are resolved. Even monitoring the traffic and analyzing the data does not always reveal the cause. You really need to make sure that you spell out in your contract the ISPs willingness to spend the time to troubleshoot, diagnose, and resolve the problem for however long it takes. Of course, something like this adds to the price of the contract, but it is better than months of dealing with a problem.

Features

Features are a very important consideration if you are one of the organizations that like to try out new technology. If your company wants to use the Internet for teleconferencing or use IP telephony, you really want to discuss this with your vendor. What happens if your company decides it needs a different setup than you originally implemented? Your ISP is responsible for hundreds of accounts, and they will try to offer you complete service, but they must be responsible for the services of the majority. You may not be allowed to implement your specific application. Redundancy, fault tolerance, synchronization and push technology are just some of the special cases.

Authorization

You need to know how and when users get added to a database that will allow them to create the VPN tunnel to your organization. Is the database on the vendor's VPN device, or is it on some internal server you control? Can you get access to it, or if not, how long will it take for user authorization to become effective? This is important in the case of a terminated employee; if an employee leaves, you want their access restricted immediately, not in a day. You don't want to come in one morning and find that person was logged on last night to a server. In these situations it is imperative that you have either immediate access to the database to revoke their access privileges or a way to contact your vendor immediately to accomplish this task.

Network Utilization

You have to be aware of how your network is doing overall. Either you or your ISP must monitor the link for bandwidth traffic utilization. Even if you are supplied a VPN by a service provider, this does not immediately guarantee that they will set up network monitoring capabilities for your company. However, most ISPs do offer some kind of VPN monitoring services. Your organization, like many others, will connect the VPN and forget about it. Then you will start to grow and request more VPN service, which drives up the bandwidth. You need a way to implement a trend analysis on those links and get ready for an upgrade long before you need it.

Device Utilization

Your VPN device is just like any machine or piece of software sitting somewhere in your organization. Someone will have to watch the performance of that machine, monitor its health, and take care of things before they happen. Remember, you don't own the machine; it's on your site but under the control of your ISP. You therefore cannot control it. The daily traffic, the number of users, and the encryption and key management processes all take up resources of the CPU. You need to keep abreast of them so you will have time to upgrade them when necessary.

Client Apps

In order for roaming laptops to create a VPN tunnel, they will need special software that is loaded on them. Who will load all these laptops, desktops, and so forth, and who will maintain them? You thought you bought a VPN service. Well, you did, but unfortunately, this is one of those gray areas your organization will have to be responsible for. It would be impossible for your ISP supplier to accomplish this task, but once you have this software loaded, they should assist you in troubleshooting connections to the VPN device. The major problem happens if some software is already loaded on these machines and conflicts with the VPN software. As mentioned previously, because of the location of the VPN software, between the data-link and network layers, there could be problems running this software. There will have to be some party whose responsibility is to correct them; the ISP wouldn't be as much help here as the original vendor would be.

Key Management

In any of the ISP VPN offering or in any of the following VPN architectures, key safety is an important issue to remember. Just as in any backup/restore procedure your company has, so must the keys of your VPN be part of a routine procedure. This is not the generation and management of keys, but where to get them if you need to duplicate them. In these architectures, the keys that are generated and managed must be stored in a safe, secure place, not only for security purposes but also for recovery of those keys. These include the public keys, device keys, and any certificates you are responsible for. The encryption keys for the tunnel must also be able to be reproduced in case the VPN device fails and a new device is needed. The common practice is that if your device needs replacing, you generate new keys for the new device; however, you still have all your old keys and certificates on servers. You really don't want all those keys sitting everywhere. You want to revoke them and issue the new ones, but you can't revoke them unless you have the original ones.

Firewall-Based VPNs

Firewall-based VPNs are probably the most common form of VPN implementation right now, and many vendors offer this type of configuration. This is not an indication that firewall-based VPNs are a superior alternative to other forms of VPNs, but more of an already established base from which to grow. It would be hard to find an organization today connected to the Internet that doesn't use some kind of firewall. Since these organizations are already connected to the Internet, all that would be needed is to add encryption software. Most likely, if your organization has recently purchased a firewall, it came with the ability to implement VPN encryption technology. When I say *VPN technology* I mean some type of encryption scheme supplied with the device. If you want a different encryption scheme, you most likely will have to pay for it. Many vendors include their proprietary encryption technology free of charge with the product.

There are many vendors to choose from when considering a firewall-based VPN, and the products are available on all different kinds of platforms. One very important security concern here is the underlying operating system. On what platform is the firewall running? Is it a UNIX-based, an NT-based, or some other platform-based device, and what are the potential vulnerabilities of that operating system? There is no device that is 100 percent secure, so if you create the VPN on that device, you need to make sure that the underlying operating system is secure. If you look back at Figure 2-1 you should see again why VPN technology should be at the lowest layer of the OSI stack. The higher up the stack it is, the more opportunities for security intrusions to occur in the lower layers that it depends on. Figure 4-3 illustrates a firewall-based VPN.

While Figure 4-3 illustrates a simple firewall-based VPN product, it is not a simple implementation. Most organizations have these systems

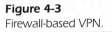

Figure 4-3
Firewall-based VPN.

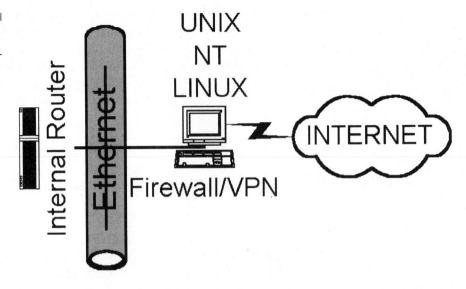

in place, so adding the VPN software is not too difficult. You must decide what type of VPN standard you want. For instance, do you want to use PPTP, L2TP, or the IPSec standard being developed. (Remember that IPSec is a framework so DES encryption could be used in an IPSec setting.) In later chapters we'll discuss DES, IPSec, and PPTP in detail, but right now it's important for you to understand that you have a choice.

If you decide that a firewall/VPN solution is the right avenue to take, it would be a good idea to look at some recent surveys on firewall products. You would then be able subjectively to compare different firewalls. Or if you have a firewall in place, you could compare that to the other firewalls on the market. You want your VPN underlying platform to be as stable as possible. A couple of good firewall surveys were recently done; you can search the Web, starting at *http://www.techweb.com/*.

There might be some confusion as to what I mean by a firewall/VPN solution. When I say that you should add VPN technology to your firewall, you might assume that I mean any firewall technology. That assumption would be incorrect, and before we move to the next section, let me clarify this. At the moment there are three types of firewall implementations you could choose: stateful-inspection, proxy, and packet filtering. When I say "add VPN technology to a firewall," I am referring to adding VPN technology to a stateful-inspection firewall only. Just as the VPN technology itself runs on the lower levels of the OSI stack, so too must the firewall or you may run into major performance problems. A proxy server runs at layer 7, the application layer of the OSI model, and the packet filtering firewall also has to examine the complete packet every time it goes by. A stateful-inspection firewall runs at layers 2 and 3. Because of this processing requirement you shouldn't add VPN technology to anything other than a stateful-inspection firewall.

Black-Box-Based VPNs

In the black-box scenario, a vendor offers exactly that, a black box. This is basically a device loaded with encryption software to create a VPN tunnel. Some black boxes come with software that runs on a desktop client to help manage that device, and some can be configured via a Web browser. It is believed that these hardware types of encryption devices are faster than software types. They create faster tunnels on demand and perform the encryption process faster. While that may be true, not all offer a centralized management feature, and they usually don't support logging themselves; you need to send these logs to another database to query. Another server is also needed if you want to do authentication, although some devices allow you to add users if you wanted to. But do you want to maintain all your users on one device?

A nice feature on some of them is that they will allow you to use an existing database. They come with management software that is usually loaded on a desktop. You configure the device to use authentication and then point it to this management server you set up. You then set up the management server to use your existing user database. For example, if you have an NT database, you can keep a single database and have your VPN device query it for user authorizations, instead of having several databases and trying to keep them in sync.

At this time, vendors should be supporting all three tunneling protocols, PPTP, L2TP, and IPSec, but don't take that for granted. Vendors have taken great strides to make dedicated encryption devices as easy as possible to implement. As with everything else in technology, if it is easy, it may not be that flexible. However, the performance may be good, which is more than enough for your company. With most black-box setups you may need a separate firewall, although more vendors are beginning to incorporate a black-box VPN with firewall capabilities. Figure 4-4 illustrates a black-box VPN solution.

The black-box VPN device sits behind the firewall. It can, however, sit on the side of the firewall, as we will see in Chapter 5 on topology. The firewall provides security to your organization; it does not supply securi-

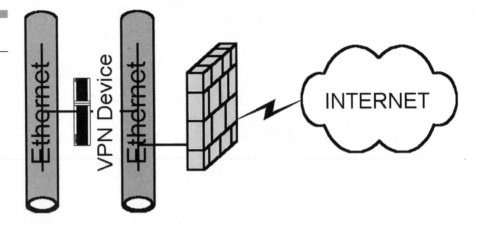

Figure 4-4
Black-box VPN.

ty to your data. Likewise, your VPN device will provide security to your data, but not your organization. Vendors are trying hard to make these devices extremely easy to use. Some have a command line syntax to configure, but most have a Web-based GUI.

SECURITY NOTE An important consideration here is what kind of VPN tunnels you are creating.

You will notice that the firewall is in front of the VPN device, and most likely you have installed a rule-based policy on the firewall. In your firewall configuration, make sure you can pass those encrypted packets. The firewall is there for protection. If you are filtering on the TCP ports and the packets come in encrypted, the firewall will try to examine the packet, realize it can't, and drop the packet. Therefore, you must make sure your firewall will pass those packets.

Router-Based VPNs

Router-based VPNs are possible for an organization that has a large capital investment in routers and an IT staff experienced with them. Many router vendors support this configuration; a visit to their Web pages will give you a sampling of what's available. There are two types of router-based VPNs. One is where software is added to the router to allow an encryption process to occur. A second method is where an external card from a third-party vendor is inserted into the same chassis as the router. This second method is designed to off-load the encryption process from the router CPU to the additional card.

Some vendors support hot swapping and redundancy, which are built into their router-based VPN products. This may be a necessity for organizations that can sustain only a very short downtime. Keep in mind that performance may be an issue with router-based VPNs. Due to the addition of an encryption process to the routing process, you may be adding a heavier burden to the router, especially if your router is handling a large number of routes or implementing an intensive routing algorithm.

Router-based VPN vendors can supply you with a list of performance statistics that might show their product encryption overhead is minimal. Will the router support all the Internet security protocols and the ones that will most likely be used in the future, such as PPTP, L2TP, and IPSec? These tunneling protocols are important for future interoperability. Also, will the router implement user authentication, or will you need a separate device that is compatible with the router to do this?

Figure 4-5 is a typical router-based VPN, where packets are encrypted from source to destination, for example, headquarters to remote offices. There are two concerns here with the router-based VPN:

1. *Interoperability.*   If you want to connect to suppliers' VPNs, will both your router and your suppliers' router operate with one another and create the VPN?

Figure 4-5
Router-based VPN.

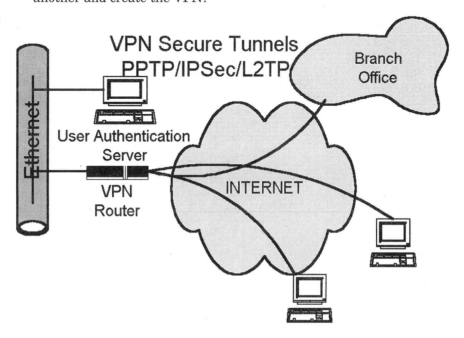

VPN Secure Tunnels
PPTP/IPSec/L2TP

Branch
Office

Ethernet

User Authentication
Server

VPN
Router

INTERNET

2. *Encapsulation.* Are you going to be transporting non-IP protocols to another site, such as IPX or SNA? Some router manufacturers only encrypt; they do not encapsulate.

Remote Access–Based VPNs

There are lot of different definitions on exactly what makes up a remote access VPN. Router manufacturers say one thing, software vendors say another, and other vendors say something else. *Remote access,* as the term applies, means that someone is out there trying to create an encrypted packet stream to your organization. So, more literally, perhaps the term applies to software running on remote users' machines, which are trying to create a tunnel to your organization, and to a device on your network allowing that connection. This tunnel could be coming in from the Internet, but it also could be coming in from a dial-up line, ISDN line, or a X.25 network. Figure 4-6 illustrates a typical remote access scenario.

This scenario has software running on a remote machine somewhere, and that machine tries to establish a connection via an encrypted tunnel to the company's internal server, or from a dial-up access line such as ISDN, to an authentication server. An access server on your network,

Figure 4-6
Remote access
scenario.

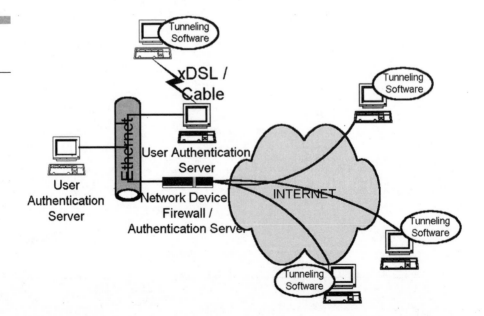

either a router, firewall, black box, or stand-alone authentication server, grants the access. This remote access device minimizes the amount of equipment of costly leased lines and remote dial-up access equipment.

Application-Aware/Proxy Toolkit VPNs

This type of VPN is not often discussed in the articles, but when you need it, you really need it, and hopefully by then you will find out that it is supported on your product. This particular situation is occurring partly because of the enormous growth of services that are being offered over the Internet. First, take a look at Figure 4-7 and try to understand what service is being requested.

The Internet is not the driving force for newer application technologies, but it is the transport mechanism to carry these newer applications. What happens, though, with these new technologies if they don't follow the old format of client/server communication? Typically in client/server communication the client is making a request to a server for a specific service on a specific port. The server responds to the client with the necessary information, and the communication takes place. Now with newer applications like IP Telephony and teleconferencing, when a connection for a specific application is made on a specific port, the response the serv-

Figure 4-7
Application-aware
VPN.

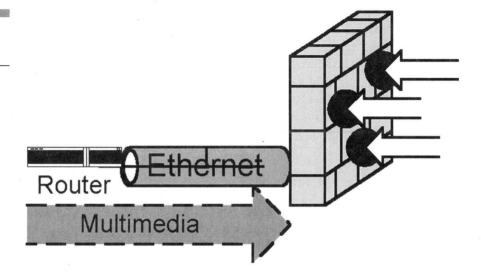

Figure 4-8
VPN toolkit.

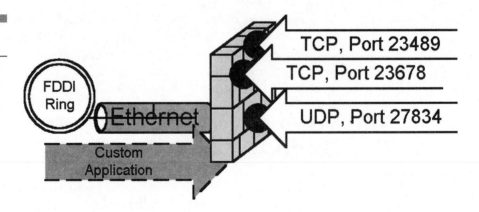

er sends back comes in on several ports. So how do you configure your VPN to handle multiple in bound connections originating from one outbound request? What happens if you have a firewall/VPN product? What ports do you open up? Look back to Chapter 1. You do not want to open any unnecessary ports due to possible security violations, but in the case of the newer technologies, you need to. If you can't open these ports yourself, you have to make sure your VPN architecture supports newer technologies such as IP Telephony, Internet FAX, and protocols H.323 and T.120. So now looking back at Figure 4-7, you are making a request for a multimedia application, and the response is coming back on several ports. This leads us into another possible consideration for a VPN architecture called a VPN proxy toolkit, illustrated in Figure 4-8.

Say, for example, you are working with a vendor and developing a new application that will need encryption support over TCP ports 23489 and 23678 and UDP port 27834. How are you going to implement this? You can just open up the individual ports, but that is an unsecured way. Remember that the packets are coming back encrypted, so how would the VPN device even know where it originated from? A better way is to have some kind of API that could be written into your VPN device that will enable you to write the functionality you need. These are called VPN API toolkits. Some third-party vendors have products for these features.

Multiservice Applications with VPNs

Vendors are beginning to come out with multipurpose applications that can reside on your firewall-based VPN device, which may be considered an added bonus or a potential problem with performance, depending, of course, on what your VPN is doing now. Some of the multiservice VPN applications are Web content filtering and antivirus checking. Web content filtering is added to your firewall/VPN device to allow you to see what kind of Web sites your internal users are visiting. It is not so much a VPN aware application, but you will need to keep track of this. The VPN encryption process itself takes a lot of processing power, so you need to keep an eye on traffic. The antivirus software, which can be loaded on the device itself or off-loaded to another server, is a very important service to implement. You need to keep viruses down to a minimum (and I say *minimum* because you can't believe how many times the same old virus gets retransmitted throughout an organization). While there may not be any VPN virus that we are aware of, you need to consider it and add that feature if the need arises.

In Figure 4-9 all traffic that is coming into the organization is first analyzed by the antivirus software that is running on the firewall/VPN device or by a server sitting on the DMZ zone. I prefer the DMZ zone since the antivirus takes a lot of processing power. When the incoming traffic has been checked, it is then passed on to the internal network. This placement is a very important concern if you are not using a firewall/VPN combination. In that case the packet that is coming in is encrypted, so it has to be first decrypted before it can be analyzed.

Figure 4-9
Multiservice VPN.

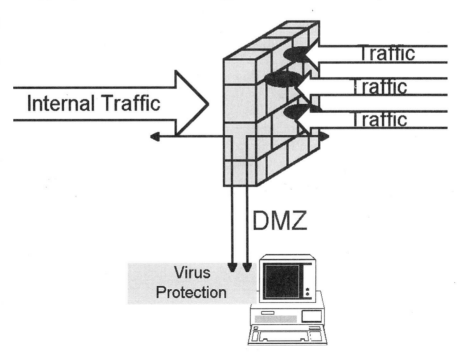

So where are you going to place the VPN device? Before the firewall? That is not the usual placement. Behind the firewall? Then the VPN device will have to be able to direct traffic to an antivirus server before allowing it to pass internally. Unfortunately, anywhere you allow the creation of a VPN tunnel, there is exposure to these types of problems—and not just antivirus problems, but security problems as well.

Software-Based VPNs

A software-based VPN is basically software that implements either tunneling or encryption to another host. It is usually used from client to server. For example, in a PPTP VPN, software loaded on the client connects to the software loaded on the server and establishes a VPN session. There are other versions of software VPNs. The appendix lists several vendors that offer software VPNs. When you choose software VPN, you will need to have a good key management process and possibly a certificate authority on your premises. With the other types of VPNs, say for example, firewall/VPN to firewall/VPN, the only keys that are needed are from VPN to VPN. This means the traffic on your internal network is decrypted, so you only need the keys for the VPN devices. But in the case of client to server, every station could possibly have their own private/public key pair; you just need to make plans for this kind of setup.

The traffic starts from a specific host in your organization and makes a connection to some server somewhere. The traffic leaving the host is either encrypted or encapsulated, depending on the VPN installed, and routed to its destination. The same occurs for someone trying to connect

Figure 4-10
A software-based
VPN.

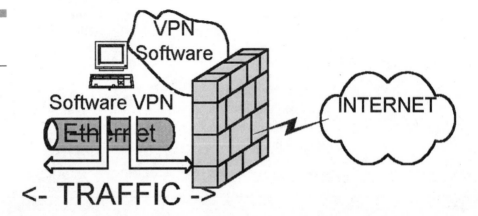

to your internal network, a client machine somewhere starts a VPN client session and sets up a communication dialog with the VPN server in your organization. This communication establishes what type of encryption and what authentication algorithms to use and other data relevant to start the communication. After that initial setup is done, the flow of data begins. In this example, if your firewall is not the VPN device, make sure it is set up to pass the encryption algorithm you choose.

Tunnel Switches for VPNs

As of this writing, VPN tunnel switches are just coming into the marketplace. Two or three vendors have announced that they have created a new type of VPN device. This one piece of equipment would give corporations the ability to streamline their VPN implementation and to create whatever type of VPN infrastructure they need. This device has all the traditional functionality of present-day VPN architecture, with the added feature of being in only one physical device. This multipurpose VPN architecture is designed to combine all the features of the traditional network devices associated with connection to the Internet. Firewall, routing, and VPN functionality are all combined into one stand-alone product to produce a one-size-fits-all scenario for a corporation, including site-to-site VPN tunneling, remote users access, and access to tunneling anywhere into your corporation. They are built to scale to thousands and possibly hundreds of thousands of users, either in an encapsulation mode or an encryption mode. They also support the dynamic encapsulation of non-IP-based protocols such as IPX and SNA. They support the traditional PPTP protocols for remote dial-up users and encryption algorithms such as IPSec for LAN-to-LAN tunnel connection. Because these devices are relatively new at this writing, there has not yet been sufficient time to examine the merits of this type of VPN architecture.

Performance Statistics/Comparisons

There have been many claims of stellar performance by some VPN vendors, so looking at some of their performance statistics and tunnel capabilities on some of their devices is important. I've also created a separate chart of advantages and disadvantages of different VPN architectures. Hopefully, this will help you to decide what type of VPN technology to implement. Remember that there is always a trade-off; you first need to understand what your requirements are: 100 users or 10,000 users, domestic or international, and so on. Also remember that VPN architecture is scalable; you can add additional VPN tunnels later.

Table 4-1 outlines some specific claims that have been made available by VPN vendors. As I have done throughout this book, I will try to keep this unbiased, so I have labeled the vendors Vendor A, Vendor B, and so on. The reason for this is that by the time you read this chapter, some of the vendors will have upgraded their products, so it would be unfair to them to list out-of-date products. In the appendix, I've listed an extensive number of VPN vendors from whom you can obtain data so you can easily visit their Web sites and obtain the necessary information. If you

TABLE 4-1 Vendor Specifics

Vendor	Type	ENC	Auth	Comp	Eth	R.U(S)	R.U(E)	S.Tun
A	HW	DES,3DES(1)	H-MD5,H-SHA,SKIP	Y	10Mbps	600	65,000	N/A
B	HW	DES,3DES(1)	MD5	N/A	Giga	N/A	N/A	N/A
C	SW	RC4	RSA	Y	N/A	16,000	N/A	2000
D	sVPN	DES,3DES(1)	PKI	N/A	100Mbps	3000	N/A	1,000
E	rVPN	PPTP	CHAP	Y	100Mbps	2000	N/A	64
F	FW	DES,3DES	H-MD5,H-SHA	N	10Mbps	64,000	23,000	N/A

Vendor Specifics (Continued)

Vendor	Auth.S	Key Mgt	Dig. Cert.	Enc&Encap.	NAT	Mgt.	Mon.	cVPN
A	R,ACE	ISAK,SKIP	X.509v3	Y	Y	Web-based	SNMP	Y
B	R	M-IPSEC	X.509v3	N/A	Y	Web-based	SNMP	N/A
C	ACE	RSA	N/A	N/A	N	N/A	N/A	Y
D	N/A	ISAK	X.509	N/A	N	prop	SNMP	No
E	N/A	N/A	N/A	N/A	N	N	N	Y
F	R	ISAK	X.509v3	Y	Y	prop	SNMP	Y

1- Only between U.S. and Canada.

like, use the chart in Table 4-1 and plug in the appropriate specifications. The following is the list of codes that are used on the table.

Code	Description
N/A	Data not available or nonapplicable to particular VPN technology
Vendor	A symbol to distinguish individual vendors
Type	Type of device (HW = hardware, SW = software, sVPN = VPN switch, rVPN = remote access VPN, FW = firewall)
Enc	What type of encryption algorithms are supported?
Auth	Authentication Support algorithm (ISAK = ISAKMP, H-MD5 = HMAC-MAC, H-SHA = HMAC SHA-1, M-IKE = Manual IPSes, PKI = Public Key Infrastructure)
Comp	Is compression supported to enable faster network throughput?
Eth	Speed of ethernet connection (giga = gigabit)
R.U.(s)	Number of simultaneous remote users that comes standard
R.U.(u)	Number of simultaneous remote users it can be upgraded to
S.Tun	Number of simultaneous tunnels allowed
Auth. S.	What type of authentication servers are compatible? (R = RADIUS, SD=Security Dynamics ACE/Server
Key Mgt.	What type of key management protocols? (ISAK = ISAKMP)
Dig. Cert	Digital certificates standard supported
Enc. & Encap	Does it support both encryption and encapsulation simultaneously?
NAT	Network address translation supported
Mgt.	System management (prop = proprietary)
Mon	System monitoring
cVPN	Client software/support for VPN

As you can see by comparing the data in Table 4-1, there is a wide range of encryption algorithms, authentication encryption schemes, and number of users and tunnels that can be supported simultaneously. Therefore, setting up the right VPN can be difficult, but there are many factors that you can look at to assist you in deciding if a vendor's product is a right for your organization. In Table 4-2 below I've listed some of the advantages and disadvantages associated with each type of VPN architecture.

By looking at Tables 4-1 and 4-2, you should now be getting a clearer picture of the VPN performance statistics and some of the associated

TABLE 4-2

Associated Advantages and Disadvantages of VPN Architecture.

VPN Architecture	Advantages	Disadvantages
Hardware	Good performance; good security; scalable; minimal encryption overhead for larger packets; some support load balancing	Limited flexibility; high price; no ATM, FDDI, or token ring interfaces; most are half-duplex; need to reboot to effect changes; some have a major performance problem with small packets (64 bytes); limited subnet functionality; some lack NAT
Software	Wide range of platforms; ease of installation; good for wide range of companies	NAT support performance problems; some have old encryption technologies; proprietary; some lack remote management capabilities; no monitoring capabilities
Router	Use of existing hardware; strong security available; low cost if using existing routers	Some may need additional encryption cards; performance problems; may need an upgrade to more powerful router
Firewall	Wide range of platforms; use existing hardware; some support for load balancing and redundant firewalls; low-cost IPSEC	Possible security problems due to operating system; not all fully interoperable with RADIUS support; some have licensing issues
Dial-up	Easy to establish VPNs; cost is low ·	Problem with compression of encrypted data, minimal RADIUS support

advantages and disadvantages of the available architectures. Of course, you will find more as you look, but they will all have the attributes I've described in Table 4-1. Now by looking at Table 4-2 you should be able to develop a set of good functional requirements on which to base your VPN decision.

Certification/Compliance

Whatever VPN solution architecture your organization decides to implement, it is a good idea to check certification. You could also rely on your vendor's word that their products are certified in PPTP, L2TP, or IPSec. One of these will be the de facto standard in the future; probably a combination of two of these will prevail.

An important point about compliance: If these protocols are not standards now, how can you be sure that your implementation will be compliant with the standard that is accepted? The real answer is you can't; however, in the appendix I've listed a set of RFCs that you should read if you really want to become familiar with the technology. No one is certain in what directions they will go but if you stick to the basics, you could probably be assured that your product will be either be compliant or easily upgraded to the standard once it is accepted. While you may not believe in certifications, they are still a little extra bit of insurance. ICSA certifies vendor's products on IPSec, which many believe will be the de facto Internet security protocol in the future. One helpful Web page to check out is *http://www.icsa.net/services/product_cert/ipsec/certified_products.shtml.*

If your organization has decided to go with PPTP as the base security platform, then you may want to take a look at the PPTP forum at *http://www.microsoft.com/.*

Compliance is also important from a security perspective. If you choose IPSec only, your solution would not be complete. The other half of the picture is key management, or the Internet Key Exchange (IKE). In order to be a fully compliant VPN technology solution, you need both. IPSec will encrypt and sign the packets, but IKE will negotiate the key exchanges between end devices. This is important, especially with regard to session keys and rekeying; if one key is compromised, only that session is affected, not all communications.

Conclusion

This chapter has taken a look at several different VPN architectures that are offered by various vendors. As you can see, different network infrastructures and different organizational requirements call for different types of architectures. Because there are just so many to choose from, you might find it difficult to decide which one is right for your organization. The answer depends on different factors, but hopefully you took a look at the first few questions and have been steered in a general direction. Those questions should have guided you toward a potential solution and got you thinking about a whole set of additional questions concerning security, user authorization and access, interoperability with your internal network infrastructure, and interoperability with external customers and suppliers. Can your proposed VPN solution be upgraded when a common set of standards is accepted? If not, can you at least upgrade the operating system to accept the new standard? Will your vendor support this? What about a network service provider-supplied VPN? Security, upgradability, and flexibility requirements all still apply.

VPNs will continue to grow. With electronic commerce and more and more business being conducted over the Internet, the need for a secure environment must be established. Every survey you read will tell you about the growth of the Internet and the future direction of growth. What most of those surveys don't tell you is that their data analysis is from the U.S. point of view. What this means is that the Internet is still considered an American concept, but more in-depth surveys are showing the enormous growth of the Internet being conducted on a global scale. This implies that Internet commerce is expanding rapidly, which will fuel the growth for VPN technology.

Services that push this global Internet growth and, subsequently, Internet-related services are IP telephony, Internet FAX, net conferencing, and multimedia applications, to name a few. Will your organization be using these new technologies? I have generally seen that there are two criteria to predict if a product will take off when it comes to information: whether it is easy to get and whether it arrives quickly. Just look around. You are more apt to use information if it very easy to get to—at the turn of a dial, the click of a mouse button, and so forth. You don't want to go through the hassle of turning on a system and pushing a bunch of buttons to get that information. You will most likely walk away from that technology.

Like the first criterion, you want the information immediately; yesterday would have been better. People don't want to wait for information; they want instant delivery. Ever read a newspaper or watch a newscast and think "That can't be right?" If you think that, do you go further to investigate it and check the source? Most people wouldn't. They just want the information now. They'll worry about the validation later.

Well, VPNs will meet those same criteria; they are fast and easy. People are so used to the Internet by now that they don't even know or care if their packets get encrypted. The speed of that information may depend on your Internet bandwidth pipe and the various ISPs you must traverse to get to that data, and like everything else in technology, the speed will increase.

CHAPTER 5

Topologies of VPNs

This chapter will show you where in your network topology you can place your VPN device. Just as in Chapter 4, you will see that there are many possible different placements. While you may think that this could be confusing, it is actually quite beneficial. All these available options give you the opportunity to take full advantage of VPN technology. VPN devices can be internal, meaning you can allow encrypted packets to pass into your network unmodified by a firewall or router (as long as the permission is granted). VPNs can also be placed where they incorporate the functions of a firewall and handle the encryption/decryption process.

Say, for example, you have a connection to the Internet and you have a dozen routers throughout your organization that you don't want to touch. In this case, you can add a tunnel switch before the router, thereby eliminating the need to add encryption software to these routers. Or, if you like, you can add encryption software from client to server, bypassing your Internet connection totally and thereby not modifying any part of your Internet network connections. You could also go with an ISP that offers you a PPTP connection via a front-end processor on their premises, thereby eliminating the need to modify any device. As you can see by just these few examples, you have a lot of options.

This chapter will explain many of the common topologies today. Firewall-to-laptop VPN, LAN-to-LAN VPN, nested topologies, and tunnel topologies are just a few of the topology setups we will look at. This chapter will attempt to cover every possible type of configuration that exists today; however, by the time this book is published, more topology setups will probably be created.

When you finish this chapter, you will have a good understanding of where these devices can be placed in your network. If you are having trouble deciding where to begin, then start with the basics. Try to figure out where the data is coming from, where it is going, and what devices it will need to get from source to destination.

Introduction to VPN Topology

Just as there were countless ways to purchase and implement VPN architecture, so are there countless ways to place this architecture into a VPN topology. In this chapter, as we go through the different topology setups, keep in the back of your mind that VPN and security must go hand in hand. You must know all the access points that lead into your network. At the end of this chapter, you will see that you probably will have more than one access point.

What you should get out of this chapter is the "how it looks and how it feels" insight. You should be able to say to yourself, "That VPN device belongs here," "Maybe we should move this authentication server over to this subnet," or "The remote access equipment belongs here." What this chapter describes is what goes where. Just like building a house, each component must go somewhere, and you need to know where the pieces go. If you can sit down and do this, it will be a great accomplishment. It will mean that you now understand that these devices and configurations all fit in their proper place, and any place you need one, you can find a device that will fit.

When considering where to place your VPN technology, first look at your network topology for your Internet connection. Then examine any other remote office that will have its own Internet connection and where you'll want to create a VPN tunnel. Try to understand that data flows as illustrated in Figure 5-1. (Don't be concerned with the numbering; just understand that the numbers represent data flows that occur throughout these components. We will revisit this numbering scheme later.)

When looking at Figure 5-1, start with the basics: how is the data going to flow between end hosts? The end host could be the firewall in

Figure 5-1
Traffic flow.

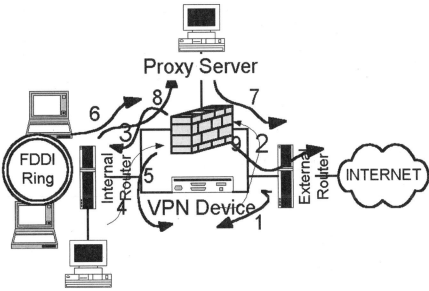

this diagram, or it could be the laptop computer on the FDDI ring. Your internal hosts may have to use the proxy server. They may have to be authenticated by the RADIUS server. Starting with the basics will help you visualize the data flow and help you see the network devices that the encrypted data will pass. You may have filters placed on some devices that are blocking encrypted data, or if the device has to examine this encrypted data, it may take a performance hit. Therefore, it would be a wise first step to examine the data flows when looking at the topology.

Firewall/VPN-to-Client Topology

The firewall/VPN-to-client topology will be the starting point for our discussion on VPN topology. We start here since this is the most commonly used topology, and practically every organization that implements a VPN will create this kind of setup. As mentioned in the last chapter, almost every organization connected to the Internet will have a firewall installed, and all that is needed will be to add VPN software to the firewall. Again, this is not implying that this is the best topology. However, it is the most common and possibly the easiest setup for those who have a firewall in place and just want the VPN functionality. Figure 5-2 illustrates this concept.

In this Figure 5-2, a user on his or her remote laptop needs to access a server that is inside the company's network, behind a firewall/VPN. The user wants to make a connection to retrieve a confidential report

Figure 5-2
Firewall/VPN-to-client topology.

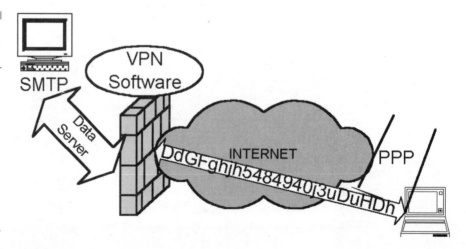

from a company server. This is the typical setup for client/VPN configuration. There are two components in this setup, which must be enabled before communications will take place.

1. The firewall/VPN device must be running some kind of VPN code. There are different ways to accomplish this; some firewalls have written into their code the ability to create the VPN, so rules will just need to be added to the firewall. With some manufacturers, you will need to add more software, e.g., if you are using an older firewall where the manufacturer did not support encryption. In this case, you will need to find a vendor whose software you can add to your existing firewall. This should not be difficult, since practically all well-known firewall vendors using UNIX or Windows will support some kind of encryption software.

2. The laptop has an installed VPN stack. It is a VPN stack since a VPN application would imply that that VPN code runs at layer 7 (application) of the OSI model. The VPN stack is actually between layers 2 (data-link) and 3 (network).

SECURITY NOTE There are different encryption technologies. If you are using some vendor's proprietary encryption and you have a different encryption on the firewall/VPN, the two will not communicate. For example, if you are using DES encryption on the firewall/VPN, you must use DES on the laptop. Vendors also differ on using encryption or encapsulation software. If you are using encapsulation on the firewall/VPN, you must use encapsulation on the laptops.

The following steps outline the communication process between the laptop and internal server once the configurations are complete:

1. The user on the laptop dials into his or her local ISP and establishes a PPP connection.

2. The laptop requests the keys from the firewall/VPN device. Either this can be a manual step by the user or an automatic step configured by the software.

3. The firewall/VPN responds back with the appropriate key.

4. The VPN software loaded on the laptop waits for the user to try to access the internal server (known by the destination IP address). If the user is visiting any site other than that of the corporate network, nothing happens. The user now wants to make a connection with the

internal server. The software running on the laptop sees the requests (again, known by the IP address), encrypts the packet, and sends it to the public IP address of the firewall/VPN combination.

5. The firewall/VPN device strips the IP address off, decrypts the packets, and sends it to the server inside the local LAN.

6. The internal server answers the request and sends back the document.

7. The firewall/VPN examines the traffic; it knows by it's tables that this was a VPN tunnel setup. So it takes the packet, encrypts it, and sends it on its way to the laptop.

8. The VPN stack on the laptop see this data stream, knows it coming from the firewall/VPN device, decrypts the packets, and hands it up to the upper-layer applications.

This configuration is what gives a VPN great flexibility; it can use the Internet as its own private network. While vendors disagree on implementation and standards, they all must support some type of client-to-VPN tunnel communication. Most of the costs savings you read about come from this setup, so when you examine your VPN options, make sure your vendor supports this configuration.

Two things that you want to watch out for in this type of setup are as follows:

1. The laptop configurations; this software has a tendency to interact with other applications and cause interoperability problems.

2. This configuration adds the overhead of the encryption/decryption process to the firewall. You may want to monitor the firewall for performance problems.

VPN/LAN-to-LAN Topology

This type of topology is the second most commonly used topology. Corporations have typically deployed the firewall/VPN-to-client topology and now want to extend that to different remote offices. This topology is also used among offices and various customers/vendors, where a VPN tunnel is created between these two sites. Theoretically if you are using both an NT-based firewall and a UNIX firewall, both using DES encryption, they should be able to communicate with each other. Of course, you should check it out to make sure.

Figure 5-3
LAN-to-LAN topology.

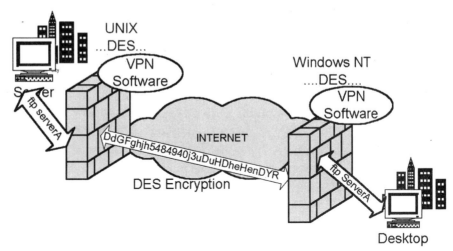

In Figure 5-3, we have an organization with a remote office. They both have their own firewalls, one is an NT-based machine and one is a UNIX-based machine. They both are running different vendors' VPN software, and the encryption algorithm used in the vendors' VPN products is DES.

The example presents a user in the remote office needing to connect to the server at another office and FTP a file. Before this communication, the components that must be enabled are as follows:

1. The administrator at each site agrees on DES encryption. The VPN software on each device creates a unique key.

2. If this is a firewall/VPN product, the administrator in each office sets up a rule, saying that if any traffic is destined for the other end, encrypt it.

3. The end user, using an FTP application on his or her desktop tries to connect to the server.

4. The packet leaves the desktop in plain text and hits the firewall/VPN device.

5. The packet is then encrypted and sent to the public IP address of the other office's firewall/VPN device.

6. The firewall/VPN accepts and decrypts the packet and forwards it to its end destination.

7. The server gets the packet and responds back.

8. It sends a packet in plain text to its local firewall/VPN device.

9. The firewall/VPN then encrypts it and sends it to the other firewall/VPN.

10. That firewall/VPN decrypts it and finally sends it back to the original user.

The beauty behind this is that the user has no idea the encryption is going on; there is nothing on the user's end that must be done to accomplish this task. As far as the user is concerned, the server is on his or her network. The server needs no special setup, since it thinks it is receiving a normal request and replies. The important concern here is routing issues; both user machines and servers must know on what addresses to route out through the firewall/VPN device.

Keep in mind, however, that addressing is a concern in this situation, as seen in Figure 5-4. For instance, suppose you addressed your network according to RFC 1918, which is the correct procedure to follow, but didn't assign different subnets to the different offices. Both the desktop and the server are on network address 10. In which direction will the traffic be routed? The desktop thinks that address 10.1.0.67 is on its local subnet, and the server thinks that the return address 10.1.0.1 is on its local network. Instead of routing the packets to their local gateway, they just place the packet on their local network, and that packet never reaches its destination. However, there are ways around this. In a later chapter we'll discuss routing issues and what you can do; creating another sub-

Figure 5-4
Addressing concerns.

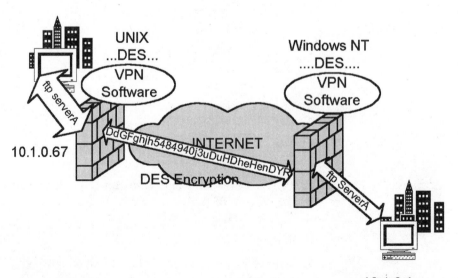

net, using proxies services, and network address translation are some options.

In the previous topology, firewall/VPN-to-client, this is not an issue, since the roaming laptops dial into a local ISP first and obtain a public routable address from that ISP. The communication goes from the public routable firewall/VPN address to the public routable temporary laptop address.

VPN/Firewall-to-Intranet/Extranet Topology

Today, intranets and extranets are common, everyday Internet services. In VPN technology, these services haven't changed, but now an additional layer of encryption is added to these services. Typically, intranets were used internally by employees, and extranets were used externally by customers. The main difference was by which direction they were accessed. Now with VPN technology, either service can be accessed internally or externally. This brings up two conditions. First, there is the flexibility to have one machine take care of both, thereby reducing redundancy. The second condition is security; now there is a way for external users to access these servers.

SECURITY NOTE   The only difference between VPN and non-VPN intranets/extranets is where the encryption process takes place. If it is on one machine, think about the Web security of typical Web servers. If not, then how far are you allowing the external traffic to penetrate your network?

In the future, we may begin to see a blurring of the lines between extranets and intranets. You now have to be concerned with how far the external traffic is allowed to travel. How will you identify employees who need the intranet services but who access them externally and the external customers who are only allowed access to the extranet?

Figure 5-5 illustrates this dilemma. In the figure, can you identify which server is the extranet or the intranet? Any one of these three servers can fill any role. When the remote desktop or a dial-up remote user tries to access these servers, which one will they be allowed to access? Figure 5-6 illustrates a possible placement for these servers. In

Figure 5-5
VPN extranet
application.

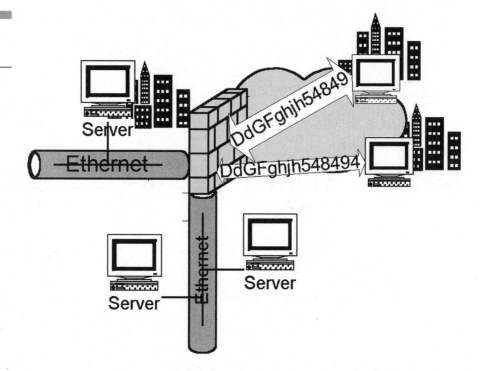

Figure 5-6
Extranet placement.

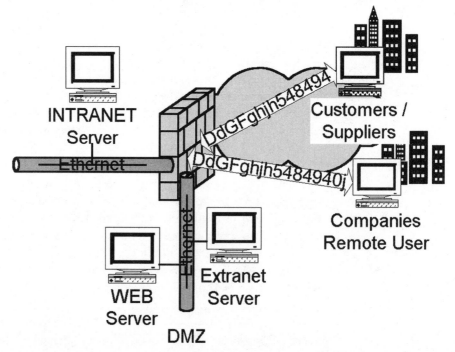

this figure, the extranet is placed on the DMZ, along with the Web server. Customers and suppliers are allowed to make connections to the extranet server. The Web server is just for normal Web traffic, available for everyone. The intranet is placed behind the VPN device and is used for internal users who are coming in from the Internet.

SECURITY NOTE   Place network servers according to their function. If public access is allowed, place them on a public DMZ. If there are external customers and suppliers, place them on their own DMZ. If employees, again, place them on their own DMZ. With multihoned machines, you can have several DMZ zones, e.g., some firewall/VPN vendors support up to 32 DMZs.

Now you have placed the extranet on the same zone as the Web server. The Web server has minimal security; the extranet server usually has more security. This is a security hazard. If someone tries to break into your Web server, he or she will typically change your HTML pages. So from the outside world, something is wrong with the way you look. This may not be a major a problem for your company; it only affects you, and the financial liability may not be that great. If someone hacks into you extranet, that someone could steal extremely important financial information. That information could be about you or whomever you allowed access to that server. You typically allow global access to the Web server, so there are no restrictions placed upon the source of the communications. Therefore, you need a way to further restrict who can access your extranet.

Figure 5-7 illustrates the proper placement for these various servers. Your Web server is kept on an untrusted network, allowing all access to this network link. Either your firewall or VPN device will allow packets to flow to your Web server unmodified.

SECURITY NOTE   To implement additional security on the Web server DMZ1 link, only allow HTTP traffic to pass through the VPN device to the Web server, denying all other types of traffic.

Your extranet is placed on its own separate network. The security you can implement here is to only allow those source addresses that you deem necessary to pass the firewall/VPN device. You are setting up an extranet between certain companies and vendors; they most likely will

Figure 5-7
Proper extranet
placement.

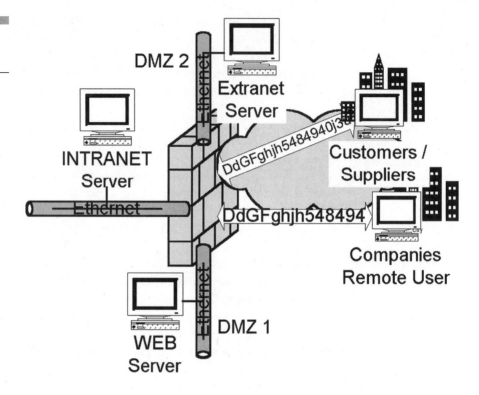

be coming from their internal network anyway. Therefore, you can restrict inbound access to only those networks. Of course, someone can spoof the source address, but when the communication was first set up, it was created using a VPN. All the data is encrypted to begin with; you are just adding a further restriction.

You may have noticed from the last three examples that there wasn't anything to difficult to comprehend about a VPN intranet or extranet. Nothing has changed, except for the fact that encryption is applied to the data stream. But where do you want the encryption to take place, on the server or a separate VPN device?

VPN/Frame or ATM Topology

A great attribute of the Internet is its flexibility to enable instant communication. However, some businesses do not want to leverage the Internet for transmitting business-critical information due to security concerns.

Figure 5-8
VPN over an
ATM/frame link.

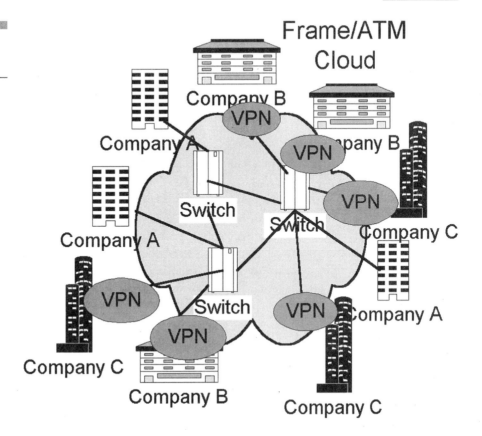

This is one reason why companies build intranets using only leased lines or frame relay links to connect their sites. Therefore, Virtual Private Networks can be configured over a shared infrastructure such as ATM or a frame relay network topology. Businesses that run their intranets over this VPN topology have some security, manageability, and reliability just as they do in their own private networks. There are different ways to accomplish this kind of topology setup, as illustrated in Figure 5-8.

Figure 5-8 illustrates a typical example of a VPN over an ISP's frame relay or ATM link. This type of topology is usually configured one of two ways. The first way is an IP over frame/ATM network infrastructure. This setup combines the application layer of IP services over the capabilities of an ATM network. Depending on the configuration of your equipment, IP packets are converted to cells and transferred over the ATM network. The encryption process is run on these packets before the conversion to cells, and the cells that contain the encrypted IP payload are switched to the final destination.

The second option is the Internet Engineering Task Force's (IETF's) Multiprotocol Label Switching (MPLS) working group. This allows service providers to peer IP and ATM integration. In this network topology, intelligent switches dynamically forward IP traffic in parallel with ATM traffic over the same ATM network. A field is applied to the packet that contains a unique identifier that identifies the end destination. All the switches in the ATM network examine this field and forward it on to its appropriate destination. The security attribute of this is that the packet is only forwarded to the destination, thereby preventing eavesdropping. Any encryption process that can be utilized here applies to the data portion only, before sending it into the ATM cloud. Since this configuration applies a field to the packet, you cannot encrypt the packet headers; however, you could encrypt the payload, which implies that the full functionality of IPSec could not be implemented. However, by encrypting the payload and switching to only that destination, security does exist.

Hardware (Black-Box) VPN Topology

Hardware, or black-box, VPNs are stand-alone devices implementing VPN technology algorithms. Some support encryption standards such as 40-bit DES (international) and 3DES (domestic and Canada). Hardware devices are believed to be able to complete the decryption/encryption process faster than software VPN devices.

Several manufacturers offer both black-box and software VPN solutions. As of this writing, hardware devices were beginning to add additional services such as firewall, antivirus, and routing capabilities. Hardware devices usually come with additional software that is loaded on a desktop to allow the configuration and management of that device; additionally, some can be configured by a Web server. Hardware device manufacturers are now making their product lines contain a full suite of services, such as digital certificates, LDAP support, SNMP monitoring, and full Internet and dial-in VPN capabilities.

GENERAL NOTE   A couple of problems with hardware devices: (1) *Performance problems.*   Several hardware devices have a performance problem with small 64-byte packets. While manufacturers are addressing those issues, it would be a concern if most of your traffic consists of small bursts of data.

(2) *Limited subnet functionality.* Some devices have a problem with granting users unrestricted internal access if the internal network is subnetted. What this means is that if you have 10 subnets in your organization and want to give users access to all 10 subnets, you'll have to create an authorized tunnel for each subnet, which could become cumbersome. However, you may consider it an additional security feature, since you can limit this access by network.

Figures 5-9 and 5-10 illustrate a couple of typical placements for these devices. In Figure 5-8, the VPN device is sitting behind the firewall on the internal network. Data packets are flowing through the firewall and the VPN device. As the packets pass through these devices, either they proceed unaltered or are encrypted, depending on the configuration of the device.

The management station sits somewhere on the internal network used to configure the device; you also may have the option of using a Web server to configure the device. If you have a geographically diverse set of VPN devices, make sure you have the ability to create management tunnels to these devices to modify them.

In this setup, the VPN device can act like a bridge or router. With bridging, the packets will flow from one interface to another, but with routing, you will be assigning IP address space and have to make sure that the other devices in your network can route to them.

The placement in Figure 5-9 has the firewall next to, or parallel to, the VPN device. This is usually referred to as a one-arm configuration. This setup allows the VPN device to scale to thousands of tunnels. The

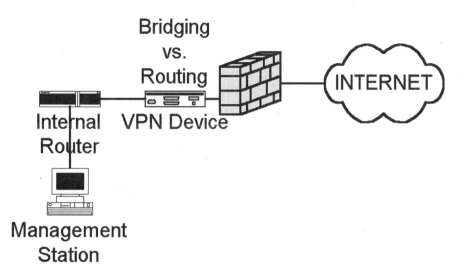

Figure 5-9
Black-box VPN
behind firewall.

Figure 5-10
VPN parallel with
firewall.

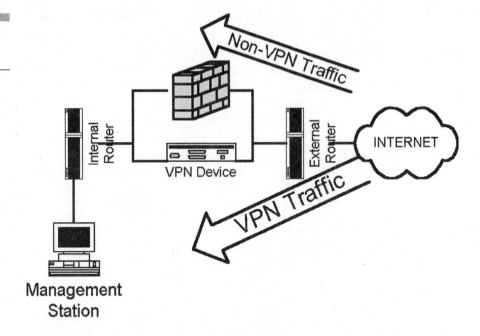

external router passes VPN traffic to the VPN device (which is directed by the VPN's address) and directs all other traffic to the firewall.

In a more elaborate setup, you can add a firewall behind the firewall device, as shown in Figure 5-11. When VPN tunnels are created and access granted, they are created to specific destinations. If you choose to do so, after the VPN device decrypts the packet, then you can have the internal firewall check that packet to see its final destination and allow

Figure 5-11
Advanced VPN
configuration.

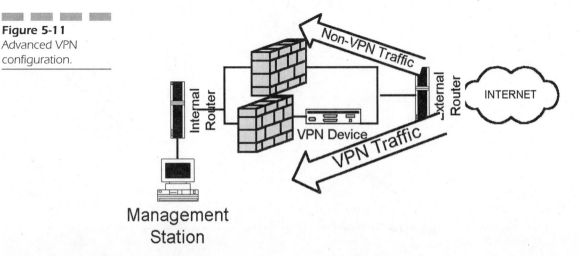

or deny access. There is also another option of having the VPN device forward the traffic back out the interface it came in on and go through the other firewall. You would need to set routing up on the device. While not the optimal solution, it can be accomplished.

VPN/NAT Topology

While network address translation (NAT) is not a VPN, there must be some discussion of NAT, since many organizations implement NAT and a VPN device is directly affected by the NAT process. Network address translation is the process of changing an IP address (usually a company's private address) to a routable public IP address. NAT provides a mechanism for hiding an organization's internal private address structure. (In some cases a company may even want to use NAT to hide its public address.) Using network address translation is not complicated, but the placement of the VPN device is important. If you implement NAT on a VPN packet, that packet may be dropped; remember that a VPN is an IP-to-IP setup. Figure 5-12 illustrates the VPN traffic flow with a firewall in place, doing NAT and the VPN device doing user authentication.

Figure 5-12
Implementing NAT with firewall and VPN.

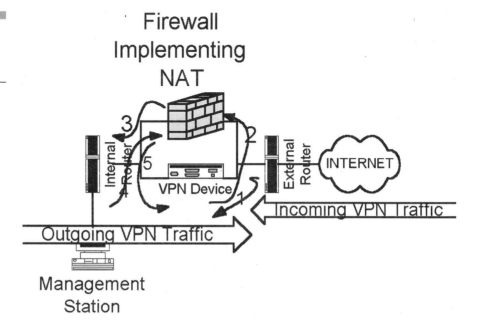

Following are a few notes regarding outgoing and incoming VPN traffic:

Outgoing VPN Traffic

1. All traffic coming from the internal router is directed to the NAT device to change the source IP address of the requesting device to a routable public IP address.
2. The NAT device then forwards that packet to the VPN device that adds the encryption process on that packet.
3. The packet is routed to the external router and finally to its destination.

Incoming VPN Traffic

1. Incoming VPN packets need to be directed to the VPN device first; the VPN device strips off the encryption overhead on the packet and checks for authentication privileges, such as user authentication. In the case of using IPSec, it would check the SPI association.
2. The packet is then routed to the network address translation device to readdress the packet back to its original (internal) IP address. NAT in this case is being taken care of by the firewall.
3. The NAT device then routes the packet (with its new source IP address) to the internal router.

Implementing NAT with a firewall is not the only setup. Instead of a firewall, you could have in place a proxy server implementing NAT. Of course, with the proxy setup, make sure your proxy can act like a firewall or, at the very least, install access lists on the router.

GENERAL NOTE   These two rules must be followed when using NAT and VPN:
(1) For outbound packets. If it is to undergo NAT and be part of a VPN, NAT must be applied before the VPN device encrypts the packet;
(2) For inbound VPN traffic. NAT must be applied after the VPN encryption has been removed from the packet.

VPN Switch Topology

Some new products on the market today are called VPN switches. They are layer-3 switches, which create tunnels on demand. As stated in the previous chapter, they are relatively new. They have the ability to create and assign tunnel characteristics and switch multiprotocol traffic. They perform encryption, encapsulation, and multiprotocol routing supposedly at wire speeds. They also have a nice feature of supporting a network protocol policy-based switching. An example of this would be if you had both a frame relay and Internet service. This device acts as the main switch device connected to these transports' mechanisms. That is, based upon the policy installed, you can have frame relay traffic switched one way and Internet traffic switched in another direction.

These VPN switches also come with a set of remote management software to provide for capacity planning, fault management, and statistical information such as tunnel utilization and quality of service monitoring. Figure 5-13 illustrates a typical tunnel setup. These tunnels are set up via a management console and are created and switched on demand to the respective destinations. While they are usually easy to set up and maintain, they are not a firewall. Therefore, they do not offer the protec-

Figure 5-13
VPN switch.

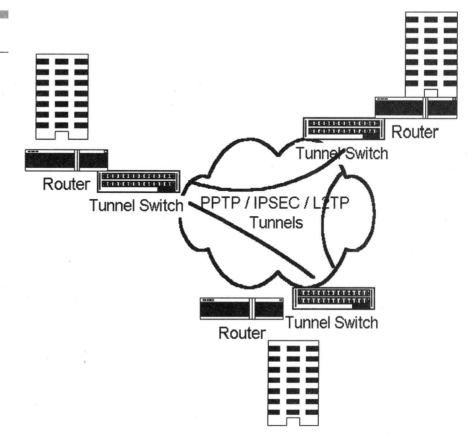

tion that a firewall would offer. However, as in the hardware VPN devices, vendors may be adding firewall capabilities soon.

VPN Nested Tunnels

VPN nested tunnels can be considered a tunnel within a tunnel. There are different ways to accomplish nested tunnels; one way they are used is when an organization wants to implement end-to-end security. Figure 5-14 illustrates a nested tunnel.

In Figure 5-14, we have a PPTP client wanting to connect to the PPTP server. The process is as follows:

1. The PPTP client performs the encryption process on the data from the application.

2. It then forwards the encrypted data stream to the firewall/VPN device, which then adds DES encryption to the packet. The DES encryption can be implemented as part of the IPSec standard.

3. The packet is then received by the far-end VPN device, which checks for authentication, strips off the DES encryption, and sends it to its final destination, the PPTP server.

4. The PPTP server then decrypts the PPTP packet and forwards the packet to the upper-layer applications.

GENERAL NOTE   Before the two firewall/VPN devices can perform any encryption/decryption process, they first have to have a VPN configured between them, as was illustrated in Figure 5-3. A common recommendation is to use IPSec and PPTP in combination.

Figure 5-14
Nested tunnel VPN.

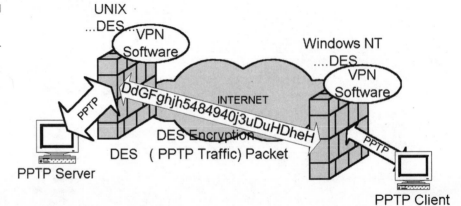

Another way to perform a nested tunnel would be with the use of a public key algorithm such as PGP. In this case, the process is as follows:

1. The client would use the server's public key to encrypt a plaintext file.

2. The encrypted data is then routed to the first firewall/VPN device to be encrypted again with DES.

3. It is forwarded to the far-end VPN device

4. The receiving firewall/VPN device performs the decryption process and sends it on its way to the server.

5. A user on that server would use his or her private key to decrypt the message.

These two ways show how a nested tunnel could be created. Of course, you can always use another algorithm to perform encryption, such as with an encryption process called Triple DES (3DES). In a later chapter we will look at the mechanics of 3DES. For now, however, we can think of it as a single DES process performed three times. This might be a simplistic view, but it is relatively accurate.

Load Balancing and Synchronization

Just as any company would institute load balancing for their critical servers, VPN technology can be load balanced. *Load balancing* is the process of off-loading VPN processing needs among the various servers. *Synchronization* is the process of synchronizing VPN devices. The one-arm (parallel) configuration mentioned earlier is a typical topology when using load balancing and synchronization. This is one reason why VPNs can scale.

Load Balancing

There are three ways to accomplish load balancing. First, you can set up some routing policy on the company routers. Second, the VPN device can query a server farm to see which servers are loaded. Say for example that you are allowing extranet VPNs, and you estimate that you may have at any time 5000 simultaneous users. In that case, you may have two or three extranets, and the VPN device queries which server will

Figure 5-15
Router policy load
balancing.

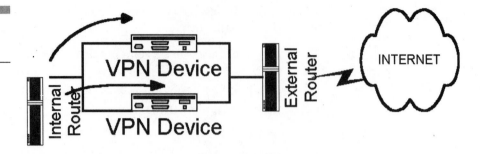

handle the request. In some load-balancing setups, the VPN device can query round-robin, looking at a load factor or determining which server responds the fastest. The third way is in the VPN device itself. When a connection is made, the fastest to respond will be the one used for all further communications, or you can set the maximum allowable connections. If, for example, you estimate that you will have to support 500 users, you can set each VPN device to handle 250 users.

As you decide what type of VPN topology to implement, whether stand-alone, black box, or a firewall/VPN combination, load balancing and synchronization may be good features to implement. Only a few VPN vendors support this setup. Figures 5-15 to 5-17 illustrate the load-balancing concepts.

In Figure 5-15, outgoing data traffic that is to be encrypted by the VPN device is balanced by a routing policy on the internal router. These packets enter a VPN device, which performs the encryption process and forwards them to the external router. On the return trip, the external router forwards the VPN traffic to the original VPN device that performed the encryption process. This is necessary due to the authentication process that is done by the VPN device. If you are doing user authentication on the VPN device, only one VPN device will know about the original connection; therefore, all subsequent traffic must be passed back to that original VPN device. This requires that the VPN devices have public IP addresses on their external links and possibly perform network address translation.

A second type of load balancing is seen in Figure 5-16. In this case the VPN device is querying the extranet servers behind it to see which one will accept the connection. The three types of criteria are round-robin, where the VPN device picks one extranet at a time. The VPN device looks at the load factor to see how busy the extranet server is, as well as the response time. The one that responds the fastest will have the connection.

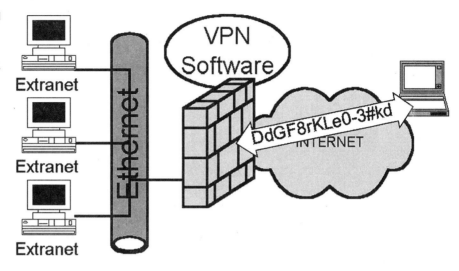

Figure 5-16
Server farm load-balancing configuration.

In this second type of load balancing, the VPN device queries the available extranets behind it and, depending on certain conditions, will forward the traffic accordingly. The VPN device can communicate with an agent that is installed on the extranet servers to keep status on them. These agents will periodically inform the VPN device of its current load conditions. Some other options that you can set are round-robin, where one extranet after another is forwarded the connection; round-trip delay, in which a ping packet is used and the first to answer takes the connection; and a random connection.

The final type of load balancing is seen in Figure 5-17. In this case, the laptop needs to make a connection to the server on the internal network. The laptop is configured to use both VPN devices. When the client attempts to make the connection, the VPN device that responds first will create the tunnel with the laptop. So in this example the laptop tried to make the connection to both VPN devices; the top device answered first, so the connection will be made with that VPN device.

Figure 5-17
Fastest response load balancing configuration.

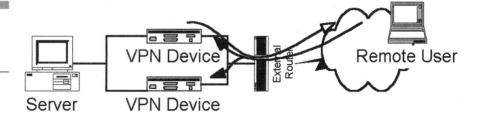

Figure 5-18
Synchronization.

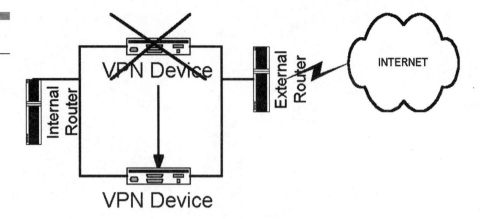

Synchronization

Synchronization is the process of having both VPN devices keep the same state tables. This way if one device goes down, the other device can answer requests that would have otherwise been answered by the device that just failed.

Figure 5-18 illustrates the concept of synchronization. The two VPN devices keep state tables of each other, and these tables are updated automatically every few seconds. State tables keep in cache such things as who has been authenticated and what IP address the user had. In this diagram, there is a third interface on the devices through which the synchronization traffic passes. This third interface is not a requirement, since some vendors claim synchronization across networks. This is supposed to keep both VPN configurations in synchronization so traffic can freely flow into either device incoming or outgoing.

Figure 5-19
Communication
problem with
synchronization.

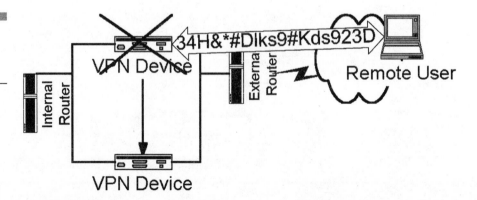

However, there is a problem associated with synchronization, which requires the user to issue another step, as illustrated in Figure 5-19. During the initial communication with the top VPN device, the laptop and the VPN device created the secure tunnel. When this device failed, the laptop has no way of knowing that the device went down. Therefore, the communications will time out, and the user needs to re-create the tunnel with the bottom device.

Conclusion

In this chapter, we've looked at many different topology configurations associated with VPN technology. These topologies range from the very simple to the elaborate. We've looked at two of the most common, firewall/VPN-to-client and LAN-to-LAN VPNs. Then we examined two of the most common applications for VPNs, the intranet and extranet VPNs; we saw that intranet and extranet VPNs just add a layer of encryption to these Web services. We also looked at where the proper placement of these devices should be to ensure maximum safety, both to your extranet and to internal networks.

These topology setups can be simple. This eases installation procedures and placements, but the trade-off is flexibility and monitoring capabilities. We could add more features such as load balancing and redundancy. This adds to the complexity, expense, and maintenance requirements, but it also adds flexibility, which may be required by your organization.

This chapter should have given you a feel for where these VPN devices go and how they play a part in the overall network configuration. Think of it as a puzzle. Each piece has a specific purpose and design, but they can be placed in different configurations. Then think about your remote offices. Plan each one individually, then decide how you want to connect. Do you want your remote offices to establish a dedicated tunnel to each other, which would require a VPN device in each office? You can also just decide to use a dial-up ISP in each remote office, which then would require you to help those users set up their machines. Remember, with the LAN-to-LAN VPN, no end-user steps are required.

Another thing you should consider is how many users will be using the VPN. There is a big difference between 10, 100, and 1000 users. If you have 1000 users, your VPN will be mission critical; therefore, you will need redundancy.

In later chapters, we will go through actual implementations of VPNs; however, you first need to understand where these devices fit into your organization. Understanding these and the components that made up a VPN setup will give you a solid foundation.

CHAPTER 6

Government
Restrictions
on VPN Technology

This chapter wraps up Part 1 of this book. While you may not learn any new technology about VPNs in this chapter, if you are thinking about creating a global VPN, you must understand your limitations. The information in this chapter comes from a variety of sources: government agencies, law enforcement agencies, privacy groups, and the federal court system.

No other area of technology has created such a storm of controversy as encryption. In this chapter we will look at why the government cares, where you can go to ask for permission to use encryption, and the economic impact of government regulations that is placed on U.S. manufacturers. (There is such an enormous impact on the financial stability of U.S. companies that it makes one wonder why the U.S. government would place this burden. What's interesting is that the data for this financial disaster comes from none other than the U.S. Department of Commerce. Because a manufacturer didn't publish this data, no one can be accused of having a personal stake in the government's policy.)

The one thing to remember is that this is not an U.S.-only policy. Almost every government has some sort of encryption policy in place. A U.S. manufacturer not only has to satisfy the laws of this country, but also those of other countries he or she deals with. In fact, after considering the amount of red tape they now have to deal with, many vendors simply give up and do not use encryption in their products. In those countries where encryption laws are relaxed, and there are many, vendors will have free reign in the marketplace to sell their goods.

Introduction to the Politics of Encryption

Soon, virtually uncrackable encryption products will be the most difficult issue facing law enforcement agencies in the next decade. All of our reliable investigative techniques, national security and the public safety of our citizens will be at jeopardy. Therefore, it is imperative that a viable key management infrastructure be adopted. We all believe that robust encryption is essential in today's telecommunication era, and in today's electronic world the ability to encrypt both contemporaneous communication and stored data is a vital component of information security.*

*J. Louis Freeh, Director, Federal Bureau of Investigation, before the Senate Judiciary Committee.

While this belief is prevalent among law enforcement officials, it is not among high-tech industries, personal libertarian groups, many members of Congress, and U.S. trading partners. According to William Murray, for jobs that move from Fort Meade to Langley, the real issue is world peace, not national security. Unfortunately, it's the National Security Agency that always wins. They are secretive and Congress usually follows their recommendations. As we move into the twenty-first century, almost all growth in trade will be electronically mediated, and if U.S. companies can't export cryptography along with their products, the market will be served by international companies. According to the FBI, of all the bills pending in Congress, only H.R. 695 addresses all the law enforcement and national security concerns for both domestic and international encryption products. One that is currently under consideration, S.R. 909, which relies on market forces, does not do enough for law-enforcement concerns. According to Phil Zimmermann, in 1991 Senate Bill 266 included a nonbinding resolution that, had it become law, would have required all manufacturers to build into their components a backdoor, so the government could eavesdrop on anyone's communication. Before that bill was defeated, Zimmerman wrote and released his Pretty Good Privacy (PGP) encryption software. Since then it has been used by thousands and is available globally. For 3 years, U.S. Customs targeted Zimmerman in a criminal investigation before finally dropping the investigation.

A good question to ask is why the use of encryption has grown. Following are four reasons that were a driving force in its growth:

1. *The availability of personal computers.* Years ago, most people couldn't afford a computer and the security risks were caused by people inside. To remedy this, computers were put behind locked doors. Today computers are everywhere; new ones can fit in the palm of your hand. Anyone with a computer could snoop on a network and capture traffic that is passing by.

2. *More and more information is being passed over the Internet.* The Internet is an unsecured network; however, it is both affordable and global, so there is a need to protect the data that is on it.

3. *Faxes needed to be replaced.* They are inherently insecure, they can be sent to the wrong number, and they can be easily compromised on some forms of transmission. Again, there is a need to scramble the data as it passes over an electronic circuit.

4. *The development in 1977 of the RSA public key system.* Two keys are used, one for public and one private. You could ship the public

key to anyone, even over insecure channels. The public key encrypted the message and only the private key could decrypt it. Up until this time, you needed to physically give this private key to your intended host, which was geographically out of reach for most people.

Now that encryption use has grown, what are the laws that govern its use? The best way to understand the law is to review each situation they're meant to address. U.S. companies are legally allowed to ship encryption products based on 40-bit DES (Data Encryption Standard) to foreign subsidiaries. Banks, whether or not they're based in the U.S., are afforded the same freedom. Banks and financial institutions are legally allowed to go up to 128-bit encryption, since 40- and 56-bit keys don't offer enough protection. Experts indicate that 40-bit DES can be cracked in a matter of hours. There's no clear consensus about the vulnerability of DES, but everyone agrees that the technology, which was originally developed by IBM and adopted as a U.S. standard in 1976, is showing its age. As of this writing, 56-bit DES was compromised.

What Role Does Government Play in VPN Technology?

Until just recently, 56-bit encryption was unavailable for export from the U.S. Encryption strength called 40-bit DES was the only allowable encryption without an export permit. There are two exceptions: Banking systems are allowed to use 128-bit encryption, and you were allowed to obtain a license if you built a backdoor into your encryption technology (also called a *key recovery*). Under the Clinton administration, the U.S. has finally eased some encryption exportable procedures. The policy also extends the exceptions to the encryption policy to health, medical, and insurance companies. They've also stated that, while the FBI will be allowed access to information that is believed to be criminal in nature, it will be only under strict court warrants. While industry is applauding the moves, they still feel the policy is lacking, especially due to the 56-bit machine that can crack DES. Companies that want to use the 56-bit or larger DES with the key-recovery feature still have to wait the 6 months for a license. The administration is trying to help out by allowing them to ship the products immediately upon their completion, except to the terrorist nations. These companies are using a recoverable technology called "Private Doorbell."

The previous exception granted to banks and financial institutions was that they could use any bit length (encryption strength) to their subsidiaries overseas (but only for financial transactions, not general use). The new policy includes insurance companies, the medical community (except biochemical and pharmaceutical), and online merchants. Moreover, the policy deals with the 45 countries that have signed treaties with the U.S., but it still does not deal with the foreign manufacturer/supplier relationships of many corporations.

SECURITY NOTE   Before this took place, companies had to submit a key-recovery plan to the government to obtain a license to export 56-bit technology. Just think of it this way: Key recovery=backdoor.

The banks and financial institutions are allowed to export 56-bit technology without the key recovery plan, but after a one-time review. In addition, they are not allowed to ship to the seven countries the U.S. government views as terrorist countries:

1. Cuba
2. Iran
3. Iraq
4. Libya
5. North Korea
6. Sudan
7. Syria

The National Security Agency (NSA), which is responsible for protecting us from the bad guys, unfortunately at times seems like the bad guy. The NSA didn't even exist for a long time, or at least no one would verify their existence (they were called the "No Such Agency"). Their job is to protect, and they want the right to read any message they deem as a threat to national security. Getting into people's personal data is like tapping a telephone; during criminal activity they want the right to be able to decrypt any messages. However, due to this stand they have made it extremely difficult for companies to compete in the global marketplace. Another little irony is that the Clinton administration is pushing for global trade, but at the same time the Administration is handicapping the very companies it wants to help. It is well known that there is a maze of rules, regulations, and procedures to go through before exporting any kind of security products. Waiting periods of over a year are not uncommon.

All the high-tech companies have been visited by the NSA. They want to make sure that these companies are aware of export rules. Some suggest that the high-tech companies are pressuring the NSA to allow them to tap into people's private communications when those people use the companies' products. It must be very frustrating for these high-tech companies to have to constantly get the approval of the NSA when working on their products.

A few years ago when the Clinton administration was trying to help these high-tech companies, Clinton signed a law allowing them export rights on the condition that they add a key-recovery feature. According to the Department of Commerce, about 50 companies have submitted plans to install key recovery into their products.

Does the Product You Are Using Have Key Recovery?

Some big companies have a key-recovery feature in their products, and most likely you weren't told that when you bought the product. If you are not sure, just find out if the manufacturer can ship their encryption product overseas and whether it is stronger than 56-bit. In these companies' defense, what other choice did they have? Moreover, if your company needs the strength for legitimate business use, key recovery may not be an issue to you.

Some high-tech companies have said no to NSA's demands; others have conceded to them. By visiting the Electronic Frontier Foundation (EFF) Web page (*www.eff.org*), you will be able to see some very disturbing documents about what the government is doing, and what the EFF and other similar organizations are trying to change.

Why Would the Government's Policy Actions Affect VPN Security?

It has always been known that 56-bit DES technology was breakable. Both the know-how and the technology existed that would make it possible. The only catch was that the machine that would have to be created to break DES was prohibitively expensive for anyone to undertake such an endeavor. However, that all changed on July 17, 1998, when a press release announced that the Electronic Frontier Foundation (EFF) broke the encryption strength in 3 days. It cost just around $200,000, and it used off-the shelf technology.

You can imagine the impact this must have had on governmental officials. All along, the government's security advocates were saying that 56-bit DES is the strongest encryption that you can get; no one has the power to break it. Therefore, the 40-bit strength was kept in place. Then all of a sudden 56-bit DES gets broken in 3 days. The 56-bit DES code has been broken before, but that attempt took 39 days. Now, 56-bit can be broken with a special machine that can be built for less than $50,000, which is within the reach of nearly every organization. Does that mean that the 40-bit encryption was extremely easy to break all along?

RSA Laboratories issued the challenge, and the EEF received $10,000, but the money is nothing compared to the concern that all 56-bit encryption technologies might be vulnerable. (The decoded message, by the way, was "It's time for those 128-, 192- and 256-bit keys.")

What's ironic is that it is mostly the government that is hacked into. Survey after survey shows that government sites have been favored targets of hackers. You would think they would insist on the strongest security procedures for everything, including encryption, so people don't use packet sniffers, analyze the data from government facilities, and possibly decode it. That, of course, is only if they are also using the same encryption strengths as everyone else.

Now imagine you are in charge of setting up an infrastructure for your organization, which has decided to conduct business with its subsidiaries and strategic partners throughout the world. Your organization is in a highly competitive market and cannot afford to have its information intercepted or compromised in any form. Therefore, as an organization, you decide to use the strongest security measures possible. If this was any other type of security product, there would be no problem, but since this security is based upon encryption technology and encryption technology is considered a munitions, things have just gotten extremely complicated for your company.

First, you need to get an encryption export license from the U.S. government. Remember, to obtain one, you must build in a backdoor, and even then you will sit and wait for months for the license. Second, this is of national concern to all countries; if you intend to use it in other countries, you need to contact those governments and get an encryption permit. Some countries, such as South Africa and Saudi Arabia, simply ban encryption. Then what can your company do? You need to think about these things all along your design process.

Where Do I Get Permission to Use Strong Security?

In order for your organization to obtain an export license to use strong security (greater than 56-bit DES), you must apply to Department of Commerce. However, how can the Department of Commerce know what products are exportable? That is, how can they know what products contain key-recovery features or only support 40-bit encryption? This means that in order to get a license, you will be working with the FBI, NSA, and the State Department, in addition to the Department of Commerce. Dealing with any agency, especially governmental agencies, would normally mean a mess of complicated forms and procedures. Now your company has to deal with all these agencies. For this reason many companies just give up trying to get an export license. Just look at the number of companies that have submitted plans; at this writing there are only 50.

So, if a company decides that they will deal with all the red tape and bureaucracy in order to use strong encryption technology in their products, is it worth it? How can they be sure that even if they go through all this paperwork, their products will be secure? From some of the information gathered, they can't.

In fact, even the Clinton administration itself agrees that key-recovery encryption techniques are inferior to the alternative privacy techniques. Therefore, where do you get strong security? As stated in the Electronic Privacy Information Center's (EPIC's) press release:

> A top U.S. official acknowledged more than a year ago that the Internet privacy technique championed by the Clinton administration is "more costly and less efficient" than alternative methods that the government seeks to suppress. The concession is contained in a newly released high-level document on encryption policy obtained by the Electronic Privacy Information Center (EPIC).*

---

*From a press release on *www.epic.org*.

This press release goes on to state that while the administration is trying to promote key-recovery techniques, they realize that this is a futile attempt. It impairs U.S. companies from effectively competing overseas, and subsequently, companies will buy products from Europe and Japan, bypassing U.S. manufacturers.

The Economic Cost of Government Intrusion

If the U.S. does not ease export restrictions on encryption technology, it is estimated that companies stand to lose up to $60 billion annually on products that do not contain strong encryption. Although 56-bit DES encryption is currently allowed, even this type of encryption is weak, as mentioned previously. In 1995 the Department of Commerce put the worldwide information technology (IT) market at $527.9 billion. This figure was based upon the revenue of primary vendors of countries in the Organization for Economic Cooperation and Development (OECD). Table 6-1 lists the members of the OECD.

TABLE 6-1

Members of the OECD.

Original Member Countries
Austria, Belgium, Canada, Denmark
France, Germany, Greece, Iceland
Ireland, Italy, Luxembourg, the Netherlands
Norway, Portugal, Spain, Sweden, Switzerland
Turkey, the United Kingdom, and the United States

Members Subsequently Through Accession (Dates of Entry)
Japan (April 28, 1964), Finland (January 28, 1969)
Australia (June 7, 1971), New Zealand (May 29, 1973)
Mexico (May 18, 1994), the Czech Republic (December 21, 1995)
Hungary (May 7, 1996), Poland (November 22, 1996)
The Republic of Korea (December 12, 1996)

SOURCE: U.S. Department of Commerce.

Between 1987 to 1995 the IT market's growth rate was twice that of other gross domestic product worldwide. During this time there was also a subtle shift from hardware to software services (from 46.6 to 52.1 percent of the market). In 1995 the market for services was placed at $161 billion, with an annual growth rate exceeding 10 percent.

OECD member countries presently control over 90 percent of the market. The U.S. by far has the largest market share; however, it has seen a slight decrease, from 46.2 to 45.5 percent. Canada, Germany, and Mexico have enjoyed extreme growth rates.

The growths in services have been the result of two important trends:

1. As more companies move toward microcomputers and packaged software, less reliance has been on customized software and more on system integration.

2. As the pace of internal reorganization increases, firms look to IT services for business process reengineering.

While the IT market has predominately remained in the OECD countries, after 1995 several nonmember countries have seen their markets equal or exceed many European nations. When IT penetration ratio is calculated (measured as market share as a percentage of GDP), nonmember countries such as Singapore have levels equal to that of OECD countries. Other countries such as China and India have ratios that are well below that of member OECD countries, and consequently, there is a tremendous growth potential in these and other nonmember countries.

The major thrust of IT will be that of client/server architecture and LAN-based connectivity. LAN-based infrastructure is varied across countries, partly because of the diffusion and acceptance of personal computers. In 1994 the U.S. accounted for 55 percent of LAN servers, Western Europe 32 percent, and the rest of the world 18 percent. The Internet has fueled an explosive growth in LAN connectivity and will continue to evolve to commercial applications from academic research. IT exportation is a major source in industrial countries, so much so, in fact, that the percentage of exportation is roughly two or three times that of other industries. While that is good news for exporting, what is even more compelling evidence of a global marketplace is that U.S. affiliates operating abroad grew at least twice as fast as U.S. affiliates operating nationally.

The IT growth is also in the delivery of services; many governments have found cost savings by delivering services via an electronic infrastructure. Such services include education, business and hospital billing, and customer processing, including stores and banks where automatic payment and security of transactions are done. Unfortunately, in order to diffuse these procedures, consumers must be ready to trust electronic commerce. And in order to garner this trust, reliability and security must be established. However, because governments deal a lot with foreigners, the question remains: Will people use these processes if the strongest security is not allowed to be used (less than 56-bit DES) and the government has a backdoor into your affairs (key recovery)?

By the year 2000, the U.S. marketplace for security software alone will be close to $5 billion. However, this potential marketplace will be a missed opportunity unless governments around the world can agree on encryption export laws, which are built into many software and hardware platforms. Global trade in computer technology has been increasing faster than any economy's gross domestic product. The data from the Department of Commerce shows the explosive growth in these industries. In the information systems industry alone, the annual growth rates projected by the year 2000 will be 9.1 percent annually, with a market of about $3,010 billion and the U.S. having about $1,470 billion in revenue.

These projections are for just one of many technology industries that are expected to grow in the next century. In 1996, there were over 1200 encryption products that were created and distributed by over 862 companies throughout the world. Almost 60 percent were from U.S. companies; the rest were produced in 28 other countries. With the number of encryption products being developed overseas, there is no reason for foreign manufacturers to buy U.S. products with key-recovery systems. In addition, with the U.S. restricting strong security products, the decision to buy U.S. products should be a moot point with many companies. This comes just as the U.S. is exporting more technology, and technology is growing faster than the GDP. The U.S. Chamber of Commerce surveyed 1600 U.S. businesses and found that 17 percent of companies used encryption in 1995. That figure is expected to rise to 60 percent by the year 2000. Not only will this hurt sales to foreign businesses, U.S. businesses that are multinationals will also be affected. Without effective encryption, U.S companies will have a tough time trying to form overseas joint ventures.

Legal Status of Encryption

The legal status of encryption is clear for an individual. Take for example the Pretty Good Privacy (PGP) program. As an individual you can download the PGP software and freely use it. If, however, you are going to be using it internationally, you should download the international version of PGP. If you are going to use it commercially, then you need to obtain a license. To play it safe, never use PGP or any encryption product and then export it.

SECURITY NOTE   Remember: The International Traffic in Arms Regulations (ITAR) will come and arrest you, and lock you up if you decide to export the PGP software.

The consequences of not abiding the laws of this country are very serious. Some of the current legal liabilities run up to a $1 million fine and up to 10 years in jail *per each unit of export,* not just the overall product. If you install a strong encryption algorithm on your Web server and don't check the country of origin of people who are downloading, you might be guilty. If 20 foreigners downloaded your product, you have just incurred 20 per-unit-of-export violations.

What if you were overseas and downloaded the product from a U.S. site that didn't check? In that case, ITAR may not be able to do anything. However, with intercountry treaties, would you really want to take the chance? Therefore, if you are in the U.S., download it from a U.S. site. If not, use the international site. There are hundreds of U.S. sites and hundreds of international sites to download it from.

Encryption algorithms are very easily obtained, and you can very easily get into trouble if you are not careful. A very common encryption algorithm consisting of three lines written in PERL is available from many Web sites that are based on PERL. It is written using the RSA algorithm and contains strong encryption properties. It is well known and available from many U.S. and non-U.S. sites (*and yes, it is illegal to export*), including many computer science departments of universities around the world. This just shows how easy it is to obtain encryption software.

International Impact on U.S. Government's Encryption Policy

Up until this point, the focus has been on U.S. companies violating the export laws concerning encryption and getting into trouble with U.S.

officials. That focus has changed in recent years. Now U.S. companies are getting into trouble abroad merely by following the rules. This may be another reason why the Clinton Administration decided to ease the 40-bit encryption standard. One story that ran in major newspapers and magazines concerned the German government ruling against U.S. encryption standards. In this case, a banking concern had issued bankcards based upon the 56-bit technology. The card was stolen from an elderly lady and used to withdraw money from her account. The bank tried to place blame on the individual for not safeguarding her PIN number, but the records showed her PIN was never used and the crackers broke the code. The bank was forced to pay only $2,699, which may be negligible for a bank. However, it has shown that even the exportable 56-bit DES is vulnerable and U.S. companies will be held liable in foreign courts.

This court ruled that the U.S. manufacturer was negligent in not providing the proper safeguards and security features that were available. This court ruling will have far-reaching implications for any company. Due to a law established by the U.S. government, U.S. companies can be held liable in foreign courts. If you are a manufacturer, what do you do? You have three options:

1. Not conduct business globally;

2. Use minimal encryption and hope for the best; or

3. Use key recovery.

One outcome is certain: Foreign manufacturers will not use U.S. products, and U.S. manufacturers will think long and hard about conducting business overseas. It's a case of Russian roulette.

What's Happening Today?

Currently, several congressional bills have been introduced that address encryption. These make it unlawful to use encryption in the furtherance of criminal activity, and they set up a process to allow law enforcement agencies to access the keys where key-recovery systems were voluntarily used. S.R. 909 is one such bill that protects public safety by encouraging the use of key-recovery systems through market-based incentives. Unfortunately, these bills do not go far enough. One of the current bills in the House is H.R. 695, which allows members of the Intelligence Committee to access encrypted files if a key is voluntarily left. This bill was amended September 24, 1997, and requires that all encryption products manufactured in the U.S. or imported have immediate access to plaintext features. In addition, the bill would allow the NSA to review all encryption products for export by destination country and require the U.S. to purchase only encryption products that have immediate access to encrypted communication.

While the U.S. places strong export limits on encryption products that protect national security and public safety, more and more emphasis is being made inside our borders. Government agencies are stating that the U.S. communication infrastructure cannot become a mechanism for criminals and terrorists to conduct illegal activity without law enforcement inhibiting them. They affirm that while Congress has allowed for electronic surveillance in many criminal situations, encryption activity needs the same level of attention, since this criminal activity is happening now. According to the FBI, computer-related cases where encryption is used have risen over 140 percent in the last 3 years. These included the 56-bit DES and the 128-bit Pretty Good Privacy (PGP) encryption.

Unfortunately, there are already many international companies that offer encryption, and businesses have problems with another agency (in this case, the U.S. government) holding their key. The NSA is behind the fight to enforce restrictions; however, the NSA thinks in terms of its own budget—more money, more personnel, but in a world context it's just a drop in the bucket. The two forms of PGP, international and national, can interoperate, and they are used because of their worldwide availability. They start at 128-bit keys, going up to an incredible 2048-bit keys, and the current thinking is that these are unbreakable now or in the future. Very few governments or companies would want to give the U.S. government an easier entry into their electronic communication. In many studies, many companies view the 40- and 56-bit keys as unsafe. Some argue that the push for limiting exports is caused by the NSA's self-preservation mindset. In the decades of declining budgets, the NSA needs more money to crack sophisticated encryption transmissions.

SECURITY NOTE   Keep in mind, however, most experts agree that frequent changing of the keys has the same effect as very long keys.

The U.S. government has been an aggressive opponent in the easing of encryption standards. So much so that the Clinton administration has gone to great lengths to squash a federal court ruling defining encryption as free speech covered under the First Amendment. The case revolved around a Ph.D. candidate in mathematics, Daniel Bernstein. The case unfolded as follows:*

Pre-1993
Ph.D. candidate in mathematics Daniel Bernstein at the University of California develops an algorithm called "snuffle," a computer program that has built-in encryption facilities. The government tells him that encryption is considered a munitions and said that he must register as an arms dealer due to the extensive export controls. Mr. Bernstein only wants to discuss his findings and algorithm with other scholars and academia. He is told that if he does he will be in violation of the Arms Export Control Act, which is punishable by 10 years in jail and $1 million in fines.

March 1993
Mr. Bernstein has a conversation with Charley Ray of the Office of Defense Trade Controls, which at the time handled export issues. The meeting is useless and Mr. Bernstein is not told whether or not he will be prosecuted if he discusses his program.

February 1995
With the help of the Electronic Frontier Foundation (EFF), Mr. Bernstein decides to sue the State Department and the International Traffic in Arms Regulations (ITAR) for violating his free speech under the First Amendment.

April 1996
Denying the government's motion for dismissal, Judge Marilyn Hall Patel declared that the code in Bernstein's cryptographic algorithm, snuffle, is speech that is protected by prior restraint by the First Amendment. The major conclusion is that computer language is just that—language, no different than that of German, French, or English— and therefore protected by the First Amendment. The judge rules that the suit can continue.

Note The government issued a letter in June of 1995 to Bernstein saying that the paper could be published and they never had denied its publication; however, they did not want it published on the Internet.

---

*Adapted from the Web site of the Electronic Frontier Foundation (EFF) (*http://www.eff.org*).

December 6, 1996

Judge Marilyn Hall Patel struck down rules on export restrictions on the privacy technology called cryptography. This is a blow to the Clinton administration's plan for manufacturers to build "wiretap-ready" computers, televisions, and consumer electronics. The Clinton administration offered a carrot to manufacturers on export restrictions in return for their cooperation on eavesdropping on their customers.

December 16, 1996

Lawyers petitioned the government to reconsider their new regulations that were issued on November 16, 1996, urging them not to put them into effect until a court could rule for their constitutionality. In an apparent attempt to circumvent Judge Patel's ruling, the Clinton administration ordered the export regulations be moved to the Commerce Department from the State Department. This, in effect, nullified the judge's ruling, since her ruling was directed at the State Department.

June 17, 1997

All the plaintiffs are in front of Judge Patel, and she is to decide if the same regulations under a different authority are still a violation of the Constitution.

August 25, 1997

The judge again strikes down regulations, ruling that they still violate the First Amendment. This again deals a blow to the Clinton's administration's plan to force companies to design government surveillance devices into computers, telephones, and consumer electronics.

As the court's decision states:

> The Court also held that the government's licensing procedure fails to provide adequate procedural safeguards. When the Government acts legally to suppress protected speech, it must reduce the chance of illegal censorship by the bureaucrats involved, for example by making the government go to a judge to decide the issue. The EAR does not require this; in fact, it precludes it.

Most important, and most lacking, are any standards for reviewing applications. The EAR reviews applications for licenses "on a case-by-case basis" and appears to impose no limits on agency discretion. The court dissected the export controls' exemption for printed materials at length, calling it "so irrational and administratively unreliable that it may well serve to only exacerbate the potential for self-censorship." The government's "distinction between paper and electronic publication...makes little or no sense and is untenable." The court not only declared that these regulations are invalid and unenforceable, but also prevented the government from "threatening, detaining, prosecuting, discouraging, or otherwise interfering with plaintiff or any other person described...above in the exercise of their federal constitutional rights as declared in this order."

The immediate effect of this decision was that Professor Bernstein may publish his encryption software, and that others may read, use, publish and review it. In addition, others in industry are studying the court's analysis, and might decide to publish their own software on the Internet as well.

However, the story does not end there:

August 26, 1997
The Justice Department is considering what further legal action it will take following Judge Patel's ruling, since another federal court upheld the export controls on encryption software. In that case, Karn v. Department of State, the district court ruled that export controls on encryption are constitutional under the First Amendment and serve important national interests. Until it is clarified, export controls remain in effect.

August 28, 1997
The government files an emergency appeal to the Ninth U.S. Circuit Court of Appeals. Judge Patel rules that after September 8, 1997. Professor Bernstein can publish his work.

September 9, 1997
The Ninth U.S. Circuit Court of Appeals stays that decision until the appeal is heard.

December 16, 1997
The three-judge panel of the Ninth U.S. Circuit Court of Appeals heard the appeal and is currently considering Patel's 1996 decision.

In a totally separate suit, Professor Peter Junger from the Reserve University Law School lost his challenge from a federal district court, severely limiting his ability to publish his encryption technology. Both challenges rely on the fact that software is considered free speech, subject to the First Amendment. Unfortunately, different courts see things differently. Arguments claim that the court could not understand the differences between source code and compiled code. The California Court's decision in the Bernstein case, which went against the government ruling, applied only to the source code, which cannot run on a computer. The Ohio Court's ruling in the Junger case that was in favor of the government's position was challenged by lawyers who said the Ohio court could not tell the difference between source code and compiled code.

However, since March of 1998, Network Associates, a U.S. company, is now shipping via a subsidiary in the Netherlands an encryption product, thereby sidestepping the U.S. law on exportation of encryption products. This first product allows strong 128-bit encryption for email and files. The subsidiary is a Swiss company called Cnlab, which developed the product using a legally available algorithm based on Pretty Good Privacy. Since this product is based and developed outside of the U.S., it is free of export restrictions, and because it is based on the PGP algorithm, it is fully compatible with strong encryption products available in the U.S.

However, things may be changing in the government's control of encryption. Two factors are influencing the government's decision to look the other way. First, products are finding their way overseas anyway. Whether it is licensing or legal loopholes, encryption products exist, and that is hurting American companies. Second, the Justice Department's decision not to seek controls on domestic products is another signal that perhaps the government has realized it can't control this area. At the moment, exporting encryption is illegal except for financial institutions, and that definition is beginning to broaden. Another bright spot introduced by Vermont Democrat Patrick Leahy and Missouri Republican John Ashcroft that is making its way states that if you can obtain the stronger encryption overseas, then you can export it.

Conclusion

This chapter brings to a close Part 1 of this book on VPN technology. By now, you should have developed a firm understanding of what VPN technology is. The underlying VPN technology should not be hard to understand. Its roots trace back 20 to 30 years, and it's based on the TCP/IP suite of protocols. Since you are reading this book, you most likely have a solid foundation of them. We looked at a definition of VPN and some of the advantages and disadvantages associated with the technology.

We also looked at the costs of VPN technology. VPNs do save money, but they also cost money to install and maintain. They do make it very easy to conduct business, both nationally and internationally. Most surveys suggest a cost saving of 60 to 80 percent for an organization; we looked at some factors that perhaps suggest it is in the range of 30 to 40 percent. VPNs are extremely flexible, and companies can off-load many of their WAN design burdens to ISPs (again, they are off-loaded, not eliminated). Much of the burden is now on the ISP. Just as if you were sitting on a local LAN, if your ISP goes down, you may not be able to work.

We looked at the different types of VPN architectures and the topologies where these devices can be placed. We saw a wide range of products, features, and implementations that you could set up to take advantage of a VPN. We also saw how flexible a VPN is; many devices in your organization can act like a VPN device. This book has been written with the security of a VPN in mind, and up until now, we suggested that:

$$VPN = f\,(security)$$

where a VPN is a function of security; by varying the values of security, you impact your VPN safety. Your data is dependent on using the most secure methods that are available and on keeping up with security measures, since outside situations can affect your security without you knowing about it.

Now let's modify this equation a little to include the following:

$$VPN = f\,(Security) + f\,(Government)$$

Everything about VPNs revolves around security and governmental oversight. If you don't think that the government will stop you, just try to work with your international customers using 128-bit DES. As seen in this chapter, the federal government is very serious about encryption.

VPNs are the future, since the Internet is the wave of the future; VPNs will grow along with the Internet. Therefore, in a few years one of several things will happen, either governments will:

1. Work secretly with every manufacturer that builds encryption products and force them to build a backdoor without letting anyone know.

2. Allow the same strength encryption technology that is available overseas already to be legally exportable.

3. Just give up and realize it is futile. The Internet has fueled such a demand for technical people. Many cryptographers who worked for the government now work in the private sector, where their salaries are 30 to 50 percent higher, leaving a drain at the governmental agencies.

The VPN
Implementation

CHAPTER 7

The Basics

As with any new technology, you need to take into account several things before implementing the technology. You are adding a new piece of equipment to an already existing infrastructure; therefore, there are always interoperability problems that surface. If you decide to add two pieces, say, a VPN hardware device and a stand-alone firewall, now you have added two devices into your network, both having potential issues of their own.

In this chapter, we look at those issues that must be taken into account, such as IP addressing, mail, routing issues, and network address translation. You are taking a network connection, breaking it into two, and sticking some device in between. Every data packet that flows through the wire will flow through that device. Therefore, you can assume the device will somehow impact every data packet it sees.

As you look at the data flows, always keep in mind where the data can be compromised. What weaknesses are there? Are you allowing inbound access, and if you are, to what devices are you allowing access? In VPN technology, you are specifically creating inbound access. Your concerns have just doubled. Normally you worry about what Web sites your users are visiting and what attacks may occur to your network. Now you also have to worry about who is coming in.

Decide on a Game Plan

When deciding on a game plan, take it slowly and deliberately. Put the pieces in place and try to picture the traffic flows. You still may not have decided on an infrastructure, but now you certainly know what devices are available. Draw a topology setting. Most likely, you have a network topology already; just place this new device or devices in the picture and try to examine the data flows. When you picture the data flows, ask yourself such questions as, how are users authenticated, what subnets will they be allowed, when will the encryption process occur? After you go through this brainstorming, step back, take a day or so off, and then come back. As you start to process this information, you will start to ask yourself different questions about this new infrastructure layout. When you come back, you will narrow it down further. In brainstorming, you don't need to come up with the solution. What you need to come up with is a comprehensive set of questions to ask potential vendors. Their answers will determine the optimum setup.

When you go through this brainstorming, the thing to remember in all of this is *think of This as a system*. Being a systems integrator for as long as I can remember, I've frequently seen the approach by managers to develop just a piece of the solution. Then by adding the pieces, they figured, you will have the whole solution. This way of thinking never worked. How can you work on one part, oblivious to the rest of the world around you, and then expect to communicate with the other parts?

Say your company is working on a new car. You are responsible for the design of the engine, and your job is to make it the most powerful engine. You design the fastest engine on earth, and its technical merits are superb. There is only one catch: After you've built the engine, you have to install it into a car whose engine compartment has been reduced by 6 inches. During the car-body manufacturing process, there was a need to reduce costs, so the engine compartment was reduced by 6 inches. You were not notified, and your engine no longer fits. This is the problem with the old way of thinking. Another example is if you are writing a TCP/IP program for a network application. How can you expect to communicate with the SNA and IPX protocols on that network? So, when it comes to a VPN, think about all the other components that you could possibly affect. Look at Figure 7-1 and think about how many aspects you need to consider.

This is probably the simplest VPN tunnel concept you could think of—a remote laptop connecting to a firewall/VPN device. The procedure should be straightforward, the setup simplified, and the connection automated. However, if you thought that, you would have made several mistakes and taken things for granted that will cause you trouble later.

Figure 7-1
Systems approach to
VPN implementation.

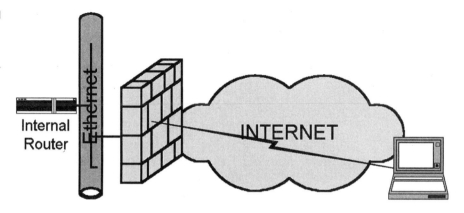

Now let's look at some items you must take into account before implementation:

IP Address Space   In any VPN scenario, you will need IP address space. Do you already have a registered IP address space that was given to your organization? You may decide to use network address translation, but you will still need a valid IP address to create the tunnel, or you will have to terminate the tunnel at an Internet border access point, such as a firewall.

DNS Issues   You may need to be concerned with who will be doing your DNS. If you are obtaining new IP address space, somewhere you will need to set up a DNS server so Internet users will be able to find your network servers. If you are using a managed VPN service, then your ISP may provide this service. As we will see later, it may be safer to have a DNS server on a DMZ zone.

Routing Issues   You need to make provisions for the routing tables that will be needed in your organization. VPNs are IP to IP; therefore, there has to be a routing algorithm in place that will allow this. Many organizations have rules about routing policies where they try to keep traffic on their local network, thereby reducing traffic across their internal WAN links. When you hook up a VPN, you will force users to use that device, which could increase traffic on that segment that contains that device.

Network Address Translation   Will you be using NAT, and if so, where? NAT gives you the ability to make a connection to the Internet. It also gives you the ability to hide your company's internal address behind one or several IP addresses. These addresses are usually implemented on a firewall machine. What this means is that every packet that comes in is terminated at the firewall and to be forwarded only by the firewall.

Encryption   If you are like a majority of VPN users, you will not even know the type of encryption you will use. Your vendor, of course, will tell you what their products support, but most likely, you will use the encryption algorithm that comes with the product. Do you know when to use DES or 3DES? In addition, how many laptops will be using the VPN? You will need the same type of encryption software loaded on them as well.

VPN Architecture Placement

After you decide what type of device to use, you then need to decide where you are going to place this device. Back in Chapters 4 and 5, we discussed the different types of VPN architectures and the different topologies. You should have some idea of where you would like to place the VPN device. You know it will be placed close to the Internet's connection point. Therefore, is there a router, a firewall, or a separate subnet you would like to use?

For Chapters 7 and 8, the example I will use is the one depicted in Figure 7-1. This setup is probably the most common and the one with the most complexity. The complexity comes in because you are implementing VPN, firewall, routing, and operating-system functionality all in one box. It is this difficulty that must be dealt with. In every other setting, you are only adding one component, which would make things easier.

One of the first questions to ask is, Where do you want to place this device? Looking at Figure 7-2, your organization has two geographically diverse departments. You could place two VPN devices if you wished, but that adds to the work and expense. Therefore, you must determine a

Figure 7-2
Different VPN geographical sites.

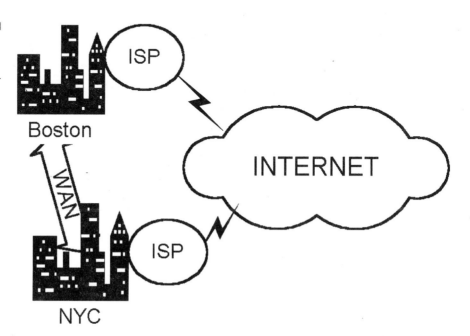

physical spot. A good spot would, of course, be where the technical talent is located, since downtime is critical and you need the talent to resolve things quickly.

Figure 7-2 illustrates an organization having two different sites (of course, you can have more than two). They are connected by a WAN link to allow communications between these two sites. They may or may not have Internet access currently. Your decision is to decide which site gets the VPN device. Once you decide that, you need to contact an ISP in the area to get Internet service or upgrade your existing service.

▬▬ ▬▬ ▬▬ ▬▬ ▬▬ ▬▬ ▬▬ ▬▬ ▬▬ ▬▬ ▬▬ ▬▬ ▬▬ ▬▬ ▬▬ ▬▬

GENERAL NOTE   Some ISPs block encrypted packets. You may not have thought this. In this case, you may want to ask your ISPs if they do before deciding on a city. You may find that your existing ISPs don't block encrypted packets. If two cities have ISP service and one does block encrypted packets, then your decision may be to go with the other city. Unless you have reasons for staying with a particular city, like technical talent, you will have to find another ISP.

▬ ▬ Routing Problems

Let's say you have decided to add this device in one city but decide to leave both cities connected by their respective ISPs to minimize traffic on the internal WAN links, as shown in Figure 7-3. The next problem you will run into is routing, as the next few illustrations will demonstrate. To correct the routing problems, you first need to understand how the traffic flows in a VPN, which we will discuss first. Then we will look at how to correct the routing problems.

Figure 7-3 looks a little convoluted, but it is typical of diverse geographical organizations that are implementing VPN technology. If we take the figure apart and look at its traffic flows carefully, they will make sense.

Outgoing VPN Traffic

In Figure 7-3, look first at the big arrows labeled "Usual Direction." Most organizations will direct the network traffic out the closest link. This is done to minimize traffic on the WAN links connecting the two cities.

Figure 7-3
NYC and San Francisco geographical VPN setup.

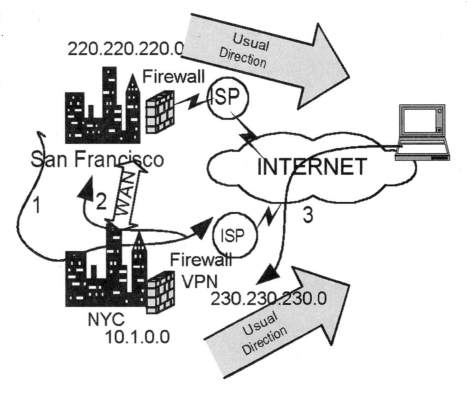

Figure 7-3
NYC and San Francisco geographical VPN setup.

GENERAL NOTE In the following examples, I will be using 220.220.220.0 as the San Francisco public routable address and 230.230.230.0 as the NYC IP public routable address. They are not valid IP addresses (230 is considered a multicast address); therefore, do not use them on your network.

San Francisco has a public routable network address of 220.220.220.0, which was given to them some time in the past. All of their equipment has been addressed according to this network number. Their main concern is that the ISP know about their public address space and routes it appropriately to their firewall. Normal Internet traffic on this network will be routed out the device labeled "firewall." The NYC area depends on its ISP to allocate them public address space. Their internal address space was addressed using the 10 address scheme and will be routed out the device labeled "firewall/VPN." For example, we will assume that NYC's ISP assigned them a public routable address of 230.230.230.0, and they will be using network address translation.

For outgoing normal Internet access, no policy change is required on any of the internal routers. All your internal data traffic will default to the next closest hop, which is usually the closest gateway or next router. This router, in turn, defaults out the firewall to the Internet.

When it comes to using VPN services, network 220.220.220.0 will not work without a change on the internal routers. Network 220 needs to default out the San Francisco firewall, with non-VPN traffic only. With VPN traffic, it has to route over the WAN to the NYC firewall/VPN device. How then can you route VPN traffic out the NYC firewall/VPN device? One way is that, since VPNs are IP based, when you set up the VPN, add the destination IP routing tables. Therefore, when users in San Francisco want to use the VPN, the internal routers will route over the internal WAN links to the NYC firewall/VPN device.

Say, for example, you are creating a VPN with a vendor who has network address 230.225.2.0. You need to add a route table entry that updates all the routers in the network. That informs the router that to get to network address 230.225.2.0, use the firewall/VPN device in NYC.

Incoming VPN Traffic

One major benefit of VPN is to allow remote users to access your internal servers. By *remote users,* we usually mean one of two types. One type of VPN user is a company employee who needs to access an internal server when he or she is on the road. The other type of VPN user is an external partner or customer who needs to access your extranet. When we are discussing routing issues, external partners are usually not taken into consideration. They are usually not worried about because they are (or should be) restricted to a DMZ zone at the Internet access point. In this case, the routing issues are restricted to that one device. However, if you want the external partners to be able to access internal servers that not part of a DMZ, then you need to treat them as internal partners. That is, if you want both internal employees and external partners to go through the firewall/VPN device in NYC and connect to servers in San Francisco, the internal routing issues are the same and must be routed by the internal routers.

Now let's consider the example of the remote laptop wanting to connect to a server in San Francisco at IP address 220.220.220.10:

1. The laptop, using its network connection setup, establishes a PPP connection to a local ISP and is assigned a public routable network address.

2. The VPN software loaded on the laptop makes a connection to the firewall/VPN device in NYC for the encryption key. This can be done either manually or by an automatic process on the laptop.

3. The NYC firewall/VPN responds back with the appropriate key. Another piece of information sent back to the laptop is the VPN domain, which consists of the IP address of the server in San Francisco.

4. The laptop now tries to connect to the server in San Francisco on network 220.220.220.10.

5. As the request works it way down the OSI stack, the software on the laptop knows that IP address 220.220.220.10 is part of the VPN domain. It then encrypts the packet and encapsulates the whole packet with a new IP address. The new IP address is the public address of the firewall/VPN device in NYC.

6. The firewall/VPN device strips the IP address off and decrypts the packet. It knows the request is for a valid server in the VPN domain. According to the user authentication processes set up, the firewall/VPN device will issue a challenge to the laptop to authenticate.

7. Once the laptop authenticates, the firewall will then check permissions to see if this user is allowed access to the server in San Francisco. If so, the firewall/VPN then sends the clear-text data over the internal WAN to the San Francisco server.

8. The server sees the requests, then responds (if appropriate permissions are set) to the destination device, which is the firewall/VPN device (this means NAT implemented).

GENERAL NOTE NYC network's address is 10. Therefore, all NYC internal routers know how to route this network, San Francisco is address 220.220.220.0, so all San Francisco routers know how to route that network. Many companies set this policy to minimize traffic on the WAN link. However, in order for the remote laptop to connect to the San Francisco network, all the internal routers must know about both networks. When the connection comes in on the NYC side, if you do not implement NAT, the destination address is that of the laptop (which is any public routable address). Since you didn't implement NAT and the internal routers only know about 10 and 220.220.220.0, the server in San Francisco would default the data packet out the closest gateway, which is the firewall in San Francisco. The end result is that the VPN communications will never work.

Step 3 Is Important

The encryption software on the laptop knows what networks are in its
VPN domain. What this means for an administrator is that you have to
set up the VPN device to "tell" the laptop what domains it will be a part
of. This is also a configuration issue; some VPNs only allow one domain,
where others allow multiple domains. Therefore, in this example, you
had a server on the 220 network that the laptop needed to access. The
firewall/VPN in NYC told that laptop that the server at 220.220.220.10
is in the VPN domain. Encrypt the packets and send them to the IP
address of the NYC firewall/VPN device, then they will be forwarded
over the WAN link to San Francisco network.

GENERAL NOTE   Routing is a two-way street: NYC has to know how
to route to San Francisco, and San Francisco has to know how to route
to NYC.

If your organization decided to segment the traffic, then you will have
to unsegment it. Of course, you only want to unsegment VPN destined
traffic, but the way routing works, you can't tell a router to forward
VPN traffic one way and non-VPN another way. The only option you
have is to know all your VPN connections outbound and add them to
your routing tables.

In our example in Figure 7-4, we have created one VPN domain, consisting of servers throughout the organization. Servers (220.220.220.10,
220.220.220.11) and servers (10.1.1.1, 10.1.2.1) are part of this domain.
When the laptop connects to the firewall/VPN device, it is told of these
four servers in the VPN domain and it caches this information. When it
wants to make a connection to any of these four servers, it encapsulates
the packet and sends it to the public IP address of the firewall/VPN
device in NYC.

Topology Placement

After taking care of the architecture placement and looking at the
potential routing problems, we next turn to the actual placement of the
equipment on the local network. As with everything else in VPN technology, there will be different ways to place this equipment. Different

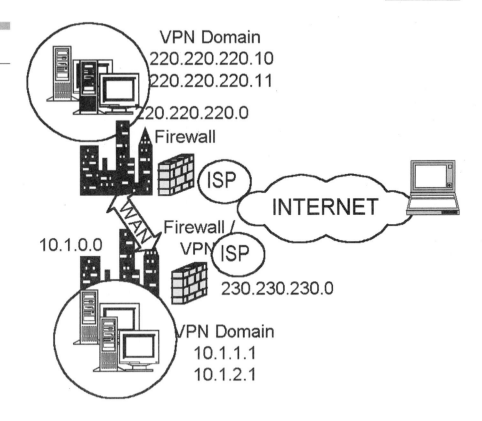

Figure 7-4
VPN domains.

types of architecture can be placed differently, but for this example, the firewall/VPN setup is used.

GENERAL NOTE Remember: Always think of the data traffic flows.

By understanding the data traffic flows, you will be able to see potential problems that may develop. Now is the time to do this, not once the device is in and functioning. Figure 7-5 shows a common placement for the firewall/VPN device.

Here we see a very common setup: from an internal router to a firewall to an external router, then to the Internet. The traffic flows here are straightforward, but the trade-off is performance. The firewall/VPN device is doing all the processing. If this is your setup, make sure you are using a high-performing platform.

Now look at Figure 7-6, which is more likely to be set up than Figure 7-5. Instead of directly connecting the firewall/VPN device to the inter-

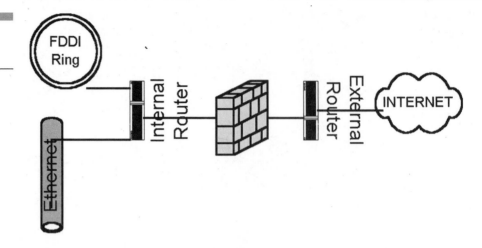

nal router, a hub is placed on the internal network. This configuration is the same as the previous example and poses no problems. The flow of traffic is still the same: internal router, firewall, external router, Internet. However, along with the performance problems, the hub could malfunction, or the cables could experience problems. The main problem here is what will mostly likely happen in the future as you add devices, as shown in Figure 7-7.

As your organization needs more services, you will place them near the VPN device. If you decide to add SMTP and DNS services, you will add them on a subnet on or near the device. If you decide to add a proxy server, again, you will place them near the device. The problem is not the services or where you want to place the devices, it is with the data flows.

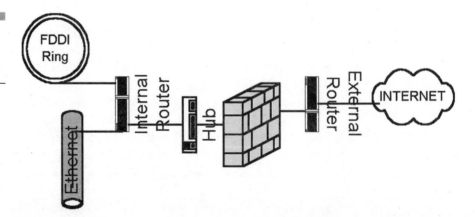

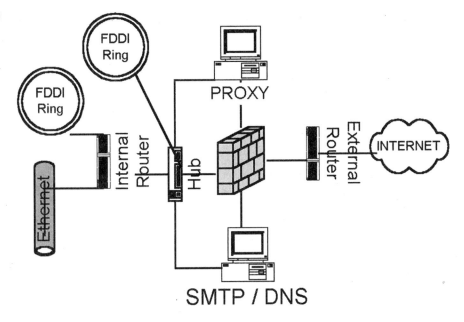

Figure 7-7
Potential firewall/VPN
placement problems.

This kind of setup will create:

- Routing loops
- Duplicate packets
- Backdoor

The hub is a multiaccess device, which will broadcast out all data packets. This will cause the proxy server and SMTP/DNS server to inspect all packets, and depending on their configuration, they may forward the packets out the firewall/VPN device to the Internet. On the return trip, there will be two sets of communications for each service requested. There is also a built-in backdoor to your network. If your proxy server or SMTP/DNS server can be compromised, then someone can get into your internal network, bypassing the firewall. If possible, do not use this type of configuration; instead, use a configuration as illustrated in Figure 7-8.

Figure 7-8 illustrates a preferred way of setting up this configuration. This helps keep routing loops and duplicate packet problems out of the picture. If due to some internal policies you cannot create this setup, then at least place filters on the internal routers to help minimize some of the routing problems. You can also shut off IP forwarding on the servers, which should also minimize the duplicate packets problems.

Figure 7-8
Placement of devices
with firewall/VPN
device.

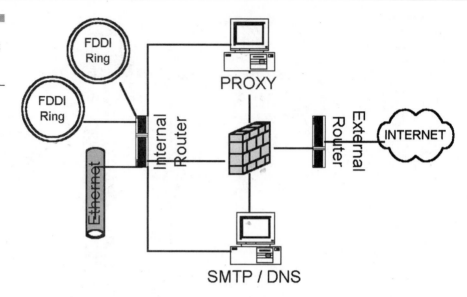

IP/NAT Addressing Concerns

IP addressing issues are some additional items you need to look at before implementing your VPN. In order to use the firewall/VPN device, you will need to obtain IP address space. You can do this one of two ways:

1. You could have obtained it from the InterNIC, which was done for the San Francisco network; or
2. You could obtain it from a local ISP, as done in the NYC network.

The problem concerns obtaining IP address space from an ISP, although it is not so much of a problem as a hassle. After you obtain address space from your ISP, you may then have to implement services such as SMTP, DNS, and Web servers according to the address space they assigned you. If, for some reason, you decide to leave that ISP, they will want their address space back. Now you have to go through the hassle of getting a new ISP, obtaining new address space and readdressing your servers. You also need to make sure that the DNS tables reflect these new IP addresses. However, if you've addressed your internal servers according to RFC 1918, there will be no need to readdress the servers. You will just need to reconfigure the NAT tables and update the DNS tables.

That brings us to another problem NAT helps to eliminate. Say you addressed your network according to RFC 1918. You cannot just connect to the Internet. Even if you addressed your network with some other IP

Figure 7-9

Static NAT.

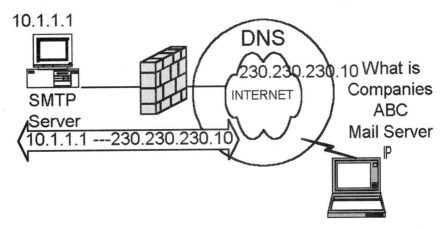

Company ABC
Mail Server

10.1.1.1

SMTP
Server
10.1.1.1 ---230.230.230.10

DNS
230.230.230.10 What is
INTERNET Companies
ABC
Mail Server
IP

addressing scheme, you still cannot connect to the Internet. You need a valid public routable address that your organization can use. Network address translation (NAT) gives your organization the ability to access the Internet behind a valid public IP address. NAT allows you several options, which makes it flexible for any organization. If your company has 10,000 nodes, you could hide those 10,000 nodes behind one valid IP address.

There are three ways of doing NAT: static, many to many, and one to many. Each one requires different setups, but all perform NAT. We will first look at static NAT (static means a one-for-one translation), with the two IP addresses never changing. Figure 7-9 illustrates a static address technique.

Someone on the Internet wants to send a message to a user named Joe at Company ABC. The laptop first has to find out what device is handling the mail for Company ABC and will query DNS servers throughout the Internet. In this example, the DNS tables reveal that IP address 230.230.230.10 is handling the mail for Company ABC. The laptop then packages the mail and sends it to "Joe@230.230.230.10"; it still has to get to Company ABC's mail server. This is shown in Figure 7-10.

Company ABC had obtained IP address space from its ISP, and the ISP assigned it the network 230.230.230.0. When the laptop sends the message, it is routed through the Internet by different ISPs until it gets to the ISP that is assigned that network block. If, however, the address 230.230.230.0 was given to Company ABC by the InterNIC, then Company ABC has to tell its ISP that it needs to route that network to them. Now the mail comes into the firewall. Address 230.230.230.10 is not the

Figure 7-10
Routed static NAT.

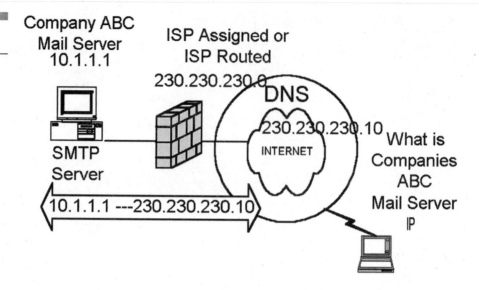

address of the mail server; address 10.1.1.5 is. The firewall strips off the 230.230.230.10 address, places the 10.1.1.5 address on the packet, and sends it to the internal mail server. The firewall has been set up for a static NAT, which is a one-for-one mapping, as follows:

```
10.1.1.5 <-> 230.230.230.10
```

The firewall/VPN changes the address to 10.1.1.5 and sends it to the mail server. This address convention cannot change; it has to remain static. The mail server has specific software running on it, and, therefore, the requests cannot be sent elsewhere. In other forms of NAT, there is many-to-one mapping. Static NAT allows for services such as mail and Web servers, but each time it allocates a single IP address.

SECURITY NOTE This should not be the placement for the mail server, since it will cause security problems. I only used it to explain static NAT. Later, we will see the best placement for the mail server and similar Internet servers.

Why and When to Use Static NAT

A company's email and Web servers are examples of devices that would use static NAT. These servers contain special software for the various functions. If you weren't using a static NAT process, the firewall would just grab an available IP address in the NAT pool and send the data to any machine. Of course, that machine would just drop the packet, since it wasn't set up to respond to these types of client/server communications. NAT is set up differently depending on your functionality needs.

There is one final aspect with NAT that you have to consider: the MAC address of the device. In typical communication, the packet is not sent to the IP address of the host, but to the MAC address. Looking back at Figure 7-1, we set up the firewall to use static network address translation to map 10.1.1.5 to 230.230.230.10. The firewall itself is probably address 230.230.230.1, but an external router wants to send the packet to address 230.230.230.10. The external router would send out an ARP request, the ARP request says, "Who is IP address 230.230.230.10?", and normally, the end device would just send back its MAC address. In this NAT example, the firewall must be configured so that when the external router sends out an ARP for 230.230.230.10, the firewall/VPN must respond to that request with its own MAC address. The firewall/VPN would then reply to the external router, saying that it has the IP address of 230.230.230.10. Then the firewall/VPN would get the packet; it knows that MAC address of the mail server at 10.1.1.5, so it just modifies the address on the data packet and sends it to the mail server.

The second form of network address translation is referred to as "pooled," or "many to many." It is a dynamic one-to-one mapping of public IP addresses to your organization's private address space. You need to obtain a range of addresses from your ISP and implement these on your firewall/VPN device. Figure 7-11 illustrates a many-to-many mapping.

In Figure 7-11, The organization has obtained another Class C IP address of 231.231.231.0 to use as their public network range for NAT translation; this consists of a pool of 255 hosts. Their internal network is addressed using network 10; therefore, their hosts are 10.0.0.1,10.0.0.2,10.0.0.3, and so on. We will forget about subnets for the moment.

The firewall/VPN device now does a mapping of the internal private network numbers to the new available public network numbers. The many-to-many translations are dynamic in allocation. Internal hosts are only locked for the session, but the session is configured on a time interval. The machine at address 10.0.0.1 is translated to address 231.231.231.1 on the first session passing through the device. The next device, the machine at address 10.0.0.2, is translated to 231.231.231.2, if 231.231.231.1 is not available. If IP 231.231.231.1 is available, it will use that one. This address translation is configurable though; you set

Figure 7-11
Many-to-many NAT
implementation.

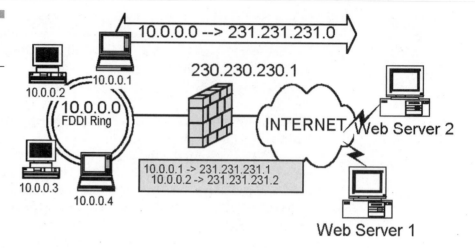

the time that the translation stays locked into the firewall/VPN device.

Since client/server communications are stateless, a device has no way of knowing if the client has finished its session with a host. Therefore, a timer is usually set in the device. When a particular communication stream stops, the device will hold that mapping for a specified time. If no further communication comes from that internal host, the IP address is placed back in the pool. A potential problem with this is, if you make the time interval too short, every time the machine passes the device, it is allocated an IP address, which lowers the available IP addresses left for other machines. If you make the time interval too large, when the communication stream is done, that particular translation is still left in the device until the timer clears, again lowering the available IP addresses left for other machines.

This type of network address translation is seldom used anymore. This setup requires you to have more public IP addresses than available internal hosts, which might be accessing the Internet. If you had 10,000 users, and at any time, 400 end users might be accessing the Internet, you would need 400+ public IP addresses. This is due to the timing interval explained in the last paragraph and because some IP addresses might not be available for immediate use.

You will see by the next NAT technique, usually referred to as "hide, port, pool" or "many-to-one," there is no limitation to the number of available IP addresses. Technically, there is a limit, but the pool is so large it is considered unlimited. Figure 7-12 illustrates a pool NAT.

This type of network address translation is becoming very common; all the internal machines are translated to the one public IP address of the firewall/VPN device. The device uses ports to keep track of individ-

Figure 7-12
Many-to-one pool
address translation.

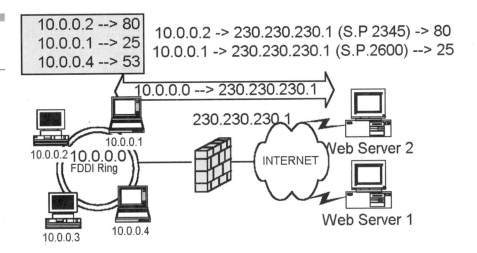

ual machines the same way a machine uses ports to signify upper-level applications, e.g., port 23 for Telnet. The device uses similar unused ports to keep track of internal host mapping. This type of translation works as follows:

1. The machine at address 10.0.0.2 wants to connect to Web Server 1.

2. The request is sent to the device on Destination Port 80 (which is HTTP) (we'll assume that 10.0.0.2 is using source port 5000).

3. The device translates that address to 230.230.230.1 (the external IP address of the firewall), inserts its own source port as 2345, and sends the request to Web Server 1, Destination Port 80.

4. The server responds back to 230.230.230.1 (Destination Port 2345).

5. The firewall/VPN device looks at the port (2345), then looks in its table and realizes that it goes to address 10.0.0.2 port (5000).

6. It translates the address and the port and sends the packet to the local machine.

7. The process is repeated over and over.

There is no timer configuration with this type of NAT, since every address is translated to that one public IP address. This type of NAT is becoming extremely common. The power of servers today allows the firewall/VPN device to handle thousands of NAT requests per minute with no performance degradation. This means that you could have a device that has a 64,000-to-1 address translation ratio.

In most situations, a combination of pool and static translation is used to accomplish network address translation.

You would use pool translation for two reasons:

1. You have a nonpublic address with a large end-user population. In this case, you don't have a choice; you need a public routable Internet IP address to transverse the Internet and that can scale to the amount of users you have; or

2. You already have a public address, but worry about security. Your organization has a public routable address, but for security reasons, you do not want your internal public addresses to be routed along the Internet. If you did, anyone snooping on the Net can see your IP traffic. In this case, they will see public IP traffic coming from your internal network, possibly see a pattern developing, and try to compromise your internal hosts. You would rather have all traffic directed to the firewall/VPN device for inspection.

Firewall/VPN Addressing

This brings us to addressing the VPN device itself. You need a valid IP address for the external side. The DMZ zones and your internal networks may or may not have public address space. You will have to set up the routing tables on the device to point into your network and to the Internet.

Figure 7-13 shows a common situation for a firewall/VPN device with public IP address space on the DMZ zones. The 230.230.230.0 network has been subnetted with two of the subnets attached to DMZ1 and DMZ2. In this figure, the organization's network address structure is, again, the 10.0.0.0 network.

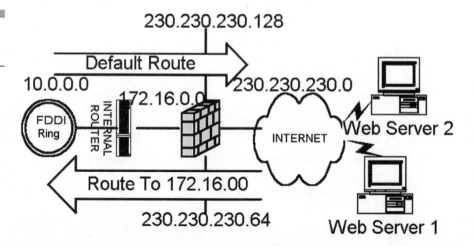

Figure 7-13
Firewall/VPN and DMZ addressing.

However, there is a new network address here, 172.16.0.0 (again network 172.16.0.0 is according to RFC 1918). Depending on your firewall/VPN device and your operating system, you may not be able to support variable-length subnet masking (VLSM). This means that if you subnetted the 10.0.0.0 network, the firewall/VPN device will know how to get to the 10 subnet it is on. It will not know how to get to the other subnets, which need to be routed to the internal router. Therefore, if your device does not support VLSM, you will have to route every 10.0.0.0 subnet to the internal router. For example, if you assign subnet 10.1.0.0 to the internal side of the firewall/VPN device, you will need to route the other 254 routes to the internal router from your firewall/VPN device. This is just for a 10 network subnetted to a Class B. If you subnet it to a Class C, 24 bits, you will need to route more than 65,000 routes to the internal router. We will revisit this routing issue again in Chapter 8.

Remote Access Issues

When considering remote access issues, you have two areas to deal with: the placement of the authentication server and what types of users you are going to authenticate. We spoke about the types of users earlier—internal employees and external customers, vendors, and so forth. You normally have three options where to set up your authentication server: the DMZ, the internal network, or on the VPN itself. Each one has its own advantages (security versus flexibility, stand-alone or integrated product, and so on).

Figure 7-14 shows the various placements for authentication servers. Each placement has different factors you have to deal with. If you put the authentication on the firewall/VPN device, that increases the processing requirements needed by that device. In addition, you will have to manually enter in every available user, both internal and external. Some vendors support a global database import. If you have a user database and can export that database to a flat file, you may be able to import that file to the authentication database on the VPN device.

If you install the server on the DMZ, you need to make sure that the firewall/VPN device can communicate with the authentication server. If, for example, you are using a RADIUS server, you need to make sure that your firewall/VPN device can communicate with the RADIUS protocol to that server. This is a two-step process: First you configure the

Figure 7-14
Placement for
authentication
servers.

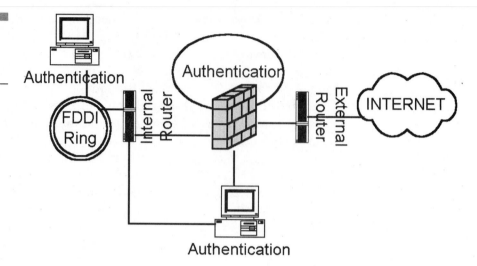

firewall/VPN device to authenticate users via a RADIUS server, and then you set up a statement to point to that RADIUS server. If you use TACAS or tokens, you need to make sure your firewall/VPN is compatible.

If you decide to install the authentication device on your internal network, you need to check compatibility, as well as timing. Some VPN devices will only allow a specific amount of time to log in. If it takes longer, the connection will be dropped. Therefore, if there is latency in your network, people may not be able to authenticate against the server. The user will attempt to access the Internet; the firewall/VPN device will query the RADIUS server. However, because of the latency in your network, when the response comes back from the RADIUS server, the firewall/VPN will time out the connection. Therefore, users will be denied outbound access, although they have permission.

There are two authentication schemes you need to consider:

1. Users going out to the Internet.
2. Users coming into the internal network.

They both use the authentication services for access, and your company may have to decide how it wants that authentication handled. This is strictly a company's policy. Some of the different authentication schemes are as follows:

- Authenticating every individual accessing the Internet
- No internal authentication, but logging every site they visit
- Authenticating and logging every site they visit

- Using an Internet Web filtering tool and only allowing certain sites to be accessed
- Authenticating users coming into the your site, normally via a VPN
- Authenticating and logging all those coming into your site

As you can see, there are many options for authenticating and logging users. That decision is best left up to management. One important thing to remember: Logging can cause a performance problem, so you need to see performance statistics before deciding where to place the authentication process.

A new product on the market that relates to user authentication and logging is "Web" importance. You set up categories on how they relate to your business. It shows which Web sites users visited and how it relates to their job function or category. Again, if you implement this, there might be performance problems.

DNS/SMTP Issues

Domain Name Service (DNS) and Simple Mail Transport Protocol (SMTP) issues are an important consideration when setting up your network devices. Careful placement of these devices is important for the security and safety of your organization's site and information. Figure 7-15 depicts a correct situation for these devices.

In this example, do not worry about public or private IP address space. Rather, watch the data flows when accessing the Internet and coming in from the Internet. You should have separate internal servers to handle DNS and mail traffic, and separate DNS and mail servers on the DMZ zone. If you leave out the SMTP/DNS server on the DMZ zone, then your internal servers will be solely responsible for the services. However, in order for them to work, you must create a hole in the firewall that allows inbound access to your network—not a good idea. All Internet traffic should go to the DMZ zone, then be forwarded to the internal network.

You should also restrict the type of data that is allowed to enter the DMZ. Only SMTP- or DNS-type traffic should be allowed to pass the firewall to the DMZ and only pass that traffic where the destination address is the SMTP/DNS server. Someone could otherwise try to compromise another server on SMTP or DNS well-known ports. The SMTP/DNS server on the DMZ will then forward traffic to internal

Figure 7-15
Placement of DNS
and SMTP server.

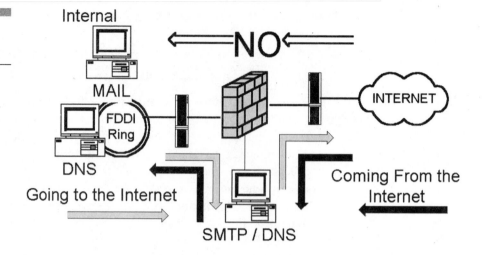

hosts. While you may not think of it, this direction also should be restricted by rules on the firewall. On the firewall, only allow DNS traffic to pass that is either to the Internet or to the internal DNS server. The same goes for SMTP. If someone should compromise your SMTP/DNS server, you do not want to allow unrestricted access internally. In this diagram, it would be hard to compromise the server on the DMZ, but in your company, you may have a hub or another server that is compromised. It's best to play it safe.

Therefore, you should never allow traffic from the Internet directly into your site. There may be times when this is necessary, as in the case of a VPN device that is behind the firewall on your local network. However, tighten those holes as much as possible. Only allow specific traffic to a specific host, and then log as much as possible.

Conclusion

This chapter tried to get you prepared to implement a VPN on a firewall device, since this is probably the most common setup today. This is not the only one, just the most common. Your organization has different requirements, so you may need a different setup. The reason for choosing a firewall/VPN setup is that it contains all the steps needed to implement security and a VPN. If the organization already has a firewall and you are just adding a stand-alone VPN device, it might be as simple as plug-and-play. If you don't need all these steps, just concentrate on those areas that you need.

You should have an understanding of the basics that will prepare you for implementing a VPN. These steps are critical, since they are the fundamental steps before you can even install the VPN. IP addressing, DNS issues, and routing issues are all major obstacles that, if not dealt with now, will cause you problems later. Think about the separate WAN links and routing between two or three different geographical areas. Think about what will be your domain (I called it a VPN domain). Then think about how many roving laptops you will have and how they will be authenticated into your network. Finally, think about users leaving your network. What types of traffic logging and what kind of monitoring and alerting do you plan to have?

The next chapter will discuss an actual implementation of a firewall/VPN running on a UNIX platform. The only thing that will not be accurate is the IP address, for obvious reasons. At this point in the book, you should be very comfortable in knowing where the device goes and what to think about for your organization's routing policy.

Every component you add onto a network has to be treated like a network device; routers, bridges, hosts, and VPN devices all have the same considerations, so all the rules of IP and name resolution apply.

CHAPTER 8

Installing a VPN, Part I

As we've now gone through several chapters, a framework should be emerging about VPN technology. This framework encompasses those aspects that make VPN technology unique. In this framework, we looked at the architecture, topology, benefits, and costs associated with the technology. Each chapter has built on the previous one, so you can gradually learn what it takes to understand and implement VPN. As can be seen by the previous chapter, there are networking items that you must deal with before implementing the VPN. Some of these items are normal, everyday networking items. You may not have even realized they were a part of VPN implementation process.

As mentioned in the previous chapter, thinking from a systems perspective is appropriate here. This way, you see firsthand all the items that you need to deal with before you can install the VPN. This systems approach applies to every situation in every technological setting.

In this chapter, we will go through a step-by-step example of installing a firewall/VPN product. We will use a firewall software package that has the VPN capabilities built-in and running on a UNIX platform. The firewall will use a separate RADIUS server on the internal network for authentication. It will be configured to allow remote access to the internal network and use the functionality of a proxy server on the internal network.

Introduction to Installing a Firewall-Based VPN

In the last chapter, we saw those things that we needed to address before installing the VPN. In this chapter, we will assume that all those things were accomplished. We've obtained the necessary IP addresses and decided what kind of network address translation to use. We've also decided on the user authentication process and what type of VPN to install. We will install both a remote access VPN and a LAN-to-LAN VPN. As done throughout this book, a particular vendor's product will not be used. This is done for two reasons. First, if a vendor's name is mentioned, this book might appear to be biased toward one particular vendor. Second, the way technology changes, by the time this manuscript is released, the vendor's product may no longer be acceptable for your organization.

The technology has been tried to be presented as black box as possible. You should be able to set up a scenario and just drop a product in place. Just remember, when you drop a VPN in place, you will be allowing an inbound connection from the Internet. Therefore, you must make sure whom you are allowing into your company.

Before beginning, let's recap the types of VPN technology and some of the important concepts that have been previously mentioned. As you go through the following example, you may question why a particular step is being done. All the steps are done to satisfy the requirements of these concepts.

VPN Configurations

VPNs come in four configurations:

1. *Intranet VPN.* A VPN that allows your internal employees to connect to an internal server from remote offices (i.e., a LAN-to-LAN intranet).

2. *Remote Access VPN.* A VPN that allows your internal employees to connect to your internal servers from the road (i.e., dialing into some local ISP and making a tunnel to your organization).

3. *Extranet VPN.* A VPN used by external customers, suppliers, and vendors to establish a tunnel to a secure server (i.e., electronic commerce).

4. *Intracompany VPN.* A VPN, not used too often yet, but that allows the use of encrypted communications inside a corporation's network to protect against internal security breaches.

Requirements

Along with the various configurations of VPNs, an additional list of requirements is necessary. These requirements ensure that your VPN implementation will be relatively easy and will help to guarantee the safety of your VPN. As stated in earlier chapters, VPNs are a function of security; if you modify security attributes, you modify the safety of your data. Whether security is internal or external, you are responsible. Internal security is how you implemented your organization's security policy, whether with a DMZ zone, restrictive firewall rules, authenticating users, and so on. External security is something that is outside of your control but still your responsibility. An external security issue would be, for instance, a particular encryption algorithm being broken.

You need to be kept up-to-date with these kinds of announcements. Once it's announced, you must take steps to minimize your vulnerability.
   the requirements are as follows:

1. *Control.*   Who has the control of your hardware, you or your ISP? If your ISP owns the equipment, then what are some response times, and what type of maintenance contracts are available?

2. *Compatibility.*   Is your VPN compatible to your internal network protocols? If you are running TCP with IPX or SNA on the same network, you will need to both encapsulate and encrypt your data.

3. *Security.*   You are ultimately responsible for security. How will you implement your company's security policy, and what types of security training will be provided for your IT staff?

4. *Interoperability.*   Will your VPN solution be compatible with your existing network infrastructure? Will your encryption algorithms be compatible with your vendors or suppliers? That is, if you are using DES, will your vendor be using DES?

5. *Reliability.*   You need to look at network uptime, bandwidth allocation, and if possible, latency. Look for quality of service (QoS) and service level agreements (SLAs) when available.

6. *Authentication.*   What types of users will you be authenticating? You have two sets: internal and external. What kind of authentication servers will you be implementing (e.g., RADIUS, TACAS, etc.), and what type of logging do you require?

7. *Accessibility.*   If internal users cannot get out or external customers cannot get in, your VPN is of no use. If you decide that your VPN must be available on a 24x7 basis, you will need 24x7 support.

8. *Maintenance.*   This is one of those gray areas where you get what you pay for. How long is the contract good for? How much support do you get? Is it on-site or just telephone support? If you are using an ISP-supplied VPN, how long is repair time if you need to replace the device?

9. *Help desk.*   Your organization will have to establish some type of help desk functionality. VPN tunneling software is not the same as the networking software used in establishing a PPP connection to an ISP. End users will have problems, and most ISPs are not equipped to handle these problems.

10. *Nonrepudiation.* You must be able to positively identify the sender, with no possible chance of error. In the future, customers will order products and services from your firm via electronic commerce. The orders will probably be fed into a tracking database for billing and record keeping purposes. If customers start denying they sent the orders, your billing, sales, and revenue charts will be inaccurate.

11. *VPN architecture.* By now you know what types are available, how they can fit into your organization, and some benefits associated with them.

12. *VPN topologies.* You should have decided where to place these devices and understand how they communicate with other network devices in your organization.

13. *VPN benefits and costs.* You've now seen most of the cost savings and the additional costs with VPN technology. As we have shown, there is more of a reduction in network support architecture than an elimination of items. You reduce the number of dial-up access lines, but you don't eliminate them.

14. *Government restrictions.* We looked at this issue back in Chapter 6. Most governments have regulations that place restrictions on the use of encryption. These regulations have a direct impact on the safety of your data.

The Firewall-Based VPN Model

The company has no Internet access; they are typical in that all their communications are over other networking infrastructures, such as Frame/ATM or leased lines. They want them replaced using the Internet. They have two main offices: corporate headquarters in San Francisco and a division headquarters in NYC. They also have a branch sales office in Chicago. The company has decided to install a firewall-based VPN running on a UNIX platform over the Internet. One reason for this decision is that the technical support of the organization is on the UNIX platform. Most of the available reports from vendors have shown that the UNIX operating systems scale better that other operating systems. Since the organization will have close to 100,000 users, 10,000 of which at any time could be using the VPN, they have decided to use UNIX.

In our model, we have decided that the firewall/VPN device will be placed in the NYC and Chicago offices. NYC was chosen because of the much larger employee base. Chicago was chosen because it had no internal WAN link and needed a way to access headquarters. Since the VPN will be available to all users, this will also help keep traffic on the internal WAN link down. Another way they are keeping the traffic on the internal WAN link down is by having two Internet connections between the headquarters. They will have a San Francisco headquarters ISP, with those users utilizing that Internet connection for non-VPN traffic, and a NYC division headquarters connection for VPN traffic. Since the Chicago VPN is new and does not have an internal link, they also will have to obtain a public IP address space. The VPN is designed so that when the Chicago users access the Internet, the VPN functionality will only occur when they are establishing communication with the NYC networks. The company's current network diagram is shown in Figure 8-1.

In our model, the company already has an internal WAN link connecting their corporate and division headquarters. They've decided to leave this link alone and replace all others by using the Internet. They also needed the additional functionality of having a VPN that could be used by both locations. They did not want the expense of having two separate VPN setups. Unfortunately, in order to connect to Chicago via a VPN, they had to duplicate the setup. Fortunately, however, the vendor supports remote management capabilities; therefore, the technical UNIX talent in NYC can monitor the Chicago configuration. They went

Figure 8-1
The company's current network topology.

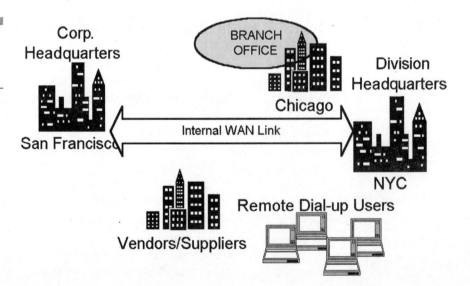

through the normal ISP comparison shopping and decided to use an ISP that has a global reach. They've also benefited in that, by having two Internet connections between headquarters, they reduced the traffic on their internal WAN link, and if one Internet link fails, they can route to their other link.

The corporate headquarters in San Francisco has had their own public registered address of 220.220.220.0; over time they used this network address for their internal machines. As a security mechanism, they did not want their address to be routed over the Internet, so they applied for a new address and decided to use pool network address translation.

The division headquarters, which has a much larger employee base, has used network 10 to address their internal clients. As with most corporations, they have subnetted their 10 network among their departments. They also need to apply to their ISP for a public routable address. They will also be using pool network address translation. It was estimated that, at the most, only 10,000 users might be using the VPN. That still is only one IP address used, and the technical specifications by the vendor assure that the VPN will easily handle 10,000 users.

The Chicago branch office also needs to obtain a valid public IP address, since the corporate policy is to hide the real addresses behind the firewall. They will also set up network address translation and address their internal network separately.

Four servers will need to be accessed by the VPN. There are two servers in San Francisco, with addresses 220.220.220.10 and 220.220.220.11, which will be accessed by internal employees on the road. Two servers in NYC, with addresses 10.0.0.11 and 10.0.0.12, will be part of the VPN.

Since the company is worried about too much unproductive time, they want the ability to monitor the Web traffic originating from inside their networks. Since the two headquarters will have a substantial number of users accessing the Internet, performance problems may affect the firewall/VPN device with the amount of logging. Therefore, they will set up a special proxy server that will have the function of monitoring Web traffic. This proxy will also act like a RADIUS user authentication server, used for incoming VPN users. The branch offices will also have to monitor traffic somehow. Since the office is small, instead of using a separate server, they will use the firewall itself to monitor traffic.

The company wanted to put in place a policy where only authorized users are allowed to access the Internet. However, what that meant was that each individual user had to be entered into the RADIUS user database. Another potential solution would be to have the RADIUS server query a central database in determining access. Neither of these options is viable. Since there is such a large mix of different platforms in the company, there is no central database. To have someone enter and delete users on this RADIUS server would require a full-time position. Therefore, since the company is not using dynamic IP addressing, they can still monitor traffic, and the logs will point back to the originating source machine inside the network.

This company has also decided the types of traffic that are allowed to flow into the organization: DNS and SMTP traffic. They have also decided to set up separate DNS and SMTP servers on a DMZ, thereby eliminating direct traffic into the organization. These are the requirements set forth by the company. By looking at the requirements, we set up a configuration that is illustrated in Figure 8-2.

This configuration establishes two firewall/VPN devices: one in the Chicago branch office and one in the NYC division headquarters. In addition, any remote users who need VPN access will need VPN tunneling software loaded on them. The chosen VPN vendor includes laptop software that allows this. However, since the local ISPs cannot help end users once they establish an Internet connection, this responsibility will fall on the company's IT department. The company assumes the current IT department will also handle this new technology. The VPN domain is also defined with servers located at both headquarters.

Figure 8-2
Firewall-based VPN configuration.

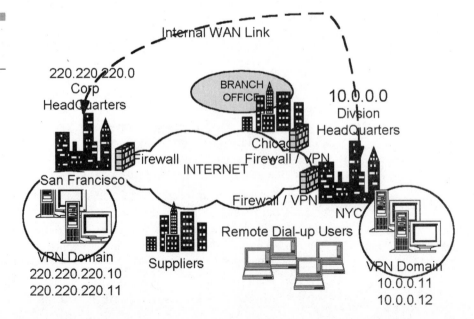

Obtain and Assign IP Address Space

Once the model has been agreed upon or dictated by upper management, headquarters and the branch office then contact their local ISP to obtain address space. Once the IP address is assigned, the technical staff then assigns the public address space to the various devices throughout the department. The following IP network addresses were assigned to the offices by the ISPs:

Corporate Headquarters	235.235.235.0
Division Headquarters	230.230.230.0
Branch Office	247.247.247.0

Just a reminder that these IP addresses are only for this exercise; they are not used anywhere and are considered multicast addresses. The local ISP usually takes care of the IP addressing between the serial link of the external router (usually labeled S0) and their connection. Starting with division HQ, we set up the firewall/VPN and associated devices as depicted in Figure 8-3.

Figure 8-3
Addressing convention for NYC-based equipment.

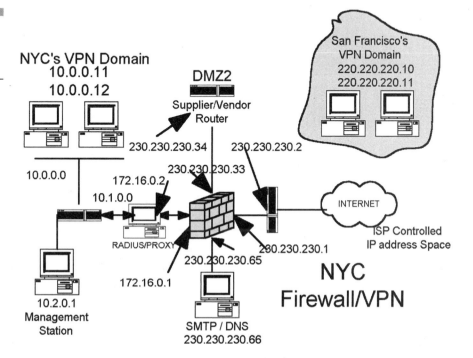

Starting with division headquarters, we have taken the address space assigned to us from the ISP and subnetted down further with a 255.255.255.224 netmask. This netmask takes the 230.230.230.0 network and breaks it into eight networks, with each network having 30 usable hosts per network. (*Usable* means actual IP addressing available for machines.) Any computer program that does subnet calculations will reveal that network, 230.230.230.0 with a netmask of 255.255.255.224, contains eight networks with 32 hosts per network. However, the first IP address of that network (230.230.230.0) is for the network number, and the last-available IP address (230.230.230.31) is for the broadcast number. Therefore, the actual usable IP addresses you have are $n-2$, where n is the total number of available IP addresses per network. You need to remember this in case you obtain from your ISP a small address range. In this example, the ISP assigned us a full Class C address, with 255 hosts or total IP addressees. If your ISP assigns you a subnet of a Class C to begin with, you have to make sure you have some valid addresses for other servers for which you want valid IP addresses. Once we subnetted that 230.230.230.0 network, we then assigned the IP addresses in the following conventions.

The External Links

Firewall/VPN device: 230.230.230.1

External router: 230.230.230.2

The IP addresses are on the 230.230.230.0 network, and the broadcast address is 230.230.230.31.

The DMZ(1) Links

Firewall/VPN DMZ1 interface: 230.230.230.65

SMTP/DNS server: 230.230.230.66

The addresses are on the 230.230.230.64 network, and the broadcast address is 230.230.230.91.

The DMZ(2) or EDI/Electronic Commerce Links

Firewall/VPN DMZ2: 230.230.230.33

DMZ2 router: 230.230.230.34

These addresses are on the 230.230.230.32 network, and the broadcast address is 230.230.230.63.

The Internal Interfaces

Firewall/VPN internal interface: 172.16.0.1

Proxy server (router): 172.16.0.2

These addresses are on the 172.16.0.0 network, and the broadcast address is 172.16.255.255.

   Now that these IP addresses are assigned, what was the reasoning for this addressing scheme?

Purpose of Subnetting the 230 Network

The ISP has assigned the NYC division a Class C network address (230.230.230.0) that contains 255 IP addresses. By further subnetting this network to a 255.255.255.224 netmask, we now have eight additional networks. The trade-off is usable IP address space; we now have 30 usable IP addresses per network. If you now think of where the IP address space is used, you might realize that you do not need a large pool of IP addresses for any of the subnets. In most organizations, there are only two, three, or maybe four devices near the Internet's connection point. It is the same way for setting up a VPN; you just don't need that many. Even if you set up a server farm and had 20 servers in that one subnet, you still have 30 usable IP addresses. As you now examine the reasoning behind the addressing scheme, you will see that this is true. As a final note, you can always use pool NAT and hide all your servers behind the one IP address anyway.

External Links

As can be seen by Figure 8-3, there is a single link between the external interface of the firewall/VPN and the external router. Therefore, you are allocating only two IP addresses for that whole network. It would be a waste of IP address space to have this whole Class C on only that link. Even this configuration is a waste of some IP addresses; in this example, there are 28 wasted IP addresses. Then the question is, why was the 255.255.255.224 subnet chosen? This problem has to do with a subnet-masking problem with many operating systems. This problem will almost certainly go away in the next few years as vendors update their code. You can set up a server to break up a network into equal parts (e.g., we broke the 230.230.230.0 into eight networks). On many operating systems you have to divide the network into equal parts; you cannot use unequal subnet masks (i.e., variable-length subnet masking). That is, you cannot have one network have 60 IP addresses and the other only 20 IP addresses. On a router, you can accomplish this configuration, but many operating systems have this limitation. However, this problem should be corrected by all vendors eventually. This has become a market demand.

DMZ1 Zone Link

Since we are using the 230 subnet on the external link, we can take the 230.230.230.64 subnet and assign it to the DMZ1 network. This will allow us 30 usable host IP addresses on this network, which would be more than enough for any corporation's needs for a DMZ zone. Most organizations will have a DNS server, Web server, and maybe a mail server or FTP server. Some of these services will probably be on the same machine. In our example we are assigning the firewall/VPN interface the address of 230.230.230.65 and our SMTP/DNS server the address of 230.230.230.66. So out of the available 30 usable addresses, we've only used two, leaving us plenty of room for growth.

DMZ2 or Electronic Commerce Links

Some organizations want to restrict their customers/suppliers/vendors to their own network. This DMZ2 link is a proper place for an extranet server, or the electronic commerce activity. In this kind of setup, you have the flexibility of segmenting noninternal traffic, checking on external authentication and having your policy checked by the rules on the firewall. On your firewall/VPN device, you can set rules that only allow certain users and restrict them to certain networks. In the case of setting up a VPN, you can restrict customers to the DMZ2 zone and allow another VPN for internal employees.

Internal Interfaces

Internal interface addressing is straightforward; you just need an available IP address to use. However, there is one major problem that occurs with the routing of internal networks. An example is shown in Figure 8-4.

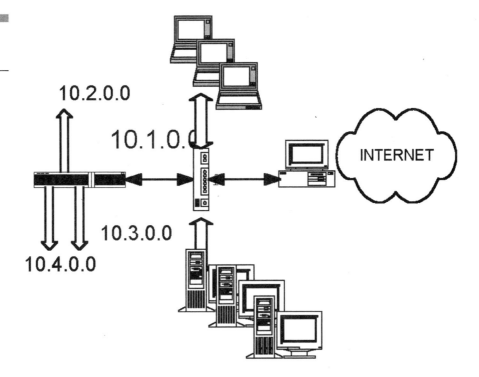

Figure 8-4
Internal routing
problem.

In this and similar situations, the internal network has been subnetted. In Figure 8-4, we see the internal network (address 10) has been
subnetted to a Class B network. What this means is that we are taking
address 10 and breaking it into 255 networks. The problem comes in
when we addressed the network with the internal interface of the fire-
wall/VPN on the subnet 10.1.0.0, and it affects incoming traffic. When
any internal user goes out to the Internet, all the gateways and routing
have been set up with a default route, to the subnet 10.1.0.0, and finally
to the firewall/VPN device to the Internet. When the traffic comes back
in, the firewall/VPN device only knows about the 10.1.0.0 network. In
order to send traffic to the other networks, the VPN device needs a route
to each and every other subnet on the 10 network. If you organization is
only using three or four subnets, this might not be a problem. However,
if you have delegated ranges of subnets to different departments, any
subnet could be used, so you have to set up each route on the
firewall/VPN device. Figure 8-5 illustrates a typical routing table
because of this problem.

The firewall/VPN device is on the 10.1.0.0 subnet, its IP address is
10.1.0.1, and the router that is directly connected to the VPN device has

Figure 8-5
Internal routing table
of firewall/VPN
device.

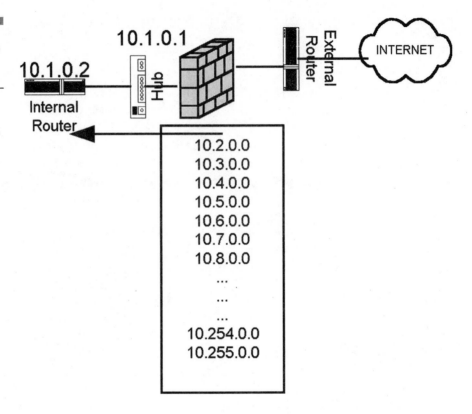

IP address 10.1.0.2. The hub that is pictured is usually connected to the department switch, so other employees on the 10.1.0.0 can get Internet access. When the traffic comes back in, the device knows where the 10.1.0.0 network is, since it's part of it, but as far as the other subnets, it has no idea how to get to them. When you configured the device, you assigned a specific IP address and netmask; therefore, the device did some calculations and derived its network. The device knows that network 10.0.0.0 has been subnetted; the problem is getting to the other subnets.

Figure 8-5 shows what the routing table would have to be on the firewall/VPN device to allow that. This is only the 10 network. If you had any other networks, you would need to add them to this routing table. You are adding additional routing processing on a device that is already doing network address translation, acting as a firewall, and implementing a VPN. You should be able to see potential performance problems with this device.

In our working model, you will notice I've introduced a network

(172.16.0.0). The firewall/VPN device knows about the network 172.16.0.0, since it is physically attached to it. However, it does not know about other subnets of that network or the 10 network that the NYC division is using. In this case, you need to route all the networks that are internal to your organization to your internal router. We've introduced network 172.16.0.0 into your company. It doesn't exist anywhere else beyond the little link, so there is no need for any routing entries. In addition, now the 10 network is completely taken care of by the internal router; therefore, the firewall/VPN device uses one route statement to send all traffic to the internal router and lets the internal router divide up and route the network 10 subnets.

As far as addressing the branch office, that should be a very simple installation. Just take one address from their assigned space and apply it to the external interfaces. On the internal interface of their firewall devices, you can apply a subnet of the public address space assigned to them. You can also choose address translation. In our example, we will use a single IP address and assign it to the external interface of the firewall/VPN device. We will subnet their assigned 247 network and install a DMZ zone. The internal address will be set to a subnet of the 172.17.0.0 network.

GENERAL NOTE VPNs have a way of bypassing the traditional norms of routing. You are aware that you cannot route on the Internet unless you have a public IP address. VPNs adhere to that, but when the data gets into your network, and if you are using NAT, a whole set of routing problems can develop.

There are other considerations that you need to address when implementing VPNs. Figure 5-3 first touched on it; here it is again in Figure 8-6. The NYC network's has been addressed using the 10.0.0.0 network. If the Chicago division was an older office, and they also used the addressing convention of network 10, changing all the internal machines would be a burden. The problem lies in the way routing works, and it is *not* a problem, everything is functioning correctly.

We set up a VPN domain in NYC of IP addresses (10.0.0.11 and 10.0.0.12). If you are in Chicago and want to establish a VPN tunnel to one of these servers, think about what would happen. Before the packet arrives at Chicago's firewall/VPN device, the server in Chicago would attempt to send a packet to one of the machines in the VPN domain. A Chicago server on the 10 network would attempt to send a data packet

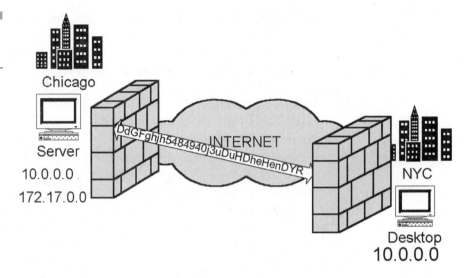

Figure 8-6
Chicago VPN
addressing concerns.

to the server on the NYC network, which is also addressed on network 10. This means the server in Chicago wouldn't direct the packet to the firewall/VPN device; it would just broadcast it out on its local network. It would never reach the NYC network. What if we could route everything out the Chicago firewall/VPN device, and as before, make a global route statement to send all 10 network traffic out the Chicago's device? No internal communication would take place. If a user in Chicago wanted to connect to a server in Chicago, a connection will not take place, since all of the 10 network traffic is being sent out to the NYC firewall/VPN device. Therefore, as can be seen from this example, VPNs can connect via the Internet two networks with the same network IP address.

GENERAL NOTE   VPNs allow the connection for networks that are addressed the same, causing routing problems.

Now, we choose the 172.17.0.0 network as our internal network for the Chicago office for two main reasons:

1. RFC 1918. In addressing any network, you should conform to the standard. Don't assume that NAT will take care of it. For example, instead of using one of the three available network ranges under RFC 1918 (10.0.0.0/172.16-172.31/192.168), you used another address, any address. What would happen is this: Say a company

out there on the Internet has authority over the IP address space you picked; it's their public address space. Now your internal users need to connect to their Web servers, or you and that company have decided to set up a VPN. When your internal users try to connect to that IP network range, they would never get out. This is the same situation just discussed in the last paragraph. Your internal network is addressed the same as the destination addresses, and your internal routers would never route the packet out the firewall/VPN device, since the routers assume that IP network is on their internal networks.

2. The only network that exists in the NYC network is the 172.16; therefore, since Chicago is addressed on the 172.17 network, this consists of a new network. The Chicago device will have no problem in placing local traffic (i.e., 172.17.0.0 on the internal network) and routing the 10 network, which is the VPN domain to the Chicago's firewall/VPN device and finally to NYC.

The laptops will need no IP configuration. They will receive their IP address from their local ISPs when they dial in.

Implementing Good Security Policy

Most organizations try to implement a good set of security policies, designed to keep data secure and confidential. However, there are always improvements that can be made, and with VPNs the same rules apply as to any good security policy you implement. If you decide that users are only allowed to access a particular service between the hours of 8:00 a.m. and 5:00 p.m., you have to have the ability to assign the VPN the same policy.

Now that we've got the IP addressing done, the next step is to describe a set of rules (usually called a "rules policy") and show you how they are implemented on a firewall/VPN device. The rules policy should go hand-in-hand with corporate policy. The VPN setup on a firewall device is different than the rules policy, but the VPN cannot function if the correct rules policy is not in place.

First, the rule you should try to apply (and I say *try* because there will be some situations when you cannot avoid it) is that you should have no external traffic coming directly into your network.

SECURITY NOTE   No external traffic should be directly coming into your network.

There was an old way of implementing a DMZ zone, as shown in Figure 8-7. Every bit of traffic went through the DMZ zone, then into the network. There was usually some device between the external router and the private network. Its purpose was to protect the private hosts. It often used access lists on the routers and proxy services to implement this type of security.

This setup did not offer the best protection. It left the routers wide open to attack, placed a heavy processing burden on this proxy device, since it did the data traffic examination at layer 7, and there was often very little reporting capability. The new model of DMZ setup is shown is Figure 8-8.

This setup ensures that all traffic goes into the DMZ only, and then the device on the DMZ forwards the appropriate traffic into the internal

Figure 8-7
Old implementation
of DMZ.

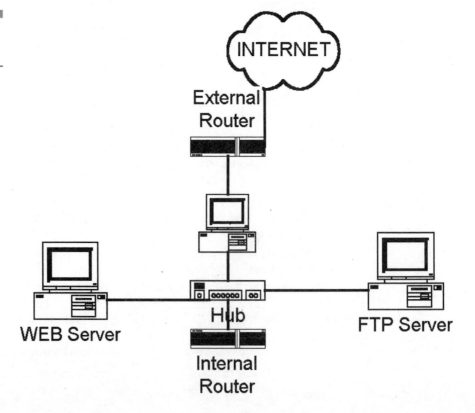

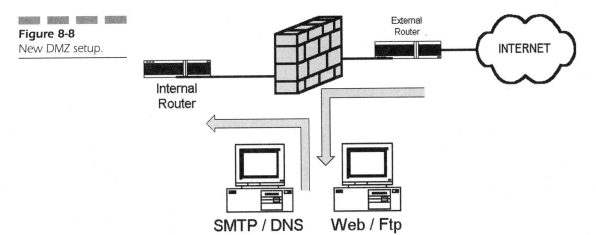

Figure 8-8
New DMZ setup.

network. For example, mail traffic is sent to the mail server on the DMZ, then the mail server forwards that traffic inside to the internal network, when appropriate. I say *appropriate,* since with this setup, you can set the mail server on the DMZ to reject or drop any mail you deem offensive (e.g., SPAM mail).

You would never want Internet traffic to go straight into your network if you can avoid it. So now with that, we are ready to set up our rules policy. I will describe a set of rules that you could first apply to your device, and then I'll explain each one. I will describe them in a format that can be implemented on a firewall. The terms applied are as follows:

- *Source.* Where the traffic is coming from. This is not an absolute source, but as seen by the firewall. Therefore, if your system is responsible for DNS traffic, on one data packet, it can be seen as the source of transmission. On the next, it can be seen as the destination of the traffic. If you picture the data flow, you will have no problem.

- *Destination.* Where the traffic is going; the opposite of source, as seen by the firewall. Just look at these two examples (→ means direction of data flow).

Internal server → Sending DNS traffic → Firewall → Internet

  - The internal server is seen as the source of traffic by the firewall.

Internal Server→Receiving DNS traffic→Firewall→Internet

  - The internal server is seen as the destination of traffic by the firewall.

■ *Service.*   What services you are allowing (e.g., HTTP, SMTP, DNS). You implement specific types of traffic that are allowed to pass. The keyword ANY implies all. Many organizations implement ANY for outbound internal employees.

■ *Action.*   What to do with that traffic. There are different options, such as accept the traffic, drop the traffic, and reject the traffic. As we look at the rules policy, you will notice where these belong.

GENERAL NOTE   A good reason for implementing the drop/reject action is for logging purposes. Many devices usually implement a specific deny all, meaning if you don't specifically allow it, it will be denied. This is a good policy; however, usually with these devices, if you don't set it up in the rules policy, you cannot log it, and you want to log all traffic. This is apparent in the Drop All rule, discussed later in this chapter.

■ *Log.*   Log traffic. Usually there are different options, such as (Long and Short) log, meaning the total number of fields that are logged, or alerting, meaning when a specific rule is triggered, an alert or email is sent to a specific host or administrator.

Implementing Management Traffic

Looking back at Figure 8-3, we set up a management station at IP address 10.2.0.1. This could either be a dedicated management server or the network administrator's workstation. You need to have an in-band access to the firewall/VPN device, and it's a good idea to put this as the first rule. You will also need a similar rule on the branch office firewall/VPN device so you can remotely manage that device.

The first rule allows the management station (10.2.0.1) to connect to the device in order to manage it. We are allowing all available services, and we Accept the action. I chose Short, but you can certainly implement Long if you like. The second rule then drops all other traffic directed at the IP address of the firewall/VPN device. This is the reason for having these as the first rules: Any traffic specifically directed at the firewall/VPN device (i.e., not VPN traffic) you want dropped and logged. VPN traffic actually is directed to the firewall, but it is a special case.

You want the action to Drop, since Drop is stealthy in nature. If you accept Reject, it will send a message back to the origination sender. While something like this may help in legitimate troubleshooting, it also gives an indication to potential hackers that something is out there and they are not allowed in.

The first two rules look like this:

Rule	Source	Destination	Service	Action	Log
1	10.2.0.1	172.16.0.1	ANY	Accept	Short
2	ANY	172.16.0.1	ANY	Drop	Long

SECURITY NOTE Drop traffic, don't Reject it.

Implementing SMTP and DNS Issues

Mail (SMTP) and Domain Name Service (DNS) Traffic

Rules 3 and 4 state that only SMTP and DNS traffic are allowed to pass through to the DMZ zone from any direction. In addition, the rule is restrictive in nature, meaning that:

■ 1. Only SMTP or DNS traffic can pass to the DMZ; and

■ 2. The SMTP or DNS traffic has to have a destination IP address of 230.230.230.66.

Now you can see how by restricting the traffic, we still allow the necessary services to work, and we add security to our network. We first make sure that only DNS or SMTP traffic is allowed to pass, thereby not giving someone the opportunity to use another service to circumvent the DMZ zone. Second, we restrict them to that IP address, not allowing an individual to comprise another machine on that port. The rules look like this:

| 3 | ANY | 230.230.230.66 | SMTP/DNS | Accept | Long |
| 4 | 230.230.230.66 | ANY | SMTP/DNS | Accept | Long |

If you have an internal SMTP/DNS host (e.g., you have a machine at address 10.2.0.2), you could further restrict rules 3 and 4 to the following:

3	10.2.0.2	230.230.230.66	SMTP/DNS	Accept	YES
4	X 10.0.0.0	230.230.230.66	SMTP/DNS	Accept	YES
5	230.230.230.66	ANY	SMTP/DNS	Accept	YES

Rules 3 to 5 further direct the traffic in specific directions. From the internal direction, only the internal server at IP address 10.2.0.2 has permission to send the SMTP and DNS traffic to the server on the DMZ zone. Coming in the Internet, the firewall will drop any traffic that is not specifically directed to the DMZ. The X 10.0.0.0 is the negate operator. This just means anyone not from the 10.0.0.0 network (which implies anyone not from the internal network) can send SMTP and DNS traffic, but only to the DMZ server.

Here is another modification to the above rule base, in case your organization is different. Assume you only have the internal SMTP/DNS server at IP address 10.2.0.2, but do not want to add a DMZ mail host. In that case, you will need to use address translation. Address, since 10.2.0.2 cannot route on the Internet. We spoke earlier about static address translation and the need for the one-to-one mapping. We installed on the external interface of the firewall/VPN device a subnet of the network 230.230.230.0 with IP addresses 1-31. In this case, you take one of those available IP addresses and create a static translation, e.g., 10.2.0.2 translates to 230.230.230.3. In your organization's DNS tables, the world will know that your company's mail server is at address 230.230.230.3, they will send mail at that IP address, and the firewall/VPN device will translate that back to 10.2.0.2. This is a setup for those special situations. You could also set the DMZ interface of the firewall/VPN device to a nonpublic address and translate it also when it's headed for the Internet. In that case, you just use either pooled or many-to-many.

Implementing Authentication

Two steps are involved when implementing authentication. The first step is to add the appropriate rules to the firewall to allow the network access. Then you need to add a user group to that network object, so the device sees that network traffic and applies the user authentication rules to it. (This process only consists of one rule; I've just broken it up into two steps so you can understand). The proxy/RADIUS server serves two functions: It monitors all internal traffic heading to the Internet so you can log it, and it serves as an authentication device to authenticate both incoming and outgoing traffic. Why would you need a proxy to do logging when you have the firewall/VPN combination? This is a good question and it borders on two issues.

1. *Performance.* While in this example we may turn on logging, you don't necessarily want to turn it on for all traffic. Again, from a performance perspective, the more rules you log, the more you are forcing your firewall/VPN device to examine every packet and send it somewhere, whether a local file or separate server. It is not necessarily a good idea to monitor every data packet from that device. That is why we introduced the proxy server.

2. *Levels of logging.* While your device may have the logging capabilities, not all logging is the same. Almost all logging supports sources and destination IP address logging, but some logging will not support user authentication to IP address. This means that if you install user authentication on the firewall/VPN device, it will force users to authenticate. However, once the user is authenticated, there is no further logging of the name, meaning you will know that a particular user authenticated at this time but have no record of sites visited.

Internal User Traffic

With internal user traffic you have several options available. For example, you could allow internal networks unrestricted access to the Internet or you can restrict them only to services.

Here we are allowing unrestricted internal traffic to the Internet:

6	10.0.0.0	ANY	ANY	Accept	No

Here we only allow internal traffic HTTP service to the Internet:

6	10.0.0.0	ANY	HTTP	Accept	No

SECURITY NOTE Remember, ANY means including the DMZ; therefore, you may choose to implement the rule as:

6	10.0.0.0	X 230.230.230.64	ANY	Accept	No

This implies that the internal network is allowed any service to the Internet. Again, the X 230.230.230.64 means NOT the 230.230.230.64 network, which implies all other networks, which implies the Internet. In this case, we turned off logging for internal outbound access, due to possible performance problems and the levels of logging mentioned earlier.

Internal User Authenticated Traffic

You have several available options when implementing user authentication: You can use the firewall/VPN device itself, use a proxy server, or use a RADIUS server. You first set up the rules to allow the network access, then you add a user group to that network object to force the users to authenticate.

Looking back at Figure 8-3, note that a small part of data flow is depicted in Figure 8-9. The example we will be using is that of implementing a RADIUS server. Figure 8-9 shows the flow of traffic when an internal user tries to access the Internet:

1. A user sends a data packet and attempts to gain access to the Internet.

Figure 8-9
User authentication data traffic flows.

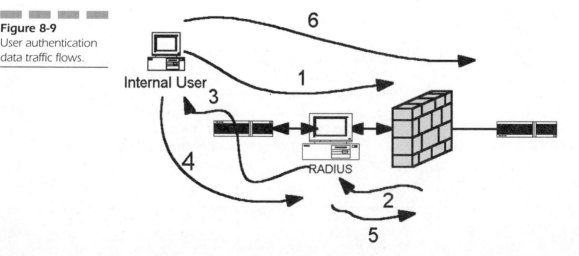

2. The firewall/VPN device has been set up to use RADIUS authentication. It first checks the network that the data packet is coming from. If the network is an allowable network, it then checks user authentication. It sends a request to the RADIUS server, verifying if this user is allowed Internet access.

3. The RADIUS server challenges the internal user for a username/password.

4. The user enters in the proper username/password combination.

5. The RADIUS server checks the permissions and informs the firewall/VPN device that this user is an authorized user.

6. The user then can go out according to the rule-based policy.

So now a typical rule-based policy would be either of the following two examples.

Allow unrestricted traffic from internal network 172.16.0.0:

8	Users@10.0.0.0	ANY	ANY	Accept	No

Only allow http traffic:

8	Users@10.0.0.0	ANY	HTTP	Accept	No

Since we are now using a database, it would be a good idea to use groups instead of individual users; otherwise, you would need a rule for each user. That brings us to the last rule, the Drop All rule.

The Drop All Rule

This rule means the device drops any traffic that is not explicitly allowed by the previous rules. You can usually use either DROP or REJECT; just remember, REJECT sends a message back to the sender, so someone knows that there is a device there. If that person is a hacker, he or she now knows there is something there that may warrant further investigation. DROP just drops the packet with no return message; the person will never receive an acknowledgment about a device at that address or addresses behind it. Now *most* devices will implicitly drop packets that you have not implicitly allowed. You may think, if they drop the packets anyway, why log them? Well, if you don't install this rule and install YES as the log option, you will not be able to log the traffic.

The Drop All rule looks like this:

9   ANY   ANY   ANY   DROP   YES

Implementing the VPN rule

This brings us to the VPN rule. Now before we can implement the VPN rule, we must set up our firewall/VPN device. You need to tell the firewall what type of encryption's algorithm you want to use, what kind of key management systems to use, and what certificate authorities to use. Once you decide on that, you apply a rule for VPN traffic, and the firewall/VPN device will apply those encryption algorithms you've already set up. This is where you have heard terms like PPTP, L2TF, and IPSec; it is here where you decide what type to implement for your organization. In our example we will consider that our firewall/VPN device will be using IPSec security, acting as its own certificate authority and using ISAKMP/OAKLEY (IKE) as its key exchange mechanism.

The actual implementation configuration setups are different for each vendor, but the following items must be implemented:

■ On your firewall/VPN device define an IPSec encryption scheme. For our example, set IPSec to use DES encryption. Each VPN setup will (or should) have the ability to create IPSec using DES encryption; here you can also choose other encryption schemes if desired. Just remember, you will need interoperability across all the devices that want to use the VPN.

■ Create a Security Parameter Index (SPI). The SPI is a used by a Security Association (SA); each end of the VPN partners uses this SA. The destination is responsible for creating a unique SPI. In some setups, you can create one SPI if you are using it between two firewall/VPN devices. The SPI is a 32-bit hexadecimal number, e.g., 0x102, 0x103.

■ You can have your firewall/VPN device act as its own certificate authority—as long as it's a trusted machine. If you feel like you need another CA, have it point to that CA.

■ Define IKE as your key-exchange mechanism. As of this writing, very few vendors have IKE implemented. Most have Manual IPSec, SKIP, or their own proprietary key-management exchange mechanism

■ Define a VPN domain on the firewall/VPN at Division. The domain consists of the hosts or networks you want to grant access to. In this case, they are the four servers mentioned earlier. The branch office firewall/VPN device is set up the same way as the NYC firewall/VPN, with the exception of the VPN domain. The reason is that between the NYC and Chicago offices, all traffic is encrypted.

Branch Office VPNs

Once the VPN devices are configured to use the appropriate encryption and key-management setups, the VPN rules need to be installed. What we will establish is a connection to the other firewall/VPN at the branch office, allowing VPN connectivity to the remote users.

The first step when creating the LAN-to-LAN VPN is to exchange keys with each firewall/VPN device, as in Figure 8-10. This accomplishes the exchanging of keys between sites and sets up a tunnel to be used on demand, in this case, an IPSec (DES) based tunnel. When a user wants to go to the division office from the branch office, the traffic will leave the branch office VPN device encrypted. When it reaches the division headquarters, it then is decrypted. The keys are changed periodically by the firewall/VPN devices.

Figure 8-10
LAN-to-LAN VPN.

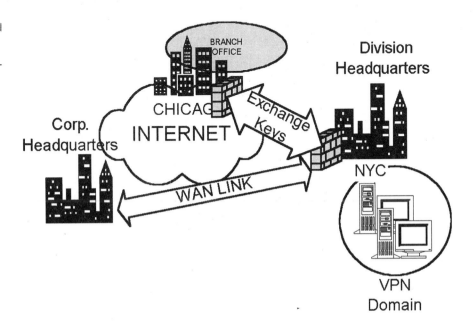

The VPN rule implemented on the Chicago's VPN device is as follows:

Rule	Source	Destination	Service	Action	Log
#	172.17.0.0	230.230.230.1	HTTP	Encrypt	YES

The network address 172.17.0.0 was the IP network we used to address Chicago's internal hosts. IP address 230.230.230.1 is the external address of the NYC's firewall/VPN device. When a user leaves the Chicago firewall/VPN and the destination is 230.230.230.1, the NYC's network, the Chicago firewall/VPN encrypts it according to the encryption policy we set up in that device. The division firewall/VPN will see traffic coming in from that IP address (247.247.247.1) and then know to decrypt it. In addition, the only service that is granted is HTTP.

The VPN rule implemented on the NYC VPN device is as follows:

#	Ch_users@247.247.247.1	230.230.230.1	HTTP	Encrypt	YES

The NYC firewall/VPN device will see traffic coming in from IP address 247.247.247.1. It has already been set up with the keys to Chicago's firewall/VPN device. The user group Ch_users@247.247.247.1 is just a user group on the RADIUS server. It will decrypt the data and then force the users to authenticate against the RADIUS server. It will check authentications, and once the users are authenticated, they will still only be allowed HTTP accesses.

SECURITY NOTE On some VPN devices, you can only install one VPN domain. That is, if you wanted some users to access one server and other users to access another server, you need to include all of them in your VPN domain. However, you can still limit them by their username, meaning that the NYC firewall/VPN device has four servers in its VPN domain, but user Joe is restricted access to only two of those servers in that domain.

You will also notice that on the last few examples of rules I mentioned, I've left the rule number out and replaced it by the # symbol. This is to indicate that this is not the last rule but should be placed somewhere close to the top of the rule-based policy.

Remote Users' VPNs

We are almost finished implementing a VPN, based upon the company's requirements, and have established a topology to allow this. The one last thing we need to do is to allow remote users the ability to establish a VPN to the NYC network. The steps involved are as follows:

1. Install vendor's VPN software on the remote laptops.
2. Configure the software .
3. Add the users into the user database.
4. Install a rule policy allowing this.

Figure 8-11 illustrates a client VPN session. The VPN software installed on the laptop is configured with the external IP address of the VPN device, in this case, 230.230.230.1. The VPN software starts up, and depending on the configuration, the laptop exchanges security keys with the VPN device. During the communication, the laptop is told that the VPN domain consists of servers 10.0.0.11, 10.0.0.12, 220.220.220.10, and 220.220.220.11.

Figure 8-11
Client VPN session.

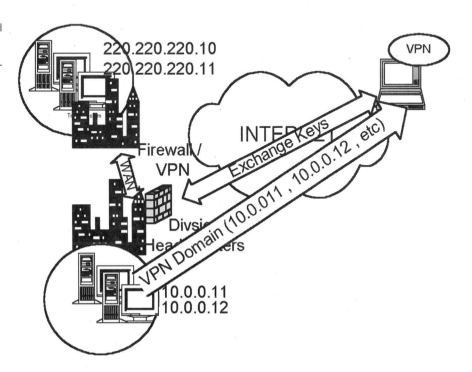

How It Works

During normal operation, the laptop is accessing Internet sites and nothing happens with the VPN software. Now, however, the laptop tries to go to *http://10.0.0.11*. The VPN software knows that IP address 10.0.0.11 is part of the VPN domain at Division. The software then encrypts the packet and possibly encapsulates it. It then puts on the IP address of the firewall/VPN device of Division (230.230.230.1) and sends it on its way. When it is received by Division, that firewall/VPN device looks at where it is coming from and looks at its rule's base to decide if it is allowed in:

#	VPN_users@ANY	230.230.230.1	HTTP	Encrypt	YES

You will notice a new source and user group, (VPN_users@ANY). This is because remote clients could be coming in from anywhere, which means any IP address, and as always, you still need to have them be authenticated. The new group, VPN_users, is just a separate database on the RADIUS server. You can use one group if you like. This rule also serves security purposes. It states that these users have to authenticate against the RADIUS server, and then they can only use HTTP traffic to the VPN domains.

A note about VPN software: In earlier chapters I said that VPN technology needs to be as far down the OSI stack as possible. With VPN software, that is between the network layer and data-link layer. With the VPN device itself, the software can be tested and optimized for particular hardware and/or operating-system capabilities. With roaming laptops it is different though; with so many applications that are usually loaded on a user machine, it is possible that the VPN software conflicts with other applications. In these situations, sometimes the vendor can be of assistance; in other cases, you may need to remove the offending application, which may be difficult to locate.

Conclusion

This chapter closes the VPN technology implementation guidelines. By now you should have a strong feel for how a VPN works, how and when data gets encrypted, and what devices are doing the encryption/decryption process.

This chapter did not deal extensively with encryption, although reference was made to it. If you could now install a VPN, or at least talk about the concept of VPNs, you would be way ahead of the game. Just think about how much you read about VPNs: how much is technical and how much is business-oriented; how much discussion is on RFCs and how much is on cost savings.

While the need to implement a good security policy is very important for any organization, I believe it is extremely important in the case of VPNs, since you are purposely opening up your network. One reason for going over the rule-based policy and describing the direction of traffic flow is, if you do not understand the basics, how can you understand the advanced material? In later chapters, we will discuss cryptography and encryption techniques, key management, and so forth. After those chapters you will see why we started with a general overview of security policy. To get bogged down in technical details when you are trying to implement something can get very frustrating. As a practical point of view, you are not going to be writing the security code for VPNs. If you are reading this book, you will be implementing VPNs and implementing security processes that already exist. Therefore, you don't need to know the specs, but you need to compare logically different encryption strengths, what's out there, and the security risks involved with each.

VPN technology is not new. It is an application derived from earlier technology. However, from an innovation point of view, it is new. *Diffusion of innovations* by Everett Rogers discusses diffusion of innovations in detail; in fact, he is considered by some to be the Father of Diffusion Studies. Innovations, like ideas, come in all forms and can be considered new if their perceived use is new. VPNs falls into this category: Encryption is old, but the perceived use is new. While there are consequences of using VPNs (as pointed out by Rogers), those consequences can be minimized.

Installing a VPN, Part II*

---

*This chapter is not the author's; it belongs to all the vendors who were gracious enough to help me develop it. I owe them a debt of thanks for taking their time out to send me this information, which I believe has added a great benefit to this book.

When I wrote this book, I tried to be as unbiased as possible in not directly saying what is the best VPN technology or what type of VPN implementation is most vulnerable to attacks. (In later chapters we will look at some of the common VPN protocols and their vulnerabilities.) However, in writing any book, there has to be a balance of practicability versus theory, real world versus textbook. During the first section of this book, we saw some different VPN configurations that are available. In this chapter, I will show you some of the actual real-life implementations that are available, so that your company can have a better understanding of the resources at your disposal.

This chapter is a continuation of Chapter 8; it will focus solely on Virtual Private Networks, but from a vendor's perspective. When we first discussed the different architectures and topologies of VPN technology, it was from a theoretical point of view. In this chapter we will take the theory and apply it into practice. This chapter is designed to show you the different types of VPNs that are in the marketplace, and by looking at these various types, you can get a sense of what type of VPN installation may be right for your organization.

There are generally two categories of VPNs: service provider VPNs and the stand-alone VPN.

Service Provider VPN Services

Service provider VPNs are a good alternative for companies that want to outsource their Internet infrastructure to a service provider. While a service provider is not the only way to achieve this outsourcing model, it is convenient; the ISP will probably control your company's access to the Internet, which will make troubleshooting that much easier. In a service provider solution, the service provider will handle all tasks of a normal Internet security staff, plus the Internet connection points, while at the same time giving a company valuable security recommendations and guidelines if necessary. The Network Operation Center, usually called a NOC, is a team of highly trained individuals who deal with Internet transport communications and security 24 hours a day, 7 days a week, freeing up the company to focus on its core business.

Figure 9-1 illustrates a typical service provider VPN. The service provider, in many cases an already established ISP, furnishes some type of VPN equipment to the customer. The equipment is either placed on

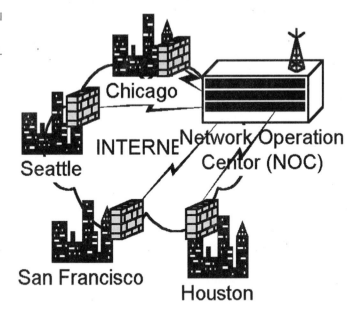

Figure 9-1
Service provider VPN.

the customer's premises or placed at the local ISP access points using devices that add encryption functionality to the data stream.

Stand-alone VPN Services

Stand-alone VPN services are also a force to be reckoned with. The sheer number of stand-alone products gives an organization leverage in what kind of VPN product to purchase and implement companywide. The rest of this chapter will deal with these standalone VPN services.

Aventail ExtraNet Center

Aventail ExtraNet Center gives you the power to control the access of partners, customers, consultants, and others to resources on your network. At the heart of our product is the ability to create a centrally defined, easy-to-manage policy. This quick start guide is meant to familiarize you with the fundamental components and concepts of Aventail ExtraNet Center.

Aventail ExtraNet Server

The primary component of Aventail ExtraNet Center is the ExtraNet Server. This is a SOCKS v5 proxy server that manages the authentication of users and processes all of the connection requests. It also contains a Secure Sockets Layer v3.0 module for encryption. Aventail ExtraNet Server can manage traffic for both incoming (external users attempting to reach internal network resources) and outgoing (internal users attempting to reach external network resources) network traffic.

Aventail Policy Console

The Aventail Policy Console is the graphical administrative tool for creating, viewing, and managing the policies for your extranet. It can also be used for starting and stopping the ExtraNet Server, as well as viewing log, audit, and license files. The Policy Console can be run locally on the machine that hosts the ExtraNet Server or remotely to manage a server that resides on another machine. When the Policy Console is being run remotely, it will establish a secure LAN, WAN, or Internet connection to the Management Server (see below). For simplicity and convenience, the Policy Console can run on either Windows NT or UNIX and can configure an ExtraNet Server on either platform.

Aventail Management Server

The Aventail Management Server is an optional service that allows administrators to remotely manage an ExtraNet Server. The Management Server and Policy Console communicate via a secure, encrypted connection. The Management Server must be installed on the same machine as the ExtraNet Server.

Aventail Management Server Config Tool

The Aventail Management Service Config Tool is a graphical user interface that allows you to modify the Management Server configuration. This policy will determine which administrators can manage the ExtraNet Server, how they must authenticate, and from which network interfaces the server will accept traffic. The policy also defines the specific directories that can be browsed remotely.

Aventail Connect

Aventail Connect is the client component of the Aventail ExtraNet Center solution. It is an application that redirects all TCP/IP application calls to the ExtraNet Server. Aventail Connect v3.0 supports WinSock 1.1 and 2.0. Aventail ExtraNet Center gives you the power to control the access of partners, customers, consultants, and others to resources on your network. At the heart of our product is the ability to create a centrally defined, easy-to-manage policy. This quick start guide is meant to familiarize you with the fundamental components and concepts of Aventail ExtraNet Center.

Product Specifications for Aventail

[See Table 9-1.]

Aventail Windows NT Installation

The following installation steps will get the Aventail ExtraNet Server up and running in a very basic configuration. The general configuration will require encrypted sessions only and require all users to authenticate against the accounts in the Windows NT Server username/password database [see Figure 9-2]. This configuration provides authenticated but otherwise unrestricted access for both outbound and inbound traffic. A sample X.509 certificate is supplied and configured during installation and should be used for nonsecure testing purposes only. Instructions on tightening access controls, configuration as a dual-homed server, obtaining "real" digital certificates, configuring the Aventail Management Server, and changing other parameters may be found in the Aventail ExtraNet Center Administration Guide located in the "\docs" directory.

Aventail UNIX Installation

The following installation steps will get the Aventail ExtraNet Server up and running in a very basic configuration. The general configuration will require encrypted sessions only and force all users to authenticate against the accounts in the UNIX "/etc/passwd" file (see Figure 9-3). This configuration provides unrestricted access for both outbound and

TABLE 9-1 *Aventail Product Specifications.*

Operating Systems	Authentication Methods	Cryptographic Algorithms
Server		**Ciphers**
Windows NT 4.0 SP 3/4	Username/Password	Data Encryption Standard (DES)
Solaris 2.6	Challenge-Handshake Authentication Protocol (CHAP)	Triple Data Encryption Standard (Triple DES)
AIX 4.2	S/Key	RC4
Linux 2.x	Digital Certificates	**Hashes**
HP/UX 10.20	Token Cards	MD4
Digital UNIX 4.0	Challenge Response Authentication Method (CRAM)	MD5
		SHA-1
Client		**Key Management**
Windows 3.1	**Supported User Databases**	
Windows for Workgroups 3.11	Windows NT Domain	RSA
Windows 95 and 98	UNIX Password Files	Diffie-Hellman
Windows NT 4.0 SP 3/4	Netware Directory Services (NDS) and Bindery	
	Remote Authentication Dial-In User Service (RADIUS)	**Access Control Parameters**
Recommended Memory	Security Dynamics ACE/Server™	Source (IP Address or Host Name) and Port
Server: 64 MB RAM		Destination (IP Address or Host Name) and Services
Client: 16 MB RAM		User Identity and/or Group Affiliation
		Time, Day, and/or Date
		Application and/or Service
		Authentication Method and/or Encryption Algorithm

inbound traffic. A sample X.509 certificate is supplied and configured during installation and should be used for nonsecure testing purposes only. Instructions on tightening access controls, configuration as a dual-homed server, obtaining "real" digital certificates, configuring the Aventail Management Server, and changing other parameters may be found in the Aventail ExtraNet Center Administration Guide located in the "\docs" directory.

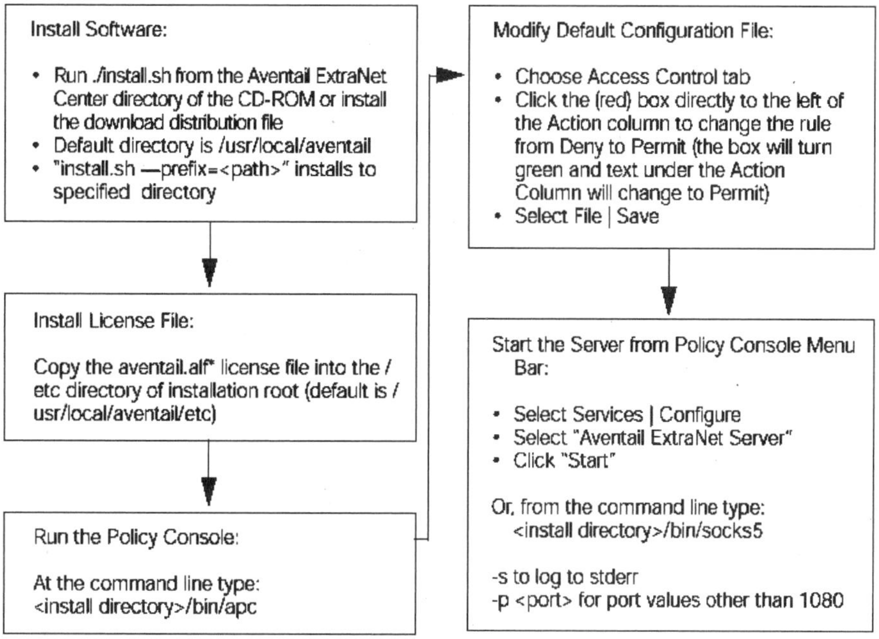

Figure 9-2
Windows NT
installation.

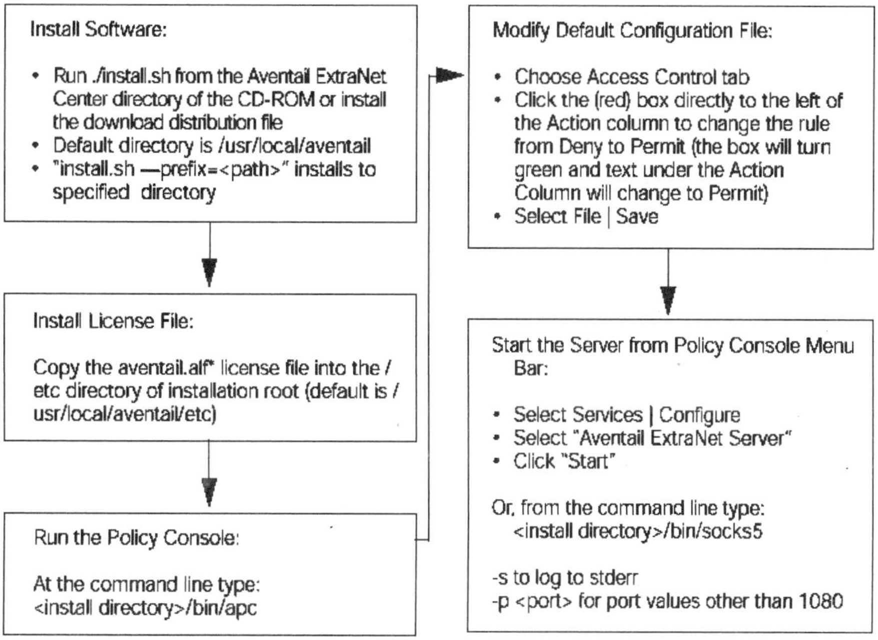

Install Software:

- Run ./install.sh from the Aventail ExtraNet Center directory of the CD-ROM or install the download distribution file
- Default directory is /usr/local/aventail
- "install.sh —prefix=<path>" installs to specified directory

Install License File:

Copy the aventail.alf* license file into the / etc directory of installation root (default is / usr/local/aventail/etc)

Run the Policy Console:

At the command line type:
<install directory>/bin/apc

Modify Default Configuration File:

- Choose Access Control tab
- Click the (red) box directly to the left of the Action column to change the rule from Deny to Permit (the box will turn green and text under the Action Column will change to Permit)
- Select File | Save

Start the Server from Policy Console Menu Bar:

- Select Services | Configure
- Select "Aventail ExtraNet Server"
- Click "Start"

Or, from the command line type:
   <install directory>/bin/socks5

-s to log to stderr
-p <port> for port values other than 1080

Figure 9-3
UNIX installation.

Install Software:

- Run ./install.sh from the Aventail ExtraNet Center directory of the CD-ROM or install the download distribution file
- Default directory is /usr/local/aventail
- "install.sh —prefix=<path>" installs to specified directory

Install License File:

Copy the aventail.alf* license file into the / etc directory of installation root (default is / usr/local/aventail/etc)

Run the Policy Console:

At the command line type:
<install directory>/bin/apc

Modify Default Configuration File:

- Choose Access Control tab
- Click the (red) box directly to the left of the Action column to change the rule from Deny to Permit (the box will turn green and text under the Action Column will change to Permit)
- Select File | Save

Start the Server from Policy Console Menu Bar:

- Select Services | Configure
- Select "Aventail ExtraNet Server"
- Click "Start"

Or, from the command line type:
   <install directory>/bin/socks5

-s to log to stderr
-p <port> for port values other than 1080

Client Windows 9x and Windows NT Installation

The following installation steps will get Aventail Connect, the client component of Aventail ExtraNet Center, up and running in a basic configuration [see Figure 9-4]. Instructions covering advanced configuration options, pubic certificates, and troubleshooting may be found in the Aventail Connect Administration and Users Guide and in the online Help.

The previous section has prepared you to build a basic extranet. The following section will enable you to take full advantage of Aventail's policy-based extranet security and management, including the ability to:

- Apply fine-grained access control rules by time, source/destination, group affiliation, etc.

- Integrate a wide variety of stronger authentication types.

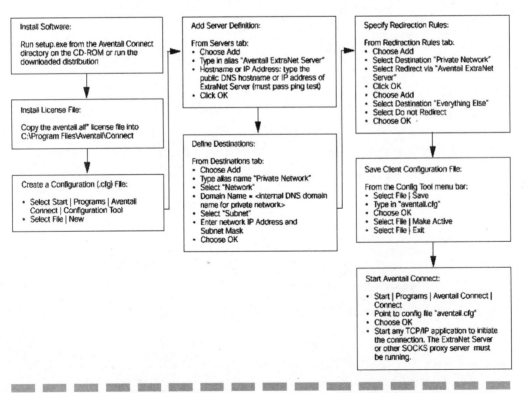

Figure 9-4 Client installation.

- Apply filters to network traffic.
- Chain multiple ExtraNet Servers together for redundancy and flexibility.

This section is an introduction to the primary components of the Aventail Policy Manager that are used to build an extranet policy. There are four types of rules that can be used to build an Aventail ExtraNet Server policy.

Access Control Rules

Access control rules define the network resources and services that are accessible to users and groups based on where they are coming from, what day or time it is, how they are authenticated, and their encryption strength.

The following are the parameters that make up an access control rule:

- Active/Inactive—Temporarily disable a rule without having to delete it.
- Permit/Deny—Defines whether the rule will permit or deny access based on the criteria selected.
- Source Networks—Defines the originating source of the connection for the rule to be applicable.
- Source Ports—Defines the originating ports (services) of the connection for the rule to be applicable.
- Destination Networks—Defines to which network resource(s) the rule will permit or deny access.
- Destination Ports—Defines which services on the Destination Networks can be used by the rule.
- Users and Groups—Defines to which users and groups the rule applies.
- Times—Defines the times or days the rule is active.
- Authentication Matching—Defines the authentication methods to be used for the rule to be applicable.
- Key Length—Specifies the encryption strength required for the rule to be applicable.
- Commands—Defines the commands that can be used on the specified Destination Networks.

Authentication Rules

Authentication rules define the authentication options available to users or groups based on their source. The following are the parameters that make up an authentication rule:

- Source Networks—Defines the originating source of the connection for the rule to be applicable.
- Authentication—Defines the authentication methods available.

Aventail has architected client/server software that simplifies administration and use of the complex and unique requirements of extranets, or inter-enterprise resource sharing over IP-based networks. Aventail ExtraNet Center gives organizations the ability to manage and secure resources from their server to an individual's local desktop, the first and last mile of the extranet. Unlike traditional remote access or LAN-to-LAN VPNs that are designed for encrypting traffic between trusted users (i.e., employees), Aventail ExtraNet Center frees organizations to connect anyone by making it easy to control individual access to specific applications and information. [See Table 9-2 for the benefits of using Aventail.]

For more information on Aventail or its products, please visit *www.aventail.com,* call 877-AVENTAIL or 206-215-1111, or email *info@aventail.com.*

TABLE 9-2

Benefits of the Aventail ExtraNet Center.

Feature/Description	Business Benefits
Superior Security	■ Protects business-critical resources
	■ Surpasses security of alternatives (e.g., leased lines or dial-on remote access)
Directed architecture	■ Provides tighter security than standard tunneled VPNs
	■ Enables secure extranet extension to customers, suppliers, and business partners
Proxy architecture	■ Eliminates direct connections from extranet to business-critical resources
	■ Prevents exposure of private addresses to public networks

TABLE 9-2

(Continued)

Feature/Description	Business Benefits
Granular access control	■ Enables definition of user access according to a wide range of parameters
Support for multiple levels of encryption	■ Allows tailoring of encryption by application and security needs
Support for multiple user authentication methods	■ Facilitates and makes best use of variety of methods, including two-factor authentication systems
SOCKS v5 session-layer protocol	■ Provides more detailed access control than lower-level protocols
	■ Easily coexists with lower-level protocols, such as IPSec, PPTP, and L2TP
	■ Functions with multiple security technologies and platforms
	■ Offers plug-and-play capabilities
Built-in Flexibility	■ Provides seamless integration into partners' and customers' IT environments
Aventail Connect	■ Minimizes impact on users and client desktops
Integration options	■ Offers compatibility with any firewall, proxy server and wide variety of databases
Application independence	■ Enables integration with legacy applications
User database support	■ Avoids replication of databases
Diverse platform support	■ Integrates into all of your IT environments
Effective Management	■ Streamlines initial roll out, normal use, and system expansion
Policy Console	■ Enables administrators to easily create and edit access control policies for users and user groups, configure the server, and add or modify authentication and encryption modules
Scalability	■ Reduces time and cost of system expansions; can grow as your extranet grows
Customizer	■ Simplifies creation of custom client software configurations for easy deployment
Remote server management	■ Facilitates management of remote servers from a single location

Compatible Systems—Access Servers

Founded in 1985 by Matt McConnell and Tim Schulz, Compatible Systems Corporation is the industry leader in Virtual Private Networking (VPN) technologies for remote access and site-to-site applications. The company's VPN Access Servers, VPN Branch Office Routers, Internet Access Routers, ISP Site Routers, Enterprise Switching Routers and Local Segmenting and Switching Routers offer complete internetworking solutions for thousands of corporate networks and Internet Service Providers (ISPs) worldwide. Compatible Systems is privately held with 55 employees.

Compatible Systems is the only vendor to offer a complete, standalone VPN product line. The company aims to become the leading supplier of VPN technology. Its innovative technology, broad distribution and sizable installed base will enable it to capture a significant initial market share and capitalize on the explosive growth expected for the VPN segment.

The company's key advantages include its technology innovations, such as internally developed multiprotocol routing and switching software, its core competency in dedicated hardware design and its easy-to-use management software for network devices. Compatible's well-developed, broad distribution channels for selling networking products to small/medium-sized businesses and close relationships with many ISPs also gives it a clear market advantage.

Compatible Systems' VPN product family delivers a complete, standalone VPN solution with superior price/performance. Compatible's products offer the widest client platform support available today, including all announced Windows® versions, Macintosh and Linux. The products also offer broad protocol support (IP, IPX, AppleTalk) and bridging of non-routable protocol.

The IntraPort Family of VPN Access Servers

The IntraPort family of VPN Access Servers provides Internet-based remote access and LAN-to-LAN solutions ranging in size from eight simultaneous tunnels to more than 2000 simultaneous tunnels. All IntraPort products feature IPSec tunneling for TCP/IP and IPX network protocols; integrated routing via RIP, RIP2 and OSPF; three encryption levels including Triple Data Encryption Standard (DES) technology; unlimited user client support for Windows 95, Windows 98, Windows NT, MacOS, and Linux; MD5/SHA, RADIUS, and SecurID authentication; and full packet filtering. CompatiView, a GUI management application for Windows and Macintosh, is included with every IntraPort. The IntraPort family includes:

IntraPort2   Designed for small to mid-size corporate networks, it supports up to 64 simultaneous remote client connections and 16 LAN-to-LAN connections. Two 10/100 Ethernet ports allow for placement behind or in parallel with a corporate firewall. It features a 175 MHz StrongARM RISC microprocessor, and software-based encryption.

IntraPort 2+   Designed for mid-size and large corporate networks, it includes all the features of the IntraPort, but adds a Triple DES co-processor. It supports up to 200 remote client connections and 64 LAN-to-LAN connections. The co-processor dramatically improves throughput in high-level encryption applications.

IntraPort Enterprise   Designed for large network applications and carrier-class operations, the IntraPort Enterprise features two StrongARM RISC processors (233 MHz) and two PCI-based Triple DES co-processors for wire-speed throughput. It has two 10/100 Ethernet ports and supports up to 10,000 simultaneous remote client connections and up to 64 LAN-to-LAN connections.

IntraPort Enterprise-8   Designed for large organizations as the anchor to an enterprise-wide VPN, the IntraPort Enterprise-8 features an 8-slot hot-swappable chassis with three I/O board options. Each board includes a 233 MHz StrongARM RISC processor and a PCI-based Triple DES co-processor. Two 10/100 Ethernet ports allow for operation behind or in parallel with an existing firewall. The largest capacity VPN access server on the market today, each of the IntraPort Enterprise-8's I/O cards support up to 5,000 simultaneous remote client connections and up to 64 LAN-to-LAN connections.

IntraPort Carrier   Carrier-class VPN switches that allow Network Service Providers (NSPs) to deliver VPN-based remote access to Frame Relay and MPLS Intranets. By integrating dial-up remote access via IPSec VPN connections with Layer-2 services such as Frame Relay and MPLS, the product allows NSPs to incorporate roving users into packed switched WAN offerings. The IntraPort Carrier is available in either a two- or eight-slot chassis. Each slot houses an I/O card supporting up to 5,000 VPN sessions for fully loaded capacities of 40,000 and 10,000 connections, respectively. Each StrongARM-based I/O card features a Triple DES encryption co-processor. LAN/WAN interface options include 10/100 Mbps Ethernet, DS3, and High-Speed Synchronous Interface (HSSI).

VPN Branch Office Routers Allow businesses to create private Wide Area Networks (WANs) using either traditional leased lines or VPN technology. These products can literally cut wide area network expenses in half by consolidating all network traffic—both private data and Internet traffic—onto a single wide area connection. The product line features full VPN routing and bridging, with IPSec compliance, allowing almost any networking protocol to be securely transported via the Internet. Customers can choose to connect to remote sites via private WAN lines and keep the option to move all or part of the network to VPN at a later time. The routers support VPN routing of TCP/IP, IPX, and AppleTalk, along with VPN bridging of other network protocols such as NetBEUI.

Internet Access and ISP Site Routers Are designed to provide painless high-speed connectivity between corporate networks and the Internet.

The VSR™ Family of Multigigabit Switching Routers Provides the strongest support in the internetworking industry for next-generation Internet services. Based on low-latency multigigabit switching fabric, the VSR family of hardware features multiple RISC processors and an innovative combination of cached and full-tabled routing. This advanced design supplies the power to support a variety of applications, from corporate networking to Customer Premise Equipment (CPE) for Internet access, to classless backbone routing.

Case Study—Adobe Systems, Inc.

Adobe Systems, Inc. is one of the world's largest developers of graphics and media software, with annual revenues of approximately $900 million. Part of Adobe's philosophy is to be flexible with its employees. On a rapidly expanding basis, this flexibility can include telecommuting. In McCreight's VPN pilot project groups, many telecommuters are project engineers who require frequent high-speed access to the central office network. The company formerly supplied ISDN lines and remote access capabilities, absorbing costs in some cases up to $1,200 per user each month. In addition, the 800 number used for low-speed and road warrior access was costing more than $1 million annually.

Solution

To reduce the 800 number costs, Corporate IS negotiated a dial-up remote access outsourcing deal with CompuServe. While this worked well enough for many users, others were more demanding. They wanted to choose their own ISP, wanted faster access speed, wanted interconnection options available only to the public Internet, such as cable modems or radio modems, or were located in places where CompuServe had no local numbers available.

McCreight wanted to offer an Internet-based remote access alternative, and began researching VPN systems. His first offering was a combination of central-site firewall software from one supplier with firmware and software clients from a different supplier. While the system worked as advertised, he uncovered a number of real-world issues he had not anticipated. The firewall/client solution required fixed IP addresses, failed to handle IPX, and featured an imperfect implementation of NAT. The software client supported only Windows and was highly invasive in the Windows IP stack. Reconfigurations were cumbersome because too many network parameters and settings had to be initiated at the client side, creating additional user support needs.

Once the first solution was in place, McCreight polled users and potential users of VPN to learn what else was needed. The strongest message in the replies was a desire for Macintosh support at the client side. A Seattle-based Adobe employee spoke with a friend at Apple, who recommended the Compatible Systems IntraPort series of VPN Access Servers. McCreight admits to being skeptical of a smaller vendor's ability to meet his VPN requirements but was very impressed with the technical sales department at Compatible Systems and decided to give the IntraPort solution a try.

A month after installation there are more than 30 pilot project users regularly connecting to the IntraPort VPN server. From the administration side, McCreight prefers the server-based administration of the IntraPort. It allows him to make changes to the VPN without having to update the client configurations individually. With a recent reorganization strongly emphasizing cost control, VPN looks to have a bright future within Adobe. McCreight relates the story of a video project developer located in San Francisco. After switching to VPN [at this point he uses a mixture of the firewall/server and the IntraPort] from his previous ISDN long-distance dial-up configuration, he has reduced monthly costs from $1,300 to $400 while upgrading access speed from 128 Kbps to 1.1 Mbps DSL. Since high-speed data communications costs are paid by the telecommuter's department, this employee's manager has been delighted with the savings. Word is spreading throughout the organization of the cost-saving and speed-enhancing benefits of having remote users connect via VPN.

McCreight is working with Compatible Systems engineers to explore some minor technical issues that have arisen, but he says his experience has been highly positive. In particular, he has come to believe that Compatible Systems' unlimited user license for client software is superior to the method he originally preferred—a minimally priced "box" plus a charge for each client license.

"The Compatible Systems approach is user-friendly at all levels," McCreight says. "And the savings are obvious from the very start. This is a good VPN system, both for the administrator and the users. And many of us are looking forward eagerly to IntraPort's support of IP-tunneled native AppleTalk, a la the IntraPort's current IPX support."

Case Study—New Hope Communications

New Hope Communications is a publishing and events management company serving the natural products industry. Headquartered in Boulder, Colorado, the company also has offices in Kansas City, New Jersey, London, and Trinidad and Tobago, along with a number of traveling sales representatives and executives who rely on remote access to enter and process orders, stay current on production issues and access email and a Lotus Domino groupware server.

Network administrator Chris Gangwish had previously provided remote access services through an 8-modem remote access server. Though the system worked in terms of allowing access to shared data, there were a number of problems. Macintosh users had to dial in using the deathly slow and outdated ARA (AppleTalk Remote Access) client. In addition, multiple users at remote offices were dialing in on an 800 number at 28.8 Kbps and staying connected for virtually the entire business day, resulting in large monthly phone charges.

VPN installation went extremely smoothly, Gangwish notes. He was able to bring the server up in less than half an hour and reports that while configuring user accounts was the most involved aspect of the installation process, the IntraPort's filtering capabilities allowed him far greater control of access permissions on an individual user basis.

Currently, about two dozen New Hope employees are using the Intra-Port VPN. Users of Macintosh computers are overjoyed at being able to abandon ARA in favor of PPP dialup to their Internet Service Provider. Windows 95 users love the simplicity of the client and the fact that they don't have to make any other modifications to their machines or dialup Internet accounts.

While Gangwish has yet to do any formal cost analysis to determine VPN savings, he notes that in the New Jersey office alone, there is a 28.8 Kbps connection to the Boulder office that is "up" all day every working day in addition to a 128 Kbps ISDN connection to the Internet. "Our plan is to eliminate the entire 800-number system over the next year and replace it with VPN," he says. "The existing system still has a future—as a backup."

For more information on Compatible Systems or its products, please visit *www.compatible.com,* or 1-800-356-0283, or email *info@compatible.com.*

Nortel Networks—Extranet Switch 4000

Although the idea of a Virtual Private Network (VPN) is an old one, its usage today commonly refers to the use of the Internet as an alternative to a traditional private network. Although the potential uses of the Internet are nearly infinite, the application most companies are exploring is remote access, using the Internet as an alternative to building a dedicated dial-in infrastructure. The appeal of this is cost savings. Although exact savings depend on a number of different factors, most studies show that savings of $1,000 per user, per year can easily be realized. However, as companies want to grow beyond this initial application, they quickly realize that they need to have more than just a connection to the Internet. To fully realize the potential of using the Internet, you must link or extend the Intranet through the Internet to the external user. This is the concept of the extranet. However, an extranet requires a degree of security, performance, scalability and policy management not found in traditional Internet VPN solutions.

Contivity™ Extranet Switches from Bay Networks, a Nortel Networks Business, offer all of the features needed to meet the challenges of a high-performance, scalable, and secure extranet in a single product. Compared to the previous solutions (external devices such as routers and firewalls), the Contivity Extranet Switch integrates all of the necessary technologies into a single platform—routing, firewall, bandwidth management, and secure tunneling. Its directory-enabled architecture allows it to determine what level of performance, access, and security each user should have, based on the needs of that user. This allows the creation of the "Personal Extranet," one that can be tailored to meet the diverse needs of a wide range of users regardless of the application each user is trying to access. Implementing an extranet with the Contivity Extranet Switch allows customers to take advantage of the Internet for today's applications such as remote access. At the same time it provides the secure infrastructure needed to support next-generation applications such as Electronic Business, linking together the enterprise with its customers and suppliers through the Internet.

Some of the VPN configurations that are available are those of VPN switches. One such switch is that of the Nortel Networks Contivity Extranet Switch 4000. The switch uses a very simple three-step design for configuration via a GUI. [See Figure 9-5.] The following will describe an installation of this VPN switch which begins with a program called ExtNetIP.exe.

Figure 9-5
Nortel's IP Address
Configuration Utility.

Configure the Switch

The Switch is so flexible that you can choose from three simple-to-use methods, including:

- Quick Start Configuration—A single display allows you to add IP addresses and establish up to three PPTP tunnel sessions.
- Guided Configuration—A step-by-step configuration method describes each display and then summarizes what you have configured on the display.
- Manage Extranet Switch—The day-to-day management method with simple, easy-to-use displays.

Complete details for configuring and monitoring the Switch are in the Nortel Networks Contivity Extranet Switch Administrator's Guide, along with a detailed checklist that describes things you'll need to properly configure your Switch.

Quick Start

The Quick Start Configuration single display allows you to add a LAN port IP Address and Subnet Mask, establish the tunnel as Private (your private LAN) or Public (public data networks), and configure up to three PPTP Users and an Administrator with User IDs and Passwords. Additionally, you can set the system's Date and Time. The Quick Start Configuration displays can be completed in as little as 15 minutes. [See Figure 9-6.]

Explanations of all fields are included in the Getting Started Guide. The Contivity Switch has been praised throughout the industry for its ease of configuration and its superior usability features.

Guided Configuration

The Guided Configuration steps you through the entire navigational menu. Each functional area begins with an objectives summary and then steps you through each subsection. On-line context-sensitive help is available to supplement the summary. The Guided Configuration can take two to three hours to complete, depending on how extensive your configuration will be [See Figure 9-7.]

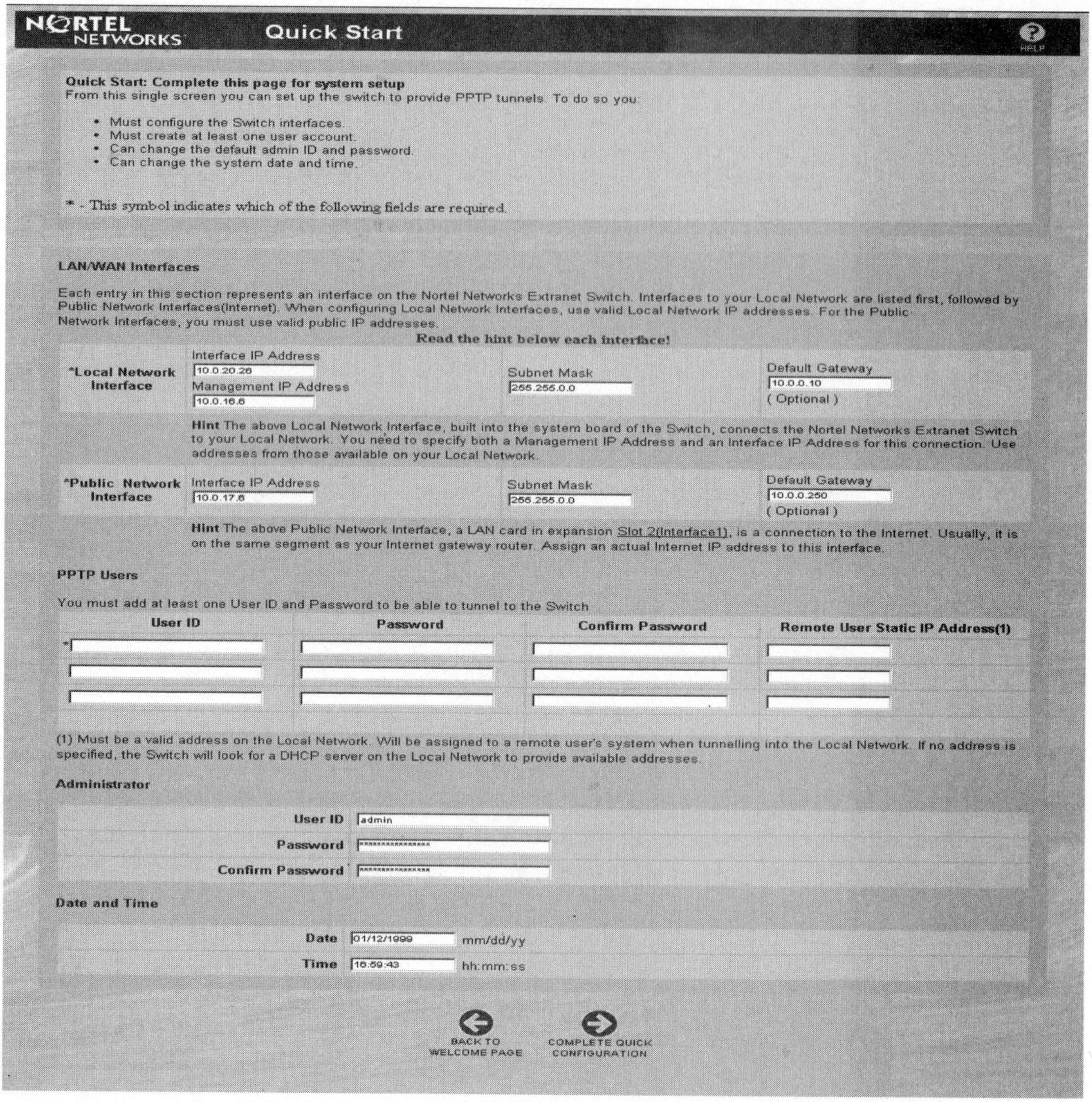

Figure 9-6   Nortel's Quick Start.

Manage Extranet Switch

The Manage Extranet Switch configuration allows access to all configuration management facilities. Once you are familiar with the Switch's navigational menu and capabilities, then you'll want to select Manage Extranet Switch. On-line context sensitive help is available for all configuration and management areas. [See Figure 9-8.]

Figure 9-7
Nortel's Guided Configuration.

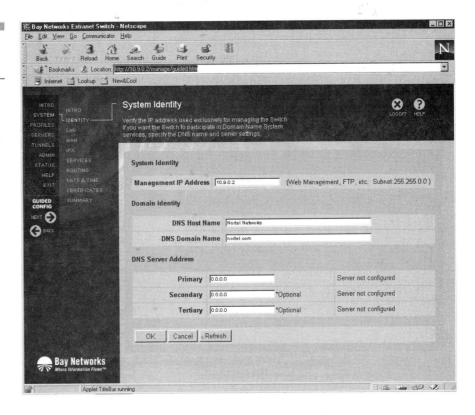

Figure 9-8
Nortel's Managed Extranet Switch.

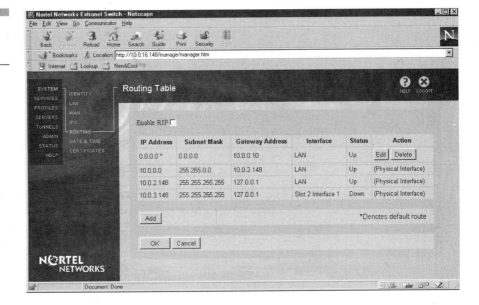

An important focus of the Contivity Extranet Switch has always been ease of use. Regardless of how technologically superior a solution may be, undue complexity can prevent its benefits from being realized. The configuration and use of the Contivity Extranet Switch has been designed to be as simple as possible so that users can realize the benefits of an Extranet as quickly as possible. This philosophy is particularly illustrated by the unlimited distribution IPSec client that's included free of charge with each Contivity Extranet Switch. Using his or her normal user name and password, the remote user can easily and quickly establish a secure tunnel through the Internet, taking advantage of the encryption and compression capabilities of IPSec.

For more information about the Contivity Extranet Switch and other Nortel Network products, please visit *www.nortelnetworks.com/products/* or 1-(800)-4NORTEL.

Radguard—cIPro System

Radguard's cIPro System is a comprehensive IP-level network security system that safeguards access to your network and protects data flow between your networks. By applying security at the network layer (IP in the TCP/IP suite), you create a secure network infrastructure—virtual tunnels—in which your applications can securely exchange data. You can be confident that your applications' data will not be modified. Furthermore, by working at the IP level, your applications do not need to be modified—the added security is transparent to your users. cIPro System integrates a variety of advanced technologies to maximize protection.

- Multiple protection levels, that enable users to safely transfer data between secure corporate hosts over public networks, resulting in a Virtual Private Network (VPN).
- Communication between your private network and untrusted, public networks is secured using cIPro System's Multi-Layered Probing (MLP) firewall technology.
- Security auditing features (e.g., alarms and logs) inform users of breaches of security and enable them to control automatic system responses.

Protecting the secure transfer of data between your private, remote networks involves ensuring that the data may not be intercepted or modified. The cIPro System solution is to create a Virtual Private

Network (VPN) in which your hosts communicate with each other through secure, virtually private tunnels over the untrusted, public network.

The cIPro System Security Solution

The cIPro System is a unique, hardware-based comprehensive security solution, designed and produced in-house by RADGUARD. cIPro System is used for securing private networks that communicate through any untrusted network, such as the Internet. cIPro System protects your private networks and the data transferred between them by:

- Creating a VPN for your private communication networks using advanced data encryption techniques.
- Using a firewall to implement your security policy for controlling the flow of clear (i.e., unencrypted) traffic, to and from the public network.
- Providing both real-time notification of policy violations and a detailed audit of security-related events.

Components of cIPro System

The cIPro System comprises the following components:

One cIPro-CA   A hardware device that serves both as the certification authority that certifies all the cIPro-VPNs in your network, and as a security gateway dedicated to protecting your master management station and management commands.

A number of cIPro-VPNs   Hardware devices that serve as security gateways by creating a VPN to secure traffic between distributed private networks that communicate over public networks. They also control access to your private network by hosts residing in the untrusted, public network.

cIPro-MNG   The management software that resides on your management station, that is protected by the cIPro-CA. cIPro-MNG is used to set up and monitor your cIPro-CA, cIPro-VPNs and network security. Optionally, other management stations can be connected to cIPro-VPNs, allowing regional or hierarchical management.

Figure 9-9
Radguard's cIPro
System.

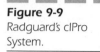

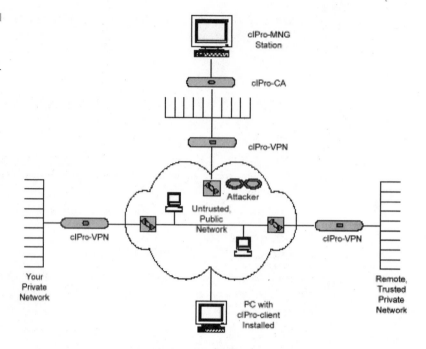

cIPro-client (Optional-component) This optional component of the cIPro System is an encryption and authentication application that may be installed on a single computer. The cIPro-client provides protection of data transfer between the computer on which it is installed and remote computers, that are protected by a cIPro-VPN. Unlike a cIPro-VPN, which can protect a number of computers in a network, the cIPro-client application provides protection only for the computer on which it is installed. It safeguards data transparently, by encrypting and signing outgoing data before directing it to trusted host destinations, and by decrypting and authenticating incoming data. [See Figure 9-9.]

Beyond the hardware-related configuration, setting up the VPN involves defining and monitoring all the cIPro-VPNs, hosts and subnets in the system and specifying various encryption parameters. This is done by the cIPro various GUI interfaces. [See Figure 9-10 for an example.]

The setup of the cIPro VPN consists of the following:

■ Which cIPro-VPNs are in my VPN? (Informative)

■ Which hosts or subnets are protected by the local cIPro-VPN? (Configurable)

■ Which hosts or subnets are protected by remote cIPro-VPNs? (Informative)

Figure 9-10
An example of clPro's
GUI interface.

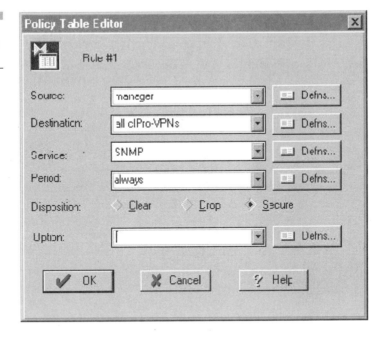

Data Encryption

▒ What type of protection do I want between sites?

▒ How often do I want the keys to be changed? (Configurable)

▒ What Security Associations are currently in use? (Informative)

Define the Policies for Network Access

▒ Multi-layer probing—Which policies define how the packets should be filtered? (Configurable)

▒ How should the packets be filtered?

Remote User Authentication

▒ Which remote, unprotected users can access my private network? (Configurable)

▒ Which protected hosts can the remote user access? (Configurable)

Network Address Translation

▒ Which local hosts or addresses are mapped to which global addresses? (Informative—except for static entries)

Defining cIPro System Responses to Policy Violations

- How will each event be handled? (Configurable)
- How should the selected event be handled? (Configurable)

Monitoring the System

The current alarm status of the cIPro-VPN is displayed in the status line. From the status indicator, you can access the HP OpenView alarm log. In addition, all the events within a predefined time frame are logged as a backup inside the cIPro-VPN itself.

- What is the current status of the system?
- What alarms have been received?
- What events are currently logged in the cIPro-VPN? [See Figure 9-11.]

The *cIPro System Conceptual Guide* is one of a suite of books provided by RADGUARD describing the concepts of network security and the features of the cIPro System. The cIPro System security services provide comprehensive IP level network protection for private networks connect-

Figure 9-11
cIPro logging.

ed via untrusted networks, such as the Internet. RADGUARD's suite of cIPro System books comprises:

- *cIPro System Conceptual Guide,* which describes the concepts of network security and how cIPro System provides a secure Virtual Private Network.
- *cIPro System Installation Guide,* which describes how to connect the devices, load the software and configure the cIPro System's initial security policy, based on a sample Virtual Private Network.
- *cIPro System Reference Guide,* which describes how to use the cIPro system's management software and the cIPro-CA and cIPro-VPN hardware devices.

For more information on Radguard or its products, please visit *www.radguard.com,* or call (201) 828-9611, or email *info@radguard.com.*

RedCreek—Ravlin

RedCreek Communications began operations in July 1996 to address the growing demand by Corporate America for more comprehensive network security solutions, especially in the Internet market. RedCreek, aware of the inherent risks in transmitting sensitive company information over public networks, has developed low-cost, high-speed products and services to eliminate those risks.

RedCreek's products and services ensure privacy of information as it is transmitted over private and public networks and provide control of access to corporate resources. RedCreek's solutions are based on a revolutionary architecture, CryptoCore®, assuring unparalleled transmission speed, transparent authentication, and network scalability. Network management of the products is through a simple Windows95/ Windows NT 4.0 configuration utility that supports industry-standard SNMP for device management.

RedCreek is dedicated to providing low-cost, high-speed, and easy-to-use network security products. RedCreek's Ravlin family of products enables the secure transmission of data between offices and from remote/mobile users to their corporate offices. Products include: Ravlin 4, Ravlin 10, Ravlin 100, RavlinSoft, and RavlinManager.

Distributed systems and extended networks make business more productive. But with this added productivity, unprotected corporate data is traveling into potentially dangerous new neighborhoods. As a result, this data is getting "mugged" on an unprecedented scale: The cost of computer crime is rising at an alarming rate according to the Computer Security Institute's annual "Computer Crime and Security Survey." 72% of the 520 respondent companies acknowledged suffering financial losses from security breaches in 1997. The combined loss from computer security crime totaled over 136 million dollars, a 36% increase over 1996 loses. (Computer Security Institute, 1998). Stung by losses, or fearful of being the next victim, corporations are encrypting data so that wherever it may travel on the distributed network (intranet) or public network (Internet) it is unintelligible and unusable to would-be data thieves. Previously known as slow, cumbersome, and expensive, encryption technology has matured to meet required design characteristics:

- Standards-based
- Fast (supporting wireline speed)
- Easy to manage
- Easy to use
- Low cost

RedCreek Communications meets these requirements in its Ravlin family of encryption products. Their scalability, coupled with Ravlin compliance with the Internet Protocol Security Standard (IPSec) for authentication, firewall access control, and encryption standards, enables network managers to address their security requirements across widely diverse environments.

The Ravlin Architecture

RedCreek Ravlin is a family of high performance encryption products. All of the products in the family are based on the fully scalable Ravlin architecture [shown in Figure 9-12].

Figure 9-12
Ravlin architecture.

The CryptoCore Engine   The Ravlin architecture is based on Crypto-Core®, a proprietary, patent-pending engine that combines optimized software and parallel processing, implemented with low cost, off-the-shelf components enabling value-priced products. CryptoCore delivers wireline speed through the encryption system. Encryption never slows network throughput, even when encrypting at the Triple DES standard.

Services   Ravlin services include encryption, tunneling, and key management. RedCreek has chosen to adhere to dominant standards, such as IPSec, in each area. This gives RedCreek Ravlin the advantage of being reliable as well as having the broadest possible industry support and interoperability.

Encryption and Authentication   Ravlin uses the DES specification for encryption. RedCreek selected DES because of its strength, its widespread use, and its position as the world's dominant encryption specification. Through the management interface, managers can specify the desired level of DES, 40-bit, 56-bit or 168-bit Triple DES. Along with DES encryption, Ravlin also supports ISO X.509 v3 digital certificates. The use of X.509 digital certificates allows customers to insert their unique X.509 certifications into Ravlin products. This is how Ravlin works within a public key infrastructure (PKI).

Tunneling   Ravlin users can implement IPSec Encapsulated (ESP) Tunneling Mode for even stronger security. In IPSec ESP Tunneling Mode, the entire IP packet (headers and data) is encrypted, with a new IPSec packet wrapped around the outside. By comparison, basic encryption encrypts the payload, but leaves the address in the clear. ESP Tunneling Mode protects against leaving the addresses in the clear and thus protects against an attacker capturing the source and destination addresses, where he could use those addresses to attack the private networks of the sender or receiver.

Key Management   One of the important considerations for building VPNs is a reliable method for automatically trading encryption keys over the Internet, a process known as key management. Ravlin implements ISAKMP (Internet Security Association Key Management Protocol). ISAKMP is the key management standard adopted for IPv6 by the IP Security (IPSec) Working Group of the IETF.

Scalable Platform   As the architectural diagram shows, each Ravlin implementation is based on a Ravlin platform. Today the

Ravlin family includes three different platforms: Ravlin 4, Ravlin 10, and RavlinSoft. All products are interoperable and provide the same levels of security. The different platforms let managers cost-effectively select encryption systems for each connected site based on specific site requirements.

Ravlin 4, with 4 Mbps throughput, is designed for LANs, WANs and workgroup environments running at up to T1/E1 speed. Ravlin 10 handles corporate network communications and delivers 10 Mbps throughput.

System Management   Network managers configure and manage Ravlin secure environments through the RavlinManager. A single RavlinManager can control any number of Ravlin units, whether local or remote. Once secure associations are defined through RavlinManager, the secure VPN operates independently and doesn't require an active RavlinManager.

RavlinManager is fully SNMP-compliant. Operations can be accessed through an SNMP-based management platform. Managers can use SNMP to perform configuration and management tasks, and also use the powerful alert and reporting features of their SNMP management platform to monitor the health of Ravlin systems.

Standard External Interfaces   Ravlin is designed to interoperate with other standard security systems on the network. A Ravlin system can be integrated transparently into existing standards-based networks, and managers can build multilayered security strategies using best-of-breed products from multiple vendors.

User/Device Authentication   In the area of user/device authentication, Ravlin supports the following:

- Authentication, accounting, auditing
- RADIUS
- Tokens: SDI SecuID, Bellcore S/Key
- Enigma Logic, Cryptocard
- PKI: LDAP, RADIUS, CiscoCA enrollment
- Services, X.509 digital certificates

Standard Firewall Interface   Ravlin operates in conjunction with firewalls. Because of this, network managers can choose a standards-

Figure 9-13
Ravlin network.

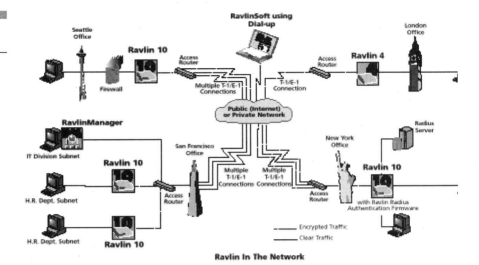

compliant firewall based on specific firewall features and know that the firewall will work with all Ravlin functions. [See Figure 9-13.]

Computer networking has entered a new phase, characterized by easy access, much heavier use of backbones and public networks, and networks that extend to remote offices, telecommuters, business partners, suppliers, outsourcers and customers. Under the pressure of these changes, many companies are re-evaluating their security policies, procedures and technology and recognizing the need to make much wider use of encryption technology to protect data wherever it may travel, and despite intrusions.

This report has presented a new model for network security based on encryption technology. To be suitable for widespread deployment, encryption must be fast, manageable, transparent, scalable, robust, standards-based, and economical. We call this model the Trusted Network. Both economy and fault tolerance tend to dictate dedicated, modular hardware devices for servers and backbones. For workstations, on the other hand, inexpensive encryption software running on the host processor may take advantage of spare processing capacity.

RedCreek Ravlin is a scalable family of encryption products designed to meet these exacting new requirements in network security.

For more information on RedCreek or its products, please visit *www.redcreek.com,* or call (888) 745-3900.

TimeStep—PERMIT Enterprise

TimeStep Corporation, a Newbridge affiliate, is a leading provider of secure VPN solutions for corporate intranets, extranets, and Internet remote access. With TimeStep's VPN technology, businesses can send sensitive data across the Internet confident that it will travel safely—unseen, unchanged, uncopied, and intact. Designed for large-scale business communications, TimeStep's award-winning PERMIT Enterprise product suite integrates secure VPN, access control, and authentication technologies in a single solution.

The PERMIT Enterprise product suite allows you to use public networks for:

- Secure Internet remote LAN access
- Secure branch office connectivity
- Secure extranet connectivity with business partners, customers, and suppliers

Administration of the secure VPN can be from single or multiple points, and handled from an internal point of contact (on a LAN) or from a remote station anywhere around the globe (via the Internet).

The PERMIT Enterprise Product Solution

The three main PERMIT Enterprise product groups are:

- The PERMIT/Gate™ family of security gateways
- PERMIT/Client™ software applications
- The PERMIT/Director™ suite

The PERMIT/Gate protects one or many nodes, the PERMIT/Client protects a single workstation, and the PERMIT/Director suite of products provides authentication through certification and access control via secure VPN group management.

The PERMIT/Gate

The PERMIT/Gate™ is a tamper-resistant gateway that secures data communications for intranets, extranets, and Internet remote access.

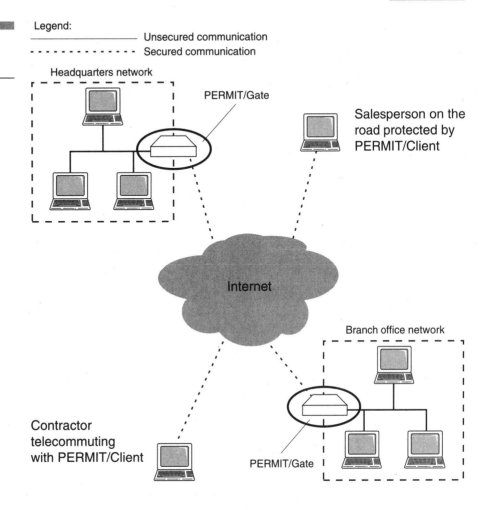

Figure 9-14
TimeStep's
PERMIT/Gate™.

The PERMIT/Gate 7520, with up to 100 Mbps throughput, is well suited for high bandwidth applications using T3 connections and internal LANs using Fast Ethernet. The PERMIT/Gate has the ability to support high volumes of remote access clients. The PERMIT/Gate 4520 and 2520, with 10 Mbps and 4 Mbps throughput respectively, are ideal for medium sized enterprises with lower bandwidth applications using T1 connections, internal LANs, and SOHO applications. You would install a PERMIT/Gate between a private network and a public network (often the Internet or a large corporate WAN). [See Figure 9-14.]

Key Benefits of PERMIT/Gate

Wire-rate performance   Fast, hardware-based DES and 3-DES encryption for wire-rate IPSec performance. The PERMIT/Gate 7520 also has a custom hardware-based packet engine that includes support for MD5 and SHA-1 algorithms.

Interoperability   The PERMIT/Gate is an IPSec-compliant solution that works with other IPSec-compliant security products. The PERMIT/Gate is also IPSec-certified by the International Computer Security Association (ICSA).

Scalable Architecture   Supports thousands of simultaneous secure sessions using a full spectrum of encryption and authentication algorithms.

Remote installation, management, and auditing privileges   Network administrator can configure, monitor, and audit each PERMIT/Gate remotely from anywhere on the secure VPN using PERMIT/Config™.

Flexible security policy   The PERMIT/Gate enables network administrators to segment their network by enforcing policy with varying degrees of encryption and security requirements.

PERMIT/Client

PERMIT/Client™ is software that secures communications for a single workstation. PERMIT/Client supports IPSec tunnel and transport modes for LAN and PPP connections. It is ideal for telecommuters and for Internet remote access by business travelers. PERMIT/Client is available for the Windows NT 4.0, Windows 95/98, and Mac OS 7.1 (or later) operating systems. Optional two-factor user authentication support is available with any Entrust-Ready™ PC card token or smart card.

Key Benefits of PERMIT/Client

Interoperability   Compliance with the full IPSec standard allows PERMIT/Client products to work with other IPSec-compliant security products.

Transparent Operation PERMIT/Client secures communications automatically and transparently to the end users and their applications.

Multiple Connection Options PERMIT/Client supports Ethernet, PPP, and tunneling connections which can be automatically reconfigured by dynamically changing connection profiles with one simple menu selection.

Reliable Security PERMIT/Client provides assurances that communications are secure by allowing the user to view, log, and trace the status of his or her secure VPN connections.

PERMIT/Director

The PERMIT/Director™ suite contains the software applications used to manage the people and resources protected by PERMIT Enterprise™ products within your secure VPN. Assigning users and resources to different groups gives you the ability to maintain multiple secure VPN partitions. This allows you to control who can communicate with whom, and the level of IPSec encryption and authentication that each party can use. The PERMIT/Director suite includes PERMIT/Director, PERMIT/Config, Entrust/Manager™, and Entrust/Directory™.

Key Benefits of PERMIT/Director

Scaleable Architecture PERMIT/Director combined with the Entrust® public key infrastructure (PKI) from Entrust Technologies allows cross-certification and LDAP-compliant directory support that enables you to protect thousands of nodes.

Multiple secure VPNs Group-based policy gives you the ability to control who can communicate with whom, allowing you to manage multiple secure VPNs under one or many PKIs.

Central Management Comprehensive management system consolidates access control, authentication, confidentiality, and data integrity to reduce the cost and complexity of network security administration.

Installation

The two main factors to consider when planning your setup are one, which users or resources do you want communicating securely and two, your current or envisioned network topology. Implementations vary widely based on each specific need, but the following steps are generally taken in each setup once you decide on a topology.

1. Set up Entrust and PERMIT/Director.
2. Install the PERMIT/Gates.
   Before setting up the PERMIT/Gate you must determine whether you will use the PERMIT/Gate as a router or use Bridge Emulation Mode.
3. Load PERMIT/Config.
4. Via a terminal console session, define Gate IP addresses and remote access parameters for each Gate.
5. Finish configuring the Gates with PERMIT/Config (for example, set management server addresses, create Entrust certificates, define the network segments on the private side of the Gates, define any groups based on IP addresses you want to control access to with PERMIT/Director, set the encryption level, define the PAR range, build the secure map).
6. Set up basic permissions on PERMIT/Director.
7. Load the PERMIT/Client software on remote user nodes.
8. Finish configuring PERMIT/Director.

Ideally you would perform this implementation at one physical site, and then deliver the components to their intended destinations, although you can implement them remotely with proper planning. If you use an Entrust CA, an X.500 server, or PERMIT/Director in your secure network, set them up before setting up the PERMIT/Gate.

With the establishment of IPSec as the universal standard for network security, you can now have all the benefits IP networks offer, universal cross-platform compatibility, an almost organic expandable quality and the peace of mind that comes with knowing your data is secure in transit.

At TimeStep, we're committed to making this promise a reality, with meaningful implementations of these new standards that are powerful, flexible, and intuitive. The scaleable architecture of the PERMIT Enterprise product line is our proof of that commitment. With PERMIT Enterprise, no network is too big, and no security requirements too complex. Finally, your secure network can grow with your business.

For more information on TimeStep or its products, please visit *www.timestep.com,* or call 1-800-383-8211 or email *info@timestep.com.*

VPNet—VPLink Architecture*

VPNet, the first company formed with a singular focus on virtual private networks, takes a comprehensive approach to VPNs. VPNet's VPLink™ architecture delivers a consistent set of security and networking services across multiple product implementations. The architecture maintains full compatibility with existing networks while providing a mechanism for rapidly embracing new technologies, scaling to higher access speeds, and incorporating emerging networking and security standards.

VPLink technology blends three constituents. Beginning with solid networking fundamentals, it then leverages existing and emerging IPSec standards for VPN security and administration. Finally, it adds system- and component-level integration expertise to enhance performance and lower costs. In this way, VPLink technology provides data privacy, integrity, and authenticity over public data networks without compromising performance, scalability, interoperability, manageability, or cost.

VPNware Products

VPNware™ products provide the first comprehensive solution for manageable site-to-site and remote end-user VPN connectivity. Based on the VPLink architecture, they target existing networks through plug-and-play ease of integration, transparent operation, wire-speed performance, and centralized configuration and management capabilities. All VPNet products are designed to minimize the implementation overhead of VPNs and thus expand the market for future VPNet solutions.

---

*VPNet, VPNware, VSU, VPNmanager, VPNremote, and VPLink are trademarks of VPNet Technologies Inc. All other trademarks and tradenames are properties of their respective owners.

The VPNware Service Units VSU™-10, VSU-1010 and VSU-1100 provide reliable intranets, remote access, and multi-partner extranets. VSUs provide superior security, performance, and flexibility for IPSec-compliant VPNs. (VSUs are ICSA IPsec certified.) Encryption is Triple DES—the highest level of security available—and runs from 10 Mbps to 100 Mbps full duplex. Furthermore, all VSUs compress data packets to raise throughput and install on any Ethernet networks in a wide variety of configurations. (See below.) VSUs support up to 5,000 simultaneous remote users, both internationally and domestically (depending on model). Additional features include support for ISAKMP key management, routing, and comprehensive Network Address Translation (NAT) capabilities.

The VPNremote™ Client Software provides end-to-end privacy, integrity, and authenticity of IP data from dial-up sites with a local call to the nearest ISP. Therefore, telecommuters, traveling executives, and mobile sales and service personnel can use ubiquitous public network facilities for private remote access to corporate VPNs. Based on standard protocols, connections require no special hardware or software at the ISP point-of-presence (POP) and operate transparently to applications that use IP to communicate. When IP packets are sent or received from designated VPN sites, the software automatically encrypts outbound traffic and decrypts and authenticates incoming traffic on the fly, without user intervention.

The VPNmanager™ Java™-based management software brings the ease and familiarity of Web browsers to the administration of VPNs. VPNmanager applications let network professionals define, configure, and manage VPNs from any location equipped with a computer. Using familiar installation and management procedures, network managers can configure and check the status of VPNware VSUs, add remote sites and dial-up users to a VPN, monitor the performance of private data transmissions, and troubleshoot existing configurations. When VPN works are being designed by VPNware™ products, two basic network topologies must be considered, those with firewalls and those without firewalls. Figures 9-15 to 9-18 illustrate some of the various configurations.

VPNet Configuration without Firewalls

Figure 9-15 shows an example of a network with VSUs installed in a simple no-firewall, in-line configuration. The VSU-10, VSU-1010, and VSU-1100 from VPNet Technologies can all be installed in an in-line configura-

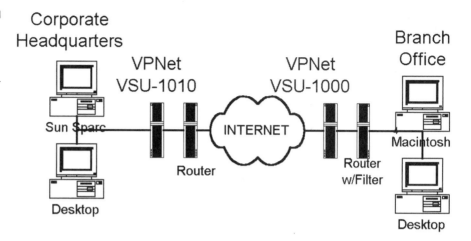

Figure 9-15
VPNet configuration,
In-line with no
firewall.

tion. This simple network is typical of many corporate networks. Where there is no firewall, either of two configurations can be used: In-Line or One-Arm. The typical placement of a VSU is in-line, on the link between the trusted and untrusted network, in the direct path of packets going to or from the untrusted network. However, occasionally, in-line placement of VSUs is not preferred in the no-firewall installation, and VSUs can be configured as a network node, similar to a workstation or host: This is referred to as "one-armed configuration" [shown in Figure 9-16].

The main advantage of a one-arm configuration is for load balancing and scaling to thousands of simultaneous VPNs with VPNremote clients. Also, note that one-arm configurations for site-to-site operation may require static routes to be configured on the associated routers.

VPNet Configuration with Firewalls

The one-armed VPN solution is good for networks that have low traffic between the router and firewall, because both the encrypted and clear traffic will be on the same network segment. This solution is especially useful for small amounts of encrypted traffic, because the solution allows a lower bandwidth for encryption, while maintaining a normal bandwidth for clear traffic. The one-armed method is a frequently used configuration that allows the router to decide which traffic to route to the VPN, and which traffic to route to the firewall. This configuration is also frequently used where there is no firewall. Figures 9-17 and 9-18 illustrate VPNet configurations with firewalls.

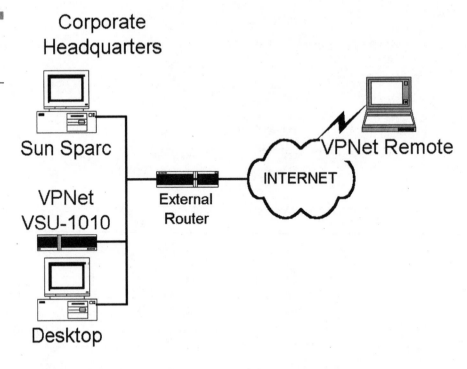

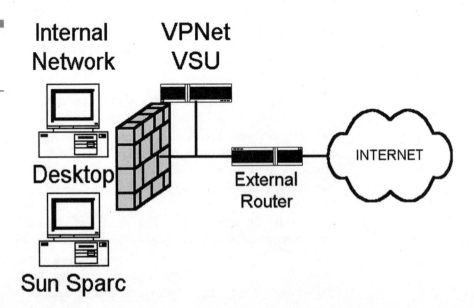

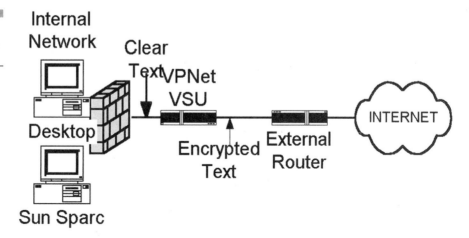

Figure 9-18
VPNet configuration,
in-line with firewall.

For the one-armed configuration the following Customer Provided Equipment (CPE) is required at the network:

- One (or more) VSU-10, VSU-1010, or VSU-1100
- Firewall
- Ethernet network between router and firewall.

For remote clients, the Client IP Address Pool, a VSU feature, must be configured in the VSU. For site-to-site VPNs, NAT must be configured in the VSU or a static route configured on the router to ensure that outbound VPN traffic is routed to the VSU. The VSU is usually placed on the public side of the firewall in the one-armed configurations.

Advantages The one-armed configuration allows internal IP addressing and minimizes change to existing networks. A Client IP Address Pool method allows for the LAN, or private network, to use private addressing schemes. With the VSU on the public side of the firewall, only decrypted traffic passes the firewall, allowing all traffic, both VPN member and non-member traffic, to have the firewall filtering and screening rules applied. Finally, if the VSU fails, non-VPN traffic will still be able to enter through the firewall from the router.

Disadvantages The disadvantage of the one-armed configuration is that all traffic must pass through the firewall, potentially causing throughput problems. Additionally, every VPN packet will appear twice on the same segment. Special care and effort must be taken to differentiate the VPN traffic from the normal traffic, thus ensuring that all VPN traffic is routed to a VSU.

In-Line VPN Configuration

When a remote site is connected to a main site via the public network and all traffic must go through the main site to be proxied or otherwise handled, placing the VSU in front of the firewall is a good solution. As with the one-armed method, this configuration is also frequently used for networks where there is no firewall.

The required customer's provided equipment (CPE) for the inline-in-front-of-firewall network configuration will be:

- One VSU-10, VSU-1010, or VSU-1000
- Router between the LAN and WAN
- Firewall (optional)
- Ethernet network between router and firewall

Additionally, the firewall may need to know about authentication traffic if an internal authentication server (such as RADIUS or a Security Dynamics ACE/Server) is being used.

Advantages Placing a VSU in front of the firewall is a simple plug-and-play effort. The firewall does not have to be aware of any VSU or encrypted traffic. All of the traffic is taken care of before it reaches the firewall. With a VSU on the public side of the firewall, only decrypted traffic passes the firewall. Thus, all traffic, both VPN member and nonmember traffic, has the firewall filtering and screening rules applied. The router does not have to be configured to differentiate between the routing of VPN member and nonmember traffic.

Disadvantages The placement of a VSU does modify the existing customer network. The bandwidth of a VSU may be affected in this configuration. All traffic must pass through a VSU, and if it fails, the network is disconnected from the WAN.

For more information on VPNet Technologies and its products, visit *www.vpnet.com* or call (408) 445-6600 or email *info@vpnet.com*.

Conclusion

Chapter 9 was an interesting chapter to write, although since I didn't write it, I guess a better way of putting it is that it was interesting to read. When installing VPNs, it's always different, there are command line syntax structures, GUI interfaces, Web browsers, and firewalls that use a rule base to implement their VPN solution.

In this chapter, out of all the implementations, how many times did PPTP, L2TP, and IPSec get mentioned? While they were mentioned, they were mentioned only in passing, such as "this product supports IPSec," or "this device supports PPTP." That brings both good and bad news. The good news is that you don't have to overly concern yourself with these protocols, since the vendors take care of that. The bad news, is that if you have two different vendors, you have to worry about inter-operability problems. So unless you are a vendor developing PPTP or IPSec products, you should be more concerned with the interoperability aspects of the products you are using.

We also discussed the types of VPN, service provider VPN and stand-alone VPN. While there isn't a definitive answer to which one is best, you should look at what you have to work with. Do you have the technical staff, do you have the expertise, do you even have the time, and most importantly, do you have the security staff that will keep up-to-date to protect your investment? While stand-alone products give you control over the hardware and access to it, you are responsible for the security. Although you give up some access with a service provider VPN, you hopefully will receive a wealth of experience and security protection in return. As with everything else, it comes down to a trade-off and what is best for your company.

Troubleshooting
VPNs

Chapter 10 covers the basics of troubleshooting VPNs. While the term *basic* may imply "simple," here it means "fundamental." As you went through Chapter 5, the topology chapter, you began to see how various VPN architecture placements can be achieved. You also saw the other components that are involved in setting up a VPN infrastructure. A VPN infrastructure consists of routers, switches, remote users, authentication devices, and so on. Therefore, if you assume that a VPN is simply an encryption algorithm, you would be mistaken and overlook the other various aspects of VPN technology.

VPN troubleshooting always starts with isolation. You are potentially taking a data packet from one end of the Internet and sending it over to a destination, passing routers along the way. Once the data packet gets to your device, it may be sent to another device for authentication and passed back to the original device for verification. Regardless of the VPN device you install, the data packet will follow this route.

In this chapter, we will look at the very common remote dial-in user VPN, the LAN-to-LAN VPN, and a mutlihoned firewall/VPN, since these three devices are the most common in today's environment. I will also spend some time on PPTP, IPSec, and L2TP VPNs and give you some clues for troubleshooting them. It's important not to lose sight of the big picture: where is the data coming from, where is the data going, and from what two points are the tunnels established? Many VPN problems are caused simply by tunnel configuration characteristics that were never set up properly.

Introduction to Troubleshooting VPNs

Troubleshooting VPNs can be very complicated, since VPNs are a mass of technologies jumbled together. Anywhere in the picture you can experience problems; unfortunately, in most cases it is not the VPN at fault. It is more often another system that interacts with the VPN that causes the problem.

GENERAL NOTE   80 percent of the problems with VPNs are not VPN problems; that is, it is not the encryption algorithm that is causing the malfunction, but another piece in the puzzle.

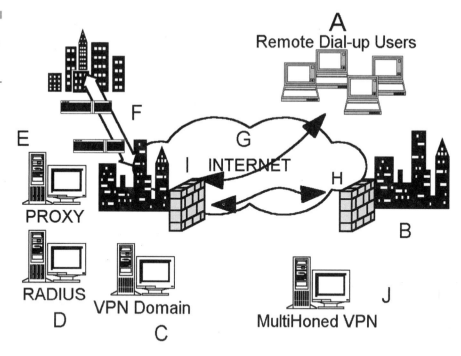

Figure 10-1
Various troubleshooting areas within a VPN.

In that case, where could the problem lie, or where could you start to look? Start by taking a look at Figure 10-1, which shows potential troubleshooting areas, and examine the various pieces. You need to understand these areas when you are troubleshooting a VPN to effectively and efficiently resolve the problem. Interestingly, nowhere on Figure 10-1 does it mention encryption or encryption algorithms; therefore, you should get an indication of how small a role encryption problems play. This is not saying encryption does not cause problems; it does, but just a small part of the problem. Let's take a look now at some of the areas.

A. Remote Dial-In Users It is very possible your remote dial-in users are not able to connect to the VPN device to establish an encrypted tunnel. This particular problem is one of the most common that can occur when implementing a VPN and sometimes the most frustrating.

B. LAN-to-LAN VPN This is another geographic site that is connected to another VPN. Here you really have to understand the setup in establishing your LAN-to-LAN VPN. Whether it's IPSec, PPTP, or L2TP, if you don't understand the protocol being used, you are not going to get the VPN working.

C. VPN Domain   If external users can make a connection to your corporation network but then cannot go any further or access any equipment, the VPN domain has not been set properly. Somehow your VPN system has to tell the remote users when to encrypt data.

D. Authentication Services   Here is another area to check, once your remote VPN dial-in connections, LAN-to-LAN VPN connections, and extranet VPN connections are set up. These users must be authenticated. If your authentication device cannot communicate with your VPN device or cannot respond fast enough, user time-outs will occur.

E. Proxy   Depending on what kind of devices you place close to your Internet's access point, you may mistakenly confuse proxy problems with VPN problems. In that case, you need to find out how far your users can get into your network.

F. Internal WAN Routing   Routing is another major cause of so-called VPN problems. By not accurately setting up a routing policy that will forward the return packets via the VPN device they came in on, communication will never occur.

G. The Internet   As mentioned earlier, some ISPs block encrypted packets. If your or anyone's router that is along the path from user to corporate network sets up a filter to block these packets, communications will not occur.

H. Encryption Problems   Between any two VPNs, encryption problems can occur. Key mechanisms, time-outs in key exchanges, problems communicating, and upgrades can all affect the communications between two sites.

I. Addressing   Before you establish a VPN, you will need to know about addressing concerns. Do you have a private or public address space? Are you using NAT? If not, and you plan to use IPSec in tunnel mode, then you will need public addresses.

J. Multihoned VPN   If you use a multihoned VPN device, like a UNIX station, decide to use it as a firewall/VPN combination, and decide to have multiple DMZ zones, then you really have to consider traffic flows, routing issues, and possible NAT issues on the same box. Being on one station allows flexibility and eases management; however, the setup can be difficult to maintain.

K. Miscellaneous   While K is not on the diagram, the miscellaneous category covers all the other aspects of VPN, PPTP, PPP, DES, SKIP, and MD5 problems. These are the kinds of problems that are directly related to VPN technology.

As you can see, there are many areas where VPN troubleshooting skills come in handy. I would say the single most important step in VPN troubleshooting is isolation. If you can't isolate the problem, it can take a long time to figure it out. In the following sections, we will go into more detail regarding some of the problems just mentioned.

Remote Dial-In Users

Remote dial-in users are potentially one of the biggest headaches administrators encounter when setting up VPN accounts. To understand how to troubleshoot problems in this area, let's first figure out how to configure this type of setup. Figure 10-2 illustrates the configuration.

In any VPN dial-in account software gets loaded onto laptop machines. This software is usually Windows 95/NT; however, some developments are being made for UNIX platforms. You configure the VPN device first, then the remote users' laptops. The VPN device is configured with the following items:

VPN Device

1. *VPN domain.*   The network or servers that users will be allowed to connect to.

2. *Key generation and certificates.*   You will configure the VPN device to create a key, e.g., Diffie-Hellman, and you will create a certificate for the device. This is when the trust factor comes in. You can use the VPN device itself as the certificate authority, or you can choose a third party as the certificate authority, since some vendors are now beginning to implement this configuration.

3. *Authentication server.*   The authentication server that users will

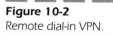

Figure 10-2
Remote dial-in VPN.

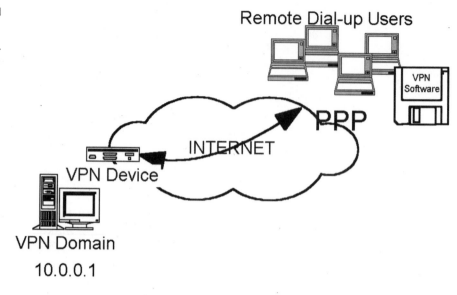

connect to. Back in Chapter 8, we placed a rule on a firewall that would allow this:

```
VPN_users@ANY | 230.230.230.1 | HTTP | Encrypt | YES
```

You are telling your VPN device that for users "anywhere"—if they are coming to the public IP address of 230.230.230.1 (the external interface)—the data is to be encrypted, and the users are only allowed access to the HTTP server. In another configuration setup option on the device, you tell it the authentication device IP address, or you set it up so the VPN device authenticates the users. As an administrator, you create a group called (VPN_users) and add the users to it.

4. *Encryption or encapsulation.* This may depend on your VPN vendor. We spoke about the differences between encryption and encapsulation earlier. Some vendors' products force all dial-in users to be encapsulated, whereas some VPNs use just encryption. Therefore, you may need an encapsulation option for non-IP traffic.

Laptop

1. The laptop needs the VPN software to be loaded on it.

2. You need to set up the configuration option of the VPN software to point to the public IP address of your VPN device.

3. You need to get the key to your VPN device.

Troubleshooting

Dealing with remote user VPN can be a headache, but usually only at the beginning. Once you know and understand the procedure, it becomes easy. Following are some of the problems associated with this configuration:

Frequently, the problems are caused by software faults on the laptop. Perhaps the software didn't load, or it loaded but it doesn't seem to work. Because of the nature of the software, it can and does interact with any other applications. Since it's between layer 2 (data-link) and layer 3 (network) layer, it can interact with any other device on the machine. If you have any problems with the software, remove it and reboot the machine. When you install it, make sure no other applications are running. In addition, make sure you have the right software—not only the correct version, but the right encryption algorithm. For example, many VPN manufacturers support multiple encryption algorithms, e.g., DES, 3DES, IDEA; however, the software you loaded on your machine might be a different algorithm. If you are using 3DES on your VPN device, you must use 3DES on the laptop. Normally if you click on Help Æ About, it will show you the version number and encryption algorithm loaded.

Now let's assume you have the software loaded on the laptop, and it seems to be working. You've created a configuration object on the laptop with the VPN's IP address, but it still doesn't work. Figure 10-3 illustrates a couple of steps to try.

GENERAL NOTE Don't mistake PPP errors for VPN errors. If you cannot even dial into your ISP and get an Internet connection, you will not make a VPN connection. Before loading the VPN software, make sure you can get onto the Internet.

If you are still having problems with the laptop, then you will need two people to diagnose the problem. First, have someone on the VPN device and monitor traffic. Due to the amount of traffic, you may want to filter on the laptop's IP address. Have someone on the laptop ping the external address on the VPN device:

```
Remote Laptop -> VPN Device ICMP Echo request
Remote Laptop -> VPN Device ICMP Echo request
Remote Laptop -> VPN Device ICMP Echo request
Remote Laptop -> VPN Device ICMP Echo request
```

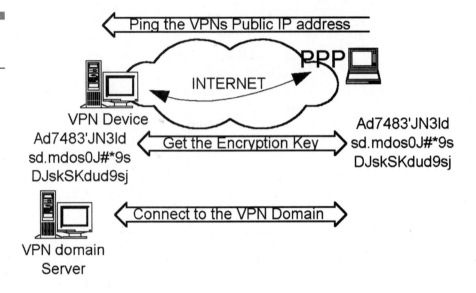

You need someone on the VPN device because for security reasons VPN devices may not send an ICMP reply back to the laptop. If you are monitoring the VPN device with a packet sniffer, you will see the packet come in and know the laptop is at least on the Internet and able to route to the VPN device.

The next step is to get the key of the VPN device. On the laptop there will be a button labeled Update, Fetch Key, or the like. On the laptop you should see something similar to the following:

```
Remote Laptop -> VPN Device TCP D=258 S=1052 Syn Seq=467 8929 Len=0
Win=8192
VPN Device -> Remote Laptop TCP D=1052 S=258 Syn Ack=467 8930
Seq=2170041381 Len=0 Win=9112
Remote Laptop -> VPN Device TCP D=258 S=1052  Ack=217 0041382
Seq=4678930 Len=0 Win=8576
Remote Laptop -> VPN Device TCP D=258 S=1052  Ack=217 0041382
Seq=4678930 Len=4 Win=8576
VPN Device -> Remote Laptop TCP D=1052 S=258  Ack=467 8934
Seq=2170041382 Len=0 Win=9112
Remote Laptop -> VPN Device TCP D=258 S=1052  Ack=217 0041382
Seq=4678934 Len=4 Win=8576
VPN Device -> Remote Laptop TCP D=1052 S=258  Ack=467 8938
Seq=2170041382 Len=4 Win=9112
Remote Laptop -> VPN Device TCP D=258 S=1052  Ack=217 0041386
Seq=4678938 Len=4 Win=8572
```

This indicates that the VPN is sending the encrypted key to the remote laptop. There is usually a GUI on the Win 95 station, and in that GUI

Figure 10-4
Laptop
authentication.

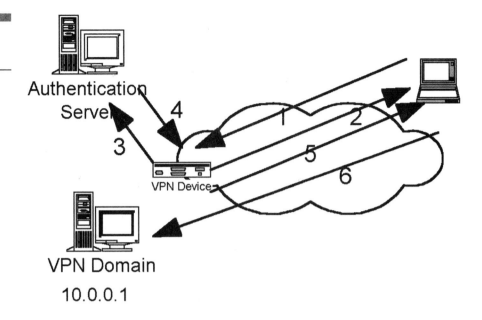

you will see a bunch of characters. That is the encryption key the laptop just received from the VPN device.

Once you get the key, the laptop is ready to establish the VPN communications. Now try to access the VPN domain device. In Figure 10-2, the VPN domain is 10.0.0.1 and the access we allowed was HTTP. On the laptop, start up a Web browser, and in the URL locator, type in http://10.0.0.1.

While you are monitoring the VPN device, you will see the encrypted packets coming in. First the VPN device will query the authentication server, then it will query the laptop for username and password, as illustrated in Figure 10-4. The events occur as follows:

1. The laptop tries to access the VPN Server at 10.0.0.1.

2. The VPN device queries the laptop for username and password.

3. If the VPN device has been set up to use an authentication server, it will query that server.

4. The server either grants or rejects the request.

5. The VPN device responds to the laptop with either a grant or deny access.

6. Finally, if access is granted, the laptop then can HTTP to the VPN server at 10.0.0.1.

As long as the laptop authentication succeeded, you can go to the next step. During this authentication step, check the logs on the authentication device, and/or VPN device, if there are messages, e.g., "User test denied access," you know your problem lies in the authentication mechanism. These types of errors occur due to wrong logins, wrong passwords, and time-outs between the authentication server. All these must be checked.

Figure 10-5 illustrates another problem with the authentication server process. On the top part of the figure, the RADIUS server has been placed further into the network on an FDDI ring. The authentication steps 1, 2, and 3 are completed, but there is a delay in step 4, (the grant or reject packet from the RADIUS server). The VPN device just times out waiting for the response and denies the inbound access to the laptop. The logs might be tricky to read in this situation: The RADIUS server will say that the user has been authenticated, but the VPN device might say that the user has been denied (the VPN implied this due to the time-out problem).

The second problem is with the RADIUS protocol itself. As you will read later, the RADIUS protocol has many packet types and attributes. If you configure the RADIUS device to use these attributes, but the VPN

Figure 10-5
Authentication
problems.

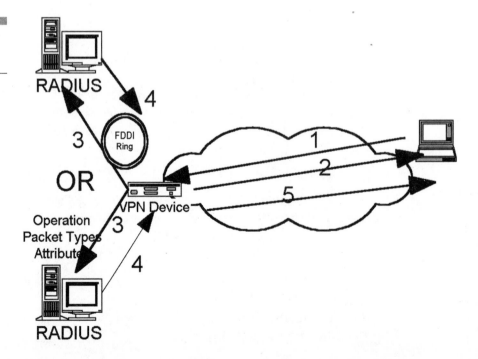

device doesn't handle all these aspects, either the RADIUS server or VPN device will just get confused and deny the login request. Therefore, whatever authentication device you plan to use, make sure your VPN device supports it.

If the authentication process succeeds, then by using the packet sniffer, you will see packets in the following format:

```
Remote Laptop -> VPN Device TCP D=260 S=260 LEN=687
Remote Laptop -> VPN Device TCP continuation ID=50180
VPN Device -> Remote Laptop TCP D=260 S=260 LEN=867
Remote Laptop -> VPN Device TCP D=260 S=260 LEN=209
VPN Device -> Remote Laptop TCP D=260 S=260 LEN=899
VPN Device -> Remote Laptop TCP D=260 S=260 LEN=899
Remote Laptop -> VPN Device TCP D=260 S=260 LEN=96
```

These are the encrypted incoming packets made by the laptop when they issue the command in their Web browser, http://10.0.0.1. Note that this particular vendor is using TCP Port 260 for both source and destination ports. Another vendor will mostly likely have other protocols and port numbers. The important thing is that you see these packets entering the VPN device.

On the other side of the device, you will see packets like:

```
VPN Device -> 10.0.0.1 80 port=33026
10.0.0.1 -> VPN Device 80 port=33026
VPN Device -> 10.0.0.1 80 port=33026
VPN Device -> 10.0.0.1 80 port=33026
10.0.0.1 -> VPN Device 80 port=33026
10.0.0.1 -> VPN Device 80 port=33026
```

This is an indication that the laptop made the VPN connection; the VPN device decrypted it properly and sent the request to the Web server.

The last data stream you would see is something like:

```
VPN Device -> Remote Laptop TCP D=260 S=260 LEN=867
Remote Laptop -> VPN Device TCP D=260 S=260 LEN=209
```

This is the public side of the VPN device returning the packet to the laptop.

The remote dial-in users configuration is by far the most common VPN application that exists today and will continue to grow. With this setup all your remote users will be able conduct business from remote offices, customer sites, and so on. Until now, if a salesperson needed a particular document, he or she would need someone to email it. Then the salesperson would have to ask the customer if he or she has a dial-up line that the salesperson could use to retrieve the document. With the remote client VPN setup, that has all changed; every company has or will have Internet access. Therefore, all users would have to do is plug into a jack and retrieve the document from a server on their company's network (of course, assuming a DHCP or some addressing scheme is set up).

LAN-to-LAN VPN

We now move into the next-most-common configuration, the LAN-to-LAN VPN configuration. The LAN-to-LAN VPN is actually closely tied to the IPSec standard being developed. IPSec, which will be discussed later, came from the Automotive Network Exchange (ANX). The goal was to connect multiple vendors, suppliers, and customers and exchange data safely. Where the remote dial-up user VPN uses protocols such as PPTP, L2F, and L2TP, IPSec concentrates on LAN-to-LAN.

Figure 10-6 illustrates a typical LAN-to-LAN VPN. Notice that not all traffic is encrypted. You will also notice the arrow is simply labeled "VPN" instead of "tunnel." If you encapsulate the data, you create a tunnel; however, a VPN can simply be encryption. Two types of communications are involved:

1. *Web server access.* When User B wants to connect to the Web server on User's A network, it is simply HTTP unencrypted traffic. The VPN device should not encrypt this traffic; it should flow untouched.

2. *VPN server access.* When User A wants to connect to the VPN server at User B's network, the VPN device should recognize that this is a VPN request and encrypt the packets.

Figure 10-6
LAN-to-LAN VPN.

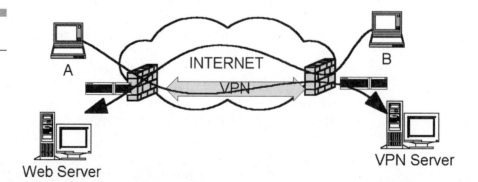

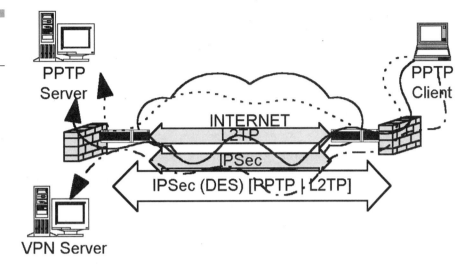

Figure 10-7
Various VPN
protocols.

You will also notice that I've left off any protocols in Figure 10-6. Now compare that to Figure 10-7 and its associated protocols. From Figure 10-7, you can see why I first showed you Figure 10-6. There are many ways to set up a VPN, with many different protocols. PPTP and L2TP are layer 2 protocols, and IPSec is a layer 3 protocol. You can therefore combine the two. If you combine them, however, problems can occur in either protocol. Before you can troubleshoot these protocols, you first need to know how to set these systems up. In the following sections, we will take a closer look at PPTP and L2TP. Then we will look at how to troubleshoot them.

PPTP VPN

Point-to-Point Protocol was designed to allow remote users to dial into their local ISPs and then tunnel their way to the company server. In this case it would be a Win 95 PPTP client tunneling to a PPTP server on the company's network. PPTP used the existing infrastructure protocols to allow for dial-up connection, namely PPP. PPTP then takes these PPP packets and encapsulates them inside of a Generic Routing Encapsulation (GRE) Header. Because of the reliance on PPP, PPTP uses encryption algorithms such as PAP and CHAP to provide the encryption. PPTP also uses Microsoft's Point-to-Point Encryption (MPPE) to provide for encryption. Due to the availability of PPTP on NT stations and the installed user base, PPTP is a VPN protocol. PPTP comes in two configurations: compulsory mode and voluntary mode.

Compulsory Mode

A compulsory mode PPTP session uses the services of an ISP with a PPTP front-end processor, as shown in Figure 10-8. Compulsory modes are made with the help of a NAS. No PPTP software is needed on the client. Any communication problems in a dial-up connection to the ISP is handled by the PPP protocol; therefore, any troubleshooting on the laptop would be dial-up networking configurations. Because compulsory modes are created without the user's knowledge, when troubleshooting these kinds of problems, you may need the help of the local ISP you are dialing into. They also restrict the users from accessing other parts of the Internet.

Voluntary Mode

Voluntary mode is where the clients established the PPTP connection straight to the PPTP server on the other side of the network to create the tunnel, as shown in Figure 10-9. In this case the ISP is out of the picture. In troubleshooting, you first need to make sure you can access the Internet. Then you should follow the troubleshooting procedures as described in the "Remote Dial-In Users" section earlier in the chapter.

Figure 10-8
Compulsory mode.

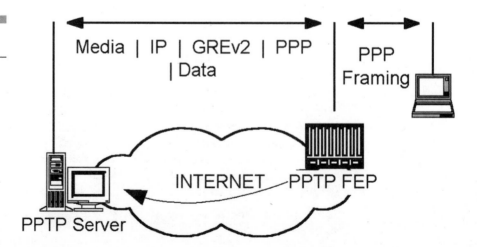

Media | IP | GREv2 | PPP | Data

PPP Framing

INTERNET — PPTP FEP

PPTP Server

Figure 10-9
Voluntary mode.

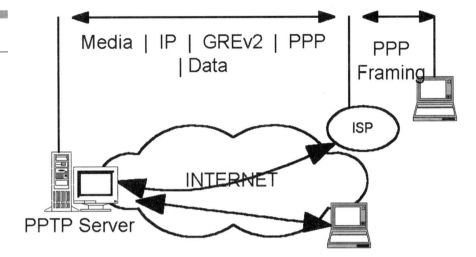

In voluntary mode PPTP, there is no longer a requirement for an ISP FEP. Connections are made straight to the PPTP server on the corporation's LAN. The laptop troubleshooting here would be that of the PPP setup communications. In addition, this form of PPTP allows a machine on the Internet to access the PPTP server without the services of a PPP connection.

In either PPTP setup, you need to understand the terminology of how PPTP establishes a connection in order to effectively troubleshoot them.

PPP Data Communication

PPP Data Communication is the initial communication needed for the laptop to connect to the ISP. The remote PPTP-enabled client connects to the ISP using encrypted PPTP datagrams and authenticates the user. PPP encapsulates all non-TCP protocols, such as IPX and NetBEUI, within these PPP frames.

PPTP Control Connections

Once the PPP protocol establishes the connection, the PPTP protocol establishes the connection between the PPTP client and the PPTP server. It uses the TCP protocol to establish what is known as the PPTP tunnel. These control messages, shown in Table 10-1 are helpful in troubleshooting PPTP connections.

TABLE 10-1

Control Messages.

Message Type	Meaning
PPTP_START_SESSION_REQUEST	Start session
PPTP_START_SESSION_REPLY	Replies to request
PPTP_ECHO_REQUEST	Maintain the session
PPTP_ECHO_REPLY	Replies to maintain session
PPTP_WAN_ERROR_NOTIFY	A PPP link error has occurred on the connection
PPTP_SET_LINK_INFO	Configures the connection between PPTP client Server
PPTP_STOP_SESSION_REQUEST	End the PPTP session
PPTP_STOP_SESSION_REPLY	Replies
WAN-Error-Notify	Errors on WAN PPP interface

Within these control messages are additional error codes that are helpful for troubleshooting. Start-Control-Connection-Reply, for example, has a list of result codes that add additional information for troubleshooting, as shown here:

1. Successful channel establishment.

2. General error—Error code indicates the problem.

3. Command channel already exists.

4. Requester is not authorized to establish a command channel.

5. The protocol version of the requester is not supported.

WAN-Error-Notify is a list of error control messages sent from the PPTP Access Concentrator (PAC) to the PPTP Network Server (PNS) to indicate error conditions on the WAN link. If you are having intermittent PPTP problem, keep an eye on these counters. They may indicate you are having WAN problems rather than PPTP problems. The error conditions are as follows:

■ *CRC errors.* The number of PPP frames received with CRC since the beginning of the session

■ *Framing errors.* The number of badly formatted framed PPP packets

■ *Hardware overruns.* The number of hardware receive buffer overruns since the beginning of the session

- *Buffer overruns.* The number of buffer overruns since the beginning of the session
- *Time-out errors.* The number of time-outs since the beginning of the session
- *Alignment errors.* The number of alignment errors

PPTP Data Tunneling

PPTP Data Tunneling is the final stage of transmission, where the PPTP protocol forms the PPP packets that have the PPTP encrypted packets and sends them to the PPTP server. The PPTP server then decrypts these packets and sends them to the intended hosts.

PPTP communications depend on the type of mode you are using, either voluntary or compulsory, so the troubleshooting would depend on how the control connections are set. In the case of compulsory mode, the ISP FEP (front-end processor) handles the PPTP communications. In the case of voluntary mode, the laptop itself handles the PPTP control messages. A typical set of steps to handle PPTP communications are as follows:

1. The laptop makes a PPP dial-in account to an ISP or an ISP with FTP.
2. The FEP would signal to the PPTP server with a PPTP_Start_Session_Request, and the server would reply with a PPTP_Start_Session_Reply.
3. The FEP then sends a call request to the PPTP server.
4. The server sends back a call reply to the FEP.
5. The data communication begins.
6. Finally, a PPTP_Stop_Session_Request is sent and a PPTP_Stop_Session_Reply is received. (See Figure 10-10.)

Before we close our discussion of PPTP troubleshooting, there is one more area we need to look at: the PPTP server behind a firewall, as shown in Figure 10-11. In Figure 10-11, we are using PPTP communication through a firewall; however, without configuring the firewall to pass the right packets, the PPTP communication will never take place. PPTP uses IP Protocol 47, which is the GRE protocol, and TCP Port 1723 or TCP Port 5678. Port 1723 is for Microsoft's PPTP service.

Figure 10-10
Control messages.

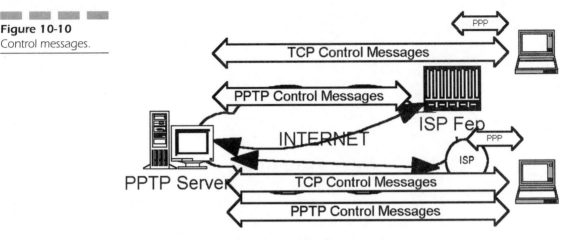

GENERAL NOTE PPTP is not confined to one port. To best troubleshoot PPTP problems through a firewall, monitor the logs of the firewall. You will see something like "Rule 5...Drop...TCP...575....Log." If you are trying to troubleshoot, this will tell you that your PPTP connection is trying to come in on Port 575.

PPTP has a lot of areas where problems could occur—not in the protocol itself, but in the infrastructure that makes it work (e.g., the firewall, the FEP, the PPP connection). When troubleshooting PPTP, you first need to isolate how far the packets are progressing. If you are monitoring the firewall and don't even see PPTP control connections coming in, the problems lie from the ISP FEP to the laptop itself.

Figure 10-11
PPTP through a
firewall.

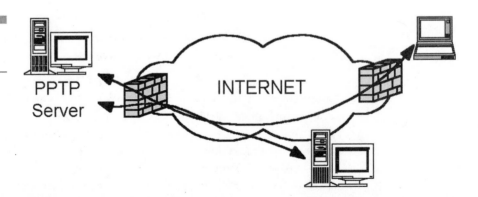

L2TP VPN

Layer 2 Tunneling Protocol (a combination of L2F and PPTP) is basically the same as PPTP. L2TP relies on PPP to establish a dial-up connection, but unlike PPTP, it defines its own tunneling protocol. It uses the PPP (PAP and CHAP) for user authentication, and since it's a layer 2 protocol, it allows for transportation on non-IP protocols. Figure 10-12 illustrates a typical dial-up L2TP VPN.

A L2TP VPN setup is very similar to the PPTP setup. The data packets include the initial PPP communications, and PPP can be used for the encrypted packets. L2TP is independent of the media, so you can use L2TP over ATM, FRAME, or IP. You will also notice that the PPTP server has been replaced by an L2TP server, and the ISP PPTP FEP has been replaced by an L2TP Access Concentrator. The L2TP VPN allows for multiple connections inside the tunnel and assigns a unique Call ID for each session inside the tunnel. Like PPTP, L2TP defines messages types. They are as follows:

- *Control.* The control messages are responsible for such things as setup, teardown, management of the sessions, and the status of the tunnel. Control messages are also used to maintain characteristics inside the tunnel, such as maintaining flow control and determining transmission rates and buffering parameters for the PPP packets for individual sessions.

- *Data.* The data messages are the PPP packet without the framing information.

Figure 10-12
L2TP VPN.

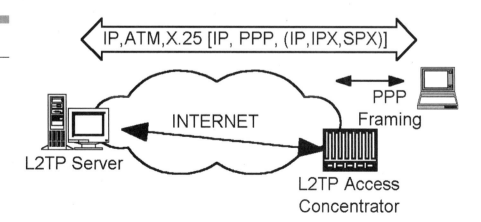

TABLE 10-2

*L2TP Control
Messages.*

Message Type	Meaning
Start-Control-Connection-Request	Start session
Start-Control-Connection-Reply	Replies to request
Start-Control-Connection-Connected	Response to reply; finishes handshaking of tunnel setup
Stop-Control-Connection-Notification	Closes control connection
HelloTunnel	Keep-Alive
Outgoing-Call-Request	LNS informs LAC an outbound call is to be established
Outgoing-Call-Reply	Reply from LAC

L2TP uses the same modes found in PPTP (voluntary and compulsory) and has its own list of control messages, as shown in Table 10-2. In addition, L2TP uses special terminology to define the endpoints where communication begins and ends. An L2TP Access Concentrator (LAC) communicates with a L2TP Network Server (LNS) to control connections.

In addition, the L2TP draft, draft-ietf-pppext-l2tp-12.txt, specifies some general messages that can be useful in troubleshooting:

0—No general error

1—No control connection exists yet for this LAC-LNS pair

2—Length is wrong

3—One of the field values was out of range or reserved field was nonzero

4—Insufficient resources to handle this operation now

5—The Call ID is invalid in this context

6—A generic vendor-specific error occurred in the LAC

7—Try another. If LAC is aware of other possible LNS destinations, it should try one of them. This can be used to guide an LAC based on LNS policy, for instance, the existence of multilink PPP bundles.

Passing L2TP through a firewall is easier than PPTP. L2TP uses UDP Port 1701; the entire payload and header is sent in a UDP datagram. Recipients can choose whatever port they like, and since they are not using GRE, IP Protocol 47 is not needed on the firewall. Troubleshooting L2TP VPNs are very similar to troubleshooting PPTP VPNs, since they either make use of an ISP (LAC or FEP) or an end server (PPTP server or LNS). Knowing the various controls messages available in the drafts and RFCs helps a great deal in troubleshooting VPN problems.

IPSec VPN

The Internet Security Protocol (IPSec) VPN could wind up being very difficult to troubleshoot. In a later chapter, I will again discuss the IPSec standard, but for now, realize that IPSec is supposed to be synonymous with interoperability. The problem is that by leaving room for interoperability, many vendors can choose their own route, which may mean interoperability problems. In the PPTP and L2TP VPNs, there are control messages, communication messages, and so on that can help you determine where the problems lie. In IPSec these message don't exist, at least not in the same detail as the other algorithms that are meant to assist in setting up and maintaining the VPN. However, the trade-off is that IPSec has IPv6 built into it, and IPSec offers more security than the other protocols. IPSec uses several technologies for establishing and therefore troubleshooting the VPN:

- Diffie-Hellman key exchange
- Digital signatures
- DES encryption
- Keyed hash algorithms
- Security Association (SA)
- Domain of Interpretation (DOI)

The major troubleshooting problems you will have in IPSec VPNs is in the Domain of Interpretation (DOI). DOI is a grouping of related protocols that are used in establishing a particular Security Association (SA). The Security Association is IPSec; since it will be vendor-specific, it can be the hardest to troubleshoot. The Security Association is that first step in establishing the IPSec VPN. Before any data transfers can begin, both parties must agree on an SA. The SA is very similar to a set of rules in a game (how long, how many players, who goes first, etc.). During an SA setup the following parameters are exchanged:

- The mode and keys used in the Authentication Header (AH)
- The mode and keys used in the Encapsulating Security Payload (ESP)

- How often to exchange keys
- Whether the data is in transport or tunnel mode
- What authentication protocols
- What encryption protocols
- The SA identifier
- The connection lifetime

As you can probably guess, the Security Association can be the biggest troublespot, since this is where the most data is being passed from one vendor to another.

GENERAL NOTE   In IPSec, a lot of communication is voluntary; that is, the receiver decides on the parameters being sent. Because of this, a receiver could either reject or accept the parameters for an SA.

IPSec is not a product, although a vendor could install an IPSec stack on a router, firewall, and so on. Figure 10-13 shows how you can apply the IPSec standards to create various tunnels on almost any device you have. However, with this flexibility comes interoperability problems. Every corporation that is connected to the Internet has some sort of firewall. You need to check whether it is a firewall or an IPSec problem, or for that matter, a problem with PPTP or L2TP.

Figure 10-13
IPSec tunnels.

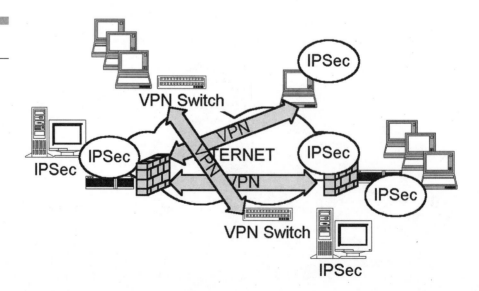

In my own experience, log file messages like the following all point to problems with the encryption algorithms and/or properties that were set up on the VPN device (e.g., not being able to activate the tunnel, the tunnel already exists, you are using DES, or the end host is using something other than DES):

- Cannot decrypt header
- Cannot define methods for DES
- Cannot obtain SA data
- Failed to create secret key
- Certificate invalid
- Illegal encryption method
- Illegal method selected
- Unknown scheme
- Cannot get session key from cache
- Tunnel activation failed

In addition, the VPN device cannot accurately communicate with the other end with the algorithm provided. Much in the same way that the PPTP or L2TP control message pointed to a problem with the tunnel, these last messages point to the algorithm involved.

One last thing should be mentioned about PPTP, L2TP, and IPSec: they are still under development. It's important to note that as these protocols are being developed, the partners you set up VPNs with will change; therefore, you cannot easily adjust your parameters to new VPN tunnels.

Figure 10-14 shows a very common scenario that exists and that will continue to grow. It is the very simple process of adding LAN-to-LAN VPNs, regardless of the protocols used. Assume you are using the SKIPv1 protocol as your key-management protocol, and you set up a tunnel with another LAN on January 1, 1998. Now during the first 6 months, everything is working fine. Then on June 1, you decide that you want to add another LAN connection, but the new VPN device is configured to use SKIPv2. How would you then configure the VPN device on the original system? Upgrade to SKIPv2 and have problems with SKIPv1, or upgrade all sites to SKIPv2?

SKIP is just one protocol I mentioned; you can use the same scenario with any protocol. The point is, with VPN technology still in its infancy and survey after survey suggesting LAN-to-LAN VPNs will increase in

Figure 10-14
VPN tunnels.

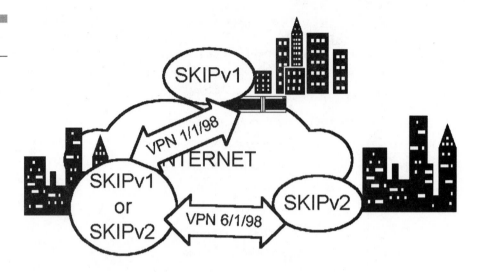

number, this situation will continue to grow. As the VPN administrator, you will have to keep an accurate eye on this.

GENERAL NOTE   Don't upgrade your VPN device without first checking the connections you have.

Any VPN device that you have that is connected via LAN-to-LAN is a two-way street, as indicated by Figure 10-14. The parameters to communicate between the two devices are set up at the initial configuration. If for some reason you have to upgrade the VPN device, you may stop communications between the devices. During the next few years, there will be many products that use VPN services. Say, for example, you have a firewall/VPN-based device. If you upgrade the firewall to fix one problem, you may cause problems with the VPN stack on the firewall. If you need to upgrade the device, first look at all the tunnels you have created and try to coordinate the upgrade with someone who can help you in troubleshooting problems as necessary.

Multihoned Firewall/VPN

Multihoned firewall/VPNs are firewalls with DMZ zones on them, and in addition to running the firewall code, they are also doing routing, encryption/decryption, and possibly network address translation. In

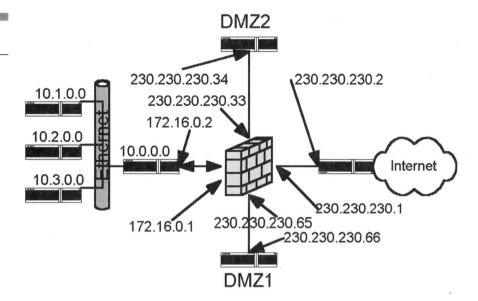

Figure 10-15
Firewall-based VPN.

Chapter 8, we went through a typical firewall/VPN configuration, but we did not cover how to troubleshoot it. In this section, we will go through the troubleshooting techniques that accompany the setup. This setup is one of the most common and most difficult—and by *difficult,* I mean in its complexity, not in its technical difficulty. Figure 10-15 shows a firewall-based VPN.

This illustration is similar to the one presented back in Chapter 8. In that chapter I showed you how to set up a rule-based policy to allow for the VPN traffic. In this section I want to concentrate first on the firewall itself and the VPN. You will also notice I've introduced three new routers in this figure (10.1.0.0, 10.2.0.0, and 10.3.0.0). Before we go into troubleshooting, we need to make sure that the routing policy is correct on all the devices. The internal network has been addressed according to RFC 1918 and given a 10 network address subnetted to a Class B:

1. All the routers in the organization have to be set up to route to 172.16.0.0 network. You'll recall that because of the variable-length subnet masking (VLSM) problem, we have to introduce another network or route all networks on the firewall back to the internal routers.

2. The routers (10.0.0.0, 10.1.0.0, 10.2.0.0, and 10.3.0.0) all have to have a default policy that points out to 172.16.0.1. The firewall's internal IP address is 172.16.0.1, and it will take care of any packets that are destined to the Internet by a routing policy that is installed on it.

3. The firewall has to have a routing policy that has a default route out to the external router at (230.230.230.2) and has an internal router for network 10 that points to the internal router's address at 172.16.0.2.

4. The external router has to know what packets to route back to the firewall (the router does not need to know about any private address space, just public). In the example, we are assuming that 230.230.230.0 is the public address given to the company and used on the firewall.

   Note: Depending on how the external address is set up on the router, you may need to route the subnets also to the firewall IP address.

5. Depending on how you are using NAT, you may also need another route on the router. For example, is you are using the firewall-external router address range (230.230.230.1-31), then you do not need another route on the external router, since it is directly connected to that network. If you obtained new public address space to use for NAT, then you will need to specify a route on the external router, pointing that network to the firewall's interface.

Once this configuration is set up, you should try routing from any internal host to the Internet, and from the firewall to any internal host. You can't route from the external router to the internal network, since that would mean you are trying to route to a 10 network, which is illegal. This step has to be accomplished first, and this must succeed. If it doesn't, no internal VPN can be established. Now let's add a couple more components to the picture, as in Figure 10-16.

In Figure 10-16 I've introduced some more components that are typical of a corporation's network infrastructure. If you are wondering why we're spending time on this configuration, first, I often find that supposed "VPN problems" are actually routing and NAT problems that are implemented on a firewall/VPN device. Second, there is nothing stopping you from creating a PPTP VPN on the SMTP server. If you want someone to access your SMTP server via PPTP to retrieve some confidential mail, that's a VPN configuration setup.

The additional components are as follows:

- Web Server 2 (172.17.0.2)
- SMTP Server (10.2.0.1)
- Web Server (230.230.230.67)
- DNS Server (10.1.0.1)

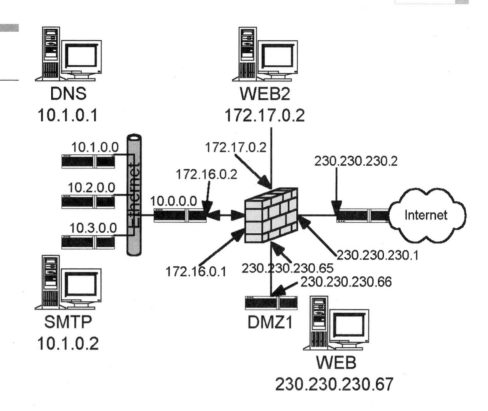

Figure 10-16
Additional
components.

I've changed the addressing around on the DMZ2 interface so you can see how NAT/routing and VPN technology work together. Let's look at each server and what is needed to get them functioning.

Web Server (230.230.230.67)

The Web server's address is 230.230.230.67, which is part of the subnet that one leg of the firewall/VPN interface is set to. There is not much to do here except for making sure that the firewall/VPN is subnetting the 230.230.230.0 network and that there are rules to allow HTTP traffic to flow to the Web server.

Web Server 2 (172.17.0.2)

We created a private address space on the DMZ2 zone; however, people on the Internet cannot route to this device. So the first thing you must do is to assign a valid Internet address to this Web server. Looking back at Figure 10-16, note that the subnet 230.230.230.0, is between the external interface of the firewall/VPN and the Ethernet connection of the external router. Since this subnet consists of 32 IP addresses (.0 for the network address, .31 for the broadcast, .1 for the firewall, and .2 for the router), we have an additional 28 IP addresses to use (32−4). So let's use 230.230.230.3 for this Web server. The translation would look like this:

```
172.17.0.2 <- -> 230.230.230.3
```

When individuals try to connect to that Web server, they will send the packet to http://230.230.230.3 and it will come into the external router. However, the router will not know what to do with it. In a typical communication, the router needs the MAC address of the device at 230.230.230.3 to send the packet to it, so it issues an ARP request. Because there is no device at 230.230.230.3, the firewall/VPN device has to specify that address to the external router. Devices on a network are allowed to have multiple IP addresses but only one MAC address, so if this were a UNIX machine, you would issue a command something like this:

```
ARP -s 230.230.230.3 XX:XX:XX:XX:XX:XX
```

where XX:XX:XX:XX:XX:XX is the MAC address of the firewall. The router will now ARP for the IP address of 230.230.230.3, and the firewall will respond, telling the router it is that address. The router will forward that packet to the firewall, and then the firewall will translate that packet to 172.17.0.2 and (after checking its rules policy) send it to the Web server.

DNS Server (10.1.0.1) and SMTP Server (10.2.0.1)

The DNS and the SMTP server are very similar to the Web server at 172.17.0.2. The steps needed are as follows:

1. Assign a public address for them.

2. Set up a translation rule in the firewall.

3. Have the firewall ARP on their behalf.

4. Set up rules on the firewall to allow the traffic to pass.

Now if want to connect a VPN connect to these devices, say for example, your Web server at (230.230.230.3/172.17.0.2), you would have to follow the same guidelines developed back in Chapter 8 in our firewall/VPN model. The steps are as follows:

1. Generate the firewall/VPN keys.
2. Pick the encryption scheme.
3. Assign or generate the certificates.
4. Set up a VPN domain.
5. Set up rules to allow traffic directed at the Web server to be encrypted.
6. Set up user authentication schemes.

As mentioned, a firewall/VPN device is a very common VPN setup, and the multihoned firewall is another very common combination. When troubleshooting this particular setup, understanding how the data flows from one point to another is the only way to effectively resolve problems.

Conclusion

This chapter covered two of the most common troubleshooting areas in VPN connectivity: the remote laptop VPN and the LAN-to-LAN VPN. As you can see, there are many other network objects that can interfere with the establishment of the VPN. Something that was assumed to be a VPN problem could likely turn out to be something else.

In troubleshooting VPNs, the most important step is isolation—determining where the data stops. As mentioned in an earlier section, the encryption algorithms themselves are often a major problem in VPN connectivity. Included in this chapter was a list of error messages that might point to VPN encryption problems (e.g., cannot obtain SA data, failed to create secret key, certificate invalid). A lot of these are initial connection problems that have to be worked out. In troubleshooting VPN tunnels, it is a very good idea to monitor any kind of counter that is available with your specific vendor, such as WAN_Error_Notify in the PPTP protocol.

The last item we looked at was the multihoned firewall/VPN device. Now that this model has been discussed in Chapters 8 and 10, you can see how much you have to consider in effectively troubleshooting this type of device. The firewall/VPN device balances flexibility with complexity, but it allows a VPN configuration to be set up by placing VPN code on the firewall. The firewall/VPN device is considered a software VPN, and because some literature states that hardware devices are faster than software devices, you need to examine them all before deciding on anything.

One last thing on troubleshooting VPNs: You need as much information as possible on such items as log files, multiple windows into the device, packet data sniffers, and multiple parties involved, since you may have to monitor the VPN device while someone tries to create a VPN tunnel. In troubleshooting VPNs, there is no such thing as too much of a good thing. Get as much data as possible.

11

Maintaining a VPN

By now, we have seen implementation of VPNs, requirements, components, and so on. Each chapter so far has brought about new components that need to be looked at and maintained. While some components may not have been specifically mentioned, it should be understood that you don't implement technology without having a way to maintain it.

Here is an example of maintenance: You install a database for internal employees, and you monitor the machine. Over time your internal employee base grows to the point where your internal employee base is too large for your original database. Now you need a second database, but you need to connect it to your original database. Such things as payroll and reporting still come from your original database. Your maintenance plan for your original database did not include room for growth, or it did and management did nothing about it. Now you have a monster of a headache to deal with. Most likely you now will bite the bullet, throw tons of money into it, and experience massive downtime as you move to the new database.

In this chapter we will look at all those things that make the maintenance of VPNs a particular problem. Just looking at the table of contents should reveal that the maintenance requirements are a little higher than other types of network devices. However, what's included in other maintenance procedures still applies to VPNs.

Introduction

Like any other network device, VPNs need maintenance, but unlike any other network device, VPNs should not be considered a "one-device" item. Even if you are using a stand-alone black-box type of configuration, a VPN takes a lot more maintenance than other devices. When you install your VPN, you set up tunnels, create user access databases, and install encryption and key-management schemes. You probably will also install some type of monitoring and alerting software, and probably some type of user authentication server like a RADIUS server. VPNs should be considered very dynamic in nature. Figure 11-1 shows just some of the maintenance requirements of VPNs.

A VPN device can and will break down and disconnect you from the Internet if that is your only way out. However, with today's high-tech devices, you are looking at mean time to repair (MTTR) in terms of years instead of months. Therefore, your maintenance requirements of VPN technology will fall into the support infrastructure, like user and

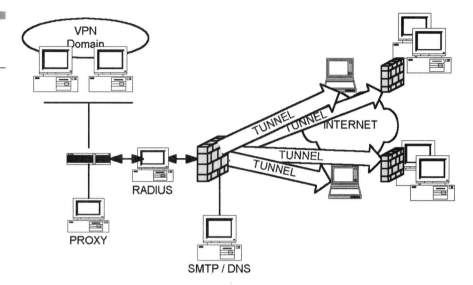

Figure 11-1
Maintenance
requirements.

data authentication, security, key management, and so on. I prefer to think of VPN technology as a concept that has many attributes, and each one of these attributes needs to be maintained. This chapter will look at those things that will make your VPN secure and those things that you need to maintain in order to utilize the full range of features that are available with the technology.

Redundant Links

Redundant links were described back in Chapter 3. In Figures 11-2 and 11-3, we can see two of the many options available for an organization.

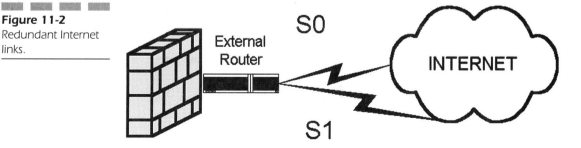

Figure 11-2
Redundant Internet
links.

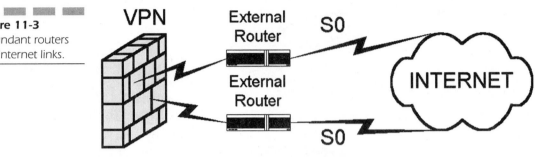

They are both redundant, but the level of redundancy changes for each setup. If you are not using a queuing mechanism on the routers, then most likely one is the primary Internet connection, and a secondary link is installed in case of primary failure.

Looking at these two diagrams, you can see how easily the network architecture can begin to get complicated. Also, there is a big difference between redundancy and single point of failure. Redundancy is just the process of backing up a main line. Redundancy is "assumed" (i.e., no single point of failure). No single point of failure is illustrated in Figure 11-4.

Figure 11-4 adds another layer of complexity to the connection, but it also adds in safeguards. This 24x7 setup is considered mandatory for many organizations where downtime is not acceptable. You will now need something or someone to monitor this setup. I have seen many situations where this worked as planned, but with one catch. One device would fail over, but there is no signaling mechanism for the failed

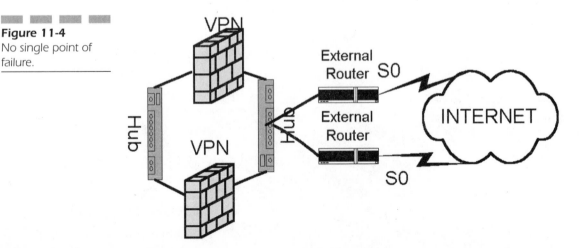

device. No one is alerted that it failed, then the standby failed and all outbound access is denied. In earlier chapters we discussed how the complicated network design is pushed off to ISPs, but since this design is on your premises, it's your concern. Now who has responsibility for taking care of this complicated design? Just by looking at these past three figures, you can see how the network design begins to grow in complexity. And, of course, the design is not fool-proof; the internal hub, the internal FDDI ring, and any switches in between could go down. When a company's requirement is "no single point of failure," is that what they really mean? You have to be sure. Now, depending on the redundancy you've built, your maintenance requirements can be calculated.

SECURITY NOTE   Each link that you build for redundancy adds another way into your company.

Growth in Your Organization

While organizations grow, the Internet traffic that your organization realizes will undoubtedly increase much faster than your physical network infrastructure can carry. Survey after survey predicts over 200 million users on the Internet by the turn of the century. Yet there is only so much room that your physical space can occupy for network equipment (e.g., routers, hubs, switches and other equipment). When the Internet traffic starts growing at unbounded rates, whose responsibility in your organization will it be to handle these new networking needs? Faster switches will be needed to replace the older switches, more powerful routers will be required, and bigger bandwidth pipes—or multiple pipes—will be needed to your ISP. What about the number of tunnels that can be presently established and the number of licenses that are in effect today? While they may be enough now, they will not be in the future. Can you easily upgrade a license to allow more users and add more tunnel capability to your VPN device? Can you add another device in parallel to handle this new load? Or will your organization be bounded by the existing hardware and need to upgrade everything?

Your Web site will also see increased traffic. Just having a presence on the Internet, along with the number of search engines available, will increase your bandwidth needs. You may think that your requirements don't require a larger pipe to your ISP, but if potential customers have to wait to see your URL, they most likely will go somewhere else. There are hundreds of suppliers for any product, and the longer customers are waiting for your Web page to load, the more likely they will go to another supplier.

Now add to this all the outbound Web traffic and the amount of SMTP and DNS traffic that passes, and you easily can get a feel for the amount of traffic generated. You can easily look on a router and see the utilization of that link. You also can get a packet analyzer to determine packet sizes and the amount of utilization. In addition, individual vendors will provide the various packet sizes that their encryption technologies add to the amount of traffic. With this information you can logically calculate the amount of bandwidth your company may need.

Software Updates

Operating Systems VPNs

Software updates can be a multistep process that will probably need support from several vendors, if you decide to take the route of operating system, firewall/VPN-based VPN service. Take for example the model in Chapter 8, the firewall/VPN device configuration. In that setup, you have an operating system, which contains a certain revision of software and a certain patch revision specifically for that system. Then add to that the actual firewall code, along with its latest patch revision. Then comes the VPN software, which can be added to the firewall product or as a program to the operating system. Considering this firewall/VPN is a security product, you should either have it password protected or implement a 2-factor authentication process that again adds another layer to the device. Now add any kind of device monitoring, web content filtering, and antivirus or intrusion detection software you would like to have. Now you can see how many pieces of software that will have to be looked at and examined.

It is well known that all operating systems, at one time or another, have a problem with security issues, but now you have to keep track of them. The VPN vendor will probably be responsible for their software, but they cannot be responsible for the operating system that you are taking care of. The operating system vendor should be responsible for their operating system, but look at your contracts carefully. Are operating system upgrades free? I doubt it.

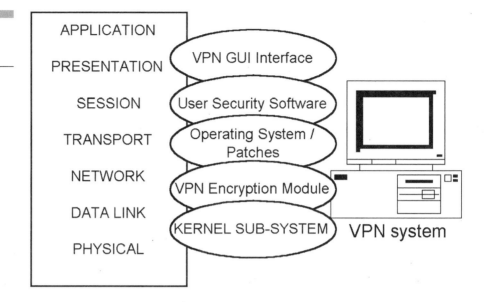

Figure 11-5
Layered VPN software concerns.

Now take all these software layers and try to imagine all the possible communication and security issues that concern each one. Think about all the vulnerabilities that each one could develop. As Figure 11-5 illustrates, each application lies on top of the previous one; therefore, if you upgrade one application, you must think about the one on top. With a typical server, if there is an incompatibility, you can back out of the upgrade, take the system off-line, and so on. With security servers, you have to know immediately, lest you give an individual an opportunity window to enter your network.

Figure 11-5 clearly illustrates the interoperability problems you could face on the VPN device. Starting from the application layer down to the data-link layer, many interoperability issues arise. One reason why black-box VPNs have an advantage is the lack of levels of software needed on these devices. However, the trade-off is flexibility, and this setup has vulnerabilities of its own.

SECURITY NOTE While it may appear that operating systems have more vulnerabilities than their black-box counterparts, with operating system VPN devices, the vulnerabilities are found and information is distributed quickly. Since black-box vendors' operating systems are proprietary, they may not be so anxious to divulge their vulnerabilities. Just a note to be made aware of, not an indication of conscious effort.

Black-Box VPNs

When using black-box VPNs you are faced with a double-edged sword. First, the underlying operating system is proprietary, which means you probably won't be able to add any features you desire unless the vendors support it. This is not to imply that vendors don't try to support the main features that customers want, but every requirement you need may not be supported, so you really must establish your requirements first. You also may have limited knowledge of the security of the system—the vulnerabilities, holes, and buffer overflow problems. You also have to rely on the manufacturers themselves to be forthcoming with the necessary security information, and then make the available updates and patches to that system. If a fix to a major security problem requires a major operating system upgrade, hopefully you wouldn't be charged for it. You need to establish this up front.

The other side of the coin is that since the operating system is proprietary to the manufacturer, it may be a very secure one, if for no other reason than lack of interest of potential hackers and lack of publicly available documentation. There are thousands of books written on UNIX and Windows operating systems, and with that comes knowledge and ideas. Most vendors also try making their operating systems as slimmed down as possible. They first optimize the system for the specific task at hand, usually working on the basic functionality first, and then they probably make it very secure. However, when customers start demanding more and more features for those types of products, holes can be developed. So it is a good idea to keep ahead of security problems in general.

Onsite Technical Support

As mentioned, VPN technology is not only a technically complex technology with regard to encryption algorithms and authentication schemes, it is also complex in that it interacts a great deal with other network devices. This being the case, onsite technical support may be needed in certain situations. If you have an operating system-based VPN, the support task may be easier. You control the operating system, and most organizations have the talent in house to deal with those issues that arise with operating system-based VPNs.

With black-box VPNs you usually don't have the expertise in-house, so you usually have to rely solely on that particular vendor who manufactured that device, or on the consulting firm that installed it. Now concerning black-box VPNs, the vendor may or may not be able to remotely manage the device, which means you have to make support plans. If you are not installing a managed service VPN, then someone needs to configure and maintain the VPN. Some black-box vendors support remote management, some don't; you just need to be aware of that and give your IT staff the needed resources.

Troubles usually arise when those intermittent problems appear. You really need to understand the data flows, as shown in the topology diagrams in the last few chapters. In this case, it would help if another set of eyes were able to look at the problem. As mentioned earlier, think of VPNs as a system; that way you will approach the problems as potential system problems.

GENERAL NOTE   I cannot emphasize enough that so many problems I deal with involving VPNs are not VPN problems, but routing problems, network address translation problems, setup problems, and configuration problems. Only a small percentage are VPN problems, such as encryption keys not being in sync.

Telephone Support

Telephone support is another one of those things you don't think about until later. What happens 80 percent of the time is that you decide on a VPN product and get all the necessary procedures and requirements in place. You hire out the expertise or install the system yourself, and then finally you get the device in. You configure it for a couple of features and then you forget about it and concentrate on doing other system and network tasks. Finally, you now need to add another feature, create additional tunnels, or implement some security or user authentication process on your VPN device, and your 90-day free telephone support is up. Or your consultant is long gone, since the original task has been completed.

Try not to get caught in this situation. Get a longer telephone support contract, if possible, or at least have all the requirements in place when you are ready to go. If it takes 3 months to get everything ready, the investment would be worthwhile. Then try to try and get all the necessary players back together again. If you need to call your consultant back in, you may get a different one who first has to look over your particular situation and try to come up reasons why things were done a certain way. It will take some time for the learning curve.

Help Desk Support to Remote Users

In many articles about VPNs, there is an emphasis on pushing off the help desk functions to ISPs and the vendors who sold you the product. From a realistic point of view, if there is a problem, your organization is going to get the calls from angry end users who cannot get their work done. If you are the manager in charge, you are going to get the brunt of email and upper-management complaints that want to know why this is happening. Irate remote users who cannot get into critical servers that they need will become frustrated and make your work environment very difficult.

Think about how help desk functionality is implemented now. Normally you have a user within close geographical range whom you can easily get to and resolve his or her problem. Now with remote users you have to dictate over the phone the steps they need to take. Normally when you get to a user machine, you take over, looking at the configuration files, setup, and so on. Now you are going to have to walk users through all this and be very patient. This means your organization is going to have to train its staff on how to handle these functions. Can you imagine trying to explain to end users the concepts of encryption, key management, and certificate authorities? Your local ISP will be responsible for getting them connected to their backbone, but beyond that, they have no responsibility to assist, unless, of course, they offer that as a service. So now your help desk not only has to handle internal users working remotely, but customers, suppliers, and vendors who you give authorization to access your data.

VPNs: Build or Buy?

You have the choice of whether to build or buy a VPN, but in many cases you also have the choice of how much you want to build or buy. Many ISPs offer services that help with the implementation of VPNs. They range from just supplying IP address space to the design and configuration of your access points, and networks to monitoring of your networks, and a whole set of services in between. You can select different levels of services, different support structures, and different maintenance contracts with your ISP. Of course, the more you subcontract to the ISP, the more the contract costs, but for many organizations, that is a viable and attractive alternative. You could also just farm out the configuration and installation to VPN subcontractors who are not ISPs; you may feel that they are less biased.

One thing to remember is that the more you outsource, the less control you have. Even with contractors, they retain the knowledge and experience. The trade-off again is that your staff will only do one VPN, whereas the ISP or contractor has done hundreds. So if you decide to go with the ISP, make sure you get guarantees on whatever you feel is necessary, and if you have contractors do all the work, make sure there are training sessions for your employees. When the contractor leaves, if your employees cannot handle the maintenance of the devices and something fails, you could be down for days.

Compatibility Issues

In your VPN setup you can have many protocols that will transverse your network and individual operating systems. In many organizations, there is usually some form of IP, IPX, SNA, NETBIOS, and so on types of traffic. Once you announce that your VPN will allow non-IP traffic from one site to another via the Internet, users will want those features. So make sure you decide from the beginning whether you need encapsulation and/or encryption and find out if your vendor supports that.

Compatibility issues also arise among the various ISPs, as shown in Figure 11-6. As mentioned, some ISPs block encrypted packets, so in troubleshooting these types of problems, it may be wise to get the ISP involved. In addition, if you want individual machines to use the functionality of the encryption, you may need to have drivers installed on their operating system. If you have a desktop machine that comes with a PPTP stack-type of encryption and you want to use some other kind (e.g., DES, 3DES), you would need to load some software to implement this encryption scheme. Is this new encryption software compatible with the software you have running already on the machine? This applies to the intra company VPN we discussed in earlier chapters. You may decide that PPTP is not secure enough for your internal data, so you will need to install a DES stack.

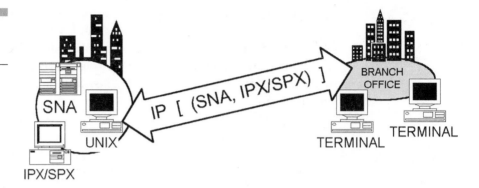

Figure 11-6
IPX, SNA VPN com-
patibility concerns.

Monitoring

Monitoring is a critical element of the overall VPN process, and it also may cause difficulties in implementation. Just think how much traffic you have coming in through this device. Back in Chapter 5 I showed you where you could place these devices. By looking at the placement, you can see the potential for the amount of traffic you would likely have to monitor. Now consider what type of traffic you want to monitor: only VPN traffic or all traffic flowing through the device? All VPN devices I have seen offer monitoring capabilities, but some offer "all traffic logging," and others offer "no traffic logging." If a vendor implements a feature with which you can monitor just some types of traffic, that means the device will have to look at all traffic and examine it. This means that all traffic, including SMTP, DNS, HTTP, and VPN, will be monitored and stored somewhere. This may not be an intensive process application on the VPN device, and if there is a server it is sending it to, the server will need the disk space.

Alerting

All logged events can trigger an alert, but it's important to distinguish between the types of alerts. Is the alert caused by someone trying to hack the device? If that is the case, what type of traffic are they using? Some VPNs devices support SNMP, and while SNMP has been around for a long time, it doesn't support all the capabilities needed to successfully trigger critical alerts to an admin person in charge of security. This leaves maybe a rules policy established on a firewall to issue an alert of some kind on denied packets. If you install a RADIUS server, when does the RADIUS trigger alerts? Does an unsuccessful attempt to log in trigger an alert, such as an incorrect password or wrong username? How about for someone trying to send encrypted data and bypassing the firewall altogether? All these alerts may be triggered from the RADIUS, but you also need to be alerted with traffic that doesn't even get that far. If you are also using a firewall, the firewall will be denying traffic, and it may be alerting somewhere. It is easy to see how alerting can become monstrous. Alerting is a big issue, and there are a lot of products that will issue alerts, send emails, send a page, and so on.

Logging

While alerting is important for any organization, logging is the most important feature that you can install. Just think about it: How do you know that one of your servers is being hacked into or your mail server is being used as a mail relay? The simple answer is, you don't—at least not directly. What happens is something is going wrong, you are not getting outside or you are not getting any mail, so you decide to investigate. If you make the alerts too sensitive, the administrator gets too many of them, so he or she promptly shuts them off or minimizes the window the alerts are coming in on. Therefore, it's the logs that tell the story: Who, what, where, when, but not why (except in spam mail when it's fairly obvious). With logging you can look back and see what has been happening, who can see the times, what IP address they came in on, and what server they tried to attack. Even if they spoofed their IP address, you can tell what ISP they were coming from, and at least the ISPs can try to help you. Don't forget the FBI either; if you decide to press charges against an individual who is using you as a target, they will want the log files to verify the attacks, and, along with the ISP's log files, the breakin can often be traced to an inexperienced spammer.

Event Correlation

The next thing to consider is event correlation. Do all the alerts that you have been getting indicate a pattern or is something serious happening?

Is the alert caused by someone doing a traceroute or extended ping? Are you looking at the traffic? Are they coming in on UDP or TCP traffic? Are they trying to make a connection on Port 25, which is an indication that someone may be attempting to hack into your mail server? When you connect to a public network, expect all kinds of traffic. Perhaps someone troubleshooting on one end has your IP address for some reason, and you think they are trying to break into your network. (One of my favorites is when someone is just learning how to use SNMP and he or she decides to do an SNMPWALK through the Internet. This sets off all kinds of alarms.)

All these conditions will trigger alerts, and like anything else, if someone starts getting hundreds of alerts a day, they will naturally shut off their alerts. No highly skilled technical person who can understand and implement a VPN will sit and stare at alerts all day. You need to set up a correlation package that will take these potential alerts, do logical processing on them, and then issue an alert, maybe to a trouble help desk with the error condition. There are several good packages that will take in as input alerts you define and assign a metric to. Say, for example, you are using the UNIX syslog; you parse the syslog file and assign numbers to individual types of messages. Then you can set up these event correlations to trigger on certain conditions that are repeated, as in Figure 11-7.

Figure 11-7

Event correlation.

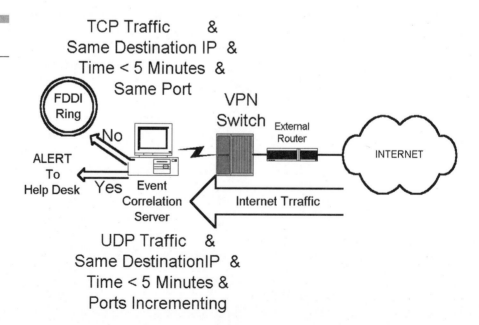

Figure 11-7 illustrates how event correlation works. If TCP traffic is directed to the same destination IP within a certain time frame—in this case, less than 5 minutes—somebody *could* be trying to hack into the system. If it is UDP traffic and the ports are incrementing, somebody might be trying to do a port scan on one of your devices or is playing with traceroute. You can see by just these two examples that you can add whatever conditions you like to trigger an alert to the help desk. Being on the Internet, you should expect all these types of traffic, therefore, your event correlation must take into account these abnormalities. The alert is usually caused by denied traffic anyway; it might be wise to capture that data, and see if it happens again. You don't want to set off too many alerts right away, which people may ignore. Instead, you want to keep track of the occurrence and see if it happens again. Of course, if it happens again relatively soon, it could be an indication of misconduct.

SECURITY NOTE   To make auditing a functional tool for your organization, you need all the components. Monitoring, alerting, logging, and event correlation must all be part of the package.

Encryption and Encapsulation

Encryption and encapsulation are often talked about in the VPN marketplace. As mentioned, encryption is the process of encrypting a data packet for transport over the Internet or some other network. Encapsulation is the process of taking some non-IP traffic and encapsulating it into an IP packet, which then may or may not be encrypted. The term "tunnel" is often used; I have seen *tunnel* referred to as encapsulation mode in which IPX, SNA, and non-IP packets get encapsulated, or packaged, into the data portion of an IP packet. I have also seen *tunnel* referred to in a VPN scenario where either an IPX or even an IP packet is further encrypted (for security reasons) to travel across the Internet. With either definition you choose, you must make sure you have the available software that will perform the translation. For example, if you have an SNA mainframe and want to communicate to a site across the country, you first have to encapsulate that traffic into an IP packet (if you are using an IP internal routed network). Then if you decide that further security is needed, you can further encrypt that packet at the

Figure 11-8
Encapsulation versus
encryption.

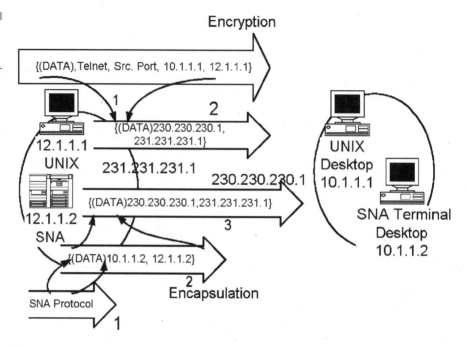

VPN device before it leaves the organization. The reverse happens when
the packet reaches the far end, as in Figure 11-8.

The difference between encryption and encapsulation can be very
subtle. On the top part of Figure 11-8, the UNIX machines are trying to
communicate with the other UNIX terminals. For security reasons that
whole packet is then layered into another IP packet. It is then transported across the Internet, where the end device strips off the outer IP
packet layer and forwards the packet to the UNIX desktop. This type of
encapsulation is called IP-in-IP, or IP-in-IP tunneling. On the mainframe, first the SNA traffic needs to be converted into an IP packet, if
you are using an IP routed internal network. Usually there is software
running on the mainframe. This SNA traffic is encapsulated into an IP
packet and then sent to the IBM terminal desktop at the far end. The
VPN device gets this IP packet, adds its own header, and sends it on its
way. The far end strips off this first IP packet header, it is then forwarded to the SNA terminal desktop, which then strips it off and hands off
the SNA data to the application running on the terminal. From a maintenance perspective, you need to understand when encapsulation and
encryption are taking place. If you are not sure where to look in the OSI
stack, the time taken in diagnosing these problems can be very long.

Key Management

As mentioned, key management deals with the process of securing, generating, distributing, and storing keys. Keys are the underlying security mechanisms in VPN technology, so a very secure method is needed to ensure their safety. While private key systems are more secure, they are also less flexible due to their nature. Public keys that are very flexible also need security protection. With public keys systems, your VPN device is taking a public key from another device, believing it is indeed the public key of that device. That's where certificate authorities come into play; they do the vouching for that key, much like a notary republic does for your signature.

Key management presents security difficulties, since keys are the basis for the decryption process. Like putting your spare key under your doormat, what happens if you put your security keys on an untrusted server? In some key systems there is only one secure key, which is usually placed on a server to allow the decryption process to take place. In other situations keys are exchanged between client and server before communication can take place. From this you should be able to see that key management is an extremely important factor to consider.

We talked about alerting earlier in this chapter, but usually that alerting is for security concerns on the VPN device itself. What happens if your key server goes down? In this case, no VPN communication will take place, or worse, your VPN uses an older key. We spoke about internal employees being the number-one security concern for an organization. In this case, are you monitoring the internal server for connections coming from inside the network? Probably not. Remember: you should monitor everything.

Random-Number Generators

The securities of the keys that are used in encryption are dependent on a random-number generator that adds security to the key. Hackers will try to find a pattern in the ciphertext so they can guess the key. As with passwords, people are predictable when generating keys. Because of this, random-number generators are used so that no set parttern is established.

The best number generators are those that mimic nature or a hum or electrical static interference. These types of things are completely random in nature. Physical movements are believed by some to be the best indicators of random generations that we have at our disposal. If you've created a PGP key on your computer, you would have noticed that you were asked to move your mouse around or type keystrokes in. This action supposedly duplicates a random motion, which the key is then based upon; also, this motion is fed through a hash generator to ensure randomness. While this action is *supposed* to produce randomness, it does not, so in these instances, a pseudorandom set of numbers is used. It determines the numbers by taking a seed value of the actual values produced and running them through a hash function to try to produce a random sample.

Certificates

Certificates are the digital documents that attest to the identity of a public key and to the identity of that person. Certificates help to validate a digital signature and make sure that that a person is not impersonating someone else. They can be hierarchical in nature, where one certificate authority validates another certificate authority. The internationally accepted standard for certificates is ITU-TX.509; the current version is 3. Certificate authorities are the servers that issue the certificate that identifies the digital signature, and the digital signature identifies the individual. In an earlier chapter we discussed the concept of nonrepudiation, which is the ability to verify a user's identity. In order for any kind of electronic commerce to be viable in the future, certificates will play an important role. Figure 11-9 illustrates a certificate in action.

When looking at the events in Figure 11-9 from a security point of view, you can see where the vulnerabilities lie. The public key server or the certificate authority could get compromised and affect the whole system. Therefore, many organizations decide to have the issuance of digitial certificates handled in-house.

Security Update

Security will undoubtedly be the biggest maintenance item you have with VPNs. You just can't drop them in place and forget about them;

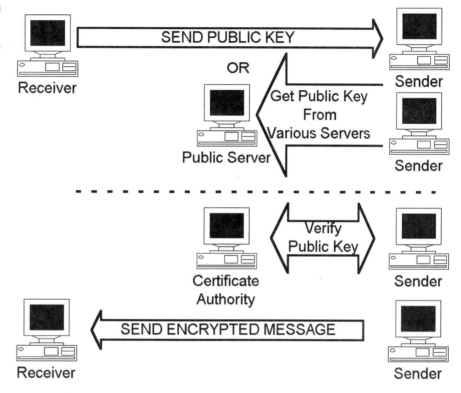

Figure 11-9
Certificate authorities.

you must keep up-to-date with the latest security alerts, vendor bulletins, their suggested corrective actions, and what is happening in the real world. During the writing of this chapter alone, three new security attacks were reported in the media: one concerning the 56-bit DES standard, one concerning a newspaper, and one concerning a new type of attack where simultaneous users working concurrently broke into a host and created a vulnerability. A good thing about security matters today is that there are many security organizations and many mailing lists. When a security event occurs, immediately it is announced in the media and on such mailing lists, so people become aware of them quickly. The problem then is in the older application you are running or not keeping up-to-date on your operating systems, Web servers, and so on. You must always keep up-to-date with security, because it is always changing.

SECURITY NOTE Security is like a leaky plumbing system. Once you plug up one hole, another hole is discovered.

Support of Major Upgrade

When your organization decides to implement a VPN, you need to decide what types of products to install and what kind of infrastructure you want to create. You can go from the very simple to the elaborate. Say, for example, you have decided that in order to implement a VPN, you want to make use of your existing routers and save on the cost. Therefore, you will need to make sure the individual installing the VPN software knows router technology and knows how to troubleshoot the equipment if it fails? Now you have either a VPN problem or a router problem. What happens if you decide to add VPN switches throughout the organization? This means a major impact to the network design, since you are adding these devices right before your Internet access points. Can you add these VPN switches? Will they interoperate with your existing equipment? Will the routers need to be upgraded to support encryption, or will the overhead be a problem?

Now suppose you installed access lists on the routers. If they are doing packet filtering, will they allow an encrypted packet to get through? Probably not, if they are looking at the port layer, as in Figure 11-10. In this simplified figure an encrypted IP packet (using IPSec) is coming in from the Internet. What can be readily seen is the destination IP address and the authentication header used in IPSec. What cannot be seen is the payload, since it is encrypted. The router, however, has an access list that is only allowing inbound Ports 25 and 53, which are SMTP and DNS traffic. What happens now to the packet? It probably gets dropped. Now you can correct the situation, but you need to correct each router along its path. Does your internal staff or an outside staff support this equipment? Are your routers being managed by a provider? If so, you will need to inform them of your VPN plans.

Figure 11-10
Router blocking encrypted VPN traffic.

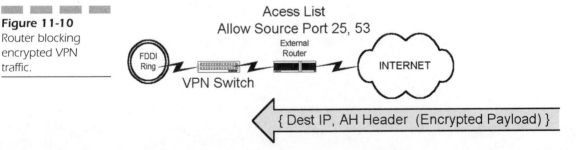

Tunneling Protocols

As mentioned, three leading tunneling protocols exist today: IPSec, PPTP, and L2TP. Which one will you decide on and when do you want to use each one? Do you want to have an implementation that combines the different types of protocols? Depending on your internal architecture and your desktops, you may not want to or cannot support the different types available. What level of support will a vendor's products have for each tunneling protocol, and when the standards are finalized, will your equipment be upgradeable? All three protocols offer security for your organization; some offer more security than others. In any case you need to make sure that if you decide to use PPTP on your desktops, your VPN device can either pass that packet, encrypt that packet, or encapsulate a security package around it.

You also need to make sure that your encryption policy allows for the different types of encryption technologies. IPSec is a framework, PPTP is encryption, PPTP offers encapsulation, and DES offers strong security and authentication. These protocols and technologies do not all interoperate, so before choosing one, make sure you know what your requirements will be.

Management Devices

In previous chapters I've mentioned that it is wise to be able to manage your VPN devices from a central location. Keep in mind, however, that not all VPN products support centralized management features. Consider, for instance, how you now configure and ship a VPN device to a different office building; you include instructions on how to install it. Or you manually configure it and carry the device to different geographical locations within your organizations.

Now you normally have one of two ways in which you can modify and troubleshoot the device. You can either create a tunnel across the public network to configure it, which implies the vendor has given you the option to install a management tunnel based on some (hopefully) standard encryption algorithm. Or, you should be able to connect a modem to the console port of that device in order to manage it. Here you've just opened a security problem by adding a modem on a security device. You need to consider the kind of modem you will be using, a standard off-the-shelf model or some type of security modem that encrypts the data

Figure 11-11
Centralized
management.

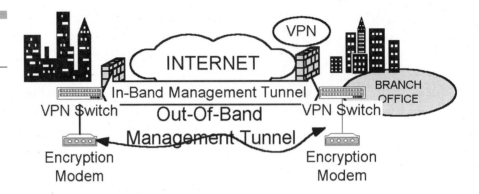

between modems. Are these modems secure? Are they tested? Do you trust them? There are several on the market that serve this purpose. What other choice do you have? If you can't create a management tunnel, your only other option is the modem. You could always have someone local look at the device, but this defeats the purpose of centralized management.

Figure 11-11 depicts a management setup. You either need to go in-band to manage the VPN device or out-of-band to manage it. Some vendors support the in-band setup; others support the out-of-band setup, with modem ports on their devices. The best solution would be to use both. If you somehow create a filter or set up something incorrectly on the VPN device, you may block your in-band access; in that case, you would need to walk someone through the configuration setup to get the device functioning again. At least with out-of-band setup, you can regain entry into the device.

Performance

What is meant by *performance* must be defined by your organization before your ISP or VPN vendor can address this issue. As with an automobile, is it the gas mileage or acceleration that defines performance? How then do you define performance—uptime, latency, utilization, number of tunnels created? In some statistics performance is the number of cycles per second your VPN device can deliver; this can be thought of as the number of simultaneous tunnel connections, or the throughput, as measured by the number of users per second. When you can accurately put a metric on performance, then at least you have a benchmark to judge it by. You can probably get performance statistics on your VPN device, but are the performance statistics understandable? How do they relate to the actual number of users passing through your VPN, pipe, tunnel, and so forth? If you define, say, 100 users passing simultaneously into and out of your Internet connection, at least you can use that as a benchmark.

Quality of Service

How can a VPN vendor define quality of service? Back in an earlier chapter, I said that quality of service is defined by latency, network uptime, and bandwidth. You can get bandwidth guarantees from your ISP. From your VPN vendor you can obtain the available bandwidth of the device itself. You can also get network uptime guarantees from your ISP, and they probably will generate weekly reports, if you like. Unfortunately, latency cannot be guaranteed unless you don't leave your local ISP's backbone. If you travel off your ISP's backbone, you enter into someone else's network, with its own performance metrics and configuration. Of course, you can ask your ISP for historical data regarding latency and get a good idea of the likelihood of future latency issues, but they are estimates at best.

You can also talk about quality of service as a specification on your network devices. Sometimes this is referred to as *policy bandwidth*; a simpler name is "queuing." You can set up policy guidelines to let certain traffic through at the expense of others. There are several drafts that talk about quality of service and some working groups. Keep in mind, of course, that the policy requirements will take processing power.

Authentication

How will you support users both internally (in-house employees) and externally (customers and externally accessing employees)? How many databases do you want to keep? Assume you have an internal database consisting of everyday users, and you have a separate database for some of those users who need Internet access. Then add in another database for external VPN users who may be employees, and maybe another for vendors, suppliers, and customers. How do you modify these databases? Some users who need Internet access might do work from home. What about those roaming users who come into the office only once or twice a month? They will need internal access. Can you see the difficulty in keeping these databases in synchronization? Then what about the people who leave the company? What databases were they in and how do you know if you deleted them from all the databases? From this view, your VPN has just created a full-time position for a database administrator.

Skilled Labor

Skilled labor is always the most overlooked asset in any organization. While you were reading all these things to consider for maintenance, you may not have even thought of technical employees. In most papers today and on Capitol Hill, you hear about the shortage of skilled labor. I don't know if that is true or if it is simply supply and demand working, but whatever it is, if you lose your key people, your organization will suffer. While everyone is replaceable, why bother going through the headaches and expense of losing them in the first place and needing to train new people? Although many organizations think training is an unnecessary evil, they now need to add security training. If you plan to do business over the Internet—and most organizations do, or at least plan to—you will need security training. You can hire your own security staff, or you can outsource. That decision has both pros and cons and depends on your company's products, markets, size, and so on. So unless you have highly motivated employees who are technically astute and enjoy their jobs, you are opening yourself up for major headaches.

Conclusion

In looking back at Chapter 11, we see that there are many maintenance requirements that VPNs depend on. Once more they are not individual, centralized maintenance items; they are interdependent upon other devices in the network. When you decide to implement a VPN or to put in place a support structure for them, you can use this chapter as a reference to check maintenance requirements. To recap, here are some of the maintenance issues:

- Redundant links
- Growth in organization
- Software updates
- Onsite technical support
- Telephone support
- Help desk for remote users
- VPNs—build or buy
- Compatibility
- Monitoring
- Alerting
- Logging
- Event correlation
- Encryption and encapsulation
- Key management
- Random-number generators
- Certificate authorities
- Security update
- Support of major upgrade
- Tunneling protocols
- Management devices
- Performance
- Quality of service
- Authentication
- Skilled labor

Most of these items can be integrated into the already-existing process infrastructure of your organization. Several others, such as encryption, security, and certificates, involve more work on your part, but they can all be accomplished with reasonable amounts of diligence and patience. The first, and most important, step in dealing with security issues is to take a look at all of your components, processes, and operating systems and compare them to the vendor's recommended patch and revision levels. After that, the next step is to keep up with security, subscribe to newsgroups, and periodically check your vendors' Web sites for updates. With all the information available today, there is no excuse for not knowing that a particular security problem exists.

As stated previously, "expect it to happen." Each one of the issues listed above is an "known unknown." Each one can happen, and you can prepare for each one to minimize the impact to your organization.

The Security
of VPNs

12

Cryptography

In this chapter we will discuss cryptography, or the art of solving difficult problems. This is just an introduction to cryptography; there is a vast ocean of knowledge and literature that you can consult for more information. I've included this chapter since VPN technology relies on cryptographic functions, and VPN security relies on the cryptographic strengths of the encryption algorithm.

In this chapter we will look at the different types of ciphers, blocks, and streams that take your message and output it as ciphertext. We will also look at public versus private key cryptosystems, digital signatures, hash functions, and the U.S. governments' Clipper Chip program.

In many articles and documents, you will read about cryptography and encryption simultaneously. They are so often used together, in fact, that it is sometimes difficult to tell them apart. When you talk about cryptography and encryption algorithms, for instance, are you talking about DES, PGP, RSA, and so on? Perhaps we should distinguish the two terms. *Cryptography* is the art of keeping things secret, the actual mathematical algorithm. *Encryption,* on the other hand, is the framework. Pretty Good Privacy is the framework (encryption), and the International Data Encryption Algorithm (IDEA) is the cryptography. Even though IDEA contains the word *encryption,* it is a mathematical cryptographic algorithm.

Finally this chapter will close with a cryptographic timeline done by Carl Ellison, et al., which will allow you to see where cryptography started until the present.

What Is Cryptography?

In simple terms, a cryptographic process takes a plaintext or clear-text file and converts it into "ciphertext" by means of an encryption process. Back in Chapter 1, we defined an encryption. Let's look at the definition again:

> Encryption is nothing more then taking a message, such as "I'll be late,"
> and converting it into some gibberish, say, for example,
> "2deR56Gtr2345^hj5Uie04." The other end of the process is called
> *decryption,* and it's the reverse of encryption, for instance, taking
> "2deR56Gtr2345^hj5Uie04" and converting it back to "I'll be late."

To restore the ciphertext back to its original form, it undergoes a process called decryption, as defined above. That process is facilitated by the use of the key, and the decryption process can only occur with the use of that key.

All encryption algorithms rely on cryptographic functions. In this chapter we will discuss cryptographic functions, and in the next chapter we will look at the encryption algorithms that rely on these cryptographic functions. An ongoing concern of Virtual Private Networks is whether the cryptographic algorithm can be broken, whether the data is safe, and whether the person who sent something *really* is that person who sent it. In these next two chapters you'll learn more about the security aspects of VPNs and compare one vendor's security products to another.

GENERAL NOTE   As you will see in the following sections, cryptography is a branch of applied mathematics. Everything in cryptography is related to mathematical operations on finite numbers.

Private versus Public Key Cryptography

With historical cryptography, the sender and receiver of a piece of text use the same key (the "secret key"). The sender uses the secret key to encrypt the message, while the receiver uses the same key to decrypt the message. This method is known as *secret-key cryptography* or *symmetric cryptography*. A main problem here is with the key; the sender and receiver not only have to agree on the same key, they also must figure out a way to exchange the key. If the sender and receiver are in different geographical locations, the exchanging of keys becomes extremely difficult. Will the sender and receiver trust a phone line or mail to exchange the keys? Can they trust a third-party courier? Since in secret-key cryptography, the keys are of extreme importance, can you be sure of their safety, especially in a large organization?

This creation, distribution, and security is called key management. To solve the key-management problem, Whitfield Diffie and Martin Hellman introduced the concept of public-key cryptography in 1976. In public-key cryptography, each party gets a pair of keys, a public key and a private key. The public key is made known to everyone, whereas the private key is kept secret to the party. In public-key cryptography, we eliminate the need for a secure channel. In addition, public-key cryptosystems allow the use of digital signatures and data authentication.

The advantage in using public-key cryptography is security and convenience. The private key need never be transmitted or trusted to a third party (i.e., courier). Therefore, there is never a chance that a key could become compromised, and transmission intercepted and decoded. Another advantage of public-key systems is they can provide digital signatures that cannot be repudiated. In earlier chapters we spoke about nonrepudiation, which is the ability to positively identify the sender with no chance of mistake. Public-key cryptosystems give us that necessary requirement.

The disadvantage of using public-key cryptography is speed. Many secret-key encryption algorithms are significantly faster than public-key encryption algorithms. However, public-key cryptography can be used in conjunction with secret-key cryptography to get the benefits of both. In doing encryption, the solution is to combine public- and secret-key systems in order to get both the security advantages of public-key systems and the speed advantages of secret-key systems. This is usually referred to as a "digital envelope." In addition, public-key encryption is vulnerable to impersonation, where a third party could act like the original sender. (This is referred to as the man-in-the-middle attack, discussed in the next chapter.)

Public-key cryptography is not always needed. Secret-key systems can be sufficient in any environment where you can be sure that secure transmission can take place, such as a closed banking system, where a single authority knows and manages all the keys. Since in this case the private keys will be known by a central authority, using public-key cryptography will offer no benefit. Of course, you can still use public-key cryptographic systems for your private mail.

Block Ciphers

A *block cipher* is a cipher that iterates several weak operations such as substitution, transposition, modular addition, multiplication, and linear transformation into a much stronger algorithm. This encryption algorithm takes place with the user key specified. The decryption process is the reverse of this algorithm.

GENERAL NOTE   A block cipher encrypts a block of data, say, for example, 64 bits at once, then goes on to the next block. DES is an example of a 64-bit block cipher.

There are many variations to these algorithms. One such class is called the "Feistel cipher." These ciphers operate on one-half of the ciphertext on each iteration, and then swap the ciphertext halves after each round.

The Data Encryption Standard (DES)

The Data Encryption Standard (DES), also known as the Data Encryption Algorithm, was developed by IBM (who originally called it "Lucifer"). The DES algorithm uses a 64-bit block size and a 56-bit key during execution (8 parity bits are stripped off from the full 64-bit key). The DEA is a symmetric cryptosystem, specifically, a 16-round Feistel cipher. A *round cipher* is a cipher that undergoes the algorithm a number of times; in this case, the algorithm is completed 16 times. During each round (also called transformation), a subkey is used with the iteration process. This subkey is a derivative of the main key the user supplied by a special function in the algorithm. The term "key schedule" is used to indicate the set of subkeys used in each iteration.

SECURITY NOTE   The number of rounds increases security, but the trade-off is performance.

Figure 12-1 illustrates how the Feistel cipher works. The text message "The signing of the document will take place tomorrow" is encrypted as follows:

1. The text that will be encrypted is split into two halves. The transformation function *f* is applied to one half of the text, using a sub-

Figure 12-1
Feistel cipher.

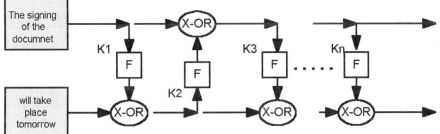

key of the key schedule. In this case, "The signing of the document" undergoes the transformation process.

2. The output of the *f*(unction) in Step 1 is then exclusive-ORed with the other half.

3. The two halves are then swapped. Each transformation uses the same pattern except for the last round; no swap occurs during this last round.

Weaknesses in DES

There is no easy attack on DES, although the mechanism to break it exists. The first solution is to use a "brute-force attack," trying every possible key combination. Another attack is called "sustained data analysis." This is depicted in Figure 12-2. Here, there are four data streams. These were the result of normal communications using a symmetric encryption algorithm. The only catch here was that the encryption/decryption key has not been changed.

SECURITY NOTE Frequently changing the DES key improves the security of your VPN data.

As you look closely at the four data streams, you notice **eem**; this is a product of the encryption algorithm using the same key. An attack can occur by guessing what **eem** stands for. In the English language, probably the most widely used three-letter word is "the." Through sustained data analysis, an attacker can guess familiar and common words. By frequently changing the key, each data stream is independent of each

Figure 12-2
Sustained data analysis.

4 Independent Data Streams

4Rtg8#sdkeopo***eem**e09!sSde9403k3cckr9402

56Thouir0wQ **eem**eotyeVghoree0e9Hg

rT0-@sm **eem**DKW2-=-1D,Oiems **eem**

RtpeoiMKswi**eem**PoejdMa0a9Em**eem**eoehR56**eem**

other, i.e., the ciphertext produced by one encryption process is totally different than the next ciphertext produced by the same encryption process.

GENERAL NOTE   Sometimes changing the key on a symmetric cryptographic system is not feasible.

Assume you have a symmetric cryptographic system that uses DES to encrypt files on a file server in your organization. Every time the DES key is changed, and that could be every minute, the server would have to reencrypt every file on the hard drive. A better solution would be to have a master DES file and encrypt that file frequently. Of course, if that master key is found out, that whole hard drive is vulnerable, but now you only have one key to worry about, not hundreds.

Weak Keys

In the DES algorithm, there is a concept called "weak keys." These are the keys that, if chosen, might make the DES encryption text vulnerable. There are 4 weak keys and 12 semiweak keys in the DES algorithm. Since DES is a 56-bit encryption algorithm, there are 2^{56} possible key combinations, and choosing a weak key is a 2^{-52} possibility.

DES 3, Triple-DES, and 3DES

The name "Triple-DES" is a bit misleading in that it might appear to be a new encryption algorithm based on DES. Rather, Triple-DES is a set of algorithms for increasing the strength of regular DES. It does this by running the DES algorithm with one or more keys. For example, a number of modes exist for 3DES. They are as follows:

- *DES-EEE3.*   This is the DES algorithm performed three times, each with a different encryption key.
- *DES-EDE3.*   This is the DES algorithm that uses three different encryption keys, but the encryption process is encrypt-decrypt-encrypt.

- *DES-EEE2.*   This is similar to DES-EEE3, but the first and third encryption process use the same key.
- *DES-EDE2.*   This is similar to DES-EDE2, but again, the first and third iteration use the same key.

There are other versions of this process—single, double, and triple iterations using one or more keys for each process. The greatest strength lies in using the DES algorithm with three distinct keys.

As a note, most will think that if one uses the DES algorithm three times with three different keys, the resulting key (encryption strength) will be 3*56, or 168. This is not the case. The way the algorithm runs is that Triple-DES is 2^{56}, which is still 72,000,000,000,000,000—more secure than 56-bit DES. Triple-DES is still the strongest algorithm for the foreseeable future.

SECURITY NOTE   DES encryption is analogous to a mathematical theorem. It is not proven to be secure, but no one has yet invented a way to break them.

Blowfish Algorithm

The Blowfish algorithm was developed by Bruce Schneier in 1993. It is similar to DES in that it is a Feistel cipher and uses a 64-bit block; however, it uses variable-length keys. Blowfish key sizes range from 32 to 448 bits long. The algorithm itself consists of two parts: a subkey expansion part and an encryption part. The key-generation part is actually a complex, time-consuming process; the normal Blowfish algorithm has to run through 521 iterations to generate all the subkeys. This must be done before the encryption process can be take place. Therefore, applications that can store these subkeys outperform DES encryption on 32-bit multiprocessors. The key expansion process will convert a key of 448 bits into several subkey arrays, totaling 4168 bytes.

Blowfish requires no license to implement and outperforms both DES and IDEA with the same key size. The main advantage of Blowfish over the others is its variable-length key sizes. With this feature, it can be added to encryption products using only 40-bits (the allowable legal exportable size), and to much larger key sizes for internal domestic products. Blowfish encryption applications are found a lot in public-domain security areas.

International Data Encryption Algorithm (IDEA)

The IDEA algorithm is a block cipher created in 1990 by a Swiss firm. It uses 64-bits with eight rounds, as compared to the Feistel cipher of 16 rounds. Like the previous block ciphers, decryption is the same process as encryption, once all the decryption subkeys have been calculated from the encryption subkeys. This cipher was designed to be easily implemented in both hardware and software. The security of IDEA lies in the use of three incompatible types of arithmetic operations on 16-bit words. In this algorithm, operations from three different algebraic groups are mixed (XOR, addition modulo 216, and multiplication modulo 216+1). IDEA uses 52 subkeys, each being 16-bits in length. The subkey generation is as follows: The 128-bit key of IDEA is used as the first eight subkeys, K1 to K8. The following eight keys are obtained the same way, after a 25-bit circular left shift. This is repeated until all of the encryption subkeys have been calculated.

IDEA is a strong encryption cipher that has withstood many challenges against it. IDEA is considered to be immune from differential cryptoanalysis, and no linear cryptanalytic attacks on IDEA have been reported. There is, however, a large class of 2^{51} weak keys, which in the process of encryption could allow the key to be recovered. However, IDEA still has 2^{128} possible keys, which makes it secure.

GENERAL NOTE Pretty Good Privacy (PGP) uses the IDEA algorithm.

RC2

RC2 is a variable-key-size block cipher. "RC" stands for "Rivest's Code," which refers to the inventor of these ciphers, Ron Rivest of RSA Data Security. It has a 64-bit block size and is approximately two to three times faster than DES when implemented in software.

Since the U.S. government restricts exportation to 40 bits, the inventor has used another method to allow for exportation. The RC2 has a special feature in which an additional (40- to 88-bit) string can be appended to the encryption key. This 40- to 88-bit string is named a "salt"; it is designed to stop attackers by using a longer encryption key.

After encryption, the salt is then sent unencrypted with the message, allowing for exportation while still abiding by the law.

RC5 Block Cipher

RC5 is different from the other RC algorithms in that it uses a variable block size, a variable key size, and a variable number of rounds. RC5 uses block sizes of 32, 64, or 128 bits. The variable key can range from 0 to 2048 bits, and the number of rounds can go from 0 to 255. It is a fast block cipher, and it can be used with a 64-bit block size that can be a drop replacement for DES. This flexibility in size gives RC5 great security. The subkey generation is calculated with the user-defined key, and the total number of subkeys is dependent on the number of rounds implemented. Then this table is used for both encryption and decryption. The encryption routine consists of the three algebraic operations, integer addition, bitwise exclusive-OR, and variable rotation. These operations make RC5 easily implemented and tested. RC5 has been tested against differential and linear cryptanalysis attacks.

Skipjack

Skipjack is the algorithm that was used in the "Clipper Chip" designed by the government and pushed by the Clinton administration. A very secretive algorithm, it was finally released by the U.S. government on June 23, 1998. The Skipjack encryption algorithm contained in the Clipper Chip uses an 80-bit key to encrypt 64-bit blocks of data and uses 32 rounds. Skipjack is expected to be more secure than DES in the absence of any analytic attack, since it uses 80-bit keys versus the 56-bit keys in DES.

Other Block Ciphers

These last few block ciphers are just a few of the ciphers available for development. It is important to understand these ciphers, since they form the underlying security of your VPN. These ciphers include the Secure and Fast Encryption Routine (SAFER) and the Fast Data Encipherment Algorithm (FEAL).

Stream Ciphers

Stream ciphers are symmetric encryption algorithms that are usually much faster than block ciphers. While block ciphers normally work on chunks of data (64-bits), stream ciphers work on individual bits. A good security feature with stream ciphers is that if using the same algorithm and the same key, the same ciphertext may not appear; it depends on when the bits are in the encryption process. Compare this to the block ciphers, where using the same algorithm and the same key generates the same ciphertext, which can be used in a sustained data analysis attack, mentioned earlier. Instead of ciphertext as in the case of block ciphers, stream ciphers produce what is known as a *keystream*. The encryption process utilizes both the plaintext and this keystream.

RC4

RC4 is another stream cipher again developed by Ron Rivest of RSA Data Security, Inc. It uses a variable-key-size stream cipher with algebraic byte-oriented operations. The algorithm is based on the use of a random permutation. The cipher has been designed to run very quickly in software, and it uses from 8 to 16 operations per byte. It, along with RC2, has special exportation status from the U.S. government.

Linear Feedback Shift Register (LFSR)

In a linear feedback shift register, a string of bits is stored in a string of memory cells, usually by an initialization vector, which is the secret key. A clock pulse advances the bits one space in that string. Then an exclusive-OR is done on certain positions in the string to produce the new bit in the string. Linear feedback shift registers can be easily implemented in both hardware and software. However, over time an analysis of these shift registers has been developed, so the bit sequences are not as secure as they should be. Therefore, LFSRs are used in conjunction with other LFSRs to make them more secure or as inputs to other algorithms.

Mixed Congruential Pseudorandom Number Generator

The mixed congruential pseudorandom number generator is usually implemented in software. It is a basic technique of producing apparently random bits. This is the same technique used to produce the numbers returned when using the random function in most languages using BASIC: modulo a constant, and replace n by a times n plus b, where a and b are constants. If a and b are large enough, the behavior of n, its most significant bits, will seem random. A common use for the mixed congruential pseudorandom number generator is to use it as part of a MacLaren-Marsaglia random-number generator.

Shift Register Cascade

Shift register cascades are a set of linear feedback shift registers, connected together in such a way that the behavior of a LFSR is dependent on the behavior of the previous LFSRs before it. A behavioral pattern is usually achieved by using one LFSR as the clocking mechanism of the following LFSR. That is, a register might advance one step if the preceding register output is one value and advance two steps if another value. Different configurations with these shift register cascades are possible.

Vernam Cipher

A Vernam cipher, often called a "one-time pad," uses a string of bits that is generated completely at random. The keystream is the same length as the plaintext message, and the random string is combined using bitwise XOR with the plaintext to produce the ciphertext. The entire keystream is random; therefore, even with very high computational resources at their disposal, they can only guess the plaintext if they see the ciphertext. These ciphers offer perfect secrecy, and one-time pads are the best security mechanism in cryptography today. Since the secret key is as long as the message, this causes serious key-management problems, and therefore, the one-time pad is impractical. Stream ciphers were developed as an alternative to the one-time pad.

Hash Functions

Hash functions take a variable-length message and output a fixed-length string, usually 128 bits or more; this is referred to as the hash value. Hash functions are one-way. A one-way hash function is said to be one-way if it is hard to invert or reverse. If you are given a string and the hash function produced a hash value, you should not be able to be given the hash value and use the hash function to reproduce the string. When a document undergoes a hashing function, this value becomes the "digital fingerprint" of the original document. So when we talk about digital signatures, we usually mean the digital signature on the hash value of the document itself. This also allows the flexibility of leaving the message digests public—something like that of a public key—and provides a way for digital timestamping.

For privacy, the message digest is encrypted with the sender's private key, referred to as the digital signature. The senders send this digital signature and the original message to the receiver. The receiver then decrypts the digital signature with the sender's public key and produces a hash of the original message. If these two messages produce the same hash value, the receiver can be sure the message is from the original user. Here you will notice that it is not the actual message that the receiver computes, but the hash value. You can think of it in very simple terms like this: The sender produces a "Garbage—Hash Value," sends it to the receiver, and the receiver needs to produce the same "Garbage" to be sure it came from the original sender.

Message Digest 2, 4, 5 (MD2), (MD4), (MD5)

Message Digest 2, 4, and 5 were all developed by Ron Rivest of RSA Labs. These are all hash functions that take a string of arbitrary length and produce a fixed-length output of 128-bits.

MD2 was designed back in 1989 and optimized for 8-bit microprocessor machines. It is described in RFC 1319. MD2 has been found to have some weaknesses in the message field if some calculations were left undone during the hash. Therefore, implementing MD2 is no longer advisable.

MD4 was designed in the 1990s and uses a 512-bit block with the message. This hashing function takes three rounds to implement. Unfortunately, attacks on MD4 were found rather quickly when leaving off the first or third round. Therefore, MD4 is not recommended for general use.

MD5 was developed in 1991, and while slower than MD4, it's considered safer. This algorithm consists of four rounds. Some people have reported weaknesses in it, but it is still considered secure and is widely used.

Secure Hash Algorithm (SHA and SHA-1)

The secure hash algorithm (SHA) was developed by the U.S. government. SHA-1, a revision to SHA, was released in 1994. It takes a string length and produces a 160-bit message digest. While it is slower than other hash functions, it is considered more secure due to its longer length.

Message Authentication Codes

Message Authentication Codes (MACs) are similar to checksums, in that they are used in encryption schemes with a secret key. They are applied to a specific message, and as in public-key systems, they can only be verified by the intended receiver. MACs fall into several different categories; they can be hashed-based, cipher-based, or unconditionally secure-based. MACs can also be used to check for data tampering. The sender and receiver share a secret key, which is embedded inside the message. The receiver can then check the message to make sure there was no tampering during transmission. MACs can also use a key together with a hash-based function. This produces a checksum that is appended to the end of the message, called a key-based MAC header. An example of a key-based MAC function is the Keyed-MD5 algorithm. Other well-known MAC algorithms are the DES-CBS, HMAC-SHA, and HMAC-MD5.

Digital Timestamps

When someone views a document, it is important for that individual to be sure of two things: the digital signature verifying the original sender and the timestamp, which shows when the document was originally created or modified. Together, digital signatures and timestamps can act like a notary public on an electronic document. Legal documents and patents all need to be timestamped. A simple example of timestamping is mailing a letter to yourself, but not opening it. Inside, the contents are safe from tampering and the timestamp put on the envelope by the U.S. Post Office is like that of a notary public.

Electronic documents stored on the hard drive of a server need another way to document date and time. As of now, by simply changing the date on the machine, you cannot affect the date of the document. Therefore, a way is needed to timestamp the electronic text, not the medium it is stored on. One solution to the timestamping problem is that of a trusted timestamping authority, similar to a certificate authority. An individual would send the document to a timestamping authority who would stamp the document with the date and time and return it. The authority would keep a record for itself; if there were ever any question as to the date of the document, the authority could be queried. There are concerns with this implementation; the document could be intercepted or the timestamping authority might be untrustworthy.

A better way of implementing timestamps is in conjunction with digital signatures. An individual would compute a hash function, sign it with his or her digital signature, and send it to the timestamping authority. The authority would append the date and time, sign the message, and send it back to the individual.

This is a simple but accurate way of looking at timestamping a document. There are additional algorithms available that protect against compromised timestamping authorities and from authorities sending back the wrong date and time.

Digital Signatures with Certificate Authorities

Digital signatures work in reverse of the normal way we think of the encryption process. The digital signature uses the private key on some block of data (and only that individual has access to his or her private key), and the recipient decrypts that data with the public key, which is well known and available. In previous chapters we talked about the concept of nonrepudiation (the ability to establish a direct link to that sender's identity). When we use digital signatures, we want to positively identify the sender; otherwise, the signature would be invalid and non-repudiation could not take place.

Digital signatures can also be used in other ways. We've already mentioned its use in timestamping a document, where another party digitally signs that data that came from a sender with his or her secret key. Now we've come to an entity that we've discussed previously called the certificate authority. The certificate authority is a third party that signs a combination of the key and the information of the original sender. What makes the certificate authority a trusted party is simply your belief that it is so. A certificate authority can be compromised and keys forged on that authority. Certificate authorities exist both in a centralized key infrastructure and a distributed key infrastructure. With a centralized key infrastructure, there are very few "roots" in the hierarchy. In the distributed key infrastructure there may not be any roots. You trust your servers or a third party to be the authority.

How Certificates Work

In Chapter 13, we will look at an example of a digital certificate, but for now, since digital certificates are part of cryptography, we'll discuss them briefly here. A document goes through a message digest (hashing mechanism). This hash value is then encrypted with the private key of the individual. This information is the digital signature, which is forwarded and stored on a certificate authority. The sender then forwards both the message and his or her digital signature to the receiver. The recipient then decrypts this hash with the public key of the sender. The receiver also queries the certificate authority for the sender's key, and again decrypts the digest. If the signature decrypts properly and the hash values match, then the signature is accepted as valid. Cryptographic hash functions (such as MD5 and SHA) are used to compute the message digest when creating the digital signature.

Strengths of Cryptographic Hash Functions

Cryptographic algorithms are designed to be unbreakable. Unfortunately, like a theorem in mathematics, that cannot be proven. Their strength lies in how difficult it is to figure out the key (known as an exhaustive key search). It is possible to try all values for keys in sequence, but the power required to do that increases exponentially. Take for example a 32-bit key: 2^{32} power is needed to try all those keys, which amounts to 4,294,967,296 combinations. Most modern computers can easily tackle this task. But when we move up to the 40-bit key, we're talking about 2^{40} power, or 1,099,511,627,776 combinations. And when we move up to 56-bit keys, a common size in DES encryption, this mean 2^{56}, or a total of 7.205759403793e+16 combinations. You can see that the number of combinations needed in a 56-bit DES encryption algorithm would take a massive amount of computer processing power to try the combinations. However, as mentioned, the 56-bit DES encryption was broken, and within a month, so the U.S. government allowed the exportation of encryption products using the 56-bit DES technology. So are the keys the strength behind cryptographic algorithms? In some algorithms they are. Some attacks on cryptographic algorithms do not try all possible keys. They use other means, such as timing attacks, known plaintext attacks, and guessing attacks.

SECURITY NOTE A major item to remember about cryptographic algorithms is that the strength of the algorithms should not rely on the secrecy of that algorithm. It has been shown that when secret algorithms were made public, they were found to be very weak.

In public key algorithms, the key lengths are usually quite large; the problem is not guessing the right key but trying to find the private key from the public key. Some algorithms require factoring a large integer into primes or computing a discrete logarithm modulo. In comparison to a DES encryption, RSA keys of 256-bit are easily broken; 384 and 512 bits can be broken with some powerful workstations' processing power. And keys over 768 bits are believed to be fairly secure for the future. An excellent book that describes cryptographic algorithms is *Applied Cryptography* by Bruce Schneier. (See Appendix.)

Random-Number Generators

One of the hardest things in keeping your cryptographic algorithms secret and your data safe is the generation of random numbers to use for your keys. A lot of work has been done with random numbers, but the trade-off is flexibility versus security. As mentioned in Chapter 11, it has been shown that the best random numbers occur in nature. Electrical noise and static are the best forms of random generators. However, these cannot be used in the everyday world. Therefore, an alternative method must be used. Devices have been made, such as diodes, or devices that measure the timing as a user types in individual keys on a keyboard. However, these have been shown to be predictable and not truly random.

Then there are pseudo-random-number generators, which are cryptographic algorithms designed to mimic a real-world environment. These are mathematical functions, just like hash functions and ciphers, that try to generate random keys. These pseudo-random-number generators work on a seed value supplied by a user and then expand that seed to generate the key. Of course, an attacker could try multiple seeds and see if there is a predictable pattern in the output. In order for these number generators to work, they have to make it computationally unfeasible to guess any of the bits patterns in the stream. There are many random-number generators on the market today.

Clipper Chip

The Clipper Chip was the U.S. government's answer to key escrow encryption. This is a microchip contained inside tamperproof hardware that used the Skipjack algorithm. Each chip contains a unique 80-bit unit key that is escrowed in two parts at two escrow agencies; both parts must be known in order to recover the key. The chip itself has been manufactured so that it cannot be reverse-engineered, meaning that the Skipjack algorithm and the encryption keys cannot be recovered from the chip. It uses three types of encryption keys: a session key, a unit key and a family key.

When two devices want to start communicating, they first agree on an 80-bit session key. The method used is determined by the implementation; public-key methods such as RAS or Diffie-Hellman can be used. The message is encrypted with the session key and another piece of data called the law-enforcement access field. Included in all of this are the session key, a unit key, and some other data, which is then encrypted with the family key.

During normal communication, sender and receiver encrypt and decrypt their respective messages with the session keys. If a law enforcement agency wants to listen to the communication, they can use the family key to eavesdrop. They then would obtain a serial number and an encrypted session key. With a warrant, the agency can obtain the two parts of the unit key and decrypt the session key, finally using the session key to decrypt the message. However, researchers from AT&T have shown that it is possible to modify a field in the Skipjack algorithm, the Law Enforcement Access Field (LEAF), which would prohibit law enforcement agencies from determining the original source of the message.

The Clipper Chip and Skipjack algorithm have caused so much opposition that they never will be taken seriously. There is the controversy about escrowed keys, particularly regarding who will hold the two keys. If this is a government solution, most likely they will choose the agencies to hold the keys, and their selection is bound to be controversial. Then there is the agency itself and how secure is it. At the moment there are not enough key escrow agencies, so if they rush to develop these agencies, again, the security of these agencies comes into play. Report after report show how many times hackers have attacked governmental sites. Are their agencies really to be trusted? And since the Clipper Chip is hardware-based, what about the manufacturing chip plant itself? Those law enforcement agencies who are in favor of requiring escrow keys see it as a way to provide encryption for public use and still allow law enforcement agencies to monitor the specific communications of criminal activity. However, there is so much opposition from free speech/privacy advocates, who feel this is a violation of their rights: Many businesses also oppose the Clipper Chip.

Which Cryptosystem Is Right For You?

Deciding on a cryptosystem is kind of like deciding what type of car you want; they all get you from place to place, but they do it differently. From a VPN perspective, you probably will not make the choice anyway. It will be implemented in your vendor's VPN solution. It's valuable, though, to be able to look at cryptographic systems and know what category they fall into: block ciphers, steam ciphers, private versus public, and so on. In thinking about security, it's especially important, since, like network devices, cryptographic functions can be attacked. In Chapter 16, we will look at various attacks, but for now, if you had to decide on what kind of algorithm, there are a couple of questions you should think about:

1. *How fast data is to be exchanged?*   Public-key cryptosystems are slower than private-key cryptosystems, so public-key systems may slow down the network performance, particularly on low-speed network devices. These kinds of networks need private-key cryptosystems, such as 56-bit DES, IDEA, and blowfish, or as mentioned above, a combination of public- and private-key systems.

2. *How long is the data going to be stored?*   Many financial transactions only last a very short amount of time. Therefore, a malicious attack would have to occur within that time and only while that session key lasted. Personal records such as personal account information, balances, and Social Security information can be stored for years. In this case the attacker would have all the time in the world to work on breaking in. To protect yourself from these types of attacks, you need to really look at the security of the servers and how they are protected (e.g., how old is the encryption strength securing these systems?). Mentioned earlier, a DES solution encrypting a master key listed every number of seconds would help in this situation.

Cryptography Timeline

So far we have talked about various cryptographic algorithms and the security within these systems. If you are like me, you enjoy reading about the history of cryptography. I've come across work done by Carl Ellison that I find extremely valuable and exciting. It is a cryptography timeline dating back to before Christ. (See Table 12-1.) It is presented here in its entirety, with the various authors who have assisted Carl in this endeavor listed.

TABLE 12-1 Cryptography Timeline.

Date	C or G	Source	Info
About 1900 BC	Civ	Kahn, p. 71	An Egyptian scribe used non-standard hieroglyphs in an inscription. Kahn lists this as the first documented example of written cryptography.
1500 BC	Civ	Kahn, p. 75	A Mesopotamian tablet contains an enciphered formula for the making of glazes for pottery.
500-600 BC	Civ	Kahn, p. 77	Hebrew scribes writing down the book of Jeremiah used a reversed-alphabet simple substitution cipher known as ATBASH. (Jeremiah started dictating to Baruch in 605 BC, but the chapters containing these bits of cipher are attributed to a source labeled "C" (believed not to be Baruch) which could be an editor writing after the Babylonian exile in 587 BC, someone contemporaneous with Baruch or even Jeremiah himself.) ATBASH was one of a few Hebrew ciphers of the time.
487 BC	Govt	Kahn, p. 82	The Greeks used a device called the "skytale"—a staff around which a long, thin strip of leather was wrapped and written on. The leather was taken off and worn as a belt. Presumably, the recipient would have a matching staff and the encrypting staff would be left home.
50-60 BC	Govt/Civ	Kahn, p. 83	**Julius Caesar** (100-44 BC) used a simple substitution with the normal alphabet (just shifting the letters a fixed amount) in government communcations. This cipher was less strong than ATBASH, by a small amount, but in a day when few people read in the first place, it was good enough. He also used transliteration of Latin into Greek letters and a number of other simple ciphers.
0-400?	Civ	Burton	The Kama Sutra of Vatsayana lists cryptography as the 44th and 45th of 64 arts (yogas) men and women should know and practice. The date of this work is unclear but is believed to be between the first and fourth centuries, AD. [Another expert, John W. Spellman, will commit only to the range between the 4th century BC and the 5th century AD.] Vatsayana says that his Kama Sutra is a compilation of much earlier works, making the dating of the cryptography references even more uncertain.
			Part I, Chapter III lists the 64 arts and opens with: "Man should study the Kama Sutra and the arts and sciences subordinate thereto [....] Even young maids should study this Kama Sutra, along with its arts and sciences, before marriage, and after it they should continue to do so with the consent of their husbands." These arts are clearly not the province of a government or even of academics, but rather are practices of laymen.

TABLE 12-1   Cryptography Timeline. (*Continued*)

Date	C or G	Source	Info
			In this list of arts, the 44th and 45th read:
			■ The art of understanding writing in cipher, and the writing of words in a peculiar way.
			■ The art of speaking by changing the forms of words. It is of various kinds. Some speak by changing the beginning and end of words, others by adding unnecessary letters between every syllable of a word, and so on.
200's	Civ	Kahn, p. 91	"The so-called Leiden papyrus [...] employs cipher to conceal the crucial portions of important [magic] recipes."
725-790?	Govt/Civ	Kahn, p. 97	**Abu `Abd al-Rahman al-Khalil ibn Ahmad ibn `Amr ibn Tammam al Farahidi al-Zadi al Yahmadi** wrote a (now lost) book on cryptography, inspired by his solution of a cryptogram in Greek for the Byzantine emperor. His solution was based on known (correctly guessed) plaintext at the message start—a standard cryptanalytic method, used even in WW-II against Enigma messages.
855	Civ	Kahn, p. 93	**Abu Bakr Ahmad ben `Ali ben Wahshiyya an-Nabati** published several cipher alphabets which were traditionally used for magic.
—	Govt	Kahn, p. 94	"A few documents with ciphertext survive from the Ghaznavid government of conquered Persia, and one chronicler reports that high officials were supplied with a personal cipher before setting out for new posts. But the general lack of continuity of Islamic states and the consequent failure to develop a permanent civil service and to set up permanent embassies in other countries militated against cryptography's more widespread use."
1226	Govt	Kahn, p. 106	"As early as 1226, a faint political cryptography appeared in the archives of Venice, where dots or crosses replaced the vowels in a few scattered words."
about 1250	Civ	Kahn, p. 90	**Roger Bacon** not only described several ciphers but wrote: "A man is crazy who writes a secret in any other way than one which will conceal it from the vulgar."
1379	Govt/Civ	Kahn, p. 107	**Gabrieli di Lavinde** at the request of Clement VII, compiled a combination substitution alphabet and small code—the first example of the *nomenclator* Kahn has found. This class of code/cipher was to remain in general use among diplomats and some civilians for the next 450 years, in spite of the fact that there were stronger ciphers being invented in the meantime, possibly because of its relative convenience.

TABLE 12-1 Cryptography Timeline. *(Continued)*

Date	C or G	Source	Info
1300s	Govt	Kahn, p. 94	`Abd al-Rahman Ibn Khaldun** wrote "The Muqaddimah," a substantial survey of history which cites the use of "names of perfumes, fruits, birds, or flowers to indicate the letters, or [...] of forms different from the accepted forms of the letters" as a cipher among tax and army bureaus. He also includes a reference to cryptanalysis, noting "Well-known writings on the subject are in the possession of the people." [p. 97]
1392	Civ	Price, p. 182-187	"The Equatorie of the Planetis," possibly written by **Geoffrey Chaucer,** contains passages in cipher. The cipher is a simple substitution with a cipher alphabet consisting of letters, digits and symbols.
1412	Civ	Kahn, p. 95-96	**Shihab al-Din abu `l-`Abbas Ahmad ben `Ali ben Ahmad `Abd Allah al-Qalqashandi** wrote "Subh al-a `sha," a 14-volume Arabic encyclopedia which included a section on cryptology. This information was attributed to **Taj ad-Din `Ali ibn ad-Duraihim ben Muhammad ath-Tha`alibi al-Mausili,** who lived from 1312 to 1361 but whose writings on cryptology have been lost. The list of ciphers in this work included both substitution and transposition and, for the first time, a cipher with multiple substitutions for each plaintext letter. Also traced to Ibn al-Duraihim is an exposition on and worked example of cryptanalysis, including the use of tables of letter frequencies and sets of letters which can not occur together in one word.
1466-1467	Civ	Kahn, p. 127	**Leon Battista Alberti** (a friend of **Leonardo Dato,** a potifical secretary who might have instructed Alberti in the state of the art in cryptology) invented and published the first polyalphabetic cipher, designing a cipher disk (known to us as the Captain Midnight Decoder Badge) to simplify the process. This class of cipher was apparently not broken until the 1800s. Alberti also wrote extensively on the state of the art in ciphers, besides his own invention. Alberti also used his disk for enciphered code. These systems were much stronger than the nomenclator in use by the diplomats of the day and for centuries to come.
1473-1490	Civ	Kahn, p. 91	"A manuscript [...] by **Arnaldus de Bruxella** uses five lines of cipher to conceal the crucial part of the operation of making a philosopher's stone."
1518	Civ	Kahn, p. 130-6	**Johannes Trithemius** wrote the first printed book on cryptology. He invented a steganographic cipher in which each letter was represented as a word taken from a succession of columns. The resulting series of words would be a legitimate prayer. He also described polyalphabetic ciphers in the now-standard form of rectangular substitution tables. He introduced the notion of changing alphabets with each letter.

TABLE 12-1   Cryptography Timeline. (*Continued*)

Date	C or G	Source	Info
1553	Civ	Kahn, p. 137	**Giovan Batista Belaso** introduced the notion of using a passphrase as the key for a repeated polyalphabetic cipher. (This is the standard polyalphabetic cipher operation misnamed "Vigenère" by most writers to this day.)
1563	Civ	Kahn, p. 138	**Giovanni Battista Porta** wrote a text on ciphers, introducing the digraphic cipher. He classified ciphers as transposition, substitution and symbol substitution (use of a strange alphabet). He suggested use of synonyms and misspellings to confuse the cryptanalyst. He apparently introduced the notion of a mixed alphabet in a polyalphabetic tableau.
1564	Civ	Kahn, p. 144 (footnote)	Bellaso published an autokey cipher improving on the work of **Cardano** who appears to have invented the idea.
1623	Civ	Bacon	**Sir Francis Bacon** described a cipher which now bears his name—a biliteral cipher, known today as a 5-bit binary encoding. He advanced it as a steganographic device—by using variation in type face to carry each bit of the encoding. [See Bacon's writings online.]
1585	Civ	Kahn, p. 146	**Blaise de Vigenère** wrote a book on ciphers, including the first authentic plaintext and ciphertext autokey systems (in which previous plaintext or ciphertext letters are used for the current letter's key). [Kahn p. 147: both of these were forgotten and reinvented late in the 19th century. The autokey idea survives today in the DES CBC and CFB modes.]
1790s	Civ/Govt	Kahn, p. 192; Cryptologia v.5 No.4, pp. 193-208	**Thomas Jefferson,** possibly aided by **Dr. Robert Patterson** (a mathematician at U. Penn.), invented his wheel cipher. This was reinvented in several forms later and used in WW-II by the U.S. Navy as the Strip Cipher, M-138-A.
1817	Govt	Kahn, p. 195	**Colonel Decius Wadsworth** produced a geared cipher disk with a different number of letters in the plain and cipher alphabets—resulting in a progressive cipher in which alphabets are used irregularly, depending on the plaintext used.
1854	Civ	Kahn, p. 198	**Charles Wheatstone** invented what has become known as the Playfair cipher, having been publicized by his friend **Lyon Playfair.** This cipher uses a keyed array of letters to make a digraphic cipher which is easy to use in the field. He also reinvented the Wadsworth device and is known for that one.
1857	Civ	Kahn, p. 202	**Admiral Sir Francis Beaufort's** cipher (a variant of what's called "Vigenère") was published by his brother, after the admiral's death in the form of a 4×5-inch card.
1859	Civ	Kahn, p. 203	**Pliny Earle Chase** published the first description of a fractionating (tomographic) cipher.

TABLE 12-1 Cryptography Timeline. *(Continued)*

Date	C or G	Source	Info
1854	Civ	Cryptologia v.5 No.4, pp. 193-208	**Charles Babbage** seems to have reinvented the wheel cipher.
1861-1980	Civ	Deavours	"A study of United States patents from the issuance of the first cryptographic patent in 1861 through 1980 identified 1,769 patents which are primarily related to cryptography." [p. 1]
1861	Civ/Govt	Kahn, p. 207	**Friedrich W. Kasiski** published a book giving the first general solution of a polyalphabetic cipher with repeating passphrase, thus marking the end of several hundred years of strength for the polyalphabetic cipher.
1861-1865	Govt	Kahn, p. 215	During the Civil War, possibly among other ciphers, the Union used substitution of select words followed by word columnar-transposition while the Confederacy used Vigenäre (the solution of which had just been published by Kasiski).
1891	Govt/Civ	Cryptologia v.5 No.4, pp. 193-208	**Major Etienne Bazeries** did his version of the wheel cipher and published the design in 1901 after the French Army rejected it. [Even though he was a military cryptologist, the fact that he published it leads me to rate this as (Civ) as well as Govt.]
1913	Govt	Cryptologia v.5 No.4, pp. 193-208	**Captain Parket Hitt** reinvented the wheel cipher, in strip form, leading to the M-138-A of WW-II.
1916	Govt	Cryptologia v.5 No.4, pp. 193-208	**Major Joseph O. Mauborgne** put Hitt's strip cipher back in wheel form, strengthened the alphabet construction and produced what led to the M-94 cipher device.
1917	Civ	Kahn, p. 371	**William Frederick Friedman,** later to be honored as the father of U.S. cryptanalysis (and the man who coined that term), was employed as a civilian cryptanalyst (along with his wife Elizebeth) at **Riverbank Laboratories** and performed cryptanalysis for the U.S. government, which had no cryptanalytic expertise of its own. WFF went on to start a school for military cryptanalysts at Riverbank—later taking that work to Washington and leaving Riverbank.
1917	Civ	Kahn, p. 401	**Gilbert S. Vernam,** working for AT&T, invented a practical polyalphabetic cipher machine capable of using a key which is totally random and never repeats—a one-time tape. This is the only provably secure cipher, as far as we know. This machine was offered to the government for use in WW-I but it was rejected. It was put on the commercial market in 1920.
1918	Govt	Kahn, p. 340-345	The ADFGVX system was put into service by the Germans near the end of WW-I. This was a cipher which performed a substitution (through a keyed array), fractionation and then transposition of the letter fractions. It was broken by the French cryptanalyst, **Lieutenant Georges Painvin.**

TABLE 12-1   Cryptography Timeline. (*Continued*)

Date	C or G	Source	Info
1919	Civ	Kahn, p. 420	**Hugo Alexander Koch** filed a patent in the Netherlands on a rotor-based cipher machine. He assigned these patent rights in 1927 to Arthur Scherbius, who invented and had been marketing the Enigma machine since about 1923.
1919	Civ	Kahn, p. 422	**Arvid Gerhard Damm** applied for a patent in Sweden for a mechanical rotor cipher machine. This machine grew into a family of cipher machines under the direction of **Boris Caesar Wilhelm Hagelin** who took over the business and was the only one of the commercial cryptographers of this period to make a thriving business. After the war, a Swedish law which enabled the government to appropriate inventions it felt important to defense caused Hagelin to move the company to Zug Switzerland where it was incorporated as Crypto AG. The company is still in operation, although facing controversy for having allegedly weakened a cipher product for sale to Iran.
1921	Civ	Kahn, p. 415	**Edward Hugh Hebern** incorporated "Hebern Electric Code," a company making electromechanical cipher machines based on rotors which turn, odometer style, with each character enciphered.
1923	Civ	Kahn, p. 421	**Arthur Scherbius** incorporated "Chiffriermaschinen Aktiengesellschaft" to make and sell his Enigma machine.
1924	Civ	Deavours, p. 151	**Alexander von Kryha** produced his "coding machine" which was used, even by the German Diplomatic Corps, into the 1950s. However, it was cryptographically weak—having a small period. A test cryptogram of 1135 characters was solved by the US cryptanalysts **Friedman, Kullback, Rowlett** and **Sinkov** in 2 hours and 41 minutes. Nevertheless, the machine continued to be sold and used—a triumph of salesmanship and a lesson to consumers of cryptographic devices.
1927-1933	Civ	Kahn, p. 802ff.	Users of cryptography weren't limited to legitimate bankers, lovers, experimenters, etc. There were also a handful of criminals. "The greatest era of international smuggling—Prohibition—created the greatest era of criminal cryptology." [p. 817] To this day, the FBI runs a cryptanalytic office to deal with criminal cryptography. [As of Kahn's writing in 1967, that office was located at 215 Pennsylvania Avenue SE, Washington DC.] "A retired lieutenant commander of the Royal Navy devised the systems for Consolidated Exporters' Pacific operation, though its Gulf and Atlantic groups made up their own as needed. "His name was unknown but his cryptologic expertise was apparent. The smugglers' systems grew increasingly more complicated."

TABLE 12-1 Cryptography Timeline. (*Continued*)

Date	C or G	Source	Info
			"Some of these are of a complexity never even attempted by any government for its most secret communications," wrote **Mrs. [Elizebeth Smith] Friedman** in a report in mid-1930. "At no time during the World War, when secret methods of communication reached their highest development, were there used such involved ramifications as are to be found in some of the correspondence of West Coast rum running vessels."" [p. 804]
1929	Civ	Kahn, p. 404	**Lester S. Hill** published "Cryptography in an Algebraic Alphabet" in which a block of plaintext is enciphered by a matrix operation.
1933-1945	Govt	Kahn, p. 422 (and many others)	The Enigma machine was not a commercial success, but it was taken over and improved upon to become the cryptographic workhorse of Nazi Germany. [It was broken by the Polish mathematician, **Marian Rejewski,** based only on captured ciphertext and one list of three months worth of daily keys obtained through a spy. Continued breaks were based on developments during the war by **Alan Turing, Gordon Welchman** and others at Bletchley Park in England.]
1937	Govt	Kahn, p. 18ff.	The Japanese Purple machine was invented in response to revelations by **Herbert O. Yardley** and broken by a team headed by **William Frederick Friedman.** The Purple machine used telephone stepping relays instead of rotors and thus had a totally different permutation at each step rather than the related permutations of one rotor in different positions.
1930s	Govt	Kahn, p. 510ff.; Deavours, p. 10,89-91	Kahn attributes the American SIGABA (M-134-C) to **William F. Friedman** while Deavours attributes it to an idea of **Frank Rowlett,** one of Friedman's first hires. It improved on the rotor inventions of Hebern and Scherbius by using pseudo-random stepping of multiple rotors on each enciphering step rather than have uniform, odometer-like stepping of rotors as in Enigma. It also used 15 rotors (10 for character transformation, 5 probably for controlling stepping) rather than the Enigma's 3 or 4.
1930s	Govt	Deavours, p. 144	The British TYPEX machine was an offshoot of the commercial Enigma purchased by the British for study in the 1920's. It was a 5-rotor machine with the two initial rotors being stators, serving the purpose of the German Enigma's plugboard.
1970	Civ	Feistel	**Dr. Horst Feistel** led a research project at the IBM Watson Research Lab in the 1960s which developed the Lucifer cipher. This later inspired the US DES (below) and other product ciphers, creating a family labeled "Feistel ciphers."

TABLE 12-1   Cryptography Timeline. (*Continued*)

Date	C or G	Source	Info
1976	Civ/Govt	FIPS PUB-46	A design by IBM, based on the Lucifer cipher and with changes (including both S-box improvements and reduction of key size) by the U.S. NSA, was chosen to be the U.S. Data Encryption Standard. It has since found worldwide acceptance, largely because it has shown itself strong against 20 years of attacks. Even some who believe it is past its useful life use it as a component—e.g., of 3-key triple-DES.
1976	Civ	Diffie	**Whitfield Diffie** and **Martin Hellman** published "New Directions in Cryptography," introducing the idea of public key cryptography. They also put forth the idea of authentication by powers of a one-way function, now used in the S/Key challenge/response utility. They closed their paper with an observation for which this timeline Web page gives detailed evidence: "Skill in production cryptanalysis has always been heavily on the side of the professionals, but innovation, particularly in the design of new types of cryptographic systems, has come primarily from amateurs."
April 1977	Civ	Shamir	Inspired by the Diffie-Hellman paper and acting as complete novices in cryptography, **Ronald L. Rivest, Adi Shamir** and **Leonard M. Adleman** had been discussing how to make a practical public key system. One night in April, Ron Rivest was laid up with a massive headache and the RSA algorithm came to him. He wrote it up for Shamir and Adleman and sent it to them the next morning. It was a practical public-key cipher for both confidentiality and digital signatures, based on the difficulty of factoring large numbers. They submitted this to Martin Gardner on April 4 for publication in *Scientific American*. It appeared in the September, 1977 issue. The *Scientific American* article included an offer to send the full technical report to anyone submitting a self-addressed, stamped envelope. There were thousands of such requests, from all over the world.
			Someone at NSA objected to the distribution of this report to foreign nationals and for a while, RS&A suspended mailings—but when NSA failed to respond to inquiries asking for the legal basis of their request, RS&A resumed mailings. Adi Shamir believes this is the origin of the current policy [as of August 1995] that technical reports or papers can be freely distributed. [Note: two international journals, "Cryptologia" and "The Journal of Cryptology" were founded shortly after this attempt by NSA to restrain publication.]
			Contrary to rumor, RS&A apparently had no knowledge of ITAR or patent secrecy orders. They did not publish before applying for international patents because they wanted to avoid such restraints on free expression but rather because they were not thinking about patents for the algorithm. They just wanted to get the idea out.

TABLE 12-1 Cryptography Timeline. (*Continued*)

Date	C or G	Source	Info
1978	Civ	RSA	The **RSA** algorithm was published in the *Communications of the ACM*.
1984-1985?	Civ	ROT13	The rot13 cipher was introduced into USENET News software to permit the encryption of postings in order to prevent innocent eyes from being assaulted by objectionable text. This is the first example I know of in which a cipher with a key everyone knows actually was effective.
1990	Civ	IACR90	**Xuejia Lai** and **James Massey** in Switzerland published "A Proposal for a New Block Encryption Standard," a proposed International Data Encryption Algorithm (IDEA)—to replace DES. IDEA uses a 128-bit key and employs operations which are convenient for general-purpose computers, therefore making software implementations more efficient.
1990	Civ	IACR90	**Charles H. Bennett, Gilles Brassard** et al. published their experimental results on Quantum Cryptography, which uses single photons to communicate a stream of key bits for some later Vernam encipherment of a message (or other uses). Assuming the laws of quantum mechanics hold, Quantum Cryptography provides not only secrecy but a positive indication of eavesdropping and a measurement of the maximum number of bits an eavesdropper might have captured. On the downside, QC currently requires a fiber-optic cable between the two parties.
1991	Civ	Garfinkel	**Phil Zimmermann** released his first version of PGP (Pretty Good Privacy) in response to the threat by the FBI to demand access to the cleartext of the communications of citizens. PGP offered high security to the general citizen and as such could have been seen as a competitor to commercial products like Mailsafe from RSADSI. However, PGP is especially notable because it was released as freeware and has become a worldwide standard as a result while its competitors of the time remain effectively unknown.
1994	Civ	Rivest	**Professor Ron Rivest,** author of the earlier RC2 and RC4 algorithms included in RSADSI's BSAFE cryptographic library, published a proposed algorithm, RC5, on the Internet. This algorithm uses data-dependent rotation as its non-linear operation and is parameterized so that the user can vary the block size, number of rounds and key length. It is still too new to have been analyzed enough to enable one to know what parameters to use for a desired strength—although an analysis by RSA Labs, reported at CRYPTO'95, suggests that w = 32, r = 12 gives strength superior to DES. It should be remembered, however, that this is just a first analysis.

Printed with permission from Carl Ellison, *http://www.pobox.com/~cme/html/timeline.html*

Authors Mentioned throughout Timeline (Table 12-1):

Bacon: Sir Francis Bacon, `De Augmentis Scientarum,' Book 6, Chapter i. [as quoted in C. Stopes, "Bacon-Shakspere Question," 1989.

Burton: Sir Richard F. Burton trans., "The Kama Sutra of Vatsayana," Arkana/Penguin, 1991.

Deavours: Cipher A. Deavours and Louis Kruh, "Machine Cryptography and Modern Cryptanalysis," Artech House, 1985.

Diffie: Whitfield Diffie and Martin Hellman, "New Directions in Cryptography," IEEE Transactions on Information Theory, Nov. 1976

Feistel: Horst Feistel, "Cryptographic Coding for Data-Bank Privacy," IBM Research Report RC2827.

Garfinkel: Simson Garfinkel, "PGP: Pretty Good Privacy," O'Reilly & Associates, Inc., 1995.

IACR90: Proceedings, EUROCRYPT '90; Springer Verlag.

Kahn: David Kahn, "The Codebreakers," Macmillan, 1967.

Price: Derek J. Price, "The Equatorie of the Planetis," edited from Peterhouse MS 75.I, Cambridge University Press, 1955.

Rivest: Ronald L. Rivest, "The RC5 Encryption Algorithm," document made available by FTP and World Wide Web, 1994.

ROT13: Steve Bellovin and Marcus Ranum, individual personal communications, July 1995.

RSA: Rivest, Shamir and Adleman, "A method for obtaining digital signatures and public key cryptosystems," Communications of the ACM, Feb. 1978, pp. 120-126.

Shamir: Adi Shamir, "Myths and Realities," invited talk at CRYPTO '95, Santa Barbara, CA; August 1995.

Conclusion

This chapter presented the various hashing functions, cryptographic algorithms, and digital schemes used in the world of cryptography. As you can see now, cryptography is such a vast topic that this one chapter could not possibly cover all of the various mathematical techniques and methods described in this field.

You also should have noticed that VPN was not mentioned much; this was a deliberate attempt to focus your attention on the technology that underlies VPNs. Your VPN solutions are focused on a particular encryption algorithm—most likely, DES encryption. You should now have a high-level grasp of how DES works, including the algebraic operations that make up DES and other ciphers. Understanding the difference will help you make intelligent choices when deciding on VPN technology. Most likely, when you receive literature from vendors, they include DES, but they also include some proprietary encryption scheme of their own. If you wanted to, you could compare their strengths and weaknesses against those ciphers that exist out there today. There are actually only a handful of categories that ciphers fall into, and you may be able to do some comparison.

Even if your VPN decision is already made, you will probably now or in the future use some sort of public-key cryptosystem, e.g., Pretty Good Privacy (PGP). Now hopefully you can understand the IDEA algorithm that PGP uses. Consider this chapter just a glimpse into the world of cryptography; there are hundreds of books and Web sites that talk about cryptographic algorithms.

CHAPTER 13

Encryption

In Chapter 12, we looked at cryptography, which is the art of solving difficult problems. In this chapter we will look at the framework where this art resides. As you go through this chapter, you will see some of the same concepts, cryptographic functions, encryption algorithms, hash functions, and so forth. This is just an indication of how intertwined cryptography and encryption is.

We will look at the latest encryption schemes, such as Pretty Good Privacy (PGP), RSA, and the Diffie-Hellman public-key encryption algorithm. Then we will look at the latest Virtual Private Network standards, such as the Internet Security's Protocol (IPSec), Point-to-Point Protocol (PPTP), and Layer 2 Forwarding Protocol (L2TP). Virtual Private Networks will take advantage of the Public Key Infrastructure (PKI) now being developed. This provides the functionality of directory services for remote users through the use of certificates and digital signatures used in today's VPNs.

As mentioned in Chapter 12, you need to understand the overall concepts about encryption. You do not have to worry about the details found in the RFCs, but you have to understand how keys are maintained, stored, and created in your VPN environment. This will help you in maintaining and troubleshooting your VPN and keeping it safe and secure.

Private-Key Encryption

In private-key encryption (symmetric) system, the same key is used for both encryption and decryption. The main security importance is to get that key to the receiver in a secure fashion. Figure 13-1 illustrates the private key process.

In the private-key encryption system, for instance, DES, the secret key encrypts the message. In this example the message is "Tomorrow at 9:00 a.m." After it is encrypted, it then gets transported over the network, where the secret key again is used to obtain the original message. As shown in Figure 13-1, the private key should not go over the same medium and should be transported separately.

In a private-key system, the integrity of the key is extremely important. It is therefore imperative to periodically replace this key. The concept called "perfect forward secrecy," where keys are refreshed on a very frequent basis, helps to limit the damage because they provide only a very small window of opportunity for attacks.

The problem with these types of systems is in the number of keys

Figure 13-1

Private-key encryp-
tion process.

that need to be managed. In systems with a very small number of keys, this may be acceptable. As more keys are needed, the management and distribution of the keys become unrealistic. Take, for example, an organization that has 100 VPN users; there would be 4950 keys to manage. And this is only with a 100 users. Say your organization had a 1,000 users; the number of keys that would need to be managed would be a staggering 499,500.

The diagram below helps to explain how the actual number of keys are calculated given the number of users in an organization using symmetric encryption. This diagram shows a company that has six users. Because the users will be using symmetric encryption, a secret key is needed between each pair of users; that is, a key will be needed between A-B, A-C, B-C, and so on. The box labeled A-B 1 is the secret encryption key between users A and B. The box labeled C-D 10 is the secret key for users C and D. Note that there are even numbers of boxes: 15 dark-gray boxes and 15 light-gray boxes. The dark-gray boxes contain no encryption key. This is because the secret key that is labeled A-C 2 will be the same secret key that is in the dark-gray box numbered 3 in the C column. In other words, the secret key for user A-C is the same secret key for user C-A. There is no number at all in the F column; this is because all its key combinations are taken care of. User F-A is the same as user A-F 5, and so on. Now we'll notice the pattern in this simple example. There will be 15 keys needed. You will see the total number of N users is one less than the actual number 5 (no F), and the number of keys needed will take up half the actual number of users (6 − 3 = 3 there is still the bottom row of F keys). Therefore, in this example of six users, we calculate 5 multiplied by 3, or equaling 15 keys. In the case of 100 users, the calculation is $99^*50 = 4950$; and in the case of 1000 users, it is $999^*500 = 499,500$.

	A	B	C	D	E	F
A	1	2	3	4	5	
B	A-B 1	6	7	8	9	
C	A-C 2	B-C 6	10	11	12	
D	A-D 3	B-D 7	C-D 10	13	14	
E	A-E 4	B-E 8	C-E 11	D-E 13	15	
F	A-F 5	B-F 9	C-F 12	D-F 14	E-F 15	

This is a major drawback when symmetric encryption is used throughout the organization. The previous example didn't even mention changing keys, which has to be done on a regular basis, thereby adding more problems. However, symmetric encryption algorithms are generally faster than asymmetric (public key) and can use smaller key sizes and generate the same security as larger key sizes in public-key encryption algorithms. What we see is that the answer to the problem is to use a combination of both. Both public-key and private-key encryption algorithms are used together to provide the speed and security of private-key systems and the flexibility of public-key systems.

Public-Key Encryption

Public-key cryptosystems use a combination of a private key that is kept secret to the individual and a public key that is made available. This private key is not the one just mentioned earlier in the private-key cryptosystem; this private key only decrypts messages that have been encrypted with the associated public key. Rivest Shamir Adlemen (RSA) and Diffie-Hellman (DH) are two well-known public-key systems that are used in VPNs today. Figure 13-2 illustrates a public-key Diffie-Hellman encryption scheme.

In Figure 13-2 both sender and receiver have a Diffie-Hellman key.

Figure 13-2
Diffie-Hellman
public-key encryption
algorithm.

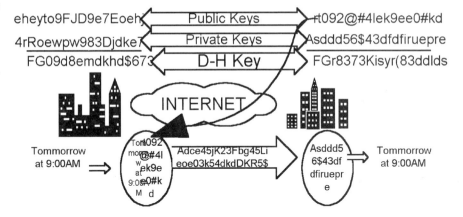

The sender obtains the receiver's public key from various sources and encrypts the message "Tomorrow at 9:00 a.m." with this public key. Then this message is sent over a public network to the receiver. The receiver then uses their private key with this message and decrypts the message. Notice that it takes both a public key and the private key to generate the D-H key, so if someone sent to a receiver a different public key, the D-H could not be generated and the receiver would know something wrong has happened. This does not mean it was intentionally intercepted; noise on the line could be the cause.

Shared Secret Key

We also may want to use a secret-key cryptosystems, since they are faster, but first, we need to find a way to establish a secure key that only the two end parties know. We don't want to give the other party our secret key, but we want something more than just relying on the public keys. This also is a feature of the Diffie-Hellman public-key cryptosystem. Figure 13-3 shows how this process works.

In Figure 13-3, User A and User B want to communicate using a secret-key encryption system using the Diffie-Hellman public-key encryption scheme first. There is a property in the D-H public-key encryption scheme wherein any two parties that use one another's public key will generate the same result. In this example, User A obtained User B's public key, and User B obtained User A's public key. When they perform a calculation function on their individual private keys and one another's public key, the results are the same; in this case, the shared

Figure 13-3
Diffie-Hellman shared
secret key.

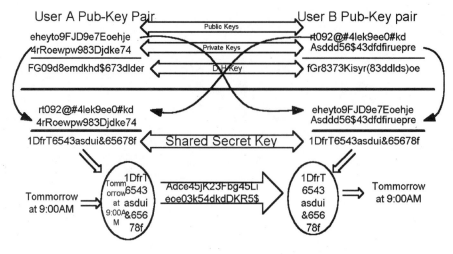

secret key was 1DfrT6543asdui&65678f. This is the secret key that the parties will use for later secure communications.

However, there still is the problem with the first initial communication between the two users: the sharing of the public keys makes the setup vulnerable to what is known as the "man-in-the-middle" attack, shown in Figure 13-4. In this scenario, User A tries to get User B's public key. The "man-in-the-middle" sends to User A his public key, claiming to be User B. He sends his public key to User B, claiming to be User A. As every bit of traffic passes back and forth between User A and User B, the man-in-the-middle intercepts it and then forwards it on without either User A or User B knowing what has happened. The way to avoid these kinds of security violations is by the use of digital signatures.

Figure 13-4
Man-in-the-middle
attack.

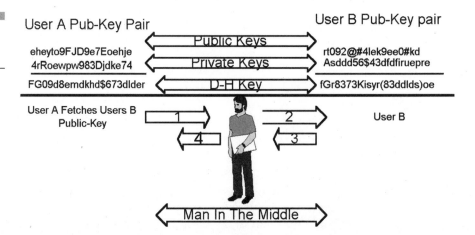

Digital Signatures

In the last chapter we have seen that a digital signature is a form of encryption, but that it works opposite of how we normally think encryption works. In encryption, only the receiver has the ability to decrypt a message that is intended for him or her. The reverse is also true. If a user encrypts a message with his or her private key, then the receiver can decrypt the message with the sender's public key. While the sender does not necessarily encrypt a message, he or she encrypts a hash value that was based on the message being sent. If the sender recalculates the same hash value, he or she knows it came from that sender. Anyone who has the sender's public key, which is readily available, can decrypt it; however, they can only decrypt the hash value, not the message itself. Therefore, if someone is eavesdropping, that person can be sure the original sender actually sent that message, but because the message was not encrypted with their public key, they cannot decrypt it. In this case, you are not worried about the security of the data, just who sent it.

Figure 13-5 illustrates the digital signature process. In the figure, User A runs the message through a hash function, which reduces it to a reasonable size, normally 128 bits. The resulting message digest is then encrypted with the user's private key; this process forms the digital signature. This resulting signature is then used together with the original

Figure 13-5
Digital signature
process.

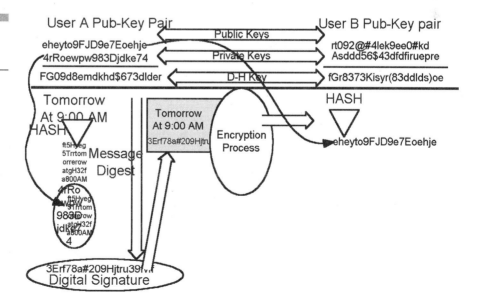

message, encrypted again, and sent to the receiver. The receiver does two things: First he or she generates the message digest using the same hash function as the sender, then he or she uses the sender public key to decrypt the digital signature in the message. If these two values are the same, the receiver knows that original user did send this message and it is intact. This process is also called a *data authentication algorithm*, since it provides a verified way to ensure the sender sent it and that the data was not tampered with. VPN users can thereby use a symmetric key encryption system, and by using the Diffie-Hellman and the RSA digital signature scheme, they can be safe from many attacks.

Certificate Authorities (CAs)

In any public-key infrastructure, there is always the opportunity for fraud. In some cases, it is the attacker pretending to be someone else, as in the man-in-the-middle attack mentioned earlier. By the use of digital signatures, we can be sure that someone signed the document, but we need a third party to make sure that signature is legitimate. That's the role of the certificate authority. It makes sure that this person is indeed the person they claim to be.

In order for a user to obtain a certificate, he or she presents his or her public key to the certificate authority, along with some unique piece of user identification. The public key, the user's unique piece of identification, and a particular CA identification forms the unsigned certificate. Next the certificate authority needs to sign this information. This is accomplished as follows: The certificate authority creates a hash code of this unsigned certificate. Then the CA takes this hash code and, together with its own private key, it encrypts them both. The CA then attaches this signature to the original certificate to form the signed certificate. Now a user could give this certificate to anyone who needs it or attach it to his or her public key. For the recipient to verify this, he or she decrypts the signature with the certificate authority, public key to recover the original hash code. Then the user recalculates the hash code of the unsigned signature, along with the one recovered from the first step. If these two match, the recipient can be sure the certificate does indeed match the original sender. This process happens the first time during communications or at an expiration date or if the sender revokes their public key. Once the receiver stores this digital signature that was verified by the certificate authority, he or she can accept any further communication from the sender with their digital signature.

The X.509 standard is becoming the universally accepted standard for formatting public-key certificates. A X.509 certificate consists of a user's public key, and a third party signs an identification of that user's block of information. This third party (certificate authority) can be a government agency, financial institution, or even a trusted server on your premises. The user gives this certificate authority his or her public key, and the certificate authority responds back with a certificate. Now the user can publish this certificate, along with his or her public key, and anyone can verify this against the certificate authority. The X.509 certificate standard also includes other items such as an identifier to point to the algorithm used to sign the document, an expiration time for the certificate, and with the latest version of X.509v3, other additional information that can be added in special circumstances. The X.509 standard also allows for the revoking of the key before it expires. Some of the applications used by X.509 are IPSec, SSL, Secure Electronic Transaction (SET), and Secure Multipurpose Internet Mail Extensions (S/MIME).

Diffie-Hellman Public-Key Algorithm

In 1976, Whitfield Diffie and Martin Hellman published an article titled "New directions in Cryptography." Since then their public-key algorithm has been used all over the world. The Diffie-Hellman key agreement protocol (also called *exponential key agreement*), is a negotiated key generation. Its strength lies in the logarithm's exponentiation finite field of mathematics. The protocol allows two users to exchange a secret key over an insecure medium without any prior secrets. The D-H algorithm also has established the security feature of a secret-key agreement, whereby even though it is an asymmetric (public-key) algorithm, the sender and receiver can use a symmetric encryption algorithm. Figure 13-3 illustrated the secret-key agreement concept. Diffie-Hellman was the first public key algorithm ever developed and is still extremely popular.

In the Diffie-Hellman key exchange, there are two global values: P (which is a prime number) and G (usually called a generator). G has a special property: It is an integer that is less than P and it can generate every number from 1 to P$-$1 just by being multiplied by itself. G is referred to as a modulo of P. Before users can communicate with each other using the D-H key exchange, they need to agree on a secret key. They do this as follows.

1. User 1 generates a private number X, and User 2 generates a private number Y.

2. They both generate public values based upon these private values and the global they've chosen, P and G. User 1's private key is G^x mod p, and User 2's private key is G^y mod p.

3. They now exchange their public keys,

4. Then they compute the secret key: User 1 would compute K_{xy} = $(G^y)^x$ mod p, and User 2 would compute K_{yx} = $(G^x)^y$ mod p. The logarithm operation has the property that the secret key K has the property K_{xy} = K_{yx} = K (the secret key); therefore, they would both have the same secret key.

The security behind this is that no one else can generate this secret key. Only the parties who know the values of X and Y can generate the secret key. Most security experts agree that in the D-H key exchange of P and G an extremely large modulus is needed; a modulus of 1024 bits is currently recommended.

The D-H key exchange is vulnerable to the man-in-the-middle attack, mentioned earlier and illustrated in Figure 13-4. This vulnerability exists because since that D-H key exchange does not authenticate users. Therefore, steps are needed to avert this, such as using digital signatures and certificate authorities.

RSA Public-Key Algorithm

In 1977, Rivest Shamir Adelman (RSA) developed what is probably the most common public-key cryptosystem in use today. It can be used for encryption and authorization and has key lengths of 768, 1024, and greater. RSA's strength comes from the difficulty in factoring large prime numbers. RSA is widely used in Internet applications such as PGP and S/MIME.

RSA uses two mathematical formulas: The encryption function, which is CT = PT^{Pub} mod N, and a decryption function, which is PT=CT^{Priv} mod N, where PT is the plaintext, CT is the ciphertext, Pub is the public key, and Priv is the private key mod N. Modulus is just the remainder of a modulus mathematical operation, e.g., 125/6 = 20.83, 125 mod 6 = 5.

The steps involved in the RSA calculations are as follows:

1. Take two large prime numbers, say, P1 and P2, and multiply them to find their product. In RSA we called this number M, or the modulus M=P1*P2

2. We then choose a number, call Pub, which is less than M, but relatively prime to (P1-1)(P2-1), which means the numbers (Pub) and (P1-1)(P2-1) have no common denominators to themselves except 1.

3. Find another number, say Priv, with the property that (PubPriv −1) is divisible by (P1-1)(P2-1).

4. Priv is the private exponent of the private key (M, Priv) and Pub is the public exponent of the public key (M, Pub).

5. The two large primes are no longer needed and can be destroyed.

RSA's security has to do with the properties of factoring large primes and finding a set of keys such that the public key "Pub" is the inverse of the private key "Priv" with respect to exponentiation in mod M. This means that the $(PT^{Pub} \bmod M)^{Priv} \bmod M = PT^{PubPriv} \bmod M = PT$. In English, the plaintext raised to the power of the public key, modulus M, is equal to the plaintext raised to the power of multiplication of the public and private key's modulus M, which equals the plaintext. Euler's Totient helps us find this key set so that the above conditions are true. Euler's Totient is the set of numbers from 1 to M − 1 that are relatively prime to M; therefore, to find ET(M), we need to know the prime factors of M.

Euler's Totient takes two theorems of arithmetic into account:

■ *Fundamental theorem of arithmetic.* This theorem states that every nonprime number (numbers that are divisible by 1 and themselves) can be represented as a product of a unique set of prime numbers.

■ *Relative prime.* Two numbers are said to be relatively prime if the condition exists such that they have no prime factors in common.

We then need to find this set of unique prime factors for N in order to calculate the Euler's quotient ET(M). Finding these primes is practically impossible for a sufficiently large M, which is why RSA is so secure. The main goal behind this is that given a modulus M (which a computer can generate) and Pub (the public key that is readily available) you can't work out Priv (the private key) and decrypt a message.

RSA is extremely secure, not because it has been proven to be secure, but rather because no mathematical algorithm has been invented yet to do so. There is some other speculation that an algorithm that could find the public root mod M could be easier than factoring M, but again no such algorithm exists yet, and RSA has withstood hundreds, possibly thousands, of attempts to crack it.

Pretty Good Privacy (PGP)

Philip Zimmerman's Pretty Good Privacy (PGP) has been utilized worldwide. Back in Chapter 6, I mentioned he had just released it before the U.S. government closed the door. Since then, many people have benefited from its use. Pretty Good Privacy (PGP) is a hybrid cryptosystem, giving you the best of both worlds. It combines both a public-key algorithm and a private-key algorithm. This gives PGP both the speed of a symmetric cryptosystem and the advantages of an asymmetric system. As far as users are concerned, PGP acts like any other public-key cryptosystem. PGP uses the RSA public-key algorithm and IDEA for encryption. A single IDEA key is used to encrypt the message, and the same key is used to decrypt the message (symmetric encryption). Then RSA is used to encrypt the IDEA key used for encryption with the recipient public key (asymmetric). The receiver uses his or her private key to decrypt the RSA-encrypted IDEA key. Then the decrypted IDEA key is used to decrypt the rest of the message. Along with PGP, Zimmermann created a set of utilities to manage a public key-ring, where users could manage multiple public keys.

Figure 13-6 illustrates an example of a PGP communication between User A and User B. The message is "Tomorrow at 9:00 a.m." The process is as follows:

1. User A encrypts the message "Tomorrow at 9:00 a.m." with the single IDEA encryption key.

2. User A encrypts the IDEA key with User B's public RSA key.

3. The message, consisting of the IDEA encrypted message and the RSA encrypted IDEA key, is sent to User B.

4. User B uses his or her RSA private key to decrypt the encrypted IDEA key.

5. Finally, User B decrypts the original message with the decrypted IDEA key.

PGP has been developed into a friendly front-end application that exists on many desktops today with all types of applications. Its popu-

Figure 13-6
PGP communication.

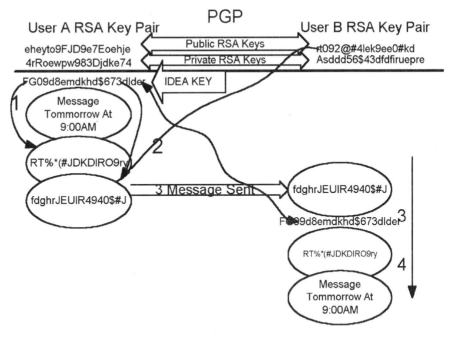

larity and ease of use, along with its RSA security strengths, make it a valuable security tool.

Internet Security Protocol (IPSec)

The Internet Engineering Task Force (IETF) has a working group called IP Security (IPSec), which is responsibile for defining standards and protocols relating to Internet security. Virtual Private Networks use these standards as part of their security measures. The IPSec working group is defining the structure of the IP packet itself and implementing a security association that will be used in VPN communications. Several of the following RFCs (which were moved to proposed standard in November 1998) associated with IPSec are as follows:

- RFC 2401: Security Architecture for the Internet Protocol
- RFC 2402: IP Authentication Header
- RFC 2403: The Use of HMAC-MD5-96 within ESP and AH
- RFC 2404: The Use of HMAC-SHA-1-96 within ESP and AH
- RFC 2405: The ESP DES-CBC Cipher Algorithm with Explicit IV
- RFC 2406: IP Encapsulating Security Payload (ESP)

- RFC 2407: The Internet IP Security Domain of Interpretation for ISAKMP
- RFC 2408: Internet Security Association and Key Management Protocol (ISAKMP)
- RFC 2409: The Internet Key Exchange (IKE)
- RFC 2410: The NULL Encryption Algorithm and Its Use with IPSec
- RFC 2411: IP Security Document Roadmap
- RFC 2412: The OAKLEY Key Determination Protocol

IPSec states that before any communication can take place, a security association (SA) is negotiated between the two VPN nodes or gateways. The security association sets up between the two devices all the information needed to ensure secure communications. Aspects such as transport and application layer services, authentication and payload encryption are set up during this security association communication. The security association is responsible for setting up several items in establishing the future secure communication between end hosts, including whether the packet is encrypted, authenticated or both. It will also specify the end point encryption and authentication protocols—for instance, DES for encryption and MD5 for authentication. It will also specify the keys used in these algorithms and other types of data.

The specific SA is identified by a 32-bit number called the Security Parameter Index (SPI). This number is just an identifier used by the end communication hosts themselves and has no meaning to anything outside this communication. The host's IP address and an SPI point to a unique SA. IANA assigns SPI numbers under 256, e.g., SKIP is 1.

The IPSec is further divided into two types of data transformation for IP packet security: the Authentication Header (AH) and the Encapsulated Security Payload (ESP). Let's look at each one individually.

Authentication Header (AH) RFC-2402

RFC-2402 describes how to authenticate IP datagram packets (data authentication) and provides for connectionless integrity, and if implemented, protection against replays. A security service in which the receiver can reject old or duplicate packets in order to protect itself against replay attacks, IPSec provides optional antireplay services by use of a sequence number combined with the use of authentication. The

sender in AH will increment a sequence number in the security association to protect against replays, but the receiver is not bound to check this
number. AH is not a full security mechanism, as the RFC itself states:

> AH provides authentication for as much of the IP header as possible, as
> well as for upper level protocol data. However, some IP header fields
> may change in transit and the value of these fields, when the packet
> arrives at the receiver, may not be predictable by the sender. The values
> of such fields cannot be protected by AH. Thus the protection provided to
> the IP header by AH is somewhat piecemeal.*

AH can be used in transport and tunnel modes. In transport mode,
AH is inserted after the original IP header and protects the upper-layer
protocols. In tunnel mode, AH is inserted before the original IP header,
and a new IP header is inserted. AH also has been designed for IPv6. In
IPv6, AH is seen as an end-to-end payload, and according to the RFC,
will appear after the routing headers (e.g., hop-by-hop, etc.). Figure 13-7
shows various modes for AH.

AH provides for data authentication by computing an Integrity Check
Value (ICV). According to RFC-2402, this should be provided and supported by MAC hash functions (HMAC w/MD5 and HMAC w/SHA-1).
Additional implementation of authentication algorithms may be implemented, but these two are mandatory.

---

*Copyright © 1998, The Internet Society. All rights reserved.

Figure 13-7
Various modes for
AH.

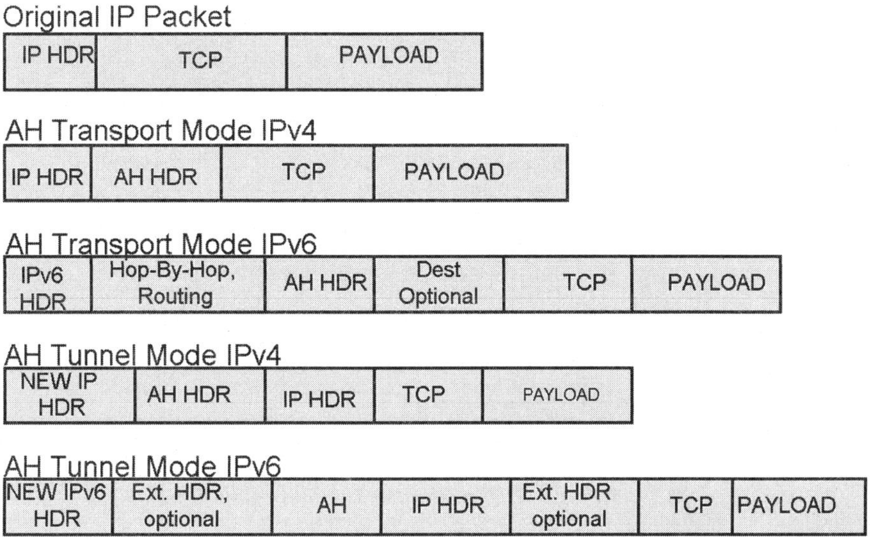

Original IP Packet

IP HDR	TCP	PAYLOAD

AH Transport Mode IPv4

IP HDR	AH HDR	TCP	PAYLOAD

AH Transport Mode IPv6

IPv6 HDR	Hop-By-Hop, Routing	AH HDR	Dest Optional	TCP	PAYLOAD

AH Tunnel Mode IPv4

NEW IP HDR	AH HDR	IP HDR	TCP	PAYLOAD

AH Tunnel Mode IPv6

NEW IPv6 HDR	Ext. HDR, optional	AH	IP HDR	Ext. HDR optional	TCP	PAYLOAD

Encapsulating Security Payload (ESP) RFC-2406

The Encapsulating Security Payload (ESP) standard provides for confidentiality, authentication, connectionless integrity, and antireplay services. This set of services in ESP is set up during the security association establishment. If you decide to set up only the confidentially of the datagram, RFC-2406 points out a potential security problem. As the RFC states:

> Confidentiality may be selected independent of all other services. However, use of confidentiality without integrity/authentication (either in ESP or separately in AH) may subject traffic to certain forms of active attacks that could undermine the confidentiality service.*

As in AH, ESP can be employed in two modes, transport and tunnel, both for IPv4 and IPv6. Also as in AH, in transport mode ESP protects the upper-layer protocols. Figure 13-8 shows various modes of ESP.

Figure 13-8
Various modes for
ESP.

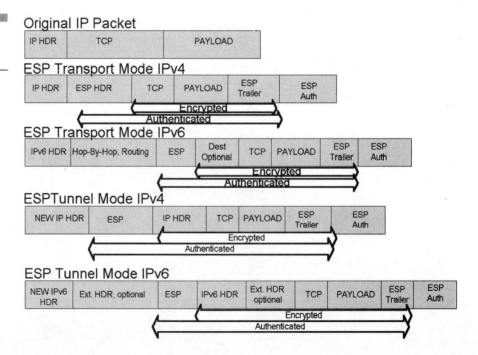

With ESP, there are encryption and authentication algorithms used. The ESP standard calls for a symmetric encryption algorithm and a hashing function for authentication. Accordingly, the ESP mandatory algorithms are as follows:

DES in CBC mode

HMAC with MD5

HMAC with SHA-1

NULL authentication algorithm

NULL encryption algorithm

The security association sets up the encryption and authentication schemes, and IPSec specifies optional, not mandatory, schemes. Therefore, support for the NULL algorithms is needed.

Problems with IPSec

IPSec has a few problems associated with it. One is that the keys are static; over the duration of the communication, there is no mechanism for exchanging these keys. Scalability has also been hard with IPSec due to the difficulty in managing enormous amounts of encryption keys in large networks. The Certificate Enrollment Protocol (CEP), developed by Cisco systems and VeriSign, has described a specific way of communicating with a certificate authority to allow the exchange of keys for large numbers of keys.

Another problem with IPSec's encapsulation approach is that it makes each IP packet bigger after the encryption process takes places. On some LANs the MTU size would force the fragmentation of these packets, which increases the network burden on devices such as routers. The other alternative is encrypting tunnels. Encrypt in Place (EIP), for instance, does not increase the size of the packet, but the trade-off is that most tunnels are proprietary, so mixing vendors may be impossible.

Many changes have been proposed to the original IPSec standard. One such major goal is to allow the support of dynamic client addresses. With dial-up users, IPSec needs to know how to handle dynamic addresses within the tunnel. The IKE protocol will also be looked at, since some security experts have uncovered a problem with the exposure of information. In addition, IKE has a problem in the way it handles the time expiration of session keys, which could cause one key not to understand the other. There is also no signaling mechanism in IPSec; therefore, if two end hosts fail to set up end communications, they can't exchange the reason why. Without IKE fully functional and implemented in IPSec, IPSec will not be the implementation of choice due to the manual key-exchange process that is unrealistic for large firms. Some features include support for IPSec client standardized dynamic addressing and additional support for additional cryptographic algorithm, such as RIPEM-160, which some European countries want to improve in the way IKE handles the key exchange.

Internet Key Exchange (IKE)

So far in the above examples, the main component of security processes has always been the keys. Whether they are freely available on a public server or on a hard drive on some unsecured server, the keys can compromise the whole system. The generation, distribution, and management of these keys fall under what is known as the key management. One of the problems with IPSec is the lack of a key-management system. The creation, exchange, and maintenance of these cryptographic keys do not exist in IPSec. However, the Internet Key Exchange Protocol (IKE) is a key-management protocol standard used with IPSec that is being developed. IKE is a hybrid protocol that implements the Oakley key exchanges inside a security association and the Key Management Protocol (ISAKMP). The framework of IKE allows for IPSec to offer such functionality as:

- Specifying a lifetime for the IPSec security association
- Allowing for the encryption keys to be updated change during IPSec sessions
- Allowing IPSec to provide antireplay services
- Allowing for the support of certification authority

ISAKMP

The Internet Security Association and Key Management Protocol (ISAKMP) that RFC-2408 specifies defines the process and packet formats to set up, negotiate, modify, and delete security associations. The security association contains information that is required for network security services, such as authentication and payload encapsulation. ISAKMP defines the payloads for exchanging key-generation and authentication data. However, ISAKMP is not bound to any specific cryptographic algorithm, key-generation technique, or security mechanism. While AH and ESP will safeguard the data, ISAKMP could be open to the man-in-the-middle attack; therefore, digital signatures are mandatory in ISAKMP. In addition, although ISAKMP requires an authenticated key exchange to be used, it does not specify one. IKE, however, specifies that the Oakley key exchange be used.

ISAKMP uses several security features for protection. Its uses a cookie, or anticlogging token (ACT), to protect against denial-of-service attacks. Session hijacking is eliminated in ISAKMP by linking the authentication, key exchange, and security association exchanges. According to the RFC, "This linking prevents an attacker from allowing the authentication to complete and then jumping in and impersonating one entity to the other during the key and security association exchanges." Man-in-the-middle attacks are eliminated by ISAKMP's authentication requirements that prevent a security association from being established with anyone other than the intended party.

ISAKMP uses two forms of negotiation. The first one is the ISAKMP SA, where they negotiate on how to protect further communications between them. This setup establishes the master key, from which all cryptographic keys will be derived. Phase One does not protect user data. These two ISAKMPs can have multiple ISAKMP SAs between them. Phase One keys are changed infrequently, maybe once a day or once a week. The second form of negotiation is used to establish security associations for other security protocols, for instance, IPSec. This second phase can be used to establish many security associations. Phase Two is used to set up protection for user data, and usually keys are refreshed every minute or two.

Oakley

The Oakley Key Determination Protocol (Oakley), RFC-2412, uses a hybrid Diffie-Hellman encryption technology to establish session keys. The Oakley protocol supports Perfect Forward Secrecy, which is used with ISAKMP protocol for managing security associations. Oakley is generic key exchange with long key lives; therefore, security could be a concern. As stated in the RFC:

> Because OAKLEY is a generic key exchange protocol, and because the keys that it generates might be used for encrypting data with a long privacy lifetime, 20 years or more. it is important that the algorithms underlying the protocol be able to ensure the security of the keys for

that period of time, based on the best prediction capabilities available for seeing into the mathematical future. The protocol therefore has two options for adding to the difficulties faced by an attacker who has a large amount of recorded key exchange traffic at his disposal (a passive attacker). These options are useful for deriving keys which will be used for encryption.*

In IKE, the ISAKMP SA establishes the first phase, which involves the authenticated key exchange between the ISAKMP entities. Oakley now protects all subsequent traffic and negotiation of SAs. Once the ISAKMP and Oakley (i.e., IKE) are set up—that is once the Diffie-Hellman public keys are exchanged and have been authenticated, and a secret key generated—the communicating systems can then establish an IPSec security association that dictates the type of AH and ESP security protocols that will be used.

Public Key Infrastructure (PKI)

The Public Key Infrastructure (PKI) is a system of digital certificates, certificate authorities, (both commercial and governmental), certificate management services, and directory services (LDAP, X.500) that verify the identity and authority of each party involved in any transaction over the Internet. PKI is the framework that provides for privacy and digital signature services in support of international commerce, balancing the needs of government and ensuring privacy.

Some uses of PKI include:

- Authentication and authorization
- Privacy and confidentiality
- Integrity of data
- Nonrepudiation
- Directory services such as X.500,LDAP
- Document transmission
- Legal and financial transactions
- Document archive and retrieval

PKI is being built into applications that support security in a wide range of Internet services, for instance, email, WWW documents, and LDAP. Certificates that bind a user to his or her public keys (and therefore can reveal the identity of that user) will play a big part in PKI. With PKI and the use of certificates, actions will be conducted electronically such as giving someone permission to write electronic checks, allowing banks to cash electronic checks, and proving identity. For this to occur, the certificate that binds a user to a public key will have to contain information about that user. Information contained in a PKI certificate will include:

- Certificate holder's identity
- Certificate's serial number
- Certificate's expiration dates
- Copy of the user's public key and/or digital signature
- The name of the certificate authority and its digital signature

While PKI promises a lot, there are unresolved issues that affect the interoperability, manageability, and scalability of using PKI on a grand scale. First off there are still several standards, including RSA Data Security's PKCS (Public Key Cryptography Standards) and the digital certificates that X.509 provides. Certificates formats differ: there are X.509 identity certificates, X.509 SET (Secure Electronic Transaction) certificates, PGP signed keys, and SPKI certificates. So which ones will be supported by vendors? A major issue with the PKI groups involves certificate management and certificate revocation. PKI systems will place revoked certificates on certificate revocation lists, but how certificate authorities will maintain these lists, and how applications and services will check these revocation lists, is still open to debate.

The long-term goal for PKI is to use certificate management integrated into a user management to create a directory-enabled management model. For example, a network administrator, we'll call him Joe, creates one account. Joe then gets a certificate, and using the LDAP protocol, he can conduct any and all business necessary immediately. If Joe is fired or quits, all that is needed is to delete his account. That way, his certificate is immediately revoked, along with all rights and privileges.

Overall, a PKI infrastructure has the security and flexibility to take advantage of the applications that are being developed today, for instance, extranet VPNs, electronic commerce, and LDAP.

Layer 2 Forwarding Protocol (L2F)

In 1996 Cisco Systems developed a protocol that was to be used in combination with Microsoft's PPTP. With the growth of dial-up services and the availability of many different protocols, a way was needed to create a virtual dial-up scenario, where any of these non-IP protocols could enjoy the benefit of the Internet. Cisco defined the concept of tunneling, meaning encapsulation on non-IP packets. Users make a PPP, SLIP connection to a dial-up ISP provider, and by the use of L2F, connect to their company's machines. This tunneling takes place at the border points to the Internet, which are routers with tunneling software called tunnel interfaces. Layer 2 Forwarding offers many benefits, such as:

- Protocol independence (IPX,SNA)
- Authentication (PPP, CHAP, TACACS)
- Address management (assigned by destination)
- Dynamic and secure tunnels
- Accounting
- Media independence, i.e., L2F over (ATM, X.25, Frame Relay)
- Both L2F tunneling and local Internet access

In the basic setup, the user makes a PPP or similar connection to a local ISP. At the request of the user, the NAS, using the L2F software, initiates a tunnel to the user's destination. The destination challenges the user for a password, and once authorized, assigns the user an IP address, just like a typical dial-up remote access device. The end point—that is, the corporate router running L2F—strips off the tunneling header, logs the traffic, and allows communication to take place.

L2F is one of the transport protocols used in Virtual Private Networks today.

Point-to-Point Tunneling Protocol (PPTP)

The PPTP Forum's (i.e., Microsoft, U.S. Robotics, et al.) PPTP protocol is a combination of the Point-to-Point Protocol (PPP) and the Transmission Control Protocol/Internet Protocol (TCP/IP). PPTP combines the features of PPP such as multiprotocol, user authentication, and privacy with the compression of data packets, and TCP/IP offers the routing capabilities of these packets over the Internet. PPTP allows for encapsulation of data by the use of a tunnel.

PPTP is an RFC draft standard (draft-ietf-pppext-pptp-06.txt). As quoted from the draft, PPTP was meant to be able to encapsulate PPP packets and forward them to their destination:

> This document specifies a protocol which allows the Point to Point Protocol (PPP) to be tunneled through an IP network. PPTP does not specify any changes to the PPP protocol but rather describes a new vehicle for carrying PPP. A client/server architecture is defined in order to decouple functions which exist in current Network Access Servers (NAS) and support Virtual Private Networks (VPNs). The PPTP Network Server (PNS) is envisioned to run on a general-purpose operating system, while the client, referred to as a PPTP Access Concentrator (PAC) operates on a dial access platform. PPTP specifies a call-control and management protocol which allows the server to control access for dial-in circuit switched calls originating from a PSTN or ISDN or to initiate outbound circuit-switched connections. PPTP uses an enhanced GRE (Generic Routing Encapsulation) mechanism to provide a flow- and congestion-controlled encapsulated datagram service for carrying PPP packets.*

PPTP can take packets such as IP, IPX, NetBios, and SNA and wrap them in a new IP packet for transport. PPTP uses the Generic Routing Protocol (GRE) to transport PPP packets. It uses encryption for encapsulated data and provides for authentication. PPTP traffic consists of two types of traffic for different data types: data packets and control packets. The control packets are used for such things as status and signaling, and the data packets are used for containing the user data. The data packets are packets that have been encapsulated using the Internet Generic Routing Encapsulation Protocol Version 2 (GREv2).

The PPTP connection first starts as a handshake between the two remote ends; they agree on the compression scheme and the encapsulation method to be used. During normal communication these packets can be fragmented if need be, and PPP header adds a serialization number to detect if a packet gets lost.

PPTP and IPSec can be thought of as the same: You can have an IPSec client establish a secure session to a firewall and create a VPN or have a PPTP client establish a session to the firewall. But PPTP will need an NT-based firewall, since it only runs on NT servers. PPTP can come in two modes. The first is compulsory mode, where the PPTP connection is made at the ISP connection point. Therefore, the ISP will need a special FEP processor to handle the PPTP connections. PPTP can also come in voluntary mode, where the PPTP connection is done at the end, a client to server, for example.

PPTP consists of three types of communications:

1. *PPTP Connection.*   This is just where a client establishes a PPP or (ISDN) link to their ISP.
2. *PPTP Control Connection.*   Using the Internet, a user creates a PPTP connection to the VPN server and sets up the PPTP tunnel characteristics
3. *PPTP Data Tunnel.*   The client and server send communications back to each other inside this encrypted tunnel.

Security in PPTP is integrated with Windows NT RAS security. Communications between remote users and their company's private networks is done by RAS encryption and authentication. Authentication protocols used are PAP, CHAP, and MS-CHAP. Encryption protocols used are 40-bit session key RSA RC4 and DES. 128-bit encryption is also available, only for use within the U.S. and Canada. However, according to the draft standard, PPTP does not provide security in its native format:

> The security of user data passed over the tunneled PPP connection is addressed by PPP, as is authentication of the PPP peers. Because the PPTP control channel messages are neither authenticated nor integrity protected, it might be possible for an attacker to hijack the underlying TCP connection. It is also possible to manufacture false control channel messages and alter genuine messages in transit without detection. The GRE packets forming the tunnel itself are not cryptographically protected. Because the PPP negotiations are carried out over the tunnel, it may be possible for an attacker to eavesdrop on and modify those negotiations. Unless the PPP payload data is cryptographically protected, it can be captured or modified.*

The security in PPTP will therefore come from other standards, some of which are listed here:

■ "Point-to-Point Tunneling Protocol—PPTP" (draft-ietf-pppext-pptp-05.txt)

- "Microsoft Point-to-Point Encryption (MPPE) Protocol" (draft-ietf-pppext-mppe-02.txt)
- "Deriving MPPE Keys from MS-CHAP V2 Credentials" (draft-ietf-pppext-mschapv2-keys-02.txt)
- "Microsoft PPP CHAP Extensions, Version 2" (draft-ietf-pppext-mschap-v2-02.txt)

Layer 2 Tunneling Protocol (L2TP)

In 1996 both PPTP and L2F were the emerging protocols. Vendors such as Microsoft, Ascend, and 3Com worked on PPTP, whereas Cisco worked on L2F. In 1998 these vendors agreed on a new IETF draft specification: Layer 2 Tunneling Protocol (L2TP). L2TP merges PPTP and L2F into a single standard (draft-ietf-pppext-l2tp-12.txt).

PPTP and L2TP offer software-based compression, which shrinks user packets. Compression techniques also add a layer of encryption, although a small amount. L2TP uses two functions: a client-like line server function referred to as LAC, which is an LT2P access concentrator and a server-side network server function called LNS. When a PC makes a PPP connection to an ISP, a LAC function will initiate a tunnel. Then the LAC adds the various headers to the PPP payload. The LAC establishes the tunnel to the LNS termination device—this device could be a router, server, or access device. After the tunnel is established, a user authentication mechanism is set up, i.e., TACAS or RADIUS tokens to establish the identity of the users. L2TP uses control messages to optimize the tunnel.

L2TP is similar to L2F mentioned in the last section, where you can install a LAC on the ISP premieres, and a remote user will make a connection (via PPP) to an ISP. Once on the ISP's network, the L2TP tunnel is created to the L2TP access concentrator.

L2TP is a layer-2 protocol, designed to encapsulate at layer 2. Therefore, IPSec, which is a layer-3 protocol, can be used with L2TP for added security. In fact, it is actually a recommended configuration if you are using L2TP to install IPSec security in an IP environment.

From draft-ietf-pppext-l2tp-security-02.txt:

> This draft proposes use of the IPSEC protocol suite for protecting L2TP
> traffic over IP and Non-IP networks, and discusses how IPSEC and
> L2TP should be used together. This document does not attempt to stan-

dardize end-to-end security. When end-to-end security is required, it is recommended that additional security mechanisms (such as IPSEC or TLS) be used inside the tunnel, in addition to L2TP tunnel security.

Simple Key Internet Protocol (SKIP)

In 1994 Ahsar Aziz and Whitfield Diffie developed the Simple Key Management Internet Protocol (SKIP). Each principal in SKIP communications is assumed to have a Diffie-Hellman public key pair. SKIP ensures a secure point-to-point communication session by encrypting all traffic with a shared secret key, illustrated back in Figure 13-3. This secret key is only known to the communicating parties and is used to derive a key. In SKIP terminology this session key is denoted as Kij. i and j are meant to denote users; therefore, Kij is the session key between those end users. Once this session key has been established, a variety of encryption algorithms can be used, for instance, RC4, 56-bit DES, 3DES, and 128-bit Safer. SKIP provides for a key-management protocol and consists of a hierarchy of keys that are constantly changing over time. The keys are created using the Diffie-Hellman algorithm, with key sizes ranging from 512 to 2048 bits. The lower-order keys, the ones that are directly encrypting the packet, are changing more rapidly that the upper-order keys, e.g., Kij. Some vendors allow you to set when these keys change, either by a specific amount of time or when a certain amount of data has been transmitted.

SKIP works with existing IP stacks, encrypting the data packets just below the IP layer. This makes SKIP transparent to network devices, applications, and even the user. SKIP uses packet-encrypted keys that are included in the packet; therefore, there is no need to establish communications to establish and change traffic encryption keys. (See Figure 13-9.)

In typical SKIP communications, the session key, Kij is known between any two Diffie-Hellman communicating parties; therefore, this

Figure 13-9
SKIP packet.

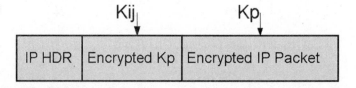

key does not need to be sent publicly. In the packet, the packet encryption key, Kp, is encrypted with the session key Kij and sent to the receiver. The receiver then decrypts the packet with his or her Kij to obtain the packet key Kp. Once they have the packet decryption key, then they can decrypt the rest of the packet. The IP header in a SKIP implementation has a protocol field value of 57, which has been assigned to SKIP by the Internet Assigned Numbers Authority (IANA).

In SKIP, the session key Kij could become compromised, say, through an attack on the server implementing SKIP. Since some implementations allow you to set a SKIP session key time-out, if that key becomes compromised, all data encrypted with the packet encryption key Kp within that time-out becomes vulnerable. Some SKIP implementations use an incrementing counter to update the master key. A counter is incremented, and once the counter has reached its set point, a new master key is updated. This eliminates the security concern of compromising earlier packet keys and playing back earlier data transmission.

Secure Wide Area Network (S/WAN)

The Secure Wide Area Network (S/WAN) is an initiative to provide for interoperability. If accepted and implemented by vendors, it will allow organizations to mix and match products from different vendors to create encrypted tunnels. Its design is to put security so low in the OSI stack that software vendors will not have to worry about security issues. Its main goal is for the interoperability of various Virtual Private Networks. S/WAN encompasses all of the encryption algorithms that are the most popular, including RSA, DES, RC4, and RC5, and key sizes of 40 to 128 bits.

The Internet Security Protocol (IPSec) does not specify encryption and authentication algorithms a vendor may use. Therefore, even if you have multiple vendors that support IPSec, they may not interoperate, due to vendors' implementation of IPSec. By lowering S/WAN in the OSI stack, upper-layer security—for instance, SSL—SOCKS will be layered on top of the S/WAN (IPSec security).

If vendors do support S/WAN, there will be VPN interoperability among various vendors who support IPSec. Unfortunately, this may be a long time in coming. Not all vendors even support IPSec, so if and when they do, then they will have to support a common-denominator set of IPSec services.

Conclusion

This chapter on encryption has touched on the major encryption algorithms that exist today, for both personal and corporate use. In the
beginning we looked at some public and private key encryption schemes,
such as RSA, PGP, and Diffie-Hellman. Then we looked at security practices, digital signatures, and certificate authorities. All throughout these
first sections, we saw how the keys (private, public, and shared-secret)
were transmitted and protected. Then we discussed the Internet Security Protocol (IPSec) and others, and we discussed the use of keys further.
In your VPN configuration, you have the same key-management concerns as you would on your personal encryption schemes.

Virtual Private Networks are therefore no different from any other
encryption framework you can think of. However, in your personal use,
the only thing that could be compromised is the safety of your personal
data. In your company's VPN, it is the safety of your corporation's data
that is at risk. Therefore, when your company installs a VPN, you'll
need to determine what framework you will use (e.g., IPSec) and what
algorithms you will use (e.g., DES for encryption, MD5 for authentication).

As a customer who installs a VPN product from a vendor, you would-
n't necessarily have any input to the kind of encryption schemes that
are implemented on that device. However, if you know that in the
future, you most likely will be doing LAN-to-LAN VPN or international
VPN, then you should be expected to at least compare the different technologies that exist.

In looking ahead at what is in store for VPN technology, just considering the Public Key Infrastructure (PKI), Lightweight Directory Access
Protocol (LDAP), and the Secure Wide Area Network (S/WAN) initiative
will give an indication of the enormous growth potential of this area.
VPN technology will change for the simple reason of PKI. Instead of
having a dedicated machine doing VPNs, a user's browser will send
encrypted packets to a service, and if using LDAP, even a global directory service.

CHAPTER 14

Secure Communication and Authentication

Authentication is the second major factor in a VPN configuration. Unfortunately, just as there were many different VPN architectures, topologies, encryption schemes, and so forth, so too are there many authentication schemes. Deciding on one is up to you; however, stick with what you know. There are two concerns: authentication ("who's allowed in?") and authorization ("what are they allowed to access?"). By the end of this chapter, you will know the major protocols and schemes available, and what's on the horizon.

This chapter will start with the basics—simple passwords—then build into some of the services you've probably heard of such as TACACS, RADIUS, and Kerberos. You don't need to worry so much about the disadvantages and advantages of these systems; usually the kind of infrastructure you have will determine your authentication requirements. In earlier chapters, we spoke about logging and audit trails; some authentication devices support auditing, some don't, and some support extended auditing. First determine what you want, then consult a few vendors. If you're not sure what you want, then look at some other sites, particularity universities. Many universities have used their infrastructure as a test bed and have documented their configuration and results. This is definitely a good starting point.

Finally, we will talk about advanced authentication protocols, certificates, LDAP, PKI, tokens, smart cards, and so on. These authentication protocols will take advantage of the applications and services written for large-scale enterprise configurations using the Internet.

Authentication Protocols

In any communications network infrastructure, there exists a need for an authentication process to allow individual users access to network services, while preventing unwarranted access to unauthorized users. This calls for a two-way trust setup: The system must trust the user, and the users must trust other users in the system (e.g., using someone's public key). In order for the system to gain a user's trust, the user will have to be able to prove that they are who they claim to be. This requires some sort of authentication process.

The framework that allows for this communication to take place is by the use of authentication protocols, many of which exist today. You encounter these when you log into your computer, when you log onto the network, when using an ATM machine to withdraw money, and so on. These protocols are of varying types, but most use the age-old principle of verification with a password, or several passwords. What is different is who has the password and how that information is transferred from client to server. In normal password systems, both the user and the system have knowledge of that password. Typically, if someone logs into a computer system, the computer has that person's password stored in a database along with his or her identity. The person supplies the password, and if the computer finds it matches the database, the login proceeds.

This, however, forces the password to be stored somewhere—in this case, a file on the server. Now you not only to have to worry about the security of the server, but that file on the server. In newer systems, a one-way hashing function is used instead of the file. A one-way hashing function is a cryptographic algorithm that allows for creating a hash value in one direction, but to go in the reverse direction (i.e., finding the clear-text password from the hash value) is computationally infeasible.

Unfortunately, even these one-way hashing functions are not 100 percent guaranteed to be invulnerable. By running a program that computes thousands of hash values based upon passwords and then comparing those hash values, it might be possible to guess what some values are. Passwords are not very large strings, so it doesn't take a massive computer system to accomplish this. Some of these hashing functions also add the value of a salt (we spoke about salts in Chapter 12) to this string to make it more difficult. If this salt is large enough, then it is widely accepted that the potential for a dictionary attack is almost eliminated.

After passwords, authentication services move into the client/server model of authentication using a network access server (NAS). This NAS server is the executor (the middle man) of the authentication and authorization of the client; the security server then just holds the configuration of the users. Therefore, there needs to be a set of rules governing how the NAS and the security server can communicate with each other on behalf of the client. This set of communication rules is often called the *authentication protocol,* and as we will see, there are many authentication protocols from all different types of vendors.

Network access servers and security servers are different; therefore, the choices you make should depend on interoperability issues and a commitment to open standards. As we will see, RADIUS, TACACS, and TACACS+ are some protocols that define this communication between the NAS and the security server. These are a few of the standards out there, and most vendors support a version of them.

Operating System Passwords

Passwords are still the most common form of the user authentication process in use today. They are used to control access to information, from simple network logins to PIN numbers we use for automatic teller machines. No matter what is written about the lack of security with password files, they are still widely used because they are simple, inexpensive, and convenient to install and implement.

At the same time, passwords are also recognized as being an extremely poor form of protection. Security advisories estimate that about 80 percent of the security incidents reported to them are related to poorly chosen passwords. Password security breaches are extremely dangerous, because a single computer may have hundreds or thousands of password-protected accounts. In today's interconnected networks, the consequences are now devastating. A skillful hacker would break into the system not to destroy it, but to use it as a starting point for attacks on other targets.

If you therefore insist on using a password file, either by choice or because of lack of resources, then at least take some necessary precautions to protect your server from attacks. *RFC-1244 Site Security Handbook* offers some guidelines for password management.*

Don't

- ■ DON'T use your login name in any form (as-is, reversed, capitalized, doubled, etc.).
- ■ DON'T use your first, middle, or last name in any form.
- ■ DON'T use your spouse's or child's name.
- ■ DON'T use other information easily obtained about you. This includes license plate numbers, telephone numbers, social security numbers, the make of your automobile, the name of the street you live on, etc.
- ■ DON'T use a password of all digits, or all the same letter.
- ■ DON'T use a word contained in English or foreign language dictionaries, spelling lists, or other lists of words.
- ■ DON'T use a password shorter than six characters.

Do

- ■ DO use a password with mixed-case alphabetic.

---

*From RFC-1244, Section 4.3.1 "Password Selection." Copyright ©1998, The Internet Society." All rights reserved.

- DO use a password with non-alphabetic characters (digits or punctuation).
- DO use a password that is easy to remember, so you don't have to write it down.
- DO use a password that you can type quickly, without having to look at the keyboard.

In selecting passwords, it's important to remember that you have to have a trade-off: you must select one that is easy to memorize so you don't need to write it down, but you also must make it restrictive enough to keep a potential hacker at bay. The objective then is to make it as hard as possible for a hacker to make an educated guess about what you've chosen. This leaves the potential hacker no alternative but to try a brute-force search, trying every possible combination of ASCII characters. A search like this might take an extremely long time, providing you with the opportunity to detect someone trying to break into your system. Therefore, RFC-1244 also recommends some guidelines for a user to select their passwords. These include:**

- Choose a line or two from a song or poem, and use the first letter of each word.
- Alternate between one consonant and one or two vowels, up to eight characters. This provides nonsense words that are usually pronounceable, and thus easily remembered.
- Choose two short words and concatenate them together with a punctuation character between them.

S/KEY

S/KEY is a software algorithm that was developed at Bellcore Laboratories and described in RFC-1760, a part of which is quoted here:

> The S/KEY system one-time passwords are 64 bits in length. This is believed to be long enough to be secure and short enough to be manually entered...when necessary. The S/KEY system applies the secure hash function multiple times, producing a 64 bit final output. MD4 accepts an arbitrary number of bits as input and produces a 128 bit output. The S/KEY secure hash function consists of applying MD4 to a 64 bit input and folding the output of MD4 with exclusive or to produce a 64 bit output.

S/KEY is a one-time password system, where each password used in the system is only used for one authentication. Passwords cannot be reused; therefore, they cannot be intercepted and used as a predictor of future passwords. Knowledge of already-used passwords in a user's S/KEY password sequence provides no information about future passwords. S/KEY one-time password scheme provides for secure authentication over networks that are subject to eavesdropping. S/KEY prevents the user's secret password from ever crossing the network during authentication. Since it is easy to integrate, many security-sensitive networks use S/KEY as their password security system. So, even if all of someone's S/KEY passwords are captured by a network analyzer as they are transmitted across the network, they will not beneficial.

The S/KEY system involves three key parts: the client, the server, and a password calculator. The client is responsible for providing the login process to the end user. The server is responsible for processing the user's login request. It stores the current one-time password as well as the login sequence number in a file. It also provides the client with a seed value. The password calculator is a one-way, nonreversible hashing function. This is defined as a function that loses information each time it is applied; it counts down after each password is used. In addition, the S/KEY server does not store the user passwords; therefore, even if someone was able to get root or administrator privileges, they could not determine users' passwords. The network protocol between the client and the host is completely independent of the scheme. Therefore, S/KEY can work with many security server software packages. An example of the hashing function is illustrated in Figure 14-1.

Figure 14-1 illustrates a typical S/KEY process, a one-time password scheme based on a nonreversible cryptographic hash of a secret string supplied by a user. It runs the pass phrase through the hashing program, and a small bunch of bytes is created through each iteration. S/KEY hashes up your pass phrase a number of times, and you supply these hashes as passwords in the reverse order from how they were generated. It is secured, since each time your pass phrase is hashed "forward," some information inside is lost, making it harder to go in reverse and obtain the original pass phrase. Since you are the only one who knows the secret phrase, only you can effectively go "backward" by starting with your known secret and continuing the process. Each hash is used as an authentication password once only; afterward, it is never valid again and, therefore, it is useless to network analyzers and hackers.

For a user to set up an S/KEY password, he or she first starts an initialization process with an S/KEY program (e.g., *skeyinit* on some fla-

Figure 14-1
S/KEY creation
process.

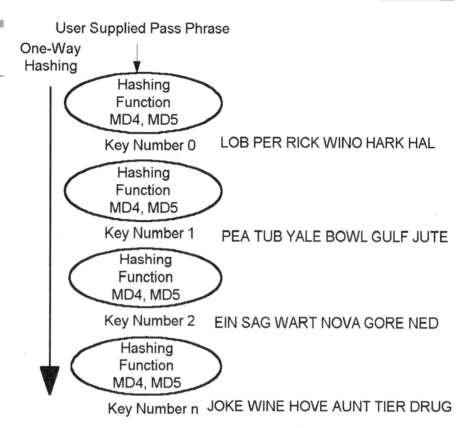

User Supplied Pass Phrase

One-Way
Hashing

Hashing
Function
MD4, MD5

Key Number 0   LOB PER RICK WINO HARK HAL

Hashing
Function
MD4, MD5

Key Number 1   PEA TUB YALE BOWL GULF JUTE

Hashing
Function
MD4, MD5

Key Number 2   EIN SAG WART NOVA GORE NED

Hashing
Function
MD4, MD5

Key Number n   JOKE WINE HOVE AUNT TIER DRUG

vors of UNIX). The user does this by selecting secret password and a number of passwords (X) to generate. Then a hash function, such as MD4 and MD5, is applied to the secret password the number of times (X) the user selected. The result is then stored on the server. When the user attempts to log in, the server issues a challenge, which is the number (X−1). The user-installed software prompts for the user's secret password, applies (X−1) iterations of the hash function to it, and sends this response to the server. The server applies the same hash function to this response. If the result it obtains in the same as the value it stored earlier, the authentication is valid and the user is allowed to log in. Then the server decrements this password counter.

S/KEY is a very valuable security process to the login solution; unfortunately, this process requires modification to existing binaries that support S/KEY challenge response that needs to be distributed throughout your company's servers. Passwords that flow on typical networks are needed for more than login—for instance, FTP and telnet, which need a username password response challenge function. Fortunately, many of these binaries exist for both UNIX and Microsoft Windows platforms.

Remote Authentication Dial-In Service (RADIUS)

Remote Authentication Dial-In User Service, or RADIUS, is a system of distributed security that secures remote access to networks and network services against unauthorized access by using the UDP protocol. RADIUS authentication includes two components: an authentication server and client protocols. The server is installed on a machine at the customer's site. All user authentication and network service access information is located on the RADIUS server. RADIUS allows for multiple formats that can be suited to an individual customer's requirements. A RADIUS server will authenticate users against a UNIX password file, Sun Microsystems Network Information Service (NIS), or in a separately maintained RADIUS database. The RADIUS model works on the client sending authentication requests to the RADIUS server, and acts on acknowledgements sent back by the server.

RADIUS authenticates users through a series of communications between the client and the server. Following is an overview of steps involved in a typical RADIUS communications using a RADIUS communication server:

1. Using his or her laptop, a user dials in to a modem connected to a RADIUS dial-in communications server. Once the setup connection is completed, the dial-in prompts the user for a name and password.

2. The dial-in server creates a data packet from this information called the authentication request. The data includes information identifying the specific dial-in sending the authentication request, the specific port that the communication came in on, and the username and password. For additional security, the dial-in server, acting in the role as a RADIUS client, encrypts the password before it is sent on its journey to the RADIUS server.

3. This authentication request is sent from the RADIUS client to the RADIUS server. RADIUS allows for multiple servers, so depending on network topology, clients can route their requests to various servers.

4. When the request is received by the RADIUS server, the server then validates the request and decrypts the data packet to access the username and password information. Then this information can be passed to the appropriate system handling security, such as a locally controlled user database.

5. Once the name and password have been verified, the server sends an acknowledgment (called an "authentication acknowledgement") that includes information on the user's network system and service requirements. That is, the RADIUS server can tell the dial-in server that the user is only allowed a specific host on the network.

6. If the username and password are incorrect, the RADIUS server sends an "authentication reject" to the dial-in device, and the user is denied access to the network.

7. To protect against hackers, particularly the man-in-the-middle attack, the RADIUS server sends an authentication key, or signature, identifying itself to the RADIUS client.

8. With this information, the dial-in server will allow or disallow network services to the client.

GENERAL NOTE The placement of RADIUS servers are important. If you only have one RADIUS server on a busy network, there may be a lot of incomplete login attempts due to time-out problems.

RADIUS service is not limited to dial-up service. Many firewall vendors support the use of a RADIUS servers. Therefore, if you choose, you could have your dial-in users and your VPN users authenticate the RADIUS server. RADIUS protocols, standards, and one-time passwords are mentioned in some of the following RFCs: RFC-2058, 2289, 2243, 2444, 2199, and 2200.

A problem may arise if your device does not support all of the operations and packet types associated with the RADIUS RFCs. An example of this is RFC-2058. Following is a small list of the operations supported in the RFC:

- Operation
  Challenge/Response
  Interoperation with PAP and CHAP

- Packet Types
  Access-Request

Access-Accept
Access-Reject
Access-Challenge

■ Attributes
User-Name
User-Password
CHAP-Password
NAS-IP-Address
Service-Type
Framed-Protocol
Framed-IP-Address

You can see by this short list that RADIUS technology has a substantial list of packet types and attributes. Therefore, when you are looking at your VPN device, you may need to find out what RADIUS components are supported.

Terminal Access Controller Access Control System (TACACS/XTACACS)

TACACS is a protocol standard specified in RFC-1492. Servers that are TACACS-aware, forward user/password information to a centralized TACACS server. The TACACS server can be either a TACACS database or a database like a UNIX password file with TACACS support. For example, a router with TACACS enabled passes user requests to a TACACS server, which can query a UNIX database to allow authorization. TACACS was originally developed by BBN Planet Corp., an Internet provider. Cisco Systems later adopted TACACS and forwarded it to the Internet Engineering Task Force for RFC status.

In TACACS authentication mode, a user requests login privileges to a terminal server, UNIX host, router, and so forth. The device will ask for a name and password and forward that request to the TACACS server in its configuration for validation. The server will validate the login and password pair with a TACACS password file. If the name and password is validated, the user is allowed to log in.

TACACS later evolved into an extended protocol, XTACACS, which includes support for some accounting and additional features on the server. XTACACS servers provide information to do audit trails, tracking user login times, and host logins, which dictate how long a particular host can be connected to the network.

The latest generation of the TACACS line is TACACS+, which was developed by Cisco Systems, incorporates increased security features such as secure communication over the network and improved access control.

Terminal Access Controller Access Control System Plus (TACACS+)

The TACACS+ protocol is another protocol developed by Cisco Systems. Despite the name, TACACS+ is very different from TACACS and XTACACS. It is a TCP-based access-control protocol using reserved Port 49. TACACS+ has several advantages over TACACS and XTACACS, as mentioned in draft-grant-tacacs-02.txt, it:

- Separates the functions of authentication, authorization, and accounting
- Encrypts all traffic between the NAS and the daemon
- Allows for arbitrary length and content authentication exchanges, which allows any authentication mechanism to be utilized with TACACS+ clients
- Is extensible
- Uses TCP to ensure reliable delivery

When the user attempts to log in, the network access server will ask the security server what to do, instead of merely forwarding the name/password to some central server. The security server will tell the network access server to initiate a command, such as prompt for the username and password. After the username and password have been entered, it will then send a permit or deny packet to the NAS.

TACACS+ has a system of attributes that are conveyed between the NAS and security server. These attributes are a set of configurations that are applied to an individual user. When the user logs in, for every command the user enters, the NAS will send an authorization request to the security server. At this time the NAS may suggest a set of attributes to be applied to the user. Based on that information in the request, the security server will either a permit or a deny the request and send the response back to the NAS. If it is a permit response, the security server may tell the NAS to apply additional attributes to that user. Examples of attributes are IP addressing, filters, date and time restrictions, and time-out values.

The attributes that are sent by the NAS are either optional or mandatory. If it is optional, the security server could propose an alternative attribute. However, if that attribute from the NAS is mandatory, the security server cannot change that attribute. In addition, if the security server does not agree to the attribute, it can only deny the user request. Each of the attributes that are returned by the security server to the NAS can also be optional or mandatory. If optional the NAS can choose to ignore the attribute. If mandatory the NAS must use that attribute. If the NAS cannot execute the attributes returned by the security server, again it has to deny the user request.

The NAS can also send out accounting start records to the security server to indicate the start of an accounting session, and an accounting stop record to indicate that the accounting session has ended. In the stop record, there will be information on the amount of time and data sent and received during the session. These authorization, authentication, and accounting messages are usually turned on in the NAS.

Kerberos

Kerberos V5 is a trusted third-party authentication protocol that allows a process running on a client to prove its identity to a Kerberos server without sending data across the network that might allow an attacker or the verifier to subsequently impersonate the principal. It was developed at MIT in the 1980s as part of the Athena project and is described in RFC-1510. The Kerberos protocol is based on the Needham and Schroeder authentication protocol, but it has been modified to support different functionality in different environments. Kerberos got its name from mythology, from Cerberus, the three-head guardian dog of Hades.

Kerberos is a symmetric DES encryption system. It utilizes a centralized private-key cryptographic functionality, and at the heart of this system is the Key Distribution Center (KDC). The Kerberos Authentication System uses a series of encrypted messages to prove to a verifier that a client is running on behalf of a user. The KDC centrally manages users and services and is the keeper of secret keys that are used with users

Figure 14-2
Kerberos
communications.

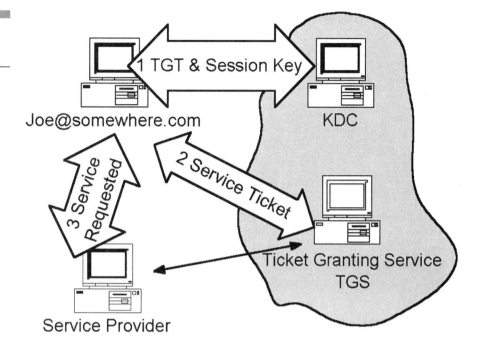

and services, which are referred to as the principals. Kerberos does not use passwords in the normal sense; instead, it uses credentials and session keys. Principals contact the KDC to acquire credentials so they can access network services. Figure 14-2 illustrates typical Kerberos communications taking place.

In Figure 14-2, the Kerberos communications is as follows:

1. User Joe at Somewhere.com (In Kerberos, Somewhere.com is considered a realm) requests a "Ticket Granting Ticket" (TGT) from the KDC. This is similar to presenting proof of identity to obtain a social security card or driver's license. The TGT is the actual mechanism used so Joe can obtain services. The KDC checks its database for the principal, fetches the client key, and generates two messages that contain the KDC session key. One message is encrypted with the client key, and one is encrypted with the KDC session key. It sends these two messages back to the client. The client now tries to decrypt both messages with the user-entered password (after the password is converted to a key). The client needs to obtain the session key in both messages.

2. Now when User Joe wants to obtain a service on the network, he (the client application) queries the KDC for a Ticket Granting Service (TGS). This message contains the TGT from Step 1, encrypted with the KDC service key, along with what is known as an "authenticator," encrypted with the KDC session key. An authenticator is just an identity to prove to the service that its contains the KDC session key. The KDC will decrypt the TGT inside of the request, confirm the authenticator, and send back an encrypted service ticket and a service session key. The client then decrypts the TGT reply and stores the information.

3. Next the client forms an application request, encrypts it with the service session key, and sends it to the application server. The service provider decrypts the message using the application service key. It then formats a service reply encrypted with the application key and forwards it to the client. This is a form of mutual authentication and gives the client the ability to verify the actual service provider it is trying to contact. The service provider also to passes messages passed to the KDC to verify the client's identity.

Kerberos is extremely flexible. With added security features, it makes the applications security-aware and provides a single sign-on with no passwords flowing through the network. It also allows the network manager to break up the network into different security realms, with different security applied to each realm. Kerberos does have some limitations, though. It is not very effective against password guessing attacks; if a user chooses a poor password, then an attacker guessing that password can impersonate the user. Similarly, Kerberos requires a trusted application in which passwords are entered. If the user enters a password to a program that has already been modified by an attacker, or if the path between the user and the initial authentication program can be monitored, then an attacker may obtain sufficient information to impersonate the user.

Kerberos has to be integrated with other parts of the system. It does not protect all messages sent between two computers; it just protects the messages from software that has been written or modified to use Kerberos. The term "Kerberized" is used to describe those applications that have been modified to take advantage of Kerberos security features. In addition, Kerberos needs the machines to be in time synchronization. Tickets contain a time-stamp; if the clocks on the various machines are off, the tickets will be useless. Therefore, a protocol like Network Time Protocol (NTP) should be used with Kerberos.

Certificates

In the last two chapters, we've mentioned certificate authorities, digital signature, and signing a certificate, but we haven't discussed exactly what a certificate is. Certificates are simply data structures that contain information. With certificates, we are not just concerned about the information, although that is needed. What we want to accomplish is to positively identify something, whether a user or device. When we talk about positively identifying something, then we are talking about the concept of nonrepudiation, and in this context, also the concept of binding a public key with a subject. You can think of digital certificates as a passport used to verify an identity.

The contents of digital certificates are as follows:

- The certificate holder's identity
- The certificate's serial number
- A valid, unchangeable date for the transaction
- The certificate's expiration dates
- A copy of the certificate holder's public key for encryption and/or signature
- The identity of the issuing certificate authority and its digital signature
- Group name
- City, state

Certificate Standards

Digital certificates are based upon the International Telecommunications Union, Series X recommendations, ITU-X509 standards, and RSA's "PKCS #7, Cryptographic Message Syntax Standard." X.509 digital certificates have been revised to the current proposed version X.509v3. Some of the modification to the X.509 standards have been:

- *X.509v1.* Version 1 defined a very simple set of attributes, *namely public-key* information. However, there were still security concerns with version 1. Very few platforms supported version 1, and it didn't scale very well.
- *X.509v2.* Added some more information about the subject and

about the issuer of the certificate authority, but still had not gained widespread acceptance.

■ *X.509v3.*   Version 3 added priority extensions; therefore public-key information and additional attributes about a user could be added if necessary. Certificate revocation lists were also added. Version 3 is accepted by government and commercial businesses.

Now with the acceptance of X.509v3 and the Public Key Infrastructure (PKI) mentioned in Chapter 13, businesses will be able to conduct business using digital certificates in the PKI framework from their workstations by using a Web browser and an LDAP-aware application (e.g., a database).

Obtaining a Certificate

For most purposes, you don't need to obtain a certificate. In most cases, you can just use the default digital certificate that is included with your secure server. Digital certificates include information about the owner of the certificate; therefore, when users visit your (secured) Web site, their Web browser will check information on the certificate to see if it matches the site information included in the URL. Sometimes a box appears warning you about a problem and warning you that someone may be trying to intercept your communications. That could be true, but usually it's more likely that the site name is incorrect, domain name is wrong, and so on.

Say that you want to get your own certificate. All you need to do is to go to one of the many sites issuing certificates (these are the certificate authorities) and buy one. Certificates are priced differently depending on what kind of certificate you want. Below is a just a small sampling of the certificates available:

■ *Class A, 1, Premium, High.*   These are digital certificates with high-level assurance. Usually used for SSL and SOCKS-enabled sites, they offer high-level security for S/MIME applications, financial transactions, enhanced electronic commerce, and other secure applications.

■ *Class B, 2, Medium, Basic.*   These are the digital certificates with medium-level assurance. Used for access to SSL-enabled sites, they provide medium-level security for S/MIME applications, enhanced electronic commerce, online shopping, newspapers, and so on.

- *Class C, 3, Basic, Freemail.* These are the digital certificates with basic security. Used for simple electronic ordering and personal secure mail.
- *Class D or 4 (chained).* This type is used for multipurpose organizations, very much like a multiuser license.

The reason there are different names is because different CA's name their certificates differently, and some overlap. Class A at one CA is the same type of certificate as Class 1 at another CA. At one site, a Class B is comparable to a Basic at another site, yet another CA's Basic is similar to a Class C from yet another CA. In addition, prices vary considerably, ranging from free to $100 per certificate, with price breaks when buying multiple certificates (this is referred to as Chained or Class D). The higher level of certificate you want, the more proof you will have to give the CA, which will incur more cost. Say, for example, that you want a digital certificate that is Class A, or Premium, and you are going to be conducting financial transactions over the Internet. The CA must be absolutely sure you are who you say you are, which involves more scrutiny of various databases to corroborate the information you gave the CA, and, therefore, more costs—and, potentially, more legal liability. We've talked about the revocation of certificates; the CA is going to have make sure they revoke a certificate once you tell them to or in the case of a security breach.

SECURITY NOTE   Certificate authorities are actual third-party companies, not concepts or software algorithms. This means CAs can be broken into and hacked just like any other site. The stronger the CA infrastructure, the stronger the protection.

Certificates, however, are not endorsed by everyone. There are those who say that certificates that verify digital signatures are extremely insecure. One such opponent is E. Gerck and the Meta-Certificate Group (MCG). This groups advocates a system of Meta-Certificates instead of other systems. The MCG system contains the following guidelines, as stated on their Web page:*

> No parts of this general work will be patented, but published—including source code—and shared under the common protection of the copyright law to avoid third-party patenting. Members of the MCG will profit by

---

*Boldface has been added for emphasis.

contributing towards a better and easier communications standard and by being at the forefront of said development. Applications will be independently developed by any individual or organization, not necessarily connected with the MCG. Presently, the entities that compose the MCG envision and are actively developing software for the following applications that will be marketed worldwide: the Meta-Certificate API, client and server, compiled in Java and in C, Internet commerce, telecommunication services using the Internet, support for SSL, SET, etc., Internet routing in a three-tier architecture, etc.

It is noteworthy that because the Meta-Certificate design avoids the international security issues it has the potential to be the vehicle of choice for international products and services—a modern "lingua franca" in Internet certification. One of the design goals is to make it as transparent as possible to any national legislation in existence or in planning.

This report goes on to imply that the functionality of identifying the user, or what is termed as a "unique distinguished name" or DN, is not the responsibility of the X.509 standard, but that of the CA, and even then it is not clear:*

Thus, X.509 focuses on defining a mechanism by which information can be made available in a secure way to a third party. However, X.509 does not intend to address the level of effort which is needed to validate the information in a certificate neither define a global meaning to that information outside the CA's management acts. The main purpose of a CA is to bind a public key to the name contained in the certificate and thus assure third parties that some measure of care was taken to ensure that this binding is valid for both—i.e., name and key. **However, the issue whether a user's DN actually corresponds to identity credentials that are linked to a person or simply to an e-mail address—and how such association was verified—is outside the scope of X.509 and depends on each CA's self-defined CPS.**

Finally, the report concludes that processing surrounding certificates authorities becomes utterly useless, and this is evident by the disclaimers. I left out this particular vendor's name and replaced it by the word company, since it is apparent that all CAs would have a similar disclaimer:

Company disclaims any warranties with respect to the services provided by company hereunder including without limitation any and all implied

---

*From E. Gerck, Overview of Certification Systems: X.509, CA, PGP and SKIP, *http://mcg.org.br/cert.htm#1.1.*

warranties of merchantability or fitness for a particular purpose. Company makes no representation....Company makes no assurances of the accuracy, authenticity, integrity, or reliability of information contained in digital IDs or in CRLs compiled, published or disseminated by company, or of the results of cryptographic methods implemented.

GENERAL NOTE   This particular disclaimer states that you will have no legal recourse against the CA. I think it is to be expected that, considering the uncertainty of standards and the legal environment that exists today, every CA will take this stand.

Smart Cards

A smart card is very similar to the credit card you carry in your wallet. It is a credit card-sized plastic card with a small chip embedded in it. Smart cards provide data portability, security, and convenience. Three terms are used in conjunction with smart cards:

1. An IC card with ISO 7816 interface
2. Processor IC card
3. Personal identity token containing IC-s

The term *smart card* comes from the French. While inventors in the U.S., Japan, and Austria were working on smart cards, it was the French who made a heavy investment in the technology. Roland Moreno, a Frenchman, made a big impact in smart card technology in the 1970s, during a period of major national investment in modernizing the nation's technology infrastructure. A company named Bull holds about 60 patents related to MP cards; they were called *carte a memoire,* or memory card. France began exporting the technology in the 1980s, Roy Bright of the French government's marketing organization Intelimatique coined the word "smart card."

A smart card is an access control device supporting different applications. It allows users to access personal and business data, make purchases, and help businesses evolve and expand their products and services in a changing global marketplace. Banks, financial institutions, telecommunications carriers, computer software companies, and airlines are just some of the companies that have the opportunity to tailor their smart card for their individual products and services. There are over a billion smart cards in the world today, and forecasts show that by the turn of the century, there will be over 2 billion. They are growing over 30 percent a year, mostly outside of the U.S. The growth in services will concentrate in areas such as digital wireless phone services, payphones, wireless telephony, Internet access, banking, healthcare, and pay-per-view television.

Smart cards are continually being developed and standardized. In addition, smart cards are employing cryptographic algorithms for security. Mondex USA formed a specification for smart technology for electronic cash, then Europay, MasterCard, and Visa formed a working group to create their own smart card specification to compete with the Mondex specifications. This first version was based on cards using symmetric encryption. Smart cards also allow users to carry digital certificates with them, thereby providing them with identification when needed.

The National Institute of Standards and Technology (NIST) is involved in setting standards for smart card technology and encryption. One of the documents available describes the encryption process of smart cards: "Implementation Guidance for FIPS PUB 140-1 and the Cryptographic Module Validation Program" can be read at their Web site, *http://csrc.nist.gov/cryptval/140-1/1401ig.htm*.

Hardware Tokens/PKCS #11

Hardware tokens are tamper-resistant, credit card-sized devices (and a type of smart card) that a user holds in his or her possession. An LCD on the card consists of six to eight digits, which usually change every 60 seconds. In user authorization, the LCD is usually combined with a PIN. Both are known only to the user, and together they serve as the password. For convenience, however, you can limit the password to just the LCD display. If you decide to use the LCD as the password, it should be used with another security mechanism, such as an encryption scheme like DES. The term "software token" is just an application on a machine that emulates a hardware token device.

Smart cards and tokens have a security feature that disables them automatically after a specified number of failed attempts to enter the correct PIN. Smart cards and tokens also provide enhanced protection of user data at the office by separating users' certificates from their hard drives and requiring a PIN, thus reducing the odds that any individual computer can be attacked.

The Public-Key Cryptography Standards (PKCS), developed by RSA in conjunction with a consortium of others, are a set of standards being developed for public-key cryptography. PKCS are compatible with the ITU-T X.509 digital certificate standards. The PKCS standard includes some defined algorithm standards such as RSA and Diffie-Hellman. PKCS also defines independent standards that can be used for digital signatures, digital envelopes, and extended digital certificates.

The current list of PKCS standards, available from RSA Laboratories at *http://www.rsa.com/rsalabs/pubs/PKCS/*, are as follows:

- #1. Mechanisms for encrypting and signing data using RSA
- #3. Diffie-Hellman key agreement protocol
- #5. A method to encrypt a string with a secret key derived from a password
- #6. Currently is being phased out and being replaced by version 3 of X.509
- #7. A general syntax for messages and cryptographic enhancements such as digital signatures and encryption
- #8. Format for private-key information
- #9. Selected attribute types for use in the other PKCS standards
- #10. Syntax for certification requests
- #11. Defines a technology-independent programming interface called Cryptoki for cryptographic devices such as smart cards
- #12. Specifies a portable format for storing or transporting a user's private keys, certificates, etc.
- #13. Mechanisms for encrypting and signing data using the elliptic curve
- #14. Standard for pseudorandom number generation

It is #11 that is used in smart card technology. RSA Data Security developed PKCS-11, which specifies the Cryptographic Token Interface Standard—an API called Cryptoki—for devices that hold cryptographic information and perform cryptographic functions. Cryptoki (pronounced "crypto-key") uses an object-based approach, specifying technology independence (any kind of device) and resource sharing (multiple applications accessing multiple devices) and presenting to applications a common, logical view of the device called a cryptographic token.

Lightweight Directory Access Protocol (LDAP)

The Lightweight Directory Access Protocol (LDAP) is an extensible network protocol for accessing information inside a directory. However, the directory structure inside LDAP is not the same as a regular directory. In a regular directory, you usually have a static view of the contents in that directory—where its contents are created, modified, and deleted over time. Compare this to an LDAP directory, where you can store such things as photos, certificates, URLs, and so on, and you can see that the LDAP structure is alive with all sorts of data that can be stored inside of it. LDAP can be defined for groups of people, thereby having one access point for multiple data types. Some of the LDAP standards define:

- The network protocol for accessing this information
- A namespace, defining how information is referenced
- How information is organization inside the directory
- A distributed model (in LDAPv3)

LDAP was born out of the X.500 Directory Access Protocol (DAP), first started in 1988. X.500 DAP defined a set of protocols in an open system that provided for users and machines to access directory services throughout the organization. X.500 used a set of directory servers (DSAs), each having a portion of the total directory service in a company. X.500 was meant to be an open standard. Unfortunately, this meant the data had to be very secure in transit through the network (later models of the X.500 protocol supported additional security features). LDAP has gone through various modifications. LDAPv2 was an Internet standard in RFC-18777. However, due to severe limitations with this version, it was not considered a viable option for the Internet community. Actually, LDAPv2 abides by the RFC standard itself; it just can't function on today's networks. LDAPv3 is now the standard of choice described in RFC-2222, 2251, 2252, and others.

LDAPv3 uses a security model that is based on the Simple Authentication and Security Layer (SASL), described in RFC-2222. This allows for secure communication and encryption between the server and the client. SASL is a framework, whereas Secure Sockets Layer (SSL) and Kerberos can be used as the security services. LDAP allows for the use of certificates, with the X.509 standard, and work is continuing to support LDAP with the latest certificate X.509v3 standard.

LDAPv3 has improved its performance over its predecessor, LDAPv2. In LDAPv2, clients who wished to access X.500 directory service first had to go through an LDAP server and make a bind request. Once authenticated, the LDAP server would then query the X.500 database on behalf of the client. In LDAPv3, a client can request searches to the LDAPv3 server without binding to it first. This was an improvement, since most of the requests were anonymous and allowed in the first place. If the X.500 database has set up security, the LDAPv3 will deny the client request, issue a bind error, and the client will try again, this time binding to the LDAP server first.

LDAP has come from the Internet community and has broad support from most major vendors supporting X.500. Like the World Wide Web, LDAP gives the user great flexibility. With LDAPv3 and its support for X.509v3, it should continue to grow like other services that exist on the Internet. Web browsers, mail clients, LDAP-aware applications and Virtual Private Network will all take advantage of LDAP.

ACE/Server with SecurID

Security Dynamics Technologies' ACE/Server SecurID is a technology implementation that ensures "strong authentication." Strong authentication in this context refers to two-factor authentication. Two-factor authentication is a combination of any two of the three available classifications of user identifications. They are as follows:

1. *Something Known.*   This is normally a password or, in some cases, a PIN.

2. *Something Held.*   This is a device, for example, a smart card, a key, or a token.

3. *Something One Is.*   This is biometrics, which means some human feature such as a fingerprint or retina scan.

When an individual is using any two of these three authentication methods, it is then defined as two-factor authentication. According to Security Dynamics, a security token consists of four attributes:

1. A physical device that must be in your hand to use.

2. It must be small enough for you to carry.

3. It must be difficult to counterfeit.

4. It must be assignable.

In the ACE/SecurID setup, a server (ACE/Server) is in "time-synchronous" mode with the smart card (SecurID). The card and the server share a common date/time stamp and what is known as a seed value. It is similar to the setup in a one-way password hashing algorithm, like in S/KEY. The server does not need to know the actual token, but with a record of the date/time stamp and the seed value, the server can generate the token and then match the token that was entered by the user. This session token can change every 30 or 60 seconds. An initial setup is used to generate the one-time password (OTP) that all subsequent tokens will be derived from.

The first part of the user authentication method is the SecurID card, which is a smart-token, two-factor authentication device. The hand-held device is the size of a credit card, containing a CPU, microprocessor, memory, and an output display (LCD). The LCD displays a four- to eight-character alphanumeric display, changing every 30 or 60 seconds. A cryptographic function runs on the microprocessor on the card, using the current time and a secret key (seed value) specific to that individual card that was initially set up by an administrator.

The second part of this method is that of the ACE/Server, a UNIX software package designed for TCP/IP networks. There are also what is termed as access control modules, which are platforms that can authenticate SecurID Tokens. These servers use the same hashing algorithm as the card. A passcode is used for access to the system, consisting of two parts: a PIN and a token. The PIN is what was assigned to the user; the token is the four- to six-digit displayed on the card.

When a user tries to log into a system with this authentication scheme, he or she will enter their passcode. The server will obtain the assigned PIN for that card and compute the token (for this time instance). It then compares this code to the two-part passcode that was entered in by the user.

In addition, the ACE/Server has a feature called a "time-slot window" to adjust for various drifts in time between it and the card. The server uses current and historic times and calculates a 30- or 60-second window. So, if the time is a bit off (meaning by a minute at most), the time-slot window will still allow a user to gain access.

The ACE/Server has a couple of security options built in. To protect against a stolen card, the server will disable the user account after three attempts. This assumes that the attacker has the card, can see the generated token, and is trying to guess the PIN. There is also a duress PIN, similar to those used in many home security systems. If a authorized user is forced to enter in his or her code, the user can enter in the duress code. The server will recognize this, allow the person entry, and automatically notify the administrator. To protect against "time-spoofing," where the server timestamp is compromised and the time rolled back, the server will not accept a token code that has a timestamp of a GMA time in the past.

SecurID is an extremely popular two-factor form of user authentication. The technology itself is compatible with all of today's user access protocols, such as TACACS, TACACS+, and RADIUS.

GENERAL NOTE The SecurID card uses a PIN and token. If the card gets stolen, it does the thief no use, since the thief doesn't know the PIN (unless of course, the user foolishly writes the PIN on the back on the SecurID card).

Biometrics

Biometrics, particularly biometrics for computing applications, is used as a form of identification. A biometric identification technique is a feature or action of a human for the purposes of uniquely identifying the human. Biometric identification systems include fingerprints, handwritten signature, voice prints, and retina scans. Biometrics is the third category of classifications: "Something One Is." By the use of a PIN, token, and biometric scan, a corporation could achieve three-factor authentication.

Lately the field of biometric identification has developed into an acceptable system for user authentication and the cost of biometric hardware and software has plummeted during the past several years. However, just like any other identification device, biometric systems can fail. They can give access to illegitimate users, or they can deny the identification of a legitimate user. Biometric systems allow for sensitivity changes to the system. Therefore, making the settings too sensitive will cause legitimate users to fail to login; making them too relaxed will cause illegitimate users to be allowed in.

Some studies done with biometric devices have found hand geometry devices to be quite reliable, while finding voice recognition devices the least reliable. None were found to be acceptable in high-security applications. A couple of terms are associated with biometric devices:

■ *False acceptance rate (FAR).* The rate at which an intruder can be recognized as a valid user. Many vendors quote the false acceptance rates of their devices by statistical analysis of field data. If a vendor's FAR is quoted as 2 percent, it means 2 out of 100 users trying to break into the system will be successful.

■ *False reject rate (FRR).*   The rate at which a valid user is rejected from the system.

Biometrics devices come in different sizes. They all accomplish the first of four major tasks of user authentication:

1. *Capture.*   The biometrics devices capture whatever it is you are trying to use, whether fingerprint, retina scan, and so on.

2. *Data extraction.*   After capturing the image, biometric recognition software creates a digital representation of the object. This uses software similar to a one-way hash function, which is loaded on a PC connected to the device. The purpose of the one-way hash function is that you don't want to go in reverse—for instance, take data and reconstruct a fingerprint.

3. *Storage.*   The data needs to be stored somewhere for authorization, for denial, and for future analysis. There are no standards for this yet, so whatever vendor you go with, you must use their complete product.

4. *Comparison.*   The software needs to do a comparison with the data representation of the object trying to gain authorization—for instance, a person's fingerprint and his or her fingerprint on file.

From a security standpoint, some forms of biometric identification suffer from one of the major security vulnerabilities: the replay attack. If someone records your voice, he or she can later use it to impersonate you—unless the system is designed to counter this type of attack, with challenge-response protocols, for example.

Biometrics devices fall under export restrictions, so if you plan to sell these systems overseas, you must concern yourself with export restrictions that fall under the U.S. State Department's national security and criminal control statutes.

Secure Modems

Secure modems are encryption-style modems designed for privacy during normal dial-up access. As on a LAN or WAN, the data that passes through the telephone system can be captured and analyzed. Figure

11-11 illustrated a placement for these encryption modems in a VPN environment.

In a typical secure modem communication, when the encrypted link is being negotiated, the modem devices first exchange user IDs. The user ID is associated with an encryption key in memory (or in the external key-management system). This key has already been set, either by a hash of a password or seed value. The encryption key is then used by the answering modem to create a random one-time session key. The session key is only used once and is immediately discarded as soon as the session is broken. Most secure modems will not interoperate with other vendors, even though they are using the same encryption algorithm.

SECURITY NOTE Secure modems are not suppose to answer to a nonsecure modem, but I have seen instances where they do, and some secure modem vendors have patches to fix this. Just make sure you implement the patched version of the secure modem you are using.

Secure modems are recommended for VPNs and all remote access scenarios, where security is at an absolute must. You can find encryption vendors on the Web; most of the modems should support a set of standards, such as ANSI X9.26 user authentication and ANSI X3.92-based DES encryption standards.

Encryption modems fall into the same category of legality as regular encryption: the U.S. government regulations. If you are doing international VPNs, you may want to look at a vendor who is compatible with international ANSI standards.

Conclusion

This chapter looked at the traditional way of authenticating (passwords), along with some dos and don'ts, and explained why passwords alone are insufficient for the new generation of secure computing and Internet applications. Most passwords are set in plaintext mode, and even if they weren't, having users choose their own password opens up security problems. Therefore, like the dinosaurs, simple passwords will become extinct.

We then looked at some of the standard authentication protocols: TACACS, TACACS+, XTACACS, Kerberos, and RADIUS. These protocols are industry standards, and most VPN implementations support them. While they are standards, some vendors may not support all of them. However, I have never seen a VPN vendor who does not support some implementation of RADIUS, both for dial-up and LAN VPN connections. If you are using one of these protocols in your environment, stay with it if you can. If, however, you cannot, look for the authentication protocol that is most widely supported. If you ever decide to add additional network components in the future, you may want to use the same authentication setup, and hopefully the most popular will be supported by the majority of manufacturers.

Next we looked at digital certificates, the X.509v3 standard, and the LDAP standard, which will allow users instant electronic access from their desktop via a standard Web browser. Of course, there was another side of the argument, that the X.509v3 standard was useless and that certificate authorities, the entities who verify the identify of the public key tied to that certificate, are not reliable. We saw an example of a disclaimer of one such certificate authority. So the question remains: If the disclaimer is so apparent, stating that the CA is not held responsible for the authenticity of the certificate, why then get a certificate and incur the costs?

Then we examined tokens, smart cards, Security Dynamics' SecurID ACE/Server solution, and biometrics. These authorization protocols are making a step into strong security—that of two-factor authentication. And, in the case of biometrics, we can set up three-factor authentication. We ended the chapter by talking about encryption modems for secure dial-up access.

As repeated throughout this book, security and flexibility are arch opponents constantly at odds with one another; until someone figures out a way to make them friends, we will have choices to make, alternatives solutions to consider, and risk analyses to perform. Remember: Expect it to happen and prepare for the "known unknown."

CHAPTER 15

VPN Operating System Vulnerabilities

Virtual Private Networks can be installed on operating systems, routers, black boxes—almost any device you have in your network. Therefore, the vulnerabilities that exist on certain platforms must be examined. In this chapter, we will look at some operating system vulnerabilities in conjunction with UNIX, Windows 95, and Windows NT. We will examine some security guidelines and some known security vulnerabilities in these systems. Then we will look at some Novell guidelines.

This chapter is not intended to list all the vulnerabilities in any operating system that could affect the safety of your VPN. This is just a single chapter on multiple operating systems, but the subject could fill a dozen books. The purpose behind this chapter is to get you thinking about what kinds of security vulnerabilities exist and how you can protect yourself against them. For example, there are hundreds of buffer-overflows security violations, and each one could allow a user to gain root access in a UNIX environment. It is gaining this root access that causes a great deal of concern. Once an attacker gains root access, the attacker may destroy the box or use it as a starting point for other attacks. In the case of a VPN compromise, the attacker would steal your secret keys, install some X-windows capturing software to capture your password, and then with that decrypt all the information flowing into your VPN. This leaves both you and your end host vulnerable. It's this type of security you need to concentrate on.

What Are VPN Operating System Vulnerabilities?

In any computing system, the operating system needs to be secure. Attacks that occur on operating systems don't occur through the front door but by a side entrance or backdoor. The buffer overflow problem is so common that it's surprising a program couldn't be written to detect this anomaly. Attacks also come in a wide range. (In Chapter 16 we will look at different types of attacks.) So then, what are VPN operating system vulnerabilities? There is no set definition of this, but if a definition had to be made, a VPN OS vulnerability would be any attack that could compromise the keys of the system.

It doesn't really matter whether you are using an operating-system-based VPN, a black-box-based VPN, a router VPN, and so on. The keys are the security in VPNs. In Chapter 12 and 13, we went through hashing functions, shared secret keys, and encryption algorithms. We learned that our main goal was to get a key to the receiving end securely. If the key gets compromised, then not only has your VPN been compromised, but you have often no idea that it was. If someone hacks onto your system, they may stay there and hack into other systems. In the case of your VPN, if they have your key, they don't need to hack into your system. If they hack into your system and steal your VPN's key, then they can just sit on the net and monitor your traffic and decrypt any data leaving your site, without the need to go back onto your system and possibly get noticed.

Therefore, a VPN vulnerability would be any vulnerability that would allow this to happen. Buffer overflows (when the root can be accessed), sendmail exploits (where attackers could mail copies of the key to themselves), and insecure file systems (where the directory that contains the key could be remotely mounted) are examples of VPN vulnerabilities.

UNIX Guidelines

The UNIX system is one of the oldest operating systems around in terms of multinetworking, access, and so on. UNIX found its home in universities around the country and was designed to be open. It was never proprietary; it's been meant to provide computing power with simple password protection. However, as UNIX grew and became more popular on the desktop and in the commercial environment, security problems began to appear. The UNIX operating system is like a two-edged sword. Since it was designed as an open system, the operating system is widely known and understood. This openness also brings about security problems.

But at the same time, the open nature of UNIX also means that security problems are found quickly and made public, and fixes are available almost immediately. Compare this to a proprietary vendor. If a security problem is made known, there is no guarantee that a fix is forthcoming. In fact, the manufacturer might not even admit there is a problem. UNIX is still by far the best-performing operating system around. Statistics will bear this out.

Common UNIX System Configuration Problems

All UNIX systems have common problems as a result of their basic design, as shown in the following list. Spending a little time going over this list can save you some major headaches later.

- *Weak passwords.* Most users, if given the chance, will use an easy password to remember. This mean that someone could use the UNIX commands (**finger** or **ruser**), obtain a user's login name, and try variations on that name to get into the user's account. Once inside the system, attackers might attempt to take advantage of vulnerabilities in that operating system to gain root access. So the place to stop them is here, by implementing a policy of strict password guidelines. (In the last chapter we looked at password guidelines.)

- *No passwords on accounts.* There are some cases where you might set up temporary accounts, say, for a university vendor to gain access. You could forget these accounts existed, and then others could try to gain access to these unknown accounts. So, on a UNIX environment, use the facilities of the CRON utility to periodically check the password file for these accounts.

- *Reusable passwords (one-time passwords).* A security measure I see mentioned a lot is not to reuse passwords. I find that in some situations, this is nonsense. If you're a company who can afford the luxury of smart cards, then you can use token and one-time passwords and have a trained staff to maintain this technology. However, in the majority of these cases, you don't have that luxury. So if you enforce this policy on your user base, two security problems can occur. One is that there needs to be a database of already used words somewhere that has to be maintained and secured. Second, if you force users to change their passwords and don't allow them to reuse the ones they have, then they will write them down.

- *Configurations in the inetd.conf file.* inetd.conf is a file that the UNIX operating system reads when a service is requested. For example, if someone tries to telnet into your system, the UNIX OS will look at this file and start up a process to have the incoming request, most likely it will be telnetd. The telnetd process is the server process that answers to the client process (telnet). From a security perspective, why is the telnetd even allowed to start up? In the UNIX operating system, a # means a comment and whatever command there is will be ignored. You may need a way to get into your system, which is expected in a UNIX environment, but why use telnet? All communications, including your username and password, goes over in clear text. Use a secure communication like ssh.

- *Shell scripts.* The standard shell scripts that come with UNIX operating systems, /bin/sh and /bin/csh may have race conditions that may be exploited to change to root, especially when you are using setuid shell scripts. Check how these scripts are run and under what user, and never allow a setuid of root on these scripts.

- *Device drivers.* Device drivers are operating system devices, so you normally wouldn't think of them as being of use to a potential attacker. The fact is, they are. Most of the devices, such as dev/audio, /dev/kmem, /dev/mem, dev/st*, /dev/mt*, /dev/rmt*, are world-writeable and -readable; since they are system-specific, they do not need world access. In fact, the device /dev/fb can be used to get screen dumps from the system console.

- *Current directory in search path of user root.* I was shown this trick a long time ago, and it's still amazing, but it exists in the UNIX environment. Usually users are allowed to write to the /tmp directory, since it is public. Say someone logs into a UNIX box as an ordinary user, creates a script called "ls," and places it in the /tmp directory; "ls" is also a UNIX command. Now say the ls script placed in the /tmp directory looks like the following:

```
#!/bin/sh
echo "sjohnsr:0:1:sjohnsr user:/home/sjohnsr/bin/csh >/etc/passwd
`ls`
rm ls
```

What happens now is sometimes the user root will be on the machine and go into the /tmp directory and may issue the command "ls" in that directory. By having the current directory in the search path of root, this script will kick off, placing the user "sjohnsr" in the /etc/passwd file. It will then issue the ls command and remove the script itself. Since the superuser root is accessing the same directory as the word on a UNIX box, these things can happen. Keeping the current directory out of the search path of root helps to minimize the problem.

- *sendmail.* sendmail has had its share of vulnerabilities identified over the years. These have been documented and made known. The best thing to say about sendmail is just make sure that the version you are using is the latest one.

- *The "R" commands.*   The "R" commands—rlogin, rsh, rcp, and so on—have a long history of vulnerabilities. Avoid these commands and use their more secure counterparts, such as ssh and scp.

- *TFTP and FTP.*   The Trivial File Transfer Protocol (TFTP) is one of those services that get started up in the inetd.conf file mentioned earlier. The problem with TFTP is that it uses no password, so if your system is allowed to start it up, a potential hacker could just TFTP your system's password file to them. The File Transfer Protocol (FTP) has had its share of vulnerabilities over the years as well, but more and more companies are making use of the "anonymous" account of FTP access. You need to check the permissions of this anonymous account; unless otherwise set, the default FTP account has additional access to accounts other than the one that should be set.

- *xhost.*   The X windowing system on UNIX uses what is termed an x-display that displays command is back to the machine that makes the x call. That machine could be the same machine or a separate machine on the network. The **xhost** command is a security mechanism that allows one machine to issue commands on another machine. Many times the command is set as **xhost +,** which means anyone can issue command on a machine. By issuing the **xhost +** command, an attacker can issue commands on a UNIX system to capture snapshots of windows, usernames, passwords, and so on. Therefore, if the xhost command is needed, just issue the command as **xhost username host**; this just means only a certain user from a certain machine can issue x commands on this machine.

- *Exporting directories.*   This is another area that affects UNIX, but, theoretically, it could affect any operating system that exports file systems. When exporting directory structures you are giving users access to those directories. Be careful in how you give those permissions (do you need to give them read access? read and write access? etc.) Just make sure the permissions are appropriate, and also tie them down to certain machines—that is, don't export them read and write to the world, unless that is absolutely necessary. You can set the export option only on those machines that need it.

UNIX Operating System Vulnerabilities

UNIX is a great multitasking, multiprocessing operating system, but it also has had its fair share of security violations. Some are minor, some major. Fortunately, they are usually identified and corrected rather quickly. UNIX vulnerabilities usually come from exploits in the applications (process) that are running on them. Since it was designed as a multiuser platform, that probably is to be expected. Now we will look at some of the specific vulnerabilities of the UNIX operating systems on various vendor's platforms. Before we do, however, I want to make some general comments:

1. *This list is extremely short.*   This book is on VPNs, not the UNIX operating system. The purpose of this list is just to examine some of the vulnerabilities in an operating system that would allow someone to gain access to your VPN keys.

2. *These vulnerabilities are old and new.*   I've taken a look at many of the vulnerabilities and concentrated on those that will give you a feel for the type of security violations that exist. Even if the vulnerability is old, that does not mean your system is up to the latest patch. The whole purpose of this is for you to look at your systems and check well-known security advisory sites for documented issues. In the appendix are lists of these sites. Start there and at your vendor's site.

3. *All of them have already been identified, and patches have been made available for each one.*   Again, if you can find known security violations on the UNIX system, these probably are already security fixes for them. By just doing a quick search on the Web, you will come up with more than you can imagine.

4. *The security advisories come from various places, not just vendors.* These advisories also come from security advisory committees, Web sites, and other sources too numerous to mention. When researching OS vulnerabilities, don't just stick with one source, consult a variety.

5. *Many vendors are not forthcoming.*   As I was trying to look for security issues, some vendors sites were extremely cooperative. Look up an operating system, click on a platform, and every known

issue with that system comes up. On other sites, however, you have to be a registered customer and pay for this information. As mentioned earlier with regard to black-box VPNs, the vendor's system may be proprietary, and they may not be forthcoming with information. Even some nonproprietary vendors are tight-lipped.

Specific Exploits

Here is a list of specific exploits that have been documented and released to the general public over the years. Again, these have all been made available and corrected. This is only intended to get you into thinking about what kind of security violations might compromise your VPN. I have gathered the following from many security Web sites. Listed are the vendor, the specific problem, and the security recommendation to correct the problem. As mentioned earlier, do not correlate the number of security violations to inferior products. A number of security violations just means they were easier to find. Being able to find these security issues readily makes you access your specific implementation and secure it all that much quicker.

AIX 4.3

"Automountd"   This allowed remote users to execute arbitrary commands with root privileges [IBM ERS-SVA-E01-1998:004.1]

"ftp"   An FTP client interprets server-provided filenames, allowing rogue servers to run commands on the system with root privileges [IBM ERS E01 1997:009.1]

"nslookup"   Leaves privileges in incorrect state; therefore, local users can gain root privileges [IBM ERS E01 1997:008.1]

"piodmgsru"   Some code in program **piodmgrsu** allows some users to gain unauthorized privileges, which may include root [IBM ERS E01 1997:007.1]

"portmir"   Buffer overflow in **portmir**; allows users to gain root access [IBM ERS E01 1997:006.1]

"libDtSvc.a"   Buffer overflow in a system library **libDtSvc.a**; allowed users to gain root privileges [IBM ERS E01 1997:005.1]

"xdat"   Buffer overflow in **xdat** command allows users to gain root access [IBM ERS E01 1997:004.1]

FreeBSD

"system call"   A **mmap** system might allow write access to some devices, allowing users who are in the group **kmem** to gain root privileges [FreeBSD SA 98:02]

"procfs"   **Procfs** allows write access to some high-level processes, allowing users to gain root privileges [FreeBSD SA-97:04]

"lpd"   A buffer overflow in **lpd** daemon allows remote users to gain root access [FreeBSD SA 97:02]

Linux

"mountd, rpc.mountd"   Buffer overflow in **mountd** or **rpc.mountd** daemona, allowing remote users to gain root access [CERT Advisory 98.12]

"at"   **at** jobs can give users root access if they are allowed to edit their scripts in /var/at/spool

HP-UX

"NIS+"   Buffer overflow problem in **rpc.nisd,** which allowed remote users to gain root access [CERT Advisory 98.06 (nisd), Sun Security Bulletin #00170]

"chfn"   Process **chfn** allows users to gain root access [CERT VB 97.04 (HP)]

"newgrp"   Buffer overrun **newgrp** allows users root privileges [CERT Advisory 97.02]

"at"   Program **at** may allow users to gain unauthorized root privileges [CIAC F-15]

"vue"   **vue 3.0**; users may gain root access [CIAC E-23]

"sd-ux"   Software distributor product **SD-UX** may allow users to gain root [CA 96.27]

"remote watch"   May allow root access to system [CA VB-96.20 HP]

NetBSD

"at"   **at** allows any file on the system to be read [NetBSD Security Advisory 1998-004]

Samba

"buffer overflow"   Buffer overflow in Samba allows remote users to gain root [CERT VB 97.10]

SCO

"mscreen"   Buffer overflow in **mscreen** allows users to gain root [CERT VB 98.10]

"at, login"   **at, login, pr_warn, sadc, pt_chmod:** can gain root [CIAC F-05]

"system call"   A system call can allow users to gain access to certain restricted files, which may lead to root [CA VB-96.15]

SGI IRIX

"autofsd"   Program **autofsd** allows users to execute commands with root ownership [SGI Advisory 19981005-01-PX]

"at"   **at** allows local users to read any file on the system [SGI Advisory 19981001-01-PX]

"mailx, mail"   **mail** and **mailx** may allow users to gain root privileges [SGI Advisory 19980605-01-PX]

"ioconfig"   **ioconfig** may allow local users to gain root privileges [SGI Advisory 19980701-01-P]

"sendmail"   **sendmail** may allow remote users to gain root privileges to a system [SGI Advisory 19980604-02-PX]

"bind"   Allows remote users to gain root privileges [SGI Advisory 19980603-01-PX]

"mediad"   **mediad** daemon allows users with access to removable media devices to gain root [SGI Advisory 19980602-01-PX]

"diskalign, diskperf"   **diskalign** and **diskperf** allows users with local accounts to gain root access [SGI Advisory 19980502-01-P3030]

"netware client"   In the NetWare client subsystem, may allow users with local accounts to gain root [SGI Advisory 19980501-01-P2869]

"license manager"   **license manager** program may allow users to gain root access [SGI Advisory 19980406-01-PX]

"suid_exec"   Buffer overflow in **suid_exec** program allows for local or remote users to gain root access [SGI Advisory 19980405-01-I]

"startmidi, cdman"   Buffer overflow exploits in several programs such

as **startmidi, cdman,** and **cdplayer** allow remote users to execute commands with root privileges [SGI Advisory 19980301-01-PX]

"df"   Buffer overrun in **df** allows users to gain root privileges [SGI Advisory 19970505-02-PX]

"inlibXt"   Buffer problems in library **inlibXt** allows for users to gain root privileges via the setuid root X programs [SGI Advisory 19971101-01-PX]

SunOS

"ping"   Buffer overflow in **ping** allows users to gain root [Sun Security Bulletin #00174]

"imap"   Buffer overflow in **IMAP** allows users to gain root [Sun Security Bulletin #00177]

"sunwadmap package"   The system application package **sunwadmap** may be compromised to gain root [Sun Security Bulletin #00173]

"libnsl"   Buffer overflow vulnerabilities in **libnsl** may be exploited to gain unauthorized privileges [Sun Security Bulletin #00172]

"mountd"   Daemon **mountd** may allow remote attackers to read any file in the system [Sun Security Bulletin #00168]

"rpc.cmsd"   **rpc.cmsd** allows attackers to overwrite arbitrary files and gain root privileges [Sun Security Bulletin #00166]

"dtaction"   **dtaction** buffer overflow allow users to gain root privileges [Sun Security Bulletin #00164]

"volrmmount"   **volrmmount** program may allow a user to read any file and possibily gain root access [Sun Security Bulletin #00162]

Solaris

"rdist"   **rdist** buffer overflow may allow an attacker to gain root [Sun Security Bulletin #00179]

"in.rlogind"   Buffer overflow in **in.rlogind** allows users to gain root access [Sun Security Bulletin #00158]

"ps"   Writes temporary files to tmp directory, which can be exploited to gain root access [CA 95:09 (Solaris ps) CIAC F-27]

"libX11"   Buffer overflow in library **libX11** may allow users to gain root access via setuid-root X11 programs [Sun Security Bulletin #00154]

"xlock"   Buffer overflow in **xlock** allows users to gain root privileges [Sun Security Bulletin #00150]

"ps" Buffer overflow in **ps** allows users to gain root [Sun Security Bulletin #00149/A>]

"nis+" Buffer overflow in a **nis+** library allows users to gain root access [Sun Security Bulletin #00148]

"chkey" A buffer overflow problem in **chkey** allows users to gain root privileges [Sun Security Bulletin #00144]

"vold" Vold may allow a user to gain root [CA 96.17]

"admintool" Administrator tool **admintool** may allow a user to gain root [CA 96.16]

The Following Affects Multiple Platforms

Since most UNIX versions have a commonality between them, the following is a small list of vulnerabilities that exist in several of the applications they have in common.

"bind" Vulnerabilities exist in **bind** through version 8, allowing denials of service and possibly buffer overruns [CERT Advisory 98.05 (bind problems)]

"rpc.statd" Buffer overflow in **rpc.statd** allows remote users to execute commands with root privileges [CERT Advisory 97.26; SGI Advisory19971201-01-P1391]

"at" Buffer overflow problem in automated job **at** allows users to gain root [CERT Advisory 97.18; Sun Security Bulletin #00160]

"rdist" A setuid **rdist** may allow users to gain root access [CERT Advisory 97.23]

"talkd" Buffer overflow problems in **talkd** allow remote users to execute root commands [SGI Advisory 19970701-01-PX; Sun Security Bulletin #00147]

"rlogin" Buffer overrun problems in many implementation of **rlogin** allow users to gain root [CERT Advisory 97.06]

"perl" Some versions of Perl before 5.004, with suidperl, may allow users to gain root [CERT Advisory 97.17]

In this section of specific documented UNIX exploits, I have concentrated on vulnerabilities where a user could gain root access or where a user could read any file. The root is where your VPN could get compromised. With root access, an attacker can do anything; therefore, you must protect your system against this. Keep in mind that if attackers can read system files, they may also be able to copy them or send them to a public directory to be copied. If they can read and copy your VPN secret key, then they can compromise any further data as long as they can derive the VPN session keys. An attacker who knows he or she is looking for the VPN key will make sure that your system stays up and will hide any indication he or she was there.

Windows 95 Guidelines

While there are several operating systems you can choose, the top three are UNIX, Microsoft's Windows 95/NT, and Novell. All three combined covers probably 80 percent of the market, and all three have security issues you must deal with. In the last section, we looked at the UNIX operating system, and to continue, we will now look at Microsoft's Windows 95 operating system. As always, there are several places you can go to obtain security advisories on a vendor's products. In this case, Microsoft is actually one of the vendors that really tries to help out and disseminate information about security matters. Therefore, a good place to start would be at Microsoft's Security Advisor Page at *http://www.microsoft.com/security/default.asp.* Some general guidelines for 95 are as follows:

■ *Do not enable file sharing.*   Windows 95 does not understand the security behind file security. When you log on to a 95 system, you are usually asked for a username/password. This is just an identifier to other machines; it is not intended to protect your machine. What this does is tell everybody on the network, "hey, somebody new is here, and that person can read and copy any files you may have on the network." This accessible data could include any public/private key you use for encryption. If you need for others to have access to your machine, then at least make sure it's password protected and restricted to only those necessary resources.

■ *Install virus software.*   Windows 95 problems come mostly from viruses. Will a virus affect your VPN and thus affect your keys? Probably not. If you are using, say, PPTP on your 95 client, then there is a possibility that a virus could attack your PPTP stack, affecting your secure key. Most likely it will just affect your one station, since the PPTP server will reject your connection request, but why go through the hassle? You should still take steps to prevent this from happening.

Windows 95 Vulnerabilities

As we did with UNIX, here is a list of known vulnerabilities that have been identified with Windows 95, along with available patches to correct these problems. As mentioned, these vulnerabilities are most likely to only compromise your local machine. The problems are all addressed and documented, and steps have been recorded to identify the infested machines and restoration of these machines.

- *Back office vulnerability.* The back office vulnerability will allow a user to remotely manage another machine. It gives the remote user more control than the person sitting at the console. This can be done over a LAN or the Internet.

- *Internet Explorer vulnerability.* This vulnerability may allow a malicious Web page to crash Internet Explorer and possibly execute arbitrary code on the browser's machine. This possibility becomes particularly worrisome as we move VPNs from public-key (PKI) infrastructure and add certificates to the puzzle. You wouldn't want someone using the certificates on someone's else browser, thereby creating a situation of compromised certificates.

- *Teardrop vulnerability.* This vulnerability occurs when an attacker sends an overlapping, fragmented IP data stream to the intended victim. Windows 95 cannot handle this, and the system hangs. Usually a reboot is needed. A Winsock 2 update is recommended.

- *ICMP vulnerability.* This is when an attacker sends a ping packet to the intended victim and specifies in the header an incorrect packet length. A reboot is the only recourse.

- *OOB vulnerability.* This vulnerability occurs if IP packets are sent to a Windows 95 machine that has an out-of-band data flag set. A common port is 139, although others can be used. A reboot is needed in this situation.

- *Newtear, bonk, boink vulnerability.* This vulnerability is similar to the older teardrop attack. Different names exist, such as teardrop 2, bonk, or boink.

- *Password-caching vulnerability.* Windows 95 stores passwords to network resources in a file (designated with the PWL extension) that is encrypted using a RC4 encryption algorithm. The problem is that the PWL files are too predictable, making a plaintext attack viable, possibly resulting in the revealing of passwords on the network.

- *File access.* When using the system's file and print services for Net-Ware, any user who has remote administration software can view files on other hard drives on the network without authorization.

- *Possible password revealed.* It may be possible to obtain the clear-text Windows 95 login password from a Windows 95 computer on a network connected directly to the Internet. There is a vulnerability when using a Samba server on Ports 137 and 139, a malicious Web page, and an NT server that tries to log in with the 95 username/password in clear text.

In this section, we've seen some well-known vulnerabilities in the Windows 95 operating system. However, to be fair, Windows 95 wasn't designed for security, unlike a device such as a firewall. As with the UNIX vulnerabilities, exploits come from attacks on processes on the system, not on the system itself. Also as in UNIX, it is important to keep up with the latest patches, revision levels, and security advisories from security groups.

Windows NT Guidelines

As in the previous section, there are some guidelines that are associated with the NT operating system. You should take more care in your Windows NT environment, since it was designed with networking in mind. In your setup, you will most likely be using 95 as a desktop OS, not a central file server. NT, on the other hand, can be your main server, file server, Web server, application firewall, and PPTP VPN server. Therefore, making sure your NT systems are as secure as possible is prudent.

- *Network security.* In the UNIX section, the **inetd.conf** file starts process-based upon client request. It is the same way in the NT world, in that you only choose those networking options that you require. Running unneeded networking protocols increases the risk of system break-in, just as in the Telnet example we discussed earlier. Most organizations need TCP/IP networking, along with NetWare resources if needed. However, it is usually not recommended that you enable the NetBEUI protocol. Whatever services you decide on, just make sure they are necessary. An approach taken by many is to shut down everything except the basic ports needed to communicate with, and then add them back in one-by-one as necessary (e.g., TCP 25, UDP 53, etc.). Just be ready to activate them if needed. Also, if possible, disable any kind of IP for-warding unless absolutely necessary.

■ *Fake administrator's account.*   It is recommended that a fake administrator account be set up with very minimal or no privileges. The real administrator privileges should then be established using a different account name. Since NT uses the administrator as the super-user, an attacker may try to break into the administrator account. Some argue that you should leave a very minimal set of privileges. That way, if someone does break into the account, he or she may not realize that this account is a fake one and think it is just a dead machine with nothing interesting on it.

■ *Block Ports 137, 138, and 139.*   If NetBIOS service is not needed, then by blocking these ports, you can prevent attacks, including Red Buttons and OOB data packets that can crash the system.

■ *Check for strong passwords.*   To prevent against certain types of guessing attacks against passwords, it is a good idea to periodically check that your users have chosen strong passwords. l0phtcrack 2.0 is a utility that can be used with password dictionaries to check this.

■ *Virus software.*   As in Windows 95, make sure you have applied the latest virus updates for your NT antivirus software. New virus-es appear daily, and you need to apply these patches as soon as they are made available.

■ *C2 Configuration Manager.*   The Windows NT Resource Kit pro-vides Windows NT the C2 Configuration Manager (C2CONFIG.EXE). This program compares the security of your NT configuration against C2-level security standards of the federal government's National Computer Security Center, then gives you the option to bring the machine up to C2 standards.

Note: C2 is run after all applications, patches, etc., have been installed. C2 allows you to set the following NT platform-specific options:

> File Systems—It is recommended that you configure all of your vol-umes to use the NT file system (NTFS). Do not use file systems such as FAT; they do not offer the same level of control over files and directories.
>
> Dual-Boot—Disable this option if possible. There is no need for it, especially on any NT server that will be a company production server or Internet server. If you have a need for dual-boot, make that machine a noncritical file server.

Authorized Users Only—However, you should use a stronger, more specific warning, such as: "Warning, the information on this computer and network is the property of company. Only authorized users are allowed to access information and are only allowed to access information as defined by the system administrators." A warning that is too vague or too brief may not stand up in court against an attacker.

Posix Subsystems—NT allows you to enable several subsystems; however, if you don't need them disable them.

Password Length—It is recommended that systems use a minimum password length of eight characters and that blank passwords not be allowed. If possible, use one of the user authorization protocols mentioned in Chapter 14.

Guest Account—The guest account allows anonymous access. It is usually recommended that this account be either disabled or deleted. If you need an extra account, don't make it "Guest." Make it something that may help you identify it if a problem arises. For example, if you need a guest account for certain vendors, make a generic vendor account. This way, if something happens with the vendor's account, at least you know how many people could have used that account.

Security Log—C2-level security requires that security logs not be overwritten, which can waste a lot of space and resources. With today's compression techniques and the use of writable CDs, however, you could store a year's worth of data on a few CDs. You just need to balance this requirement.

Don't Display Last Username—NT displays in the logon window the last username that logged on the system. This can give an intruder the identity of the last person who signed on, giving the attacker the opportunity to try some plaintext or dictionary guessing attacks.

Windows NT Security Objects

Windows NT uses certain objects on which to base security for users. These objects allow operations for users and set permissions to system objects for users. A thorough understanding of these security objects will help you to secure your system. The security objects are all interrelated, to a certain degree, and are as follows:

- *Security identifier (SID).* The security identifier is the most basic security object in NT. The SID is used to identify a user or group of users. These users can exist on one or more machines, e.g., a domain.

- *Access control entry (ACE).* An access control entry (ACE) is a two-part authorization object. It uses Access Allowed and Access Denied to allow or deny requests. An ACE contains a SID, which dictates permissions, and a permission mask, which indicates a set of generic or specific permissions to particular objects. They also point to file system specific permissions, which you should pay close attention to.

- *Access control list.* Access control lists are used to define multiple-user access to particular objects. They combine ACE into an ACL, thereby granting groups and users different permissions on the same object. When access to an object is requested, it does a two-pass function. During the first, it looks for all denies; during the second, it looks for allowable access. As it checks the permission against the SID, it makes a continuous permission list for future access.

- *Security descriptor.* The security descriptor is a group of security attributes for a particular object. When modifications are required, they are made through the security descriptor, not the object itself.

- *Access token.* An access token is similar to a database of security attributes about the user. It contains items such as a user's SID, primary group, permissions, and so on that were created through various login services under NT. They are used throughout the system for various objects to identify a SID that it is running under.

Windows NT Vulnerabilities

Like 95 and UNIX, Windows NT has it share of vulnerabilities. Therefore when dealing with the NT operating system, the same situation applies to that of the UNIX systems: You have to know your operating system and its limitations. Again, these vulnerabilities are well documented, and you can visit the security advisory Web page for more information.

- *Pipes vulnerability.* A denial of service can occur if an attacker uses the Windows NT 4 named pipes. The way NT handles pipes over a remote procedure call is the cause of this problem.

■ *ICMP vulnerability.* This vulnerability is similar to the one in the Windows 95 operating system. A ping packet is sent to the victim, and the packet size does not match the actual size of the packet. A reboot is needed to correct this problem. A fix for this is available from Microsoft.

■ *Internet Explorer vulnerability.* An attacker can use malicious code on a Web page to crash and execute a teardrop denial of service on a machine. By executing this code, the NT machine hangs after receiving corrupted UDP data packets and a reboot is necessary.

■ *RPC spoofing vulnerability.* A vulnerability exists where an attacker can send spoofed RPC datagrams to Port 135 to the victim. The server would then send reject packets to the spoofed machine. This would continue, and a loop would occur. In addition, if multiple machines were targeted, network bandwidth would be wasted.

■ *Out-of-band (OOB) vulnerability.* Similar to the Windows 95 vulnerability.

■ *Anonymous login vulnerability.* Windows NT Explorer and ACL use account names for various functions. Explorer uses account names to decide whether to grant access to an object, and the NT ACL uses it to decide whether to grant access rights to specific objects. However, because of this functionality, anonymous logon users can list domain usernames and identify share names. For enhanced security, this functionality should be restricted.

As demonstrated in the previous few pages, no operating system is safe from attacks, vulnerabilities, and compromises. They all have security issues that must be dealt with effectively. The reason I've included each is to cross-functionalize the problems with each operating system and to point out that there are no secure systems.

Novell Guidelines

In this last section, we will look at some guidelines for the Novell operating system. As we have seen by now, all operating systems will have some type of security concerns, and by now you should know where to begin to look for them. Following are some guidelines for Novell, but many apply to any OS:

- *Location.*   Don't place your server where it accessible by various people; it only takes a general knowledge of NetWare to cause damage to your server.

- *Processes.*   Set up all processes on the system so that they run at the highest levels (if possible, set them up higher than the administrator). It is possible by loading various NLMs that someone could create a supervisor account and access those processes.

- *Console security.*   To prevent unauthorized access to the console, use the **secure console** command, and add it to the autoexec.ncf bat file. This will prevent loading unauthorized NLMs and keep someone from the DOS prompt.

- *Encrypt passwords.*   It is good policy to have any passwords encrypted. Therefore, set "allow unencrypted passwords" to OFF in the autoexec.ncf file.

- *Intrusion detection.*   It is a good idea to enable NetWare Intrusion Detection. This will monitor the number of times an account is accessed and perform a lockout of that account if too many failed attempts occur.

- *Virus software.*   Virus scanning software should be run on the server and updated as regular updates are released. Any viruses found should be eliminated as soon as possible after detection.

- *Account management.*   It is recommended that the following user system parameters be set: Set up user accounts so that they have to change their passwords, set them to at least eight characters, and set it up so the passwords change every few weeks. You may also want to set workstation restrictions, so users must use a specific machine, and set allowable times for logging in (e.g., normal working hours). In addition, as in the Windows guidelines, remove the guest account.

- *Logs.*   Setting up and monitoring security logs is imperative. NetWare comes with several logs available. The accounting log will keep track of users logging in and out of the system. The system error log will indicate lockout accounts, as well as volume mounts and dismounts.

- *Security.*   The security program that comes with the system is a utility to review how the security is installed on the system; it checks various security components installed, such as users permissions and attributes.

- *RCONSOLE.*   RCONSOLE is an extremely useful utility to remotely manage NetWare servers; however, be aware when remotely managing these devices, the password is sent in clear-text mode. NetWare has a solution, where the password is now sent in encrypted format, while not knowing the encryption strength, it is better than plaintext.

Conclusion

In this chapter we've gone over several operating systems and looked at their guidelines and vulnerabilities. As this chapter evolved, the guidelines came first, and in the case of the Novell operating system, I didn't even mention vulnerabilities. This is important, since time and time again, security scanners always produce some of the same findings: The security implemented doesn't even meet with today's standards. That's ironic, since now we are talking about VPN security, and we have to both secure internal network access and worry about the data that is flowing on the Internet.

As mentioned in this chapter, an attacker doesn't always attack the system, but attacks a process on that system. In the UNIX vulnerabilities examples, we saw multiple buffer overflow problems, where an attacker would use an exploit in a process to gain root access on a UNIX system. It may be the same way for a VPN data stream (why bother trying to crack the mathematical code used in VPNs?). First, an attacker may identify his or her target, try to find where the data stream is heading, hack into that system, and then use information stored on that system to make the cracking of the VPN data stream easier.

VPN security is like any other security you have in your organization. It's just an extension of the already-applied security functions and processes that any organization should have. As always, look at the VPN from a system perspective—what is actually on the box, operating system, revision levels, and applications. (Any application is open to attack.) Then look at the communication of that box. Will it be by encryption only (DES), or can it be accessed by a browser? In other words, will there be a server on it, and if so, will you be using it as a proxy? What revision of proxy software will you use? Think of it as security in your house: You need to make sure all the windows and doors are shut and locked.

CHAPTER 16

VPN Security
Attacks

This chapter can be thought of as a continuation of Chapter 15. While it is not an operating system vulnerability checklist, it does look at the attacks that occur on VPNs. In this chapter, as I've done throughout this book, I will try to help you in implementing a secure VPN.

There are two major VPN protocols that exist today: IPSec and PPTP. We will look at the weaknesses of both. I say "weaknesses," since each one of them is a framework to accomplish a VPN. Neither PPTP nor IPSec do encryption; neither PPTP nor IPSec offer the security of data packets. So if an attack were to occur, it would occur on what these frameworks rely on.

We will also take a look at cryptographic functions. We first looked at them in Chapter 12, and we will revisit them. We will see how they are broken, and what kinds of attacks are placed upon them. Then we'll discuss some very well-known user authentication protocols: RADIUS and Kerberos. Finally, we'll finish up the chapter by looking at some other attacks that may or may not be considered VPN attacks per se. However, as with the buffer overflow problems mentioned in Chapter 15, if these attacks can compromise a system, they can logically be placed in the general category of VPN attacks.

Introduction to VPN Attacks

This chapter deals with various attacks, and as was done in Chapter 15, we need to think about whether there is such a thing as a specific VPN attack or whether any attack is merely a VPN vulnerability. Say, for example, you have an operating system that allows you to gain access over all files on that drive, including the public/private key pair. Another example would be that of a hardware VPN device with remote management capabilities. What if this capability gives an attacker a way into the system to capture and read any of the VPN keys? Take another example: You choose an insecure VPN protocol, and the attacker is able to use some logical operations to break into your specific algorithm. Here are three different attacks that weren't expressly aimed at your VPN, but nevertheless compromised it. Therefore, in this chapter, we will consider any attack that could eventually lead to your VPN data being revealed as a VPN attack. If attackers break the algorithm, it's a VPN attack; if they get into your server and read your keys, it's an attack, and so on.

At this point in the book, you should realize VPNs are a framework more than anything else. It is this framework that allows a company to use the Internet as a business asset. Business opportunities, markets, and so forth are all opened up by the use of VPN technology. However, as we've learned, the security aspects of VPNs must be addressed. Let's take a look at the various kinds of VPN attacks.

Cryptographic Algorithms Attacks

Cryptographic algorithms are subject to vulnerabilities and attacks just like any other piece of hardware or software you may have on the network. There are generally three ways of attacking a cryptographic algorithm:

- Attacks against the protocol
- Attacks against the algorithm
- Attacks against the implementation

Attacks against the Protocol

A cryptographic system is only as strong as the encryption algorithms and the hash functions it is based on. By breaking any of these, you break the whole system. It's possible to design a very weak cryptographic system. Such things as not using the right random-number generators, reusing values, and so forth hurt the integrity of the whole design, allowing someone to potentially break into the system. The encryption algorithms and the key-exchange protocols don't necessarily guarantee safety by themselves, and choosing an insecure seed for the key to be based on destroys the integrity of the protocol.

Attacks against the Algorithm

The algorithm, or the mathematical operations that are performed on the data, could make the whole system weak. Proprietary encryption algorithms don't make a system secure; most of these have been shown to be weak. Many previously secret algorithms have been made public, reverse-engineered, and, as a result, were shown to be ineffective. Using weak keys, using an insufficient amount of data size, and altering hash functions all contribute to the weakening of the system.

Attacks against the Implementation

This type of attack is particularly disturbing, since it's probably the easiest to have avoided. Some implementations leave temporary files, plaintext messages, and data stored in buffers where they can easily be retrieved. Using a combination of keys is also a vulnerability. Conventional thinking would lead you to believe the more keys there are, the more secure the system; however, by combining a strong key with a weak key, the strong key becomes compromised and, thus, the whole system gets compromised. Unfortunately, in many of these types of failures, flexibility and security were trade-offs. The vulnerabilities of key recovery, mentioned throughout this book, are a major contributor to implementation attacks.

Common Attacks on Cryptographic Algorithms

One of the main problems with cryptographic attacks is that you may not be aware that you've been attacked. Think about it: If you send an encrypted data stream to a person in another company, you really have no idea that the data arrived in one piece and unmodified. You place your trust in the cryptographic algorithms themselves. Remember back in Chapter 1 I said that "encryption is nothing more than taking a message, such as "I'll be late" and converting it into some gibberish, such as '2deR56Gtr2345^hj5Uie04.' You are hoping that the encryption is sufficiently strong so that no one can take "2deR56Gtr2345^hj5Uie04" and convert it back to "I'll be late." Luckily, though, by using multiple layers of security, we can feel confident that our data will get there safely.

However, like attacks against other systems, cryptographic algorithms are subject to attacks themselves. Following are several of the common categories of algorithm attacks.

Ciphertext-Only Attack   In a ciphertext-only attack, the attacker knows nothing about the plaintext message, but, given the ciphertext, tries to make guesses about the plaintext. A ciphertext-only attack is usually assumed to be possible, and a code's resistance to it is considered the basis of its cryptographic security. The attacker is trying to find a common pattern where he or she can identify a set of commonly used words. In practice, it is usually possible to make educated guesses about the plaintext, since many types of messages have fixed-format headers.

Ordinary letters and documents begin in a very predictable way, and that pattern is useful in many attacks. Say, for example, the attacker knows his or her target well, and possibly what that person is likely to communicate, such as a particular business issue. The attacker might be able to guess at certain patterns of characters. Back in Chapter 12, Figure 12-2 illustrates a ciphertext attack.

Known Plaintext Attack   In this attack, the attacker knows part of the plaintext document or can make an educated guess about it. This plaintext can be guessed because it may be a standard greeting, a header, or a trailer. Because the attacker has the ciphertext, he or she can use the plaintext to decode the rest of the text. In a known plaintext attack, the attacker has some part of the plaintext and corresponding ciphertext. Say for example that there is a rumor your company is about to merge. The attacker can assume certain phrases exist in the document, such as payoff, stock price, and capitalization costs, since these are all relevant to any buyout discussion. Now, by using the same encryption algorithm and, if possible, by determining the key used to encrypt the message, the attacker may be able to decode the rest of the message.

Chosen Plaintext Attack   In a chosen plaintext attack, the attacker takes some text and encrypts it with the unknown key. Working backwards, the attacker tries to guess the key used for that encryption. In these types of attacks, the attacker has the capability to find the ciphertext corresponding to an arbitrary plaintext message of his or her choosing. The cryptanalyst feeds data into the encryption mechanism in the hopes of determining some common ciphertext output to decipher future ciphertext. Some believe that RSA is vulnerable to this type of attack.

Chosen Ciphertext Attack   In a chosen ciphertext attack, the attacker has the advantage of choosing an arbitrary selected ciphertext and can find the corresponding decrypted plaintext. Some public-key cryptographic systems are vulnerable to this type of attack, and in some cases, may reveal the private key.

Man-in-the-Middle Attack   We looked at this attack in Chapter 13. This attack is practical for cryptographic communications and key-exchange protocols. Here, two parties exchange their keys for later communications. The "man-in-the-middle" hijacks the sender's and receiver's keys and substitutes his or her own, thereby giving the attacker the ability to intercept all future communication without either the sender or receiver knowing about it. The only way to prevent this is by the use of digital signatures and the shared secret-key mechanism described back in Chapter 13. The Photuris key-exchange algorithm uses this safeguard.

Timing Attack   This type of attack is relatively new and is based on measuring the execution times of a modular exponentiation operation that is used in cryptographic algorithms. Cryptosystems take slightly different amounts of time to process different inputs. When the CPU performs optimization routines, branching, loops, conditional statements, and so forth, different amounts of a machine's cycle are used. It is known that during these timing channels, data is leaked, although a minimal amount. However, attackers can exploit timing measurements from vulnerable systems to find the entire secret key. Performance statistics depend on both the encryption key and the input data (i.e., ciphertext or plaintext). Against a vulnerable system, this attack is inexpensive and often requires knowing the ciphertext. Apparently, it can be used on RSA, Diffie-Hellman, and the elliptic curve algorithms.

Brute-Force Attack   A brute-force attack is popular with attackers who have a lot of computing power at their disposal. In simple terms, a brute-force attack would be, for example: If $f(x)=y$, where y is the ciphertext, $f(x)$ is the plaintext, and x is the key. Say in this case that the ciphertext y is 125, the $f(x)$ which $||^3$, the absolute power of a number cubed, then x is the key. In this case x is 5 and -5. 5^3 or -5^3 equals 125. This is a simple example, but now consider the 56-bit DES encryption algorithm. The strongest algorithm available was cracked in record time by the Electronic Frontier Foundation (EFF) by using a brute-force method.

Differential Cryptanalysis   In differential cryptanalysis attacks, an attacker uses an iterative mapping process—that is, the mapping that is based on a repeated function. By basing the results on a large number of ciphertext pairs whose counterpart plaintext pairs satisfy a known component-wise XOR difference, the attacker then can determine the key. It is the number of rounds that allows for this type of attack to occur. For example, in a DES implementation with eight rounds, the key can be recovered; in a full DES implementation, this attack is impractical.

Strength of Cryptographic Algorithms   Saying that good cryptographic systems should always be designed so that they are as difficult to break as possible is like saying that when driving, you should always use your seat belt. Therefore, you can't prove a cryptographic algorithm is not secure, except by trial and error. In theory, any cryptographic algorithm can be broken by trying all possible keys in sequence (a brute-force attack). Fortunately, the number of steps needed for brute-force attacks increases exponentially with the length of the key. Below are the number of steps required for each key size:

- 32-bit key takes 2^{32}, or about 4.2×10^9 steps
- 40-bit key takes 2^{40}, or about 1.09×10^{12} steps
- 56-bit key takes 2^{56}, or about 7.2×10^{16} steps
- 64-bit key takes 2^{64}, or about 1.8×10^{19} steps
- 80-bit key takes 2^{80}, or about 1.2×10^{24} steps
- 128-bit key takes 2^{128}, or about 3.4×10^{38} steps
- 160-bit key takes 2^{160}, or about 1.46×10^{48} steps

The first two key sizes (32 and 40) are readily available to anyone with access to a high-end computer. The 56-bit key has been compromised, and 64- and 80-bit keys are breakable by the government and universities. The 128- and 160-bit keys are probably safe for now. However, as we seen in the previous section on cryptographic attacks, only one was a brute-force attack, all the other attacks used a different method. Since most attacks are not brute-force attacks, you must look for another way to verify the security of the cryptographic algorithm on which your VPN data relies.

SECURITY NOTE Be wary of unpublished or secret algorithms. Generally, no algorithm that depends on the secrecy of the algorithm is secure.

In public-key cryptographic systems, The key lengths are usually much longer than those used in symmetric ciphers. In public-key systems, most security breaches come not from the brute-force method, but by deriving the secret key from the public key. As an example, a public-key cryptosystem of a 256-bit modulus is broken quite easily by anyone with a powerful computer. Universities and governments can break 318- and 512-modulus keys. Keys with 768- and 1024-modulus are probably safe.

SECURITY NOTE Remember, your VPN data is as strong as its weakest link. If you are doing international VPN, you may have to adjust your encryption strength appropriately.

Random-Number Generator (RNG) Attacks

Before we talk about attacks on random-number generators, we need to talk about what random-number generators are. A random-number generator (RNG) is a device that randomly picks a number. This certainly sounds simple enough, but if you think about what makes up a random number, you would be amazed at just how hard it is to pick one. For example, try this exercise.

1. Enter 10 random numbers into a computer.

2. Enter in another 10 random numbers.

3. Repeat step 2.

4. Repeat step 2 again.

5. Repeat step 2 again, but now do it 100 times.

Did you complete the process? It doesn't really matter. What matters is, at any time did you think about the numbers you were selecting? Most likely, even if you only did step 1, you used your mental powers, and once you did that, the process is no longer random.

Now take it another step, say you are a designer of a cryptographic function. You know that the key the user will use is somehow based on a random number. How do you get that person to enter in a random number? In the case of a VPN, there are hundreds of keys. How do you make sure they are all random? You can't. Unfortunately, the only true random numbers exist in nature, for instance, in static electricity and white noise in electrical circuits. Since obviously we can't use a real RNG from nature, we employ the services of a pseudorandom number generator (PRNG) to generate supposedly random values. The PRNG collects supposed randomness from various low-entropy input streams and tries to generate outputs that are in practice indistinguishable from truly random streams. If you've ever loaded an application on a desktop computer and it told you to move your mouse around or enter in keystrokes, you were then generating some randomness input (a low-entropy input stream) that feeds into a PRNG, which then produces a genuine random-number generator.

The reason for this introduction to RNG is that RNG is a common dominator in many cryptographic functions. Therefore if your algorithms are not designed correctly, they can be the weakest link in the chain. Just as there were categories of attacks on cryptographic functions, there are categories of RNG attacks:

- *Cryptanalytic attack.* This attack occurs if the attacker is able to see a correlation between the PRNG and the random outputs. This attack is feasible on cryptographic functions where the PRNG outputs are actually visible. Therefore an RNG where the RNG outputs cannot be seen or captured does not fall victim to this type of attack.

- *Input attack.* Input attacks occur when the attacker may have knowledge about the input to the PRNG in order to predict some PRNG outputs. These kinds of attacks may occur on systems that use various kinds of predictable inputs, such as user passwords and phrases. An example of this would be a designer assuming that a motion input, such as typing on a keyboard, is randomized when in fact it is not.

- *Timing attack.* The timing attack on an RNG is similar to the timing attack on a cryptographic function. During mathematical operations that count the number of machine cycles for each operation, the attacker may gain some information. It is believed that the attacker can determine when certain Boolean operations occur. For example, bitwise additions can be detected by counting machine cycles. Then, by determining the total number of bitwise additions and the length of machine execution time, the attacker may be able to predict the number of zeroes in the other bytes, thereby revealing some information about the cryptographic function.

- *Perfect Forward Secrecy.* Perfect forward secrecy is a mechanism whereby if a key is stolen sometime in the future, no communication that has been conducted in the past can be revealed. Perfect forward secrecy is what every cryptographic algorithm should be designed for. Unfortunately, implementing this kind of algorithm takes a lot of resources, since every packet requires a new key. Most cryptographic algorithms use a session key in each packet that is derived from a shared secret key. However, while these are good measures to take, they still are no substitute for secrecy.

Government Attacks via Key Recovery

This may seem like a strange title for a section on attacks, but it is a situation that is possible. The concept of key recovery, pushed for by major governments, eliminates any chance of perfect forward secrecy, just mentioned. In fact, some argue that key recovery impinges on individual rights. If the FBI obtains a wiretap warrant, they then can wiretap any *future* communication. In key recovery, not only is future data communication in jeopardy, but any previously captured data, since the key exists to decrypt it. Safe, secure cryptographic systems are hard enough to design, but key recovery has just made a hard task even harder. In key recovery, a backdoor is purposely built in, and if a door exists, someone else will find a way in.

Another major problem with key recovery is the determination of who will hold the keys. What agencies will be responsible for the safeguarding of data? Will these be agencies under governmental control or commercial private agencies? What would be better: to allow the government to hold the keys or some enterprise you know nothing about? Now consider how many law enforcement agencies exist in the world and recall that encryption is used worldwide. Who will be allowed access to your keys? You can see how many people could potentially use your keys.

Then ask yourself how a law enforcement agent would get your key. The agent would probably get a subpoena. Now, is the agent going to travel across the state, country, or world to serve your subpoena in order to get your company's key? The answer is, obviously, no. This means the agency will have to request and receive your key electronically—probably over the Internet, since all law enforcement agencies will not have leased lines to each other. In addition, all agencies will not be using the same encryption algorithms, so your key either goes plaintext or over the fax. Neither solution, of course, is acceptable.

How does this affect your VPN? Simple. If you choose a product that has a key-recovery feature built in, you are susceptible to the compromising of your key and data—not just by the government during legitimate subpoenas, but by attackers breaking the algorithms that use key recovery, intercepting data as it passes from key-escrow agency to key-escrow agent. In addition, one government agency implied that even if they were at fault for the compromising of your key, there is nothing you can do. So it is not the government attacking your VPN, but the policy in place that acts as a catalyst for these types of attacks.

Internet Security (IPSec) Attacks

The Internet Security Protocol (IPSec) is *not* an encryption algorithm, and it is *not* an authentication algorithm. IPSec is a paradigm in which other algorithms protect data. In the various articles on IPSec, as well as in the introduction to IPSec in Chapter 13, nowhere does it state (or, at least, nowhere should it state) that IPSec protects data. That's an important distinction: If you buy an IPSec-compliant product, you are not necessarily buying security. You are only buying a product that is able to do the encryption and authentication algorithms that are specified in the RFC, along with some other particular conditions specified in the IPSec RFC. Therefore, like any other security protocol, IPSec can be attacked and compromised. If one had to guess, the biggest kinds of attacks that will occur on IPSec will be those in the category of "attacks against the implementation" mentioned earlier. After reading the rest of this section, you should see why you need to protect against these types of attacks.

GENERAL NOTE At the end of this section, before deciding on whether or not to use IPSec, read the section on PPTP that is coming up.

Implementation Attacks

Implementation attacks are such a common form of attack in security systems that you'll also see them in the next section on the PPTP standard. The IPSec standard only calls for one encryption algorithm (DES-CBC) and two authentication modes (HMAC-MD5 and HMAC-SHA-1); however, it calls for the additional "NULL" algorithms, since AH or ESP may be optional. When a standard calls for an optional algorithm, it is trying to balance flexibility with security. Yet the interpretation is that even if one end of the communication was to use DES-CBC, the other end should still be able to use the NULL, or no, algorithm and still communicate. The RFC on IPSec allows both the encryption and authentication to be set to the NULL algorithm, but not at the same time. The security association (SA) sets up future communication, but how will it handle one side specifying one algorithm and the other side specifying NULL? Will it just convert back to NULL? The SA is usually specified by the receiving end, but in order to be compatible with other systems, it must allow the NULL algorithm. Vendors could decide on how to implement this choice, thereby increasing the security exposure.

In the IPSec key-management protocol IKE component, both ends of the communications channel decide on how often the encryption keys should be changed. Given that many vendors support weaker, 40-bit keys for backward compatibility, changing these keys now becomes critical, but this is still a negotiated session. If it's a weaker implementation, it's probably using a longer time period, which, in turn, gives an attacker more time to break the 40-bit key. Considering that 56-bit keys are now broken in three days, 40-bit keys shouldn't have even been part of the standard. However, at the time the IPSec standard was created no one knew the 56-bit key would be compromised.

Key-Management Attacks

There is a recently discovered problem with how the key-management protocol (IKE) handles the cryptographic keys in IPSec. The protocol specification specifies how these keys should be exchanged, but it usually refers to the start of the communication, not the end of it. There is a "time-out" mechanism in the public-key exchanges, and it was discovered that there isn't true interoperability between the vendors. In addition, under the IKE specification, any side could terminate a session, but there is no way for the other end to know that the session has been terminated; the sending end would keep sending data. If the station is still sending data, what's to stop another station from receiving that data and, if weak keys are used, spoofing the identity of the original host? This type of attack is similar to TCP session hijacking.

Key-Recovery/Export Law Attacks

There is really no such thing as a key-recovery/export law attack, but if an IPSec implementation is available in an international standard, it has one of two serious weaknesses: either it will be IPSec using 40-bit keys (although, as of this writing, 56-bit IPSec was being released) or it will support key recovery. There is only one problem. IPSec does not support key recovery. None of the standards call for key recovery, and if they modify the standard to allow for it, we fall back into the problems mentioned in the previous section (on government attacks). Therefore, in an international IPSec configuration, we fall into the weak-key (40-bit) category, with only a couple options. If you adhere to the U.S. government's policy on encryption, you use 40- or 56-bit keys, both of which are easily broken. You could use a perfect forward secrecy mechanism, whereby you change the 40- or 56-bit key every packet, but that's not feasible in the real world. Or you could implement key recovery.

SECURITY NOTE Some vendors support one-ended key recovery. If your organization doesn't want to use key recovery and you choose a product that doesn't support it, the other end of the channel (which supports one-ended key recovery) can still allow your data to be compromised by authorities.

Administrator and Wildcard Attacks

In IPSec there is a provision for an administrative interface and a provision for wildcard matching. As per the RFC:

> For every IPSec implementation, there MUST be an administrative interface that allows a user or system administrator to manage the SPD....It is expected that through the use of wildcards in various selector fields, and because all packets on a single UDP or TCP connection will tend to match a single SPD entry, this requirement will not impose an unreasonably detailed level of SPD specification. The selectors are analogous to what are found in a stateless firewall or filtering router and which are currently manageable this way.*

While there hasn't been a direct attack yet (at least none reported), some have argued that by even having an administrative interface to the SA (security association), you can potentially increase the chance that the interface can be attacked and the SA compromised. Since there is no provision for such as interface, it is left up to the vendor's implementation. In client/server technology, it would then be some sort of TCP communication, and that communication may be vulnerable. In addition, by the use of wildcards in the SA database, you increase the chance of malicious attacks, since the ports will not be checked and authorized.

IPSec Weaknesses

This section concerns a weakness of IPSec, rather than a type of attack protocol. Problems will occur as more vendors push for features that customers demand. This will push the development of IPSec into areas it was not originally designed for, thereby causing "unknown unknown" problems.

Client Authentication

IPSec has no mechanism for user authentication of any kind: no access rights, no verification, and so on. IPSec doesn't address client support; it was basically designed around LAN-to-LAN VPN. The field is then wide open for vendors to push their IPSec toward client-compliant support. LDAP and the PKI standards are still being worked on regarding the use of certificate authorities. In order for IPSec to become client-compliant, the standards will need to be modified. Since IPSec is not encryption, what user authorization protocol will be used, and how secure is it?

Certificate AuthoritFies

In IPSec's key-management protocol IKE, there are two phases. The first is the Oakley key determination protocol, whose job is to establish the first phase of the SA communications, which involves the key-exchange protocol to protect all future communication. Oakley uses the Diffie-Hellman (D-H) public-key algorithm to generate the shared secret key between parties.

The ISAKMP standard requires that the SA be authenticated by use of digital signatures. The security concern is that the ISAKMP standard does not specify a particular signature algorithm (obviously for flexibility) and does not indicate what type of certificate authority to employ. It does specify an identification of certificate types and the exchange of certificates.

If the receiving end (which established the CA) uses an unsecured CA, or possibly acts as its own CA, what security procedures are then in place on that CA? If an attacker compromises the CA, all future communication is vulnerable.

Network Address Translation

Network address translation is not often discussed, but it exists in the IPSec standard. When using tunneling in ESP and AH modes, the original IP header is replaced by a new IP header. The problem is, where is the NAT being performed? On a router, firewall, or a desktop? What device will physically change the IP address of the packet? Will that device have to be IPSec-compliant? For example, say you have a firewall that will perform NAT, and you have your IPSec VPN behind it. You then have to pass encrypted packets through the firewall, defeating the purpose of the firewall. If you choose a firewall/VPN that is IPSec-compliant, you will be doing encryption, packet filtering, and network address translation all on that one device. Then you will need to be sure that the firewall is secured.

Necessary Features

A big shortcoming in IPSec is that it supports only a very small set of algorithms and protocols in its default setting. In order for IPSec to become a mainstream business entity, it will have to move into more support, such as client support, LDAP, and multiple default encryption algorithms, as well as support for other authentication mechanisms such as smart cards and tokens. At the moment, IPSec only supports digital signatures and digital certificates. IPSec will have to move into more desktop and browser support to continue to make it a truly interoperable Internet standard. Unfortunately, as we've discussed so many times throughout this book, flexibility and security are trade-offs. Businesses don't want to support many different security platforms and protocols, but to try to use just one platform and one protocol increases the risk.

Point-to-Point Tunneling Protocol (PPTP) Attacks

In an earlier section, I stated that attacks against cryptographic algorithms fall into three categories: attacks against the algorithm, attacks against the protocol, and attacks against the implementation. The PPTP protocol attack is an attack against the implementation. The Point-to-Point protocol is a good protocol, but, apparently, Microsoft's implementation needs improvement, like any other cryptographic algorithm. If you search on the Web for PPTP and security, you will undoubtedly find many articles on this topic, and as mentioned earlier, by the time you read this chapter, Microsoft could have easily fixed this implementation. (For this reason you should always double-check the vendor for new information.)

I've tried throughout this book to keep vendors' names to a minimum. When you are discussing installing a PPTP VPN, however, bringing up

Microsoft is unavoidable, since PPTP is free with Microsoft's Remote Access Service in Windows NT 4.0, and this is PPTP's most common implementation. Microsoft PPTP VPN consists of several components, and similar to IPSec, PPTP is a framework. It does not mandate encryption and authentication algorithms—that is left up to the other protocols, such as PAP, CHAP, and MS-CHAP. The protocols used are as follows:

- *GRE*.   This is Microsoft's version of the Generic Routing Encapsulation protocol.
- *PPP*.   A point-to-point networking protocol used to provide for TCP/IP services over dial-up serial connection lines.
- *PPTP*.   The PPTP uses GRE to tunnel PPP and adds a connections setup and control protocol.
- *MS-CHAP*.   This is Microsoft's version of CHAP. It is responsible for the challenge-response authentication algorithm; it has nothing to do with encrypting the data.
- *MPPE*.   Microsoft Point-to-Point Encryption protocol; this is the protocol in charge of generating a key and encrypting the session.

The Point-to-Point Protocol is used to secure PPP connections over TCP/IP—that is, making a VPN connection from client to server, either by a dial-up ISP connection or directly over the Internet. PPTP encapsulates PPP packets, which are encapsulated in Generic Routing Encapsulation (GRE) packets. PPTP creates a connection setup and control channel to the PPTP server over TCP Port 1723. Also, this connection is not authenticated in any way.

Attacking the GRE

PPP packets are encapsulated inside a GRE and tunneled via IP to their destination. GRE uses protocol number 47. GRE packets may carry a sequence number and an acknowledgment number and may use a sliding window to avoid congestion. This has some important implications. It means that if we want to try and spoof the PPP packets encapsulated in GRE, we just need to desynchronize the GRE channel. This may be avoided by the use of the sequence number; unfortunately, originally GRE didn't mandate the use of this sequence number, and it is therefore up to a vendor's particular implementation. The GRE didn't have a way for the end host to react to a bad or duplicate sequence number. It's possible that it can be just ignored, and then the PPP packets can be spoofed.

SECURITY NOTE The GRE draft left many options available, so if you allow PPTP packets to enter through your firewall, an attacker can ride in on the GRE packet itself.

Attacking the Passwords

The PPTP authentication implementation supports three types of user authentication. The two that are concerned with security are the hashed method and the challenge response method. Hashed password authentication is based upon two one-way hashing functions. During the first hashing function, all passwords entered are converted to uppercase, which reduces the data space. Second, the hashing functions produce the same hash output, given the same password. In Chapter 12, we talked about the concept of a salt, which is an extra number of bits added to a hash function, thereby eliminating duplicate hash outputs from the same input. Unfortunately, there is no salt, so the hash output is the same. Therefore, in this authentication model, PPTP is open to dictionary attacks. In addition, both hash outputs are sent together in the communication string. An attacker can attack the first hash function to compromise the second hash function, thereby finding the password.

The second security authentication method uses the Challenge Handshake Authentication Protocol (CHAP). CHAP works by the client contacting the server and the server sending back a challenge. The client then performs a hash function, adds some extra information, and sends this back to the server. The server looks in its own database and computes the hash with the challenge. If they are the same, authentication succeeds. While this eliminates the dictionary attack, the hashing functions could still be attacked.

The PPTP framework calls for Microsoft's Point-to-Point Encryption (MPPE). The encryption is based on the user's password. After the initial communication is set up, only certain PPP packets are encrypted. RFC-1700 lists those packets that are sent in the clear and those that are encrypted. MPPE then does not encrypt all the PPP packets. This means you can attack the PPP protocol itself—for instance, spoofing the configuration packet containing certain DNS server information. MPPE uses the RC4 cipher in either 40- or 128-bit key size. One of the main security problems lies in the fact that since there are no lowercase characters, a good selection of passwords from which to choose is eliminated. Therefore, claiming that PPTP is either 40-bit or 128-bit secure is incorrect. The session key is derived from the user's password. The password will have a much lower entropy. The only way to reach true 40-bit or 128-bit security is by generating a random session key.

Moreover, since there is no salt, and since PPP uses common headers and trailers, it makes it a target for known-plaintext types of attacks. In addition, since encryption is based on the user password, not a public-key/shared secret-key encryption algorithm (mentioned in Chapter 13), authentication cannot be assured.

In PPTP communication, there is a tremendous amount of traffic that passes by that can be used for analysis. One such device is called L0pht-Crack, which is a PPTP packet sniffer designed to analyze PPTP authentication packets and produce the challenge passwords hashes. L0phtCrack is a registered trademark of LHI Technologies, and it's available at *http://www.l0pht.com/index.html.*

SECURITY NOTE One vulnerability with PPTP is that it relies on PPP. Prior to any communication, PPP sets up and initializes the communication parameters, and since PPP has no authentication against these packets, attacks like the man-in-the-middle and spoofing may occur.

GENERAL NOTE PPTP is used from client to server, and in many organizations, this means it will be from an NT server to a Windows 95 client. Since Windows 95 has minimal security, an attacker could attack the Windows 95 clients. A recommendation if using PPTP is to upgrade all Windows 95 clients to NT stations.

It can be argued that the Point-to-Point protocol is technically a good protocol. However, the implementation of it needs more work. Microsoft is fixing these problems, and hopefully they will be corrected in NT 5.0. Security is constantly changing, and to say you will not use PPTP because of these problems would be a mistake. We've mentioned IPSec being secure, but since there isn't real interoperability among vendors, how can it be? Since IPSec doesn't mandate authentication and encryption algorithms, what's to stop one vendor from having an insecure product? These things just need to be worked out.

SKIP Attacks

Simple Key Management Protocol, or SKIP, is similar in concept to the ISAKMP protocol described earlier. It is a mechanism to exchange the cryptographic keys between communicating parties. Like other cryptographic algorithms, it suffers from vulnerabilities also.

The concept of perfect forward secrecy (PFS) does not exist in SKIP. If an attacker can discover the secret key, he or she can use that key to decrypt messages sent in the past. If SKIP employed PFS, an attacker could not decrypt messages. SKIP does, however, give some protection against these attacks. The SKIP protocol uses a hierarchy of keys. A key usually labeled as Kijn is the session key used to decrypt the data. A time mechanism in SKIP usually changes this key every hour, although some vendors have installed in their product a timer you can set. If an attacker discovers the secret key, Kijn, he or she can only decrypt the past data during that hour, since this key is changed at least every hour. In addition, the attacker would have to decrypt the key right before it was about to change, in order to decrypt all of the previous hour's communications. This provides you with additional protection when using SKIP.

There is also a denial of service attack in SKIP, called the "clogging attack." An attacker can bomb a SKIP implementation on a host with SKIP packets from multiple hosts (or one host with forged source addresses). The SKIP process of the secret-key computation is very CPU-intensive. This drains resources on the attacked host until no other services are available, resulting in denial of service. Some implementations of SKIP have a potential solution to this type of attack, namely, the SKIP certificate discovery protocol. When seeing this first packet the SKIP protocol will then challenge the sender before starting the intensive CPU key computation process. If the response to the challenge is authenticated, the CPU process begins. If rejected, the communications are halted.

Certificate Authority Attacks

Certificate authorities are no different than any other device in the chain of trusted third-party communication. If an attack occurs on a certificate authority, attackers can impersonate whomever they wish by binding any key of their choice to the name of another user and using the certificate authority to verify it. Certificate authorities use other authorities as needed when certificates are chained. If chaining is used, we are again back to the concept of the "chain being as strong as the weakest link." It only takes one insecure CA to compromise the whole chain. Following are several theoretical ways in which a certificate authority could be attacked.

Cryptanalytic Attack

Cryptographic attacks against CAs will be much like the attacks on protocols mentioned earlier. Therefore, CAs will have to use extremely long keys and change them frequently. Unfortunately, CAs may not be able to do this so easily. We've mentioned that CAs form a hierarchy structure, with the top-level CAs being at the root of the CA hierarchy. Any CAs below the top wishing to use a chaining certificate structure will use the public keys of the CAs above it. To facilitate this structure, many of the lower CAs will write the top CA's public keys in software, thereby enhancing functionality. However, if the top CA, or for that matter, any CA higher than the one in question, changes its public key, the lower CA will have to get the new keys and will need a way to verify these keys. A lower CA should not let the higher CA it's getting the public key from verify that it is indeed the public key of that CA. This defeats the whole purpose of the CA. What this means is that the higher up the chain you go for chaining certificates, the less time the top CA will have to change its key. Attackers can use this time delay to their advantage.

Timestamp Attacks

A timestamp attack is caused by the lack of a timestamp on a certificate. Assume an attacker is able to compromise a certificate's key, but the certificate authority is no longer using that key. The attacker could create a key, sign it with someone else's public key, generate a certificate-compromised CA key, and backdate the time to some time in the past when the certificate was valid. This is very similar to forgery—for instance, a bank account has your name on it; someone changes it to his or her name, and withdraws the money. To protect against this, timestamps are inserted into the certificate that indicate when this certificate was made valid.

Hardware Attack

If an attacker can gain access to the device on which a certificate authority resides, its private key could become known if the attacker reverse-engineers the device to reveal the key. This is one reason why CAs must take extreme care in protecting their keys. If the CA is compromised, every certificate is compromised as well. Earlier in this book, I recommended personally visiting the CA you will be doing business with. You would be surprised at the differences in protection in various CAs.

Weak Attacks

This section is called "weak attacks." However, its original name was "dumb attacks." These types of attacks should never occur, but they could. And if they do, they can point back to the original authentication methods used by the CA itself. Now, this far in this book, you know about public keys, digital signatures, and certificates binding the signatures to public keys. What we haven't looked at is what proves to the CA you who are you say you are. When we think about the most globally accepted document for proof of identity, we think of a person's passport. CA authorities aren't going to force you to come down and show your passport to them so they will issue you a certificate. What that means is that the security measures the CA takes in establishing the user's identity is the maximum amount of security you can expect from that CA.

Say I create a public key and send it to a CA for a certificate. What kind of identification documents will the CA ask for? Typically, a drivers license and birth certificate (both easily forged). Most likely, since CAs are not in every area, I will fill out a form and fax it to them. Now if on the public key I impersonate another person, I then take that certificate and wire that person's bank and request money to be deposited into another account. The bank will look at the certificate, verify the person on it, and wire the money. This is what is meant by a weak attack. The original CA should have demanded more identification, and the bank should have used more that just the CA as the authority.

During the first couple of chapters I pointed out that internal attacks are one of the worse types of attacks. Not to pick on the employees of certificate authorities agencies, but if someone wanted to, he or she could create a forged certificate with someone else's name and do the same type of bank attack mentioned in the previous paragraph. This is why many CAs will require two or more persons to generate certificates—to thwart such an attack from occurring. Unfortunately, there are other ways to generate forged certificates, say, by bribing an employee. A person requesting a certificate could bribe the bank employee to issue an authenticated reply that really should have been denied. Good, reliable CAs will take every precaution to stop such attacks.

RADIUS Attacks

The Remote Authentication Dial-In User Service (RADIUS) was designed with two protocols in mind—authentication and accounting—and with the idea to centralize these services. RADIUS was initially designed to run on UNIX operating systems. Therefore, attacks that could occur on a RADIUS server are similar to the attacks on the UNIX operating systems mentioned in Chapter 15. When a user dials in to a remote access device using RADIUS, it communicates with the central RADIUS server to find out if the user is authorized to be allowed access. The RADIUS server performs the authentication and responds with an accept or a reject. If the user is accepted, the remote access server routes the user onto the network; if not, the RAS will terminate the user's connection.

A vulnerability was found in RADIUS technology that caused a buffer overflow problem, and by this point, you should have read many examples of vulnerabilities caused by such problems. It's important to note that this particular vulnerability was found and corrected, but depending on the version of RADIUS you have running, you still could be affected. Therefore, it would be a wise decision to check your RADIUS manufacturer and version number and see if you have the correct version installed.

This vulnerability allowed an attacker to remotely gain superuser access to a machine running the RADIUS server. The problem manifested itself as the result of an inverse-resolution operation of IP addresses to host names. The RADIUS software would copy the host name to a buffer on its stack without first checking the length of the host name. In the attack, an attacker would set up an extremely long host name, and the RADIUS software would place the name on the stack, causing it to overrun its buffer. Any malicious code could then be run on the server.

The RADIUS is a very good protocol, and some implementations use a keyed MD5 algorithm for authentication. Apparently, this was the only place in the code that would allow this type of attack. In addition, there were found to be many places where string sizes were unchecked, possibly leading to more vulnerability. RADIUS also supports several other user authentication protocols, such as PPP, PAP, CHAP, and UNIX login. However, these user authentication protocols are not as strong as a keyed MD5; therefore, checking to see what protocols your implementation is using is a good idea.

Kerberos Attacks

Kerberos is a distributed authentication system that allows organizations to handle password security for the entire organization. The most common forms of Kerberos today are Kerberos V4 and V5. Unfortunately, both are susceptible to dictionary attacks. An attacker can attack a Kerberos V4 system with the help of a local machine, and a packet sniffer helps in the attack of Kerberos V5. The most serious of these is the susceptibility of its passwords, and therefore the Kerberos Ticket Granting Ticket, to guessing attacks against protocol. Unfortunately, these protocols are vulnerable to dictionary-type attacks. There are some available patches for "Kerberized" systems; therefore, check with your vendor.

All entities in Kerberos have a secret key, which is shared only with the central Kerberos authentication server. To obtain services from an application server in a Kerberized environment (programs modified, FTP, telnet, etc.), a client first obtains a Kerberos ticket from the authentication server. This ticket contains various items, along with the encrypted secret key belonging to the service provider. The client presents this ticket to the application server, which then verifies the ticket. In Chapter 14, we showed how this authentication is a two-step process. First, the client obtains a TGT (Ticket Granting Ticket), then the client presents this ticket to a Ticket Granting Server (TGS), which finally issues the ticket for that particular service. This is done so the user would have a ticket that would grant access for a specified time without having to communicate with the central server again.

The tickets in a Kerberos V4 system contain many "string" data formats that do not contain any kind of padding or structure alignment, thereby allowing a user to construct an invalid packet, since the server cannot verify it from a legitimate packet. So the Kerberos server sends back an encrypted packet back to the client. The packet is encrypted using DES encryption with a key derived from the user's password (an attack against the implementation). When the attacker tries to log in, the attacker will be denied and the server will send back the encrypted packet and deny the request. Since the TGT has a fixed, publicly known format, an attacker would just send packet after packet, keeping all the encrypted packets that were sent to him or her and just use a dictionary to keep trying new passwords until allowed access.

KerberosV4 systems actually help the attacker in a way. There is a service name field in the decrypted TGT ticket, and for TGT packets, it is always the same. This means decrypting the ticket only requires decrypting a small part of the ticket. It is also known that the first block in a plaintext TGT has a DES session key that has odd parity. This means that in many cases only one DES encryption is needed instead of two. Kerberos also lacks the "salt" concept in its password structures.

KerberosV5 has made significant security improvements over KerberosV4. KerberosV5 introduces something known as preauthentication; this requires users to provide some information to the server that they know the secret key before they can get a ticket. KerberosV5 also introduces timestamps; the Kerberos server will send its reply to the client only if it decrypts to the correct time, allowing for drift. While this stops the online dictionary attack, an attacker with a sniffer can initiate an offline dictionary attack against any authentication requests captured over the network earlier.

Pretty Good Privacy (PGP) Attacks

Pretty Good Privacy (PGP) has a long list of users, myself included. After all, the protocols involved, IDEA, RSA, and MD5, are all very reliable, secure protocols. Still, the question remains, can PGP be broken into? After looking at IPSec, PPTP, Kerberos, and RADIUS, how secure can PGP be? The truth is that PGP is very secure—probably one of the best security frameworks. What's more interesting about PGP is not its strength, but the government's attitude toward it. If you look back at the various articles on PGP, you will probably read a lot of cloak-and-dagger-type stuff.

It's now known that the new so-called secure encryption algorithms used by digital phones that were supposed to make it impossible for anyone to gain your code and use your ID have actually been compromised, and your communications can be intercepted. Some people have the same suspicions about PGP and are accusing the government of building backdoors into it. Fortunately, most people disagree with these beliefs. After all, if PGP did have a backdoor built into it, by this time it would have been uncovered.

PGP uses four components: a symmetric cipher (IDEA), an asymmetric cipher (RSA), a hash function (MD5), and a pseudorandom number generator (PRNG). Each one of these devices could be attacked.

IDEA

The IDEA cipher uses a 128-bit key, and the only known form of attack that could be attempted on it would be a brute-force attack. Therefore, someone would have to try at least half the key space, which is roughly 2^{127}. This comes out to 1.7×10^{38} steps. There aren't many machines that can go through this key space.

RSA

The RSA cryptosystem, developed by Rivest, Shamir, and Adleman, gets its strength from the difficulty involved in factoring large prime numbers, as described back in Chapter 13. No attack has been successful on RSA to date. And with sufficiently large key sizes, no attacks are expected to succeed.

MD5

The MD5 hashing function was found to be vulnerable if a small number or rounds were used. There have been attempts to break MD5, using brute-force, birthday, and differential cryptanalysis methods. Out of these, differential cryptanalysis had some success out of one round of MD5 and only affected an operation not related to the security of MD5.

PRNG

PGP uses two pseudorandom number generators (PRNGs): the ANSI X9.17 generator and the trueRand generator. The trueRand generator measures the latency of the user's input, and then uses that pool for a seed to the X9.17 generator. By using two generators, PGP has added security mechanisms to produce true randomness.

It would seem that PGP is a very secure algorithm that has experienced no forms of attack; however, that would be an incorrect assumption. After all, if you can't attack the protocol, you can attack the implementation. An attacker could snoop the window (like in an X-windowing environment) or set up an application on a user's machine to capture keystrokes. An attacker could even set up a small electronic receiver nearby that senses the video signals that the computer screen produces and feeds these as inputs to another computer. By subtracting the horizontal and vertical sync signals, the attacker could display the user keystrokes on another computer screen.

Denial of Service (DoS) Attacks

Denial of service (DoS) attacks cover a wide range of attack categories. So, what exactly are DoS attacks? Denial of service attacks cause the system or network to stop servicing legitimate users. An example would be if an attacker caused a broadcast storm on a network; the effect would be no network availability to other users, i.e., a denial of service to legitimate users for network resources. There are several types of DoS attacks, including TCP SYN attacks, smurf attacks, UDP diagnostic attacks, ICMP redirect attacks, teardrop attacks, and spoofing attacks. In this section we will look at these types.

TCP SYN Attacks

The TCP SYN, also referred to as syn_flooding attack, stops a server from communicating with other users. To understand TCP SYN, we need to first look at normal communication in a client/server communication process. The steps involved in setting up a TCP client/server communication is usually referred to as a three-way handshake.

1. *SYN.*   First, the client sends a server a SYN (synchronize) packet to request a service from a server.
2. *SYN ACK.*   The server responds back to the client with a SYN ACK (synchronize acknowledge) packet.
3. *ACK.*   The client then sends back an ACK (acknowledgement) to

the server, and communication begins. (The server needs this third packet before it will allow the client to send it anything.)

In a TCP SYN attack, during the process of SYN ACK and ACK, a small buffer queue is established to keep track of these incoming SYN packets. The attacker spoofs the source address, so the destination machine sends SYN ACK packets back to false addresses, while still waiting for the ACK for the three-way TCP communication to complete. The problem is that the ACK never arrives, and the destination buffer keeps filling up to handle these connections. As the buffer fills, it eventually reaches a point where no legitimate TCP connections can occur, and therefore results in a denial of service attack.

Not much can be done in TCP SYN attacks. A firewall or router can stop the SYN ACK packets from entering a network, but then the attacker can just send these packets to that network device. This would cause that device to increase its processing load, and possibly increase the utilization on your network, reducing the available bandwidth and creating another denial of service attack.

Some things you can do to help minimize the impact are as follows:

1. Increase the size of your SYN ACK queue.

2. Decrease the time-out waiting period for three-way handshakes.

3. Access list outbound on router (protects others).

Steps 1 and 2 combined will help you by increasing the available space for holding connection requests and dropping those that are invalid more quickly, thereby giving the destination server some more time before causing denial of services to legitimate machines. The third step is to help you avoid becoming a host of these attacks. Since the source addresses are spoofed, if you only allow valid addresses to leave your network, you are helping others not become victims.

Smurf Attacks

A smurf attack has three players: the attacker, the intended victim, and the bounced (or amplified) network. The attacker sends an ICMP packet to the broadcast address of the bounced network, spoofing the source address in the packet to match that of the victim's network. Since the packet contained the broadcast address of the bounced network, all hosts on that network will reply to the victim's network. This results in a packet storm originating from the bounced network and directed to the victim's network. The attacker could send several spoofed packets to different amplifier networks, causing massive network utilization problems on the victim's network.

You cannot deal with smurf attacks effectively by yourself; it is important to get your ISP involved as soon as possible. By working backwards, an ISP can filter their routers and tell where the packets are coming from. This takes a while and may involve multiple ISPs, so early warning is critical.

Let's look at an example of a smurf attack. In this example the three players are the attacker, who is on address 1.1.1.1, the victim, who is on address 2.2.2.2, and the bounced (amplified) network, which is on address 3.0.0.0.

Step 1. Attacker sends ICMP (e.g., ping) to address 3.0.0.0.

It's important to note that the attacker (1) "spoofs," or forges his or her address to be that of the victim. In other words, the bounced network thinks that the packets are coming from address 2.2.2.2, and (2) sends it to the network address of 3.0.0.0. When a packet like a ping is sent to the network address, all hosts will respond with a reply.

Step 2. Bounced network replies to the victim.

The bounced network (3.0.0.0), believing that the packet originated from address 2.2.2.2., begins pinging that address, all hosts on the 3.0.0.0 network reply back to address 2.2.2.2

Also, this is just one packet, so one ping request from the attacker can cause over 250 replies from the bounced network. The attacker would normally ping several networks at once, and all the networks would reply back to this one network, causing a massive DoS attack.

Smurf attacks are extremely disruptive to a network. I am fortunate enough to work with Todd Zickefoose ("Rusty"), who is one of the leading experts in counteracting this type of attack. His work on IOPS and the IETF will hopefully develop effective ways to stop smurf attacks.

UDP Diagnostic Attacks

Many network devices use UDP services as diagnostic ports. Echo-request, echo-reply, and discard are various types of diagnostic services performed. An attacker can send a barrage of these UDP packets to various ports on a device, again with spoofed source addresses, thereby increasing the processing load on that device. The best measures that can be taken to protect against this are (1) to have the device behind a firewall or (2) to shut them off completely on the device.

ICMP Redirects/Redirects Bombs

ICMP redirects are very common in routing networking topology. Routers inform each other that a router no longer exists and there is another way to get to the same destination. However, if an attacker can forge the address in the redirect packet, an unknowing host may send data in the other way than was intended. Denial of service can occur when a spoofed ICMP redirect packet tells a host or router that a network no longer is reachable and connectivity to that network is gone.

Teardrop, Ping of Death, Boink, and Land Attacks

Teardrop, ping of death, boink, and land are all variants of the same form of attack. They each use information in the header that doesn't agree with the actual contents of the packet, thereby confusing the server when it is trying to reassemble the packet. This usually causes the operating system to fail.

Teardrop   The attacker sends an IP packet of two fragments to the victim; the header information has a packet size of x. When the server tries to reassemble the packets, one of the packets is different from the original information, thereby causing the server to overwrite a large amount of memory and halt.

Ping of Death   The ping of death attack is vulnerable to many systems and many IP stacks. The attacker sends fragmented packets to the server. When the server tries to reassemble these packets, it turns out that the packet size is greater than 65,536 bytes, causing buffer overflows on the server.

Boink   Boink, or its counterpart, Bonk, works in reverse of the Teardrop. instead of sending a packet that is smaller than that specified in the header, they send a packet size larger than specified in the header. Bonk originally only attacked Port 53 DNS, which is usually open. Boink attacks all ports.

Land   The land attack is where the source address/source port parameters are the same as the destination address/destination port parameters. The source address and TCP information is spoofed, and usually they are identical to the destination address/destination port parameters, causing the server to lose control connections, crash, halt, and so forth.

Spoofing Attacks

Spoofing attacks are nothing more than forgery: The attacker assumes the identity of a third party. Spoofing attacks can occur across a wide range of services and protocols. IP addresses, remote procedure calls, the X-windowing system, DNS, and the UNIX "R" services can all be spoofed. However, a majority of attacks use the IP spoofing mechanism.

Spoofing can easily be prevented by configuring a network router not to pass unauthorized addresses. For example, if a router has on one of its interfaces the network 1.0.0.0, you would configure the router so that if any source address (not destination) is *not* 1.0.0.0, it would drop the packet. This implies that if the router knows that network 1.0.0.0 is on its interface, then only network 1.0.0.0 should be coming from any host on that network. If it is not 1.0.0.0, it could be spoofed. With companies today having hundreds of networks, however, you need to be very careful of how you apply this filter. Remember, though, if you filter on every packet, you increase the load on the router, which could decrease the router's performance.

DNS spoofing involves an attack on the domain name server, in which the attacker modifies the IP/host name database. Some services use DNS for authentication information, so if an attack on a DNS is successful, the service requesting authentication information would be told to allow access when it should have been told to deny access.

Some spoofing is actually good and is implemented in many applications. It is usually done to minimize the traffic on WAN links and usually involves "keep-alives." If you have a server on one end of the WAN that needs to remain aware of the status of another machine on the other side of the WAN, it will usually send a keep-alive to that machine, usually a simple ping. In order to reduce the traffic on the WAN, the network device, firewall, router, and so on will reply to the server that sent the keep-alive. Therefore, the server will still think that the other machine is up and there is no traffic placed upon the WAN link, which is usually a slow link compared to a LAN.

Other Attacks

There are some other attacks that don't fall into the category of denial of service but can impede a company's ability to conduct business. These attacks are no less damaging than the DoS attacks, and some of these attacks will affect any device on your network, including your VPN device.

Trojan

A Trojan is an unauthorized program hiding within a legitimate program. The hidden program performs functions unknown to the user. When a legitimate program has been altered by the placement of unauthorized code within it, it's considered a Trojan. Trojans are usually written to find out vital information about a system or user. These programs are hard to detect, and since many are binaries, assessing them is extremely difficult. In the case of a buffer overflow vulnerability, a Trojan could be placed on the resulting machine data segment and instructed to run.

Remote Attacks

Remote attacks are simply attacks that come from another machine. These attacks are successful because the victim usually supplies the information to be attacked in the first place. Utilities such as "host," "finger," "whois," "showmount," and "rpcinfo" can give an attacker important information about the victim. The attack itself is not a remote attack, but with this information, the attacker is able to remotely try any type of compromise that is possible on that machine. A simple example is if an attacker telnets to Port 25 (the SMTP port) of your company's mail server, which is easily found by a name query and cannot be blocked by firewalls. I mentioned this back in Chapters 7 and 8. If you do not protect your mail server, it will reveal what type of mail server it is. Now an attacker just has to look at any of the security advisories (the same ones you could have consulted) and see if this particular version of mail has been correctly patched.

Telnet-Based Attacks

Telnet is one of those utilities that was designed for simple communication. Even the original specification (RFC-764) describes it as a "fairly general, bidirectional, 8-bit, byte-oriented communications facility." Security considerations were never built into telnet. In fact, telnet is so buggy, no work is done to secure it. Buffer overflows, Trojans, shared libraries, capturing logs, and usernames and passwords being sent in clear text are so common, why even use telnet?

My personal opinion is that telnet is still a great utility. If used in the context it was designed for—simple communication—it works wonders. When all the security algorithms, password protection devices, and servers fail, you can still rely on telnet to get the work done.

Birthday Attack

A birthday attack is a brute-force type of attack on a cryptographic hash function, such as MD5. Basically it tries to find two messages that hash to the same value, causing a collision. It is called a "birthday" since the attack is usually demonstrated by using a population of people. It recognizes the fact that it is easier to find a matching pair set, such as people's birthdays, than an individual item. For instance, say you have a group of 23 people. The birthday attack simply states that given a size of 23 people, there is a 50 percent chance they will have the same birthday. That we have an even chance of success with 23 different days is called a paradox.

The birthday attack is basically a statistical probability problem. If you were given x possible inputs and Y possible outputs (MD5 converts X to Y), in the set of X inputs, there are $X(X-1)/2$ pairs of X, and for each X, there is a probability that $1/Y$ (hashed outputs) will produce the same output. Therefore, if you look at $Y/2$ outputs, there is a 50 percent chance that a matching pair will be found. If you now consider the MD5 algorithm, there are 2^{64} messages that would need to be tried. It is generally believed that this type of attack is computationally infeasible given the number of cycles and computer resources needed.

Conclusion

This chapter has described the most common forms of attacks on VPNs. You can probably recall earlier in the book that I mentioned thinking about VPNs in a systems context. After Chapters 15 and 16, you should now know why this is helpful. A breakdown or attack on a VPN will also affect the underlying technology.

One major problem with VPNs is what is usually referred to as the "VPN protocol proliferation." Four different protocols are currently being used for VPNs: PPTP (Point-to-Point Tunneling Protocol), L2F (Layer 2 Forwarding Protocol), L2TP (Layer 2 Tunneling Protocol), and IPSec (IP Security Protocol). To determine which one is right for your company and which one provides the best security, you would have to look at where they came from. PPTP, L2F, and L2TP came from dial-up VPN usage, while IPSec was born out of the Automotive Network Exchange (ANX) LAN-to-LAN VPN.

In this chapter, we looked at the security concerns with the two leading VPN protocols, IPSec and PPTP. After reading those sections, are you more inclined to choose one over the other? Both have shortcomings and advantages. They each have their place. I would agree with the PPTP specifications that recommend using IPSec in combination with PPTP.

Probably as interesting to you as it was to me is the way cryptographic functions can be broken. When I started doing research on this topic, I found the fact astonishing that an extremely strong cryptographic algorithm in an improper implementation could be rendered incredibly weak. As with everything else, there is always a trade-off, such as money versus research, security versus flexibility, and so on.

CHAPTER 17

Security Toolbelt

Throughout this book, we discussed Virtual Private Network technology, and we've looked at some attacks that can be placed upon VPN systems. We've looked at the details of what makes them function and how that functionality is broken by attacks on the very technology intended to make them safe: cryptographic systems. We also looked at the other attacks, or so-called side-attacks, including capturing keystrokes, capturing X-windows screen shots, and so on.

We can therefore conclude that anything that could cause a potential hazard to your VPN safety should be examined, but the question is, what can be done? This chapter will help you look at some of the measures that can be taken to ensure the safety of your VPN environment.

As you go through this chapter, think about where could you apply each recommendation. With this chapter in hand, you can begin to develop a roadmap to security. By the end of the chapter, you will have a list of at least 10 items that you could do to secure your site free of charge. You will know where to go to get helpful information and what to do in case of being attacked.

A very important piece of advice is that if under attack, when you are tempted to immediately shut down a system or reboot a machine, don't. Instead, think first. By the end of this chapter, you will have some guidelines to help you.

What Is a Security Toolbelt?

A security toolbelt is a global term that refers to protecting your company's resources. It doesn't necessarily mean knowing every single vulnerability that exists on the Internet. It does mean, however, knowing what you are vulnerable to. Various security toolbelts have many of the same things in common but differ on the fine points. Therefore, a security toolbelt could be defined as those components that make your network safer, and if an intrusion occurs, it lets you know where to go for help.

SECURITY NOTE   Perfect security does not exist. If someone tells you that he or she is a security expert, can protect your network 100 percent, and if anything goes wrong, they will be liable, become skeptical. Go instead with security experts who have knowledge in many areas, who will protect you 99 percent of the time, and who will know where to go for help for that 1 percent when they can't.

Training

Companies often put training last on the list, but I think it should go first. You would not bring your car to a mechanic who hasn't been properly trained, and you wouldn't go to a doctor who hasn't been trained. However, companies expect their IT employees, because of their technical skills, to stop security attacks. IT personnel can learn security skills, but I wouldn't expect a server administrator to automatically become a security administrator; it's just too broad an area. It's not impossible, though. Any technical person can learn security; he or she just needs to be willing, since learning about security takes a lot of time on an individual's part.

Management Training

Management training is a must. Not meant to pick on managers, but article after article says the security policy must come from the top. Even I sometimes advocate this view—that is, until reality sets in. Say a company has a security team on staff who is solely responsible for the protection of the company's IT resources. They have years of experience in IT, including networking, security, operating systems, and so forth. Then, as many articles advocate, the top executives set the security policy, and the security staff implements it. Is there any logic in this? A manager who has to worry about costs, profits, human resources, and capital outlays now has to decide what the security policy of the company should be.

It's not their fault. Even technical people can't keep up with the changes. So how then can top management be expected to keep abreast of security technology? Through training. Not the kind of intensive training that IT security people receive, but the "big-picture" kind of training. This type of training would include how access is granted to a network, how and why logging is good and what to log, what kind of environment does the company have, and perhaps how some simple attacks can occur. With this knowledge, top management can sit down with IT security staff and work out a solution that gives management what they want and allows the IT staff to still secure the network to the best of their ability. What I have heard from many managers is they are just not sufficiently briefed on what their security options are.

Security Advisories

You can subscribe to many security advisory Web sites that disseminate security information. There are both nonprofit and for-profit Web sites, but most of them don't charge anything for advisory statements. It is a simple process to visit and query them on known vulnerabilities of various systems. If you use a Web search engine and enter in the keywords "security vulnerabilities advisories," you can come up with thousands upon thousands of Web sites offering security advice.

Newsgroups/Mailing Lists

Newsgroups and mailing lists, and even IRC chatlines, are some of the best sources of information concerning security issues. What often occurs is that someone is working on a system, and something happens. Perhaps they noticed something strange, or for some reason, their authentication server is down, or they are getting weird messages on the console on one of their servers. They look into it for a while but can't figure it out. So they visit the vendor's site, checking the patch and revision levels. Nearly all of the time, after they have exhausted their options, they will post a message to a newsgroup or mailing list in the hope that someone has seen this problem before.

Now why would an administrator post a message to a newsgroup or mailing list? Simple. It's free. You may be using a vendor's product, but if you didn't purchase maintenance from that vendor, you don't have support. Newsgroups and mailing lists are free, easy to get to, and usually a reply comes back rather quickly. After the problem has made its way through the newsgroups and mailing lists, then vendors look at the problem to determine if it is a legitimate vulnerability. And if so, a patch is released and announced by the security advisories. Unfortunately, this is the only logical choice a vendor and security advisory can make. But consider the alternative. Say a vulnerability is discovered, filtered through the newsgroups, and made known to the vendor. The vendor acknowledges this vulnerability and issues an alert that says, "A vulnerability was found in [x area], and by the way, there is no patch yet, so shut down your system." Obviously, this wouldn't work.

Phone Support

You may already have phone support, and you probably have contact numbers for various technical support teams for the various manufacturers' equipment that you use. Now what if you are attacked, and the attack is coming from the Internet? The attack could be coming from across the state, across the country, or across the planet. Whom would you call? You probably would start with your ISP, but if you think of it, many smaller ISPs are too small to help stop an attack—although I am sure they will try. If you are using a larger ISP, the number you were provided for Internet access is probably not the security group, and in big organizations, the Internet access group may not even know who the security group is. Therefore, before this situation can occur, be prepared. Get any and every number you possibly can. If your ISP is going to want specific information first, know what type of information they will want. Confusion on such matters can mean massive delays, resulting in hours of attacks.

Vendor Security Page/Mailing Lists

Every vendor's product you use should have some informational Web page that you can access. In addition, many vendors have email forms on their pages that you can fill out to receive automatic updates on products, as well as security alerts. There are also mailing lists throughout the Web that are geared to specific types of products. The only problem with the mailing lists in this case is that if you get on an active list, you will receive hundreds of emails a day, first from the original query, and then from all the replies. Most newcomers to the Web don't realize that it is proper to read the FAQ first, and if their question is not answered there, then post it.

Governmental Departments

Most people may not be aware of it, but there are branches of the government that actually have some very good, reliable information on security, procedures, vulnerabilities, and so on. So far throughout this book, it seemed like the government was the enemy. Well, perhaps with regard to encryption. However, they have many good sites for computer security and are free and willing to share that information. Even some of the armed forces offer computer documentation and security advice.

Escalation Procedures

Escalation procedures are important and, from a legal point of view, are your next step. Say you have all the numbers of ISPs, vendors, and so on, and someone breaks into your system. With the help of the ISP, you track them down. Now what will you do? Prosecute? Remember that your ISP will not prosecute on your behalf. They will, however, help you gather data, and even then it's often difficult to get that data. If during a search, an ISP turns over some information to you that is incorrect, they are liable. For example, an attacker steals a victim's credit card and creates an account using the victim's identity. The attacker then attacks your network, your ISP incorrectly identifies the victim as the attacker, and you prosecute the victim. After the mess is all cleared up, the victim now has a legal issue with the ISP. Therefore, you will most likely need a subpoena to get that information from the ISP. Your escalation procedures have to include what you are going to do and who you are going to call. Since computer crimes are a federal offense, you need to contact the FBI. The FBI will require the appropriate information available to aid in their investigation. You will need to get that information from the ISP, which will require a subpoena. As you can now see, such things are best left up to your legal department. You should be aware of what is to be required, however.

The Need for a Security Toolbelt

Every organization needs to protect itself. Some companies allocate more financial resources on security measures than others. This allocation must take into account all those things that need to be protected. When you implement Virtual Private Networks, you add another security factor. Let's look at some of those security issues that cause companies problems in the first place. Once you secure these items, then you can concentrate on protecting your VPN.

Current Vendor Patches Not Installed

This problem exists in many corporations. Installed patches are not to current specification. Patches are constantly being added and updated, which is why I have not specified exact revision numbers. If I were to specify such and such a version, you probably would look at your operating system, see that it was different, and end there. Instead, first look at the operating system's build level. Many make the mistake of doing a "show revision," come up with something like "Revision 3.02," and leave it there. Rather, look at the command itself. Many commands have extra options that will indicate a build level. For instance, "show revision -p" will reveal something like "Revision 3.02 (build 10.034)." It's this revision/build level you need to compare against the vendor's or security advisory's Web page list. Second, don't just look at the operating system. As I've mentioned earlier, each application that runs on a machine will be a certain revision/build level and a recommended patch. When you begin looking at your company's vulnerabilities, start where you are most at risk—probably the Internet connections, including the router, firewall, and authentication server. Start with these devices and work back.

GENERAL NOTE   Don't install a new security platform until you've made sure that what you have is secure. The new security platform will just reveal weaknesses that you already have, and it would be like putting a Band-Aid on top of a Band-Aid.

Initial Poor Default Security Configurations

When you install a product, many times it comes with a default configuration that is prone to vulnerabilities. In Chapter 15, we mentioned that the guest and administrator accounts are potential targets and, therefore, shouldn't exist. The guest account, usually used for simple access, can be broken into. The administrator's account shouldn't be called "administrator," and a fake administrator account should be set up. In UNIX systems, the default access is for the starting of services, e.g., FTP, telnet. These are automatically set up, and unless you take preventive measures, they are targets for attacks. In addition, many email systems set relay to ON, meaning anybody can use your email server as a spam relay, thereby sending hundreds of thousands of messages through your mail system and causing it to crash. Therefore, whenever you add a new system to your network, make sure you know the vulnerabilities of that system. Any system that you add can either be attacked or used as a starting point to conduct other attacks.

Lack of Sufficient Resources for Security

Unfortunately, in many companies, security resources are usually kept at a minimum compared to those needed. Throughout this book, I said that VPNs and security must go hand in hand. If you can't handle security, you shouldn't implement a VPN. However, this is not implying that a company must spend ridiculous amounts on security. But security encompasses so much, network infrastructure, server infrastructure, and WAN/LAN infrastructure, that it's too difficult a job without the necessary resources. In addition, a company should not expect the person who handles the administration of the equipment to also be responsible for its security. In fact, some companies have an entire department just to manage security.

Dynamic Policies and Standards Not Enforced

Many companies do not have dynamic standard policies and guidelines. The word "dynamic" is used here, since most policies and procedures are static and short-lived. Virus software is only as good as the last known virus, and the same goes for patches and revision levels. Everything changes. If this is true, how then can a company have a static security policy? Unfortunately, many do. What usually happens is a security policy is established and agreed upon by all parties. Then after some time a new device is added that requires some additional resource not originally thought of when the security policy was designed. Sometimes for the sake of flexibility, security guidelines are skipped, intended to be addressed in the future.

In addition, perhaps the head of security has not kept up with security issues and therefore dictates iron-rule adherence to the security policy. What happens time and time again is that the person who is doing the actual work cannot get the work done because of this inflexible policy. That person informs his or her manager, and the complaint goes up the chain of command. Finally 3 months later a meeting is held between upper management and security. Each party bends a little and agrees on a compromise. Then, the one who has to do the security upgrade is too busy and has to reschedule this particular job. This is real life, and it happens every single day in companies. A dynamic, flexible security policy must be used instead of the rigid one so often found in companies.

Too Much Secrecy Instead of Security

When you examine security through the eyes of a third party, it usually appears to this third party that the company has no idea who its enemies are. Most times the company is protecting itself from employees instead of attackers. While security policies are defined, procedures implemented, and authentication devices installed, the end user has no idea of what is going on. No input is ever requested; no advice is ever asked for. The problem is that the end user is the interface to the customer and is the person actually doing the work. In too many situations, security problems arise, and there is nowhere to turn to for help. In many cases, due to the stealthy nature of security, it's not even known that there's a security problem. There has to be some training for the end users. They need to know what is happening and where to go for help.

RFC 2196 Site Security Handbook

In any organization, security should start with RFC 2196, *The Site Security Handbook*. It can be thought of as guidelines or a checklist for those things that must be done in order to secure your network. Use it as a starting point and continue from there. In this section, we will discuss some very practical advice from the RFC that applies to any organization.

The Basic Approach

Start with the basic approach, identifying who your enemies are, determining whether the threats are real, and so forth. Above all, keep your security program dynamic. According to *The Site Security Handbook:*

- "Identify what you are trying to protect.
- Determine what you are trying to protect it from.
- Determine how likely the threats are.
- Implement measures which will protect your assets in a cost-effective manner.
- Review the process continuously and make improvements each time a weakness is found."

Assets

When determining what your vulnerabilities are, start from the Internet and work back. Look at your external router and its operating-system revision level. Then look at your firewall, along with its operating-system revision level. Next, look at the authentication schemes, including where that server is placed and its OS revisions.

SECURITY NOTE   The further you place the authentication server away from the Internet connections point, the more damage an attacker can accomplish.

If you place the authentication server deep inside your network, somewhere inside of the local networks segment, then if someone who was authenticating against that server discovers a vulnerability that exploits a buffer overflow problem, they could potentially attack any system. The closer the authentication server is to the Internet, the better chance you have of minimizing the damage by using internal access filters on internal routers.

According to *The Site Security Handbook,* you should look at the following when accessing your setup:

- "Hardware: CPUs, boards, keyboards, terminals, workstations, personal computers, printers, disk drives, communication lines, terminal servers, routers.
- Software: source programs, object programs, utilities, diagnostic programs, operating systems, communication programs.
- Data: during execution, stored on-line, archived off-line, backups, audit logs, databases, in transit over communication media.
- People: users, administrators, hardware maintainers.
- Documentation: on programs, hardware, systems, local administrative procedures.
- Supplies: paper, forms, ribbons, magnetic media."

Security Goals

The Site Security Handbook offers the following security trade-off:
- "Services offered versus security provided
- Ease of use versus security
- Cost of security versus risk of loss"

These are extremely valid points. Every new service you add carries its own weighted security risks. Don't just add something since it's new; find out what you need. Even as the RFC states itself, you need to balance security with flexibility. The costs involved with security can be expensive. Therefore, if you are on a budget, determine what are the most important computer-related items, and start protecting them first.

Involve Multiple Parties

As mentioned earlier, allow those who are going to be affected by the security to have some input to what is going to be implemented. One person does not know what it takes to develop a good security policy for an organization. However, do not make the group too large, either. Including too many is just as bad as including too few. *The Site Security Handbook* recommends that the following people be included in security decisions:

- "Site security administrator
- Information technology technical staff (e.g., staffs from computing center)
- Administrators of large user groups within the organization (e.g., business divisions, computer science department within a university, etc.)
- Security incident response team
- Representatives of the user groups affected by the security policy
- Responsible management
- Legal counsel (if appropriate)"

Flexible Security Policy

Consider the following quote from *The Site Security Handbook:*

> It is also important to recognize that there are exceptions to every rule. Whenever possible, the policy should spell out what exceptions to the general policy exist. For example, under what conditions is a system administrator allowed to go through a user's files. Also, there may be some cases when multiple users will have access to the same userid. For example, on systems with a "root" user, multiple system administrators may know the password and use the root account.

This cannot be overstated: Keep your security policy flexible. Unfortunately, for the most part, this section is largely ignored.

The RFC 2196 Site Security Handbook should be considered a staple in any organization's security infrastructure. It is well-written, well-detailed, and well-documented, covering all the practical steps involved in security. The sections we looked at are just a small part of this handbook. It is written by experts in the field and provides a good look at what makes up a security policy.

Security Escalation Procedures

What would happen if you underwent an attack. Do you have any idea who you would call or what items you would need? The truth is, unless an attacker does something to impact the performance of a network, server, and so on, or if you notice something by monitoring logs, you might not even know you were the victim of an attack. If you were, however, where would you go? This section looks at some places you can contact for help.

FBI Field Office

Due to the Federal Computer Fraud and Abuse Act of 1986, the FBI has the responsibility for investigating various computer crimes. As posted by their Web page, some of these crimes included:

- Intrusions of the Public Switched Network (the telephone company)
- Major computer network intrusions
- Network integrity violations
- Privacy violations
- Industrial espionage
- Pirated computer software
- Other crimes where the computer is a major factor in committing the criminal offense

You can find your nearest FBI field office by contacting the FBI's National Computer Crime Squad. This information can be found at the FBI main Web page at *http://www.fbi.gov/programs/compcrim.htm*. On this page is a list of items that may help in identifying an attacker and may be required by the FBI, including:

- Place a login banner to ensure that unauthorized users are warned that they may be subject to monitoring.
- Turn audit trails on.
- Consider keystroke level monitoring if adequate banner is displayed.

- Request trap and tracing from your local telephone company.
- Consider installing caller identification.
- Make backups of damaged or altered files.
- Maintain old backups to show the status of the original.
- Designate one person to secure potential evidence.
- Evidence can consist of tape backups and printouts. These should be initialed by the person obtaining the evidence.
- Evidence should be retained in a locked cabinet with access limited to one person.
- Keep a record of resources used to reestablish the system and locate the perpetrator.
- For notices to alert users to potential security problems and information on related subjects, contact the Computer Emergency Response Team (CERT) or the Forum of Incident Response and Security Teams (FIRST). CERT and FIRST are separate organizations not affiliated with the FBI. Persons desiring to contact the FBI's National Computer Crime Squad regarding a computer crime matter should do so by calling the telephone number listed on this page. Do not send e-mail to CERT or FIRST intended for the FBI.

The FBI also recognizes the need to share information about possible violations. The two sites listed in the last bullet item are important sources for the dissemination of computer-related security information. Do not contact them if you want to press charges; they cannot help. However, they can help you in identifying various attacks.

SECURITY NOTE   If you notice you are under attack, *do nothing* (at first). If you reset a connection or reboot a router or firewall, the attacker may see a "connection reset by peer" message, assume you are doing something, and not come back on until later. Then they probably will use another forged source address. Be prepared for this and initiate a plan to get as much information as possible before resetting the connection.

Building a Secure Site

Before you can build a secure site, you need to secure what you already have. Any new product you could install that will supposedly increase security will actually do the opposite if you don't secure your existing infrastructure. Start with maintenance, and use the following bullets as a list of items that will help you secure your site:

- *Be familiar with your equipment.*   Know what your system's operating revisions are, along with their revision levels and any patches.

- *Understand the data flows.*   Knowing the logical data connections helps you understand how the data flows in the network, thereby allowing you to create possible attack scenarios (e.g., if an attacker broke into this machine, the attacker could jump to this server, this router, etc.)

- *Stay on top of security.*   You do not have to be the leading edge in the latest differential cryptanalysis techniques, but you do have to know what cryptanalysis means. If you see an alert from a security advisory Web site saying something similar to "...differential cryptanalysis techniques have led to many cryptosystems being compromised...", you should understand what that means. In addition, know that your VPN is a cryptosystem, and if there is a potential for your data to be decrypted, investigate.

- *Test patch levels.*   There has been more than the occasional patch release that fixed one problem and created two more. See if you can test the patch on a noncritical system first, and if you can't, see if you can at least undo the patch if necessary and restore the system to its original state.

- *Keep up with training.*   The only way you are really going to be able to keep up with security is to keep up with training. Unfortunately, training is a low priority in many companies. If that is the case, then do selective training and cross-train in-house.

- *Monitor and audit.*   You have to keep monitoring and auditing the critical systems you've identified. Be careful not to over-alert, thereby causing a situation where someone ignores them or turns the alerts off altogether. Use common sense and set the alerts where they will be most effective.

- *Monitor performance.*   You usually don't get triggered and see a message like "...IP intrusion alert...". Instead, you normally get a call from an end user who can't get any email or other network resources. Then after investigating, you notice unacceptable performance on these devices, and soon thereafter, you realize you are under attack. This is all wasted time. Instead, monitor the server's health so that it will alert if something happens.

- *Audit files.*   Attacks are not always damaging to the original system. Many times when attackers break into a system, they use that system as a jumping-off point. Therefore, they will not damage that system, but they will modify system files and install a "root-kit." (A root-kit is a public utility that will allow them to remove any trace in system files that were there, such as log files.) Therefore, by comparing sizes and checksums of various files, you may notice a file has changed and begin to investigate.

■ *Check new systems.*   Just because a system is new does not mean it's secure. Check for guest accounts, default services started, and so on.

■ *Automate procedures.*   There is no reason why an administrator has to waste time going from system to system to check logs. Automate as much as possible, and set up triggering to alert for possible problems.

■ *Perform random checks.*   This is not meant to imply that an administrator has not set up the right procedures. However, just because technology is so dynamic, with new applications, new code revisions, new equipment, and turnover, things might get overlooked. Random checks at least help in these situations.

■ *Authenticate and authorize.*   Authentication is the process of determining if someone is allowed in the front door; authorization specifies how far inside the house can they go. Don't confuse the two. It's perfectly all right if your company says all authorized users have access to everything; just realize you have the option to restrict access. If you install a security server, get one with the option to authorize later; you may change your mind.

■ *Know what directories are being shared.*   In both Windows and UNIX environments, you have the ability to share directories. In both of these environments, the protocols that enable file sharing have security issues behind them. Therefore, make sure you understand them, and if possible, share them in read-only format.

■ *Audit accounts.*   Make sure you audit user accounts and terminate accounts that have not been activated for 60 or 90 days. Sometimes an attacker can get information from various systems about when the last time someone logged on. If an attacker sees a user has not logged on in the last 50 to 100 days, they would probably guess it's an old account that's not being used anymore. If they crack this account, it may go unnoticed, and then that attacker can keep infiltrating other accounts.

■ *Create Web pages.*   It is extremely difficult to get people together for meetings at times, but it will always be possible to set up a Web page. Therefore, set up security procedures, escalation call lists, even revision levels and pointers to vendors on the Web. Then let employees know they can consult the Web page to get security information. Find out the kinds of information needed, and put it on a Web page.

■ *Product evaluation.*   Before installing any new piece of equipment on a network, take time to understand what impact it will have. Attaching a router to a network is more of a security issue than adding PC. In addition, just because you are adding something new, it doesn't mean it's brand-new. There already may be security advisories with it. Don't assume you are getting the latest code/patch level.

These bulleted items represent a collection of measures that major organizations should conduct to start building a secure site. A problem is that as you start collecting these items, they grow and grow. Therefore, go through them, find some more on the Internet, read RFC 2196, and then set up a policy where everyone agrees on a certain number of items to include. Don't collect as many security items as you can and try to implement them. Each item may seem simple, but they take time and resources.

Security Tools

One major benefit of the Internet is that there are many freely available tools that can protect a network, server, or host. The tools consist of both freeware and commercial-grade software. The commercial tools, which have the financial resources behind them to develop and add new features to them, are usually preferred by organizations, the freeware tools are also a great set of tools. Anyone who has used Linux or Perl can attest to quality of this freeware. Some of the tools that were once considered freeware have gone commercial; others require a small registration fee. However, as with implementing new systems, new programs can introduce problems and may even be susceptible to them. Therefore, be sure to understand these programs before implementing them. UNIX tools are shown in Table 17-1. Windows tools are shown in Table 17-2.

These two tables should give you a sense of what's available for your company to install. Whether freeware, shareware, commercial, all these

TABLE 17-1

Security Tools for
UNIX

Category	Tool Name	Description
Authentication	Anlpasswd	Refuses to allow users to enter in bad passwords
	Crack	Password cracking
	Kerberos	Network authentication system
	Npasswd	Refuses to allow users to enter in bad passwords
	Opie	One-time passwords
	Sra	RPC authentication for FTP and Telnet.
Chrptographic checksum	MD2	Verifies message digest sizes
	MD4	Verifies message digest sizes
	MD5	Verifies message digest sizes
	Snefru	Verifies message digest sizes
Firewalls	Gateway Access Utilities	Packet filtering program
	SOCKS	Secures connectivity through a firewall
	tcpr	Runs commands through a firewall
	Tis	Toolkit for building firewalls
	xforward	Relays X commands through a firewall
Network	Argus	Generic IP network transaction auditing tool monitoring
	Courtney	Identifies the source machines of SATAN probes/attacks
	Gabriel	SATAN detector; similar to Courtney
	Netlog	Logs TCP and UDP traffic
	Netman	Suite of network monitoring and visualization tools
	Nid	Suite of network monitoring and visualization tools
	Nocol	Monitors network protocols
Network security	Ipacl	Accesses list for TCP and UDP packets
	Logdaemon	Modifies "R" programs
	Portmap	Closes portmap holes
	Rpcbind	Secure rpcbind program
	SATAN	Analyzes network security

TABLE 17-1

(Continued)

Category	Tool Name	Description
	SATAN extensions	Extensions to the SATAN scanning program
	Strobe	Checks for listening TCP ports
	Synkill	Responds to sync floods
	TCP wrappers	Controls and monitors connection services such as telnet, FTP, and RSH
	Xinetd	Controls the Internet service's daemon.
System monitoring	Arpwatch	Monitors Ethernet activity
	argus	Prepares network activity reports
	authd	Maps user to TCP connection
	COPS	Checks vulnerabilities in systems
	cpm	Checks network interfaces
	ifstatus	Checks network interfaces
	ISS	Checks vulnerabilities in systems
	Merlin	Adds GUI flexibly and enhances security tools
	RIACS	Tracks changes against a baseline
	Scan-detector	Monitors port scans processes
	Ssh	Secures authentication
	Swatch	Monitors system
	Tamu	Security scanning tool
	Tiger	Enhanced COPs
	Tripwire	Computes digital signatures for files
	Trojan	Checks for Trojans
	Watcher	Monitors System

programs have their strengths. These two tables are also just a small sampling, and as you probably noticed, there are a lot more freeware applications for the UNIX platform.

There is one more table I would like to present, that of mail tools, shown in Table 17-3. There has never been such a proliferation of email

TABLE 17-2

*Windows 95 and
NT Tools*

Category	Tool Name	Description
System administration	BCM Detect	Tests system
	Data Advisor	System diagnostics
System security	Ballista	Network security auditing tool
	BoDetect	Checks for back orifice backdoor
	Crypto for 95/NT	Encryption for PC files
	Desktop 98 Surveillance	Monitors system and network usage
	DIRT	Data interception tool/available only to law enforcement and government
	METZ Lock	Prevent the Ctrl-Alt-Delete key
	NT Crack	Audits NT passwords
	PWDump	Used with NT Crack
	Revelation	Saves passwords in encrypted files
	OfficeLock	Locks various application files
	WinU	Security and administration functions

abuse on the Internet than there is today. Spamming has caused more headaches for system administrators than any other single computer or network application. In fact, it has become such a problem that the federal government is getting involved to enact laws to punish these individuals. At the time of this writing, AOL had decided to take legal action against one particular abuser.

TABLE 17-3

Email Security Tools

Category	Tool Name	Description
Spam	Advanced E-mail Protector	Multistage filter
	Bounce Spam Mail	Sends a fake bounced message back to spammer
	Spam Hater	Tracks down the senders
	Spam Killer	Adds your address to the spammer's blacklist

Mail Relay

Mail relay is one more area in mail that you should address when securing your site. In this attack, an attacker is using your email server to spam victims. Unfortunately, this is easy to accomplish and has therefore become a major problem. The attack works like this:

1. An attacker buys a list of credit card numbers somewhere.
2. The attacker creates hundreds of various account on different ISPs.
3. The attacker obtains email lists, usually containing hundreds of thousands of email addresses.
4. Then the attacker sends mail directly to the victim, bypassing the victim's local ISP and causing the victim's machine to overload and crash.

This has become such a major problem that many ISPs will start taking legal action against the abusers. One major contributing factor to this attack is that many email servers are configured incorrectly. Although there is an option in the relay to turn relaying off, unfortunately, many organizations have theirs turned on. If you are in charge of your company's email server, check your vendor's Web site for the documentation that came with the product.

SECURITY NOTE   Unless you absolutely need others to relay mail through your mail servers, shut the mail relay option off.

I've tried to present a thorough list of security tools that are available on the Internet. I am sure some of these you know about, while others may be new to you. If the security budget in your company is not large, there are low-priced products that could still help you. Keep in mind that matching the product to the service is very important. If you are interested in network security, obtain a network security product. If you have a mix of NT and UNIX machines, then get a product that can either monitor both or the one that will monitor your critical system.

GENERAL NOTE   Use the product for the application it is intended for. If you buy a product to monitor certain machines at the Internet connection, don't use it to monitor the whole internal network.

Incident Response Centers

Incident report centers should be one of your first lines of defense in protecting your network. They offer advice, patches, vulnerability listings, contact numbers, security tools, and so on. They also have a section that usually contains white papers that will help you secure your network. Incident response centers try to alert the Internet community to the latest threats and vulnerabilities. In addition, they usually have a mailing list you can join to receive automated updates on incidents, Some of the response teams are as follows.

Forum of Incident Response and Security Teams (FIRST)

http://www.first.org
first-sec@first.org
The Forum of Incident Response and Security Teams (FIRST) is a collection of security response teams brought together to protect and disseminate information to the Internet community concerning security incidents and to take steps to deter these potential vulnerabilities quickly as possible.

Australian Computer Emergency Response Team (AusCERT)

http://www.auscert.org.au
auscert@auscert.org.au
The Australian Computer Emergency Response Team or AusCERT, provides an Australian contact for the Internet community to deal with computer security incidents. AusCERT is a member of FIRST.

CERT® Coordination Center

http://www.cert.org
cert@cert.org
The CERT Coordination Center publishes a variety of security alerts, research, and survivability tactics in WAN computing, among other things to help improve the security of your site.

Computer Incident Advisory Capability (CIAC)

http://ciac.llnl.gov
ciac@llnl.gov
The Computer Incident Advisory Capability provides security information to the Department of Defense and users of the Internet community. It offers a valuable resource for computer-related security information, including documentation, tools, databases, and more.

Automated System Security Incident Support Team (ASSIST)

http://www.assist.mil
assist@assist.mil
The INFOSEC Incident Response supports the Defense Information Infrastructure (DII).

Federal Computer Incident Response Capability (FedCIRC)

http://www.fedcirc.gov
fedcirc@fedcirc.gov
The Federal Computer Incident Response Capability (FedCIRC) provides a point of contact for incident reporting and prevention. It provides security tools, documentation, patches, and so on.

The German Research Network Computer Emergency Response Team (DFN-CERT)

http://www.cert.dfn.de/eng/dfncert
dfncert@cert.dfn.de
Sponsored by the German Ministry of Science, Education, Research and Technology, this center assists the German Research Network.

NASA Incident Response Center (NASIRC)

http://www-nasirc.nasa.gov/nasa/index.html
nasirc@nasirc.nasa.gov
The NASA Incident Response Center provides security management, analysis, and technical support for the computer and network systems and is a member of FIRST.

Federal Bureau of Investigation National Computer Crime Squad

http://www.fbi.gov/programs/compcrim.htm
nipc.watch@fbi.gov
The FBI National Computer Crime Squad is a national resource for computer crime incident reporting and offers programs to help combat computer crime.

European Contact List

http://www.cert.dfn.de/eng/csir/europe/certs.html
This is a list of European incident reporting contact points.

These incident reporting sites have a wealth of information concerning security, procedures, and documentation. If you want to learn more about security, you can start here. But before downloading all the possible documentation that is available, think about what you have and what may be vulnerable. For example, we all know that you shouldn't download applications from the Internet without first going through a virus-checking program. In addition to this, be careful about Java and ActiveX traffic, as they have been known to infect applications.

Mailing Lists/Newgroups

One of the security items in your toolbelt would be to subscribe to a mailing list and monitor the newsgroup for your appropriate environment. Don't make the mistake of subscribing to more than a handful of mailing lists. If you subscribe to more than, say, three newsgroups, you will not be able to handle the load. I've subscribed to multiple newsgroups, only to unsubscribe soon after. You normally start by subscribing to a particular newsgroup, then diligently read the emails. After about a week, you get tired of all the mail. First you get the original question, then you get the corresponding replies. Now multiply this by three or four newsgroups, and you can easily see how this would become uncontrollable. If you really need to subscribe to multiple newsgroups, send all the messages to a mail folder and use some filtering software to filter only those things you really need. If, for example, you want to monitor security vulnerabilities in the UNIX system, filter on words like security, vulnerability, attack, root, and compromise. If you are monitoring for security, you really don't want to see messages about adding a user to the network.

The following is a listing of available newsgroups and mailing lists. By no means is it an exhaustive list. It is only intended to get you familiar with what is out there.

Mailing Lists

Best of Security—*majordomo@suburbia.net*

Bugtraq—*listserv@netspace.org*

CERT Advisories—*cert-advisory-request@cert.org*

CIAC Advisories (ciac-bulletin)—*Majordomo@tholia.llnl.gov*

COAST Security Archive—*coast-request@cs.purdue.edu*

Firewall Wizards (firewall-wizards)—*majordomo@nfr.net*

Intrusion Detection Systems (IDs)—*majordomo@uow.edu.au*

Linux Security Issues—*linux-security-request@RedHat.com*

Legal Aspects of Computer Crime (lacc)—*majordomo@suburbia.net*

NT Security Issues (ntsecurity)—*majordomo@iss.net*

The RISKS Forum (risks)—*majordomo@csl.sri.com*

WWW Security (ww-security-new)—*majordomo@nsmx.rutgers.edu*

The Virus Lists (virus-l & virus)—*LISTSERV@lehigh.eduSecurity*

Security Mailing List FAQ—*http://www.iss.net/vd/mail.html*

Web Security—*http-wg@cuckcoo.hpl.hp.com*

SSL Security—*ssl-talk-requests@netscape.com*

RSA Developers—*smime-dev@rsa.com*

IETF ietf—*smime@imc.org*

News Groups

alt.security

alt.security.pgp

alt.security.keydist

alt.security.ripem

comp.security.pgp.resources

comp.security.unix

comp.security.misc

comp.security.announce

comp.protocols.kerberos

comp.virus

comp.risks

talk.politics.crypto

sci.crypt

sci.crypt.research

Web Security

One of the reasons I've placed a discussion on Web security in the security toolbelt chapter is because of the enormous impact Web security has on your organization and possibly your VPN. A few of the major concerns are as follows:

1. *Web server security.* Web browsers are the prominent transport mechanism for accessing the Web. If both your Web server and client are not secure, you are opening your organization to security problems.

2. *Active-X/JavaScript.* There is a lot of information about the security (or lack of security) in these protocols. You need to know if they are being transported across your organization from the Internet, and if they are, whether they are carrying malicious code.

3. *Public-key infrastructure.* The public-key infrastructure will be using certificates (either X.509v3 or Meta-Certificates) to access LDAP service directories in the future. If your company wants to take advantage of these technologies, you must allow them to pass your firewall; therefore, you have to decide how to secure them.

Web Servers

Web servers have the unfortunate attribute that while they are extremely flexible and meet every organization's needs, they have been a host to many problems. Like any other application, network device, or authentication server, Web servers have their own set of problems. One of their major flexibility assets, the ability to run CGI scripts, also opens up a host of problems. Some of the security risks associated with Web servers include the interception of sensitive information, such as credit card numbers and financial records. Another security risk is the server's ability to allow malicious code to enter and damage the system or destroy documents.

The Common Gateway Protocol (CGI) is a set of protocols written by a programmer to undertake a specific task. CGI scripts could be thought of as miniature Web servers running on the main server. While the protocol is not as insecure as the program itself, it is easily exploited. The recommended way of running a CGI script is with a user permission of "nobody." That way, if an attacker were to compromise the server, his or her authorization would still be "nobody," and, therefore, the attacker couldn't do much damage. However, even "nobody," in some cases, will allow the attacker to mail themselves sensitive systems files such as password information.

Web Server Vulnerabilities

The following vulnerabilities are well known. They have been documented, and patches have been released for them. This list is just a sampling
to illustrate how Web server attacks and vulnerabilities can be very similar to the attacks list in Chapter 15. These same kinds of attacks happen everywhere—in all systems, in all programs. Understanding what
you have and whether it's up-to-date is one of your best defenses.

http-apache-cookie
An older version of this Web server had an optional module that could
be loaded (modulemod_cookies), which allowed an attacker to create an
overflow buffer attack and run bytecode on the server.

http-iis-crash
The attacker was able to create a denial of service attack on a Windows
NT Web server. An attacker was able to crash the Web server, running
GET commands when connecting to Port 80.

http-cgi-nph
A program called "nph-test-cgi" contained a hole that would allow an
attacker to read any file on a readable directory. This allowed the
attacker to scan other files to locate more vulnerabilities.

http-cgi-count
A problem developed with a popular program, "count.cgi." This CGI program keeps count of hits to the Web page. It contained buffer overflow
problems that allowed remote users to execute commands on the server.

http-website-uploader
The program "uploader.exe" allowed a remote attacker to upload a file to
a "cgi-win" directory, which could be executed and possibly cause security problems.

http-cgi-phpbo
A program called "php.cgi" program allowed a remote user to create a
buffer overflow problem and execute code on the server.

http-website-winsample
The program "c-win-sample.exe", allowed a remote attacker to overflow
a buffer and execute arbitrary commands on the Web server machine.

http-scriptalias

Creating a directory with the directive "ScriptAlias" allowed a situation where some remote attackers could read the cgi-bin scripts on the Web server.

xitami-execute

A vulnerability was found on this server that would allow for a remote attacker to execute code on the Web server.

In some regards, Web servers are like a complete network infrastructure by themselves. The typical Web server will have an underlying operating system, then a particular Web server software on top of that will be CGI scripts that an administrator loads. Moreover, this particular Web server is sitting out there for the world to access. Therefore, there are potentially many security holes where it could be attacked.

Some of the common-sense steps you should take to avoid attack are as follows:

- *Secure the access.* You may decide that this is an extremely important piece of hardware; therefore, you might want to keep this server under lock and key. If this is an extranet server and you are setting up a VPN to a customer, you may be depositing financial records on this server.

- *Secure the operating system.* Look at the operating system. Is it the correct revision? The correct patch level? The vendor can tell you this.

- *Secure any authentication system you have installed.* You will most likely have a way to get into the box. Are you using telnet, (remember, this uses clear-text passwords), SSH, administrator login, RADIUS, and so forth? Each one of these has issues. Just be aware of the issues for the one you are using.

- *Secure the server software.* There are multiple vendors who supply Web server software; contact your vendor and make sure you are running the latest version.

- *Secure any CGI scripts.* Keep these to a minimum. While you may have a need for these scripts, just review them, and if possible, learn about CGI programs in general. CGI is just the framework, which supports a program such as Perl or even the shell in UNIX. Learn about the security in the program itself.

ActiveX/Java

Microsoft's ActiveX and Sun Microsystems's Java were designed so that developers could attach computer programs to Web pages. People like these systems because they allow Web pages to be much more dynamic and interactive, and they can incorporate a wide array of impressive effects such as scrolling banners, tickers, and animation. ActiveX uses ActiveX controls and Java uses Java applets. In order for these applications to work, users need access to your hard drive. Providing access allows users to run many wonderful applications, but also opens the door for malicious code developers.

ActiveX

Microsoft's ActiveX uses a control protocol that allows Web browsers to download and execute ActiveX programs. ActiveX programs run on a machine in the same user permission space as the user sitting at the console. First, a digital signature with the program that is verified. After that, users are prompted to run the program if they wish. The main security behind these programs is the developer coding. The developer has to make sure there is no malicious code in the ActiveX controls. Some Web browsers allow you to shut off ActiveX controls or create a domain of trust for trusted sites.

One security concern with ActiveX is the use of digital signatures. The digital signature could be valid, but if that person is not as trustworthy as you thought, you could invite a malicious piece of code to be loaded onto your machine. Second, the program may be signed by someone you don't know anything about, but who wants to use that program.

Java

Sun Microsystems' Java is a programming language in an execution environment. It is designed to be platform-independent. Although originally intended for embedded systems, it can be used for many different applications. Java Web browsers automatically download Java applets, which execute locally to provide display and interaction in a region of a Web page. Java provides security by eliminating many of those programming items that are considered security hazards, such as pointers. Java is meant to run what's known as a "sandbox." This sandbox supposedly acts like four walls around the program, not allowing anything to interact with the machine's internal components. This sandbox approach is both good and bad. While being secure, it restricts the number of applications that can be run. Signed Java applets are becoming commonplace; they allow more access to the machine, since they are verified by a digital signature. However, they introduce some of the problems associated with ActiveX.

Malicious Code

Java applets and ActiveX controls are types of mobile code applications and are very powerful tools for delivering many useful applications. In the wrong hands, however, they can be extremely dangerous. There have been demonstrations on the vulnerabilities associated with irresponsible developers. After all, developers who write these controls and applets are no different from the attacker; they hurt the organization's ability to conduct business and cost the company money in correcting the situation. Some Web servers had to redesign the Web servers to help restrict some code from passing.

Mobile code like ActiveX and Java script can cause problems, but so can PPTP, IPSec, RADIUS, and Kerberos. Every possible device has security problems. Some good news is that most of the security issues brought to light with Java scripts and ActiveX controls have been demonstrations rather than real attacks, although there have been some actual attacks.

 GENERAL NOTE As mobile code evolves, Web servers will only allow Java applets and ActiveX controls that have been digitally signed by a certificate authority to enter a site. Therefore, unless the attacker can compromise the CA, the code will point back to the public key of the attacker, which will eventually point back to the user. This will lead to safer mobile code applications.

Conclusion

This chapter has looked at some of the things that will make your environment and eventually your VPN safer. We started by looking at what makes up a security toolbelt and discussed some of those components that an organization needs to consider. Training, security advisories, newsgroups, and mailing lists all made up part of the toolbelt. The security toolbelt also included such things as escalation procedures, phone support, and management training. Management has to determine the security policy of an organization, but they need the training and the tools to make informed decisions.

We then discussed RFC 2196, *The Site Security Handbook* and saw how any site should have this RFC as a standard with which to implement its security policy. The RFC is filled with many real-world conclusions on how to implement security for an organization. They include the "basic approach," or identifying what you are trying to protect. Then we discussed the possibility of involving multiple parties, which many organizations decide not to do, believing they cause more security-related problems among internal staff than necessary. Finally, we looked at how to keep the security policy flexible. This is a must; the security must be a dynamic, living policy.

We then looked at some of things that help you to build a secure site, like training, monitoring, and checking new systems as they are installed. The main point was to stay on top of security and keep abreast of the mailing lists and newsgroups that offer valuable information to potential new methods of attacks. There was also a list of tools, including freeware and commercial software, that are available to help you secure your site. Finally, we looked at Web server security and what you must consider with regard to Web security software. We learned that if you don't undertake the necessary steps to secure your servers and networks—especially near the Internet connection point—you cannot secure your VPN.

CHAPTER 18

Intrusion Detection and Security Scanning

So far throughout this book, we have discussed Virtual Private Networks and the security behind them. We have looked at different types of attacks and vulnerabilities that may hinder the safety and security of your data. As we have seen, there may be no specific attacks against VPNs themselves, but any generic attack that could somehow reveal your data should be considered a VPN attack.

In this chapter, we will look at some of those things that will help you determine if something has happened to your network. Until now, security has always been reactive rather than proactive, following instead of leading. This chapter will take a look at some of the things that are out there today that will help your organization keep abreast of security intrusions.

Intrusion detection systems are software placed throughout the organization that will help you and your company determine if an intrusion has taken place. Some intrusion systems are designed to run in real time, meaning a signal will alert someone if an attack is going on. Other intrusion detection systems are after-the-fact systems; by examining certain files on a system, you can determine if they were modified and if there was an intrusion. We will look at some characteristics of intrusion detention systems, along with their strengths and limitations.

Finally, we will discuss scanners and how they relate to intrusion detection systems. We will see that a scanner is a form of intrusion detection systems and that it is meant to complement, not replace, IDS.

Introduction to Intrusion Detection

As technology and global networks have rapidly expanded and evolved, attacks on these types of information systems have skyrocketed in the last several years. At one point, security attack teams used to attack systems just as a testing procedure to inform the would-be victim that they were indeed subject to such attacks. Victims are anyone, anywhere; if it's an Internet-connected network, it is subject to attack. This rapid growth has often meant sacrifices in establishing security and privacy in such systems. For example, there was the case of the Internet worm that spread across the Internet and caused millions of dollars in damage.

Intrusion Detection Systems (IDS) are a set of programs and algorithms used against a reference set; this set could be static objects or a predefined set of rules. It is designed to ensure that the usage of a computer environment is according to a predefined security policy.

Networks are vulnerable since their identities can be revealed simply by doing "whois" queries to the InterNIC. Once a "whois" query is accomplished, the next step for the would-be attacker is to map the internal network topology. It is not difficult for an attacker to do this; a firewall will not block this query. The only way to block this is to have a DNS server sitting on a DMZ at your Internet connection point, and have all DNS queries go through that machine. The attacker would then attempt a "traceroute" to the network to see where the packets are finally dropped and use that IP address as a possible starting point.

The DNS queries also can reveal a large company's topology map. DNS servers that are considered "untrusted" (i.e., those sitting on the DMZ) should not have any DNS mapping of the internal architecture. They should only know about what has to be done for the Internet community at large. In other words, an untrusted DNS server should only know about Web servers, FTP servers, and HTTP servers that people outside your organization will need to know about.

SECURITY NOTE   If you implement a firewall using NAT and allow DNS queries through, an attacker can still map your network's topology. In a DNS data packet, the internal host's information is included inside the data packet and will not be modified by the firewall.

After an attacker has queried the InterNIC and various DNS servers for information about your site, the next step is DNS mapping. If you have an internal DNS server handling both internal and external information, an attacker can still map your network. The reason is the firewall does not modify the data packet, which can contain an IP address of an internal host.

Figure 18-1 describes what many companies try to accomplish. They already have a valid public routable address that they obtained long ago. They are connecting to the Internet, and for security reasons, do not want this address routed on the Internet. Therefore, they obtain IP address space from their ISP and install network address translation on the firewall. The firewall's only function is to map internal address to external address. Now, in order to have DNS working and have people find your Web server, FTP server, and so on, many companies allow DNS traffic inbound. If this DNS server, is also used for the internal DNS mapping, an attacker can query this server and obtain a mapping of the network. The only way to avoid this is to use a third party as a

Figure 18-1
DNS queries.

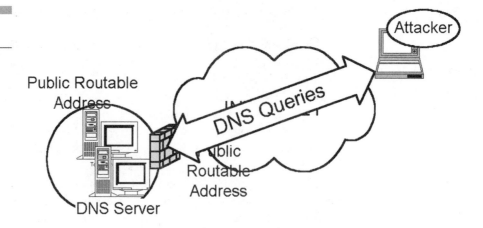

DNS host for your company or install a separate DNS server on a DMZ zone, as we discussed back in earlier chapters.

The next step in the process would be to use a strobe to perform port scans on the various devices that exist on the DMZ and, if possible, through any DNS mapping made available. The attacker's next step would then be to try to cause any machine to reveal its password file in order to list names on user accounts. At that point, if possible, the attacker would then use a variety of password guessing programs to try and crack any user identity and, finally, try to crack into the administrator's account.

SECURITY NOTE   Port scanning is not the only vulnerability to block. If you allow unauthorized protocols (e.g., the GRE protocol) to pass a firewall, attacks could ride in on them.

Early intrusion detection systems used a variety of home-grown scripts and programs designed to penetrate detection. Intrusion detection systems are a form of expert systems, in the same category as artificial intelligent systems, rule-based logic systems, and neural nets. COPS, mentioned back in Chapter 17, is such an intrusion detection system designed to check for vulnerabilities in a system. COPS used a set of tools that automated the process of gathering information for analysis.

The Need for Intrusion Detection Systems

Most organizations assume that a firewall is the best type of device against intrusions and attacks. Unfortunately, this type of logic is not true. There have been and there still are daily reports of new attacks, new vulnerabilities, and new compromises revealed. If firewalls were the answer, then these attacks would not have happened. Firewalls are part of the picture—a good part, but not the whole part. Firewalls block internally directed attacks, if configured properly, but attacks can occur on the devices that are accessible by the public—for instance, Web servers—and attacks can occur by traffic that is allowed to pass the firewall—for instance, DNS queries. Intrusion detection systems do not replace firewalls but complement them.

Authentication devices are supposed to provide an access mechanism to users, so in addition to firewalls, users now have to be authenticated to obtain resources. However, even authentication systems have failed, allowing intruders to obtain access. Intrusion detection systems can complement these types of systems also. Network and system intrusion detection systems can monitor servers and the network itself, so even if an attacker cracked an account on an authentication server beyond the firewall, the IDS may still catch suspicious traffic.

Categories of Intrusion Systems

All intrusion detection systems have in common an engine and a set of rules (or data objects) that are acted upon by the engine. An engine could act upon a set of rules to check for intrusion, or it could use a baseline object set to act against. IDS engines fall into two categories: misuse, or pattern, engines and anomaly engines.

Misuse (Pattern) Engines

These engines are categorized by well-known attacks on known weak points of a system—for example, known vulnerabilities in an operating system leading to a buffer overflow problem. They are usually detected by monitoring certain objects and noticing a deviation from the norm. These systems usually use some form of pattern matching to look for deviations.

Some of the benefits of this class of systems are efficiency and centralization. They can be set for a specific server and only require a limited set of rules to function. The limitations with this class are lack of scalability, the need to set up new pattern matching, and a narrow target area. You cannot take this type of system and expect it to match your whole infrastructure. In addition, in order to set up a new class of attacks, you need to program a whole new set of patterns into these systems. Also, these systems are usually implemented for one specific target.

Anomaly Engines

Anomaly systems are those established by observing deviations from the norm; usually a profile is built and deviations from this profile are signaled. For example, a base file, whose size and checksum are known, is then checked to determine if a change has occurred to the original file size and checksum. These types of system usually use some metric to establish the baseline. Anomaly intrusion systems can be thought of as systems that could use artificial intelligence. The system itself should evolve with its existing knowledge.

The benefits of these types of systems include the ability to set thresholds and their ability to work in real time. You can see things as they are happening; you don't have to wait until an alert is triggered or until you have a chance to monitor the logs. They also are set to allow for threshold setting; therefore, it is possible to detect that an attack is occurring before any real damage is done.

They do, however, suffer from the "incorrect baseline" problem: who decides what the baseline is and how is this baseline defined so that the engine will accurately detect intrusions? In addition, an attacker who knows that an anomaly IDS is being used can possibly circumvent it. The attacker can use different accounts and conduct multiple attacks; in other words, he or she attacks with one particular attack on one account, then in the next go-around, attacks a different account with a different type of attack. The sensitivity with these systems needs to be addressed too, since it is up to the system to decide when a user has too many open files and has attempted too many logins. Anyone who uses an authentication server device on their network where the time is a little off between client and server knows how an attacker can easily try to access their system a number of times.

Anomaly-type systems have a harder time detecting intrusions than their counterpart, misuse systems. There are no fixed patterns that can be monitored, and if a new attack is attempted, there is no baseline for the engine to function against. Therefore, these systems need to combine a human reasoning pattern with a computer-like program. Some intrusion systems base their analysis on an audit trail. This pattern is built up over time, and data is used from them as a source of reference. Such things as CPU cycles, memory usage, and disk space are measured.

While there are the two categories of IDS engines, there are also different types of systems available that are used with those engines: those that monitor the network, those that monitor the system, and those that monitor the log files.

Network Intrusion Detection Systems

This type of system monitors the data packets on the network. These systems look for anomalies on the circuit, such as denial of service attacks, which may start out with a large number of TCP SYN requests, or when someone is conducting a port scan on one of the machines. NIS systems monitor a large number of machines.

System Intrusion Detection Systems

This type of system monitors systems files. It watches for changes in a file that deviates from an established baseline. Such changes can occur if an attacker has built in a backdoor to the system via one of these main system files.

Logging Intrusion Detection Systems

This type of system monitors the log files generated by various services on the machine. It looks for a pattern of traffic that may dictate that an attacker has been trying to gain access into a system via a known vulnerability.

Deception Intrusion Detection Systems

These systems are actually traps; they are designed to act like a well-known service to entice an attacker and entrap them.

GENERAL NOTE   Intrusion detection systems cannot monitor the type of traffic in Virtual Private Networks, which is normally encrypted. Therefore, placement must be after the encryption/decryption device.

Data packets that come across a VPN stream are usually encrypted, for instance, DES, IDEA, etc. Therefore, an IDS could not perform the necessary analysis of the data stream. The situation gets more complicated in tunneling mode, where the whole packet is encrypted behind a new IP address. In order for intrusion detection systems to work properly, they must come after decryption. In the case of an end-to-end PPTP encryption stream, that would mean the intrusion detection system would have to reside on the host itself.

Characteristics of a Good Intrusion Detection System

A lot has been written about what makes a good intrusion system. Some of the items mentioned are as follows:

- *Secure.*   The system you are using has to be secured itself, or it cannot be secure enough to monitor other systems. If an attack on an intrusion system succeeds, any data that it would produce cannot be considered reliable.

- *Deviations from the norm.*   Intrusion systems must signal when deviations from the norm are encountered.

- *No human intervention needed.*   Intrusion systems need to run unobstructed to the main system. They should not interfere with the system or network that is being monitored. However, they should be accessible from the outside so their results can be monitored.

- *Impose minimal overhead.*   You cannot install an intrusion detection system if it will create a situation where the system is spending more resources on the intrusion system software than the purpose it was designed for.

- *Alerting.*   The intrusion detection system should be configurable to issue a set of alerts or pages to the appropriate personnel. These would include SNMP traps, NT events, writing to syslog, email, pages, and launching another program to initiate a procedure to minimize the impact of the attack.

- *Flexible.*   Just as a security policy must be flexible, so too must the intrusion detection system. There must be a way to add to its baseline, through metrics or whatever else you are using as the mechanism to trigger intrusions.

- *Client/server.* You want to choose system and network intruder detection systems that are heterogeneous and can work across several environments, e.g., UNIX and NT.

- *Reporting.* It makes no sense to install an IDS and have no reporting capabilities or have reporting that is difficult to read. You want reporting that is clear and that can be divided into only those pieces of information you need.

Intrusion Detection/Footprint

In order for intrusion detection systems to work, they must be placed properly in the network. Once an intrusion has occurred, whether or not the IDS picks it up, it usually leaves a footprint.

In any organization, the network is usually divided up into subnets, separated by switches, routers, and any other network device that can route traffic—for instance, a firewall. Traffic is directed by the destination address and by a routing policy placed upon routers throughout the organization—in other words, the default route. Network intrusions detection systems work by examining data packets that pass on the wire.

GENERAL NOTE Intrusion detection systems do not modify the data packet; they are not a store-and-forward type of software. In order for them to be effective, they have to be where they can monitor the most traffic that the company deems critical.

SECURITY NOTE Intrusion detection systems will not work across switched networks; therefore, placement is critical to the success of spotting intrusions.

Placement is a critical step when implementing an IDS system. Network intrusion detection systems usually have their network adapters in promiscuous mode, meaning they listen to all data packets passing on the wire. Switched networks are not broadcast networks; therefore, they

Figure 18-2
IDS placement.

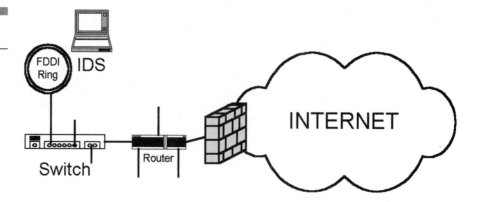

segment the traffic, as illustrated in Figure 18-2. In this figure, the intrusion detection system is placed behind the firewall, the internal router, and the switch, and it is placed on the FDDI ring. The IDS will only monitor traffic that is on the FDDI ring; every other device is still vulnerable.

Now compare this with Figure 18-3. This figure shows two placements for the intrusion detection system. The first placement is on a

Figure 18-3
IDS placement.

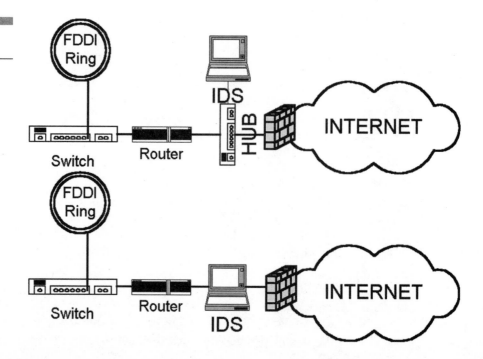

hub that is connected between the firewall and internal router. In the second placement, it is acting as a gateway that will be forwarding traffic in both directions.

Using either configuration gives the IDS access to all data traffic that is passing on the wire, thereby allowing it to monitor all data, but at the same time, increasing its resource utilization. On the top part of Figure 18-3, the IDS is just listening and capturing the packets. On the bottom part, it becomes like a router itself. Although its load is increased in the bottom configuration, this configuration may provide more flexibility to the system. In addition to the firewall, the IDS can act like another filter, authentication device, or a Web-based filtering machine. In the real world, however, IDS is just another piece of software, and many companies have a server that performs these multiple functions. You just need to decide if this configuration is an appropriate setup for your company.

Figure 18-4 illustrates where intrusion detection systems may be headed. Instead of an IDS being installed at a specific location on the network where you think it will do the best, IDS agents are spread across the network. An IDS master will sit somewhere on the network and collect information from various hosts, routers, switches, and firewalls on the network. Then it will undergo a correlation process on the traffic to check for intrusions. In this type of configuration, you can have multiple masters sharing data and collecting information from machines for processing. The IDS master would use its resources for analysis of data, and the other machines would just report their information to the master.

Figure 18-4
IDS agents.

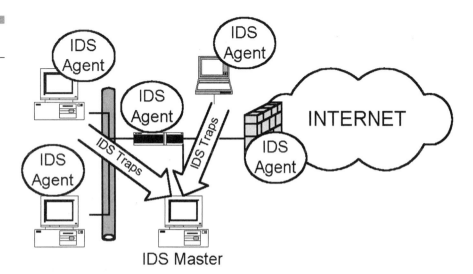

Attack Recognition

In order for a network intrusion system to work, it must be able to detect and log network specific services and protocols. If you need to monitor non-TCP/IP networks, you will either need an IPX or SNA IDS, or you will need to place the IDS right behind the device that converts between these protocols.

GENERAL NOTE Intrusion detection systems are TCP/IP-based, since the Internet is TCP-based. However, attacks still can occur on IPX and SNA networks, since these networks can be connected to the Internet via gateway devices.

Network intrusion detection systems need to detect many of the attacks that are common today, such as:

- IP spoofing
- IP fragmentation
- Syn flooding
- Sequence number guessing
- Teardrop
- Test.cgi
- Sendmail
- NFS
- Buffer overflows
- FTP and TFTP bugs
- Smurf attacks
- Session hijacking

Intrusion Footprint

An intrusion footprint is simply a way for you to identify that someone has been in your system. This does not mean that the system has been damaged in any way or that files were modified or that Trojans were left on your machine. It simply means someone was in the machine. There are things that, as an administrator, you can examine to see if the system has been infiltrated.

■ ■ ■ ■ ■ ■ ■ ■ ■ ■ ■ ■ ■ ■ ■ ■ ■

SECURITY NOTE   Some attackers use a package called RootKit that removes any trace from system files that might show someone was in the machine.

Some of the things an administrator should examine are as follows:

■ *Servers left in promiscuous mode.*   It is possible for an attacker to hack into a server and reconfigure the network driver to run in promiscuous mode. In this case, the attacker can come back later and examine the logs of the machine to catch all data on the network. Recheck the machines periodically to see that drivers are in default mode.

■ *last* command.   This is a systems command available in many flavors of UNIX. It will display the last persons who have logged into the machine. It will also show how long they were logged in for and where they came from. By examining this file closely, you might be able to find if an attacker was successful in cracking this particular machine, or whether the attacker compromised another machine and is using that machine as a starting point. When examining this file, you are looking for abnormal connections such as short login times, logins during nonworking hours, and the use of disabled accounts.

■ *lastcomm* command.   This command is similar to the **last** command, but it shows what commands are issued by the user. If you know something has happened, you can check for activity for around a certain time and see what commands were entered. You would not see a comprehensive detailed set of things that happened, but you might be given some general direction.

■ *NT events log.*   Windows NT provides some potentially valuable information concerning items that may affect security. Periodically checking this event log for such things as administrator logins, permissions changes, and new users added all point to a potential intrusion.

■ **syslog** *command.*   This command, found on many devices, produces a set of data that can be very helpful in tracking intrusions. It lists IP addresses, protocols, services, and other useful information. In addition, products are available that take syslog messages as input and create a database with this information. Then by using a front-end GUI, an administrator can query the database for specific times and addresses.

- **netstat** *command.*   This command keeps a list of protocol connections, including TCP and UDP. It lists a foreign host, which is the end host that is making the connection.
- **history** *command.*   Enabled by shell scripts on a UNIX machine, this command keeps a list of commands that have been executed by an individual. A disabled account should have no history, but an attacked disabled account may contain a history file. Therefore, you should inspect the history account from disabled accounts.

SECURITY NOTE   Any one of these commands or log files could have been compromised. So the security you place in your system should also be applied to these items.

Fooling an Intrusion Detection System

There are errors in any system and intrusion systems are no different. In Chapter 15, when we discussed biometric authentication methods, we made note that it is possible for a biometric device to allow access when access should have been denied. It is the same way with intrusion detection systems. Following are categories of errors in intrusion systems:

- *False positive.*   This is when the system indicates that an action is anomalous. In other words, an intrusion is reported as having occurred (or is occurring) when in fact a legitimate action occurred.
- *False negative.*   A false negative is just the reverse of a false positive. The intrusion has occurred, but the system indicated it was an authorized action (or failed to indicate it was an unauthorized action).
- *Subversion error.*   In simple terms, the intrusion detection system has been compromised. The attacker is forcing false negatives to occur.

The errors in any intrusion detection system need to be minimized; unfortunately, doing so is not always easy. In a false positive error, an alarm has been indicated when in fact no alarm as occurred. If too many false positives occur, these alarms will simply be ignored in the future. Analogous to this would be a home security system where, if too many alarms are triggered, the local police will simply ignore the alarm and stop coming to the house. False negative errors, on the other hand, allow an intrusion to occur when it should have been denied. These are potentially more dangerous than false positives. After all, false positives are merely an inconvenience to the user; in a false negative, an attack could be occurring. A potentially major problem in not detecting false negatives is that an attacker can circumvent the system, thereby completely hiding any future communications.

Intrusion Detection System Limitations

Intrusion detection systems also suffer from some serious limitations, which will require more work on them before they can be considered a very reliable, accurate method of detecting intrusions. Some of the weaknesses are as follows.

Inaccurate Identification of Attacker   Due to the very nature of these attacks, it is almost impossible to identify the attacker. Attackers with a good knowledge of TCP/IP and spoofing will simply spoof their source address, thereby making it impossible for the intrusion detection system to provide an accurate identification. Moreover, in the smurf attack, the attacker uses the bounced network address in the packet, making it appear to the victim's intrusion detection system that the bounced network is the attacker. If the attacker has broken into another network (other than the victim's) and launches the attack from there, the victim's IDS would incorrectly point to the identity of the attacker.

Resources Needed   Intrusion detection systems use a lot of CPU, memory, and disk space to detect intrusions. Detecting real-time intrusions would require examining every packet and creating a table to use as a counter for the next packet. If an attacker is changing his or her data stream to point to different hosts with different forms of attacks, this becomes a challenge for the IDS. In real-time mode, the device has to keep up with the traffic on the network. With 10Base-T Ethernet that may not be a problem. For higher speeds, however, such as 100Base-T, FDDI, and Gigabit Ethernet, this may be a problem for some devices. In the packet filtering IDS, logs will have to be maintained for some time, and if an attacker is attacking intermittently, the logs will have to be monitored and stored for a long time. This is especially critical in anomaly systems. In these systems, there is a learning process, so if the attack occurs over a period of time, the system may incorrectly assume that the cause is more traffic and more users, and it will readjust itself to higher levels of tolerance.

Missed Packets   Network intrusion detection systems are meant to monitor all network traffic; however, this means all network traffic that passes through them, not all network traffic in general. Depending on the placement of IDS, network packets can be missed. In Figure 18-5, traffic is directed on the FDDI ring in a counterclockwise direction. If A is an internal hacker and is trying to hack into server B, the IDS system will never see the packets, since station B will pick up the packets off the ring before the intrusion detection system gets a chance to monitor the packet.

Only What Is Known   While intrusion detection systems are trying to evolve into some type of artificial intelligence where they can think and learn, the current situation is that they are like virus detection software. They can only detect anomalies or check for inconsistencies that they are programmed for. Every new type of attack, new mechanism for intrusion, or new buffer overflow problem must be programmed into the IDS for it to be effective. That means as an administrator you have to

Figure 18-5
Missed packets.

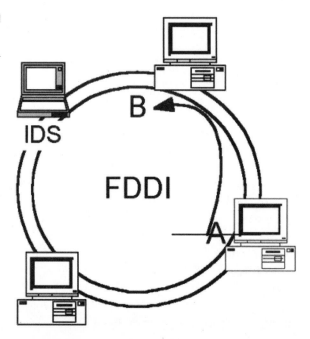

keep up with the latest threats and security vulnerabilities out there. Some vendors offer subscription intrusion detection reports, where they keep track of all the new vulnerabilities and help you keep up-to-date.

Intrusions Detection Tools

Many intrusion detection tools are on the market today, both freeware and commercial, including system IDS, network IDS, and deception IDS. They all have benefits, and what you want to monitor determines which one to use. The following is a small list of the available tools:

- *Advanced Security Audit Trail Analysis (ASAX).* Developed by Abdelaziz Mounji, this program allows you to customize and analyze the format of your data trail. It will analyze a large number of files without the usual burden of needed resources.
- *Argus.* Developed by Carter Bullard and Chas DiFatta, Argus is a IP network auditing tool.
- *Arpwatch.* Developed by Network Research Group, this tool monitors network traffic and maps Ethernet MAC addresses to IP network addresses.
- *Hobgoblin.* Hobgoblin checks file consistency against a known baseline. It is both a language and an interpreter, and can be used on a large number of systems.
- ***md5check.*** Developed by the University of California, **md5check** is a cryptographic function to check the binaries against a known baseline hash value.
- ***netman.*** Developed by Schulze and Farrell, this is an X-windowing display tool, displaying both IP and MAC packets in real time.
- ***nfswatch.*** This tool looks at the NFS traffic in an environment and maps client-to-server requests for analysis.
- ***nid.*** This is a set of tools designed to detect and analyze network intrusion.
- ***nocol.*** This monitors and reports on various types of traffic on the network, e.g., SNMP traps and ICMP unreachables.
- ***noshell.*** Developed by Crabb, this tool is designed to keep track of who is logging into disabled accounts by using a **noshell** program instead of the normal **/bin/null** put in disabled accounts.

- *swatch.*   Designed to monitor a large number of systems, this also modifies their login capabilities.

- *Tamu.*   Developed by Texas A&M University, Tamu validates the files in a file distribution package to make sure they are unmodified from their original version.

- *Tripwire.*   Tripwire uses digital signatures to compare file integrity. It uses the first-time run-through as a baseline for further comparison

- *X Connection Monitor.*   This is a system developed to monitor X connections. It allows a user to execute kill commands on the window and also checks for X-window requests of a questionable nature.

There is some work being done to simulate IDS agents, much in the same way SNMP agents run today. If that situation is possible, then you could possibly place an IDS agent on multiple hosts and have the agent send to a master IDS server some information regarding the data packet (e.g., original IP address, protocol, service, etc.). One such system is the Adaptive Intrusion Detection system (AID) being developed by Brandenburg University of Technology at Cottbus. It is designed for network audit-based monitoring of local area networks and is used for investigating network- and privacy-oriented auditing. The system itself is a client/server based architecture consisting of a central monitoring station and monitoring hosts. It uses an RTworks real-time based expert system on the central monitoring station and receives operating system-independent data from agents on monitoring hosts. Figure 18-6 is an illustration of the AID system.

To learn more about AID and to see a larger list of intrusion detection systems, take a look at Michael Sobirey's Intrusion Detection Systems page *http://www-rnks.informatik.tu-cottbus.de/~sobirey/ids.html)*, where there are links for the following intrusion detection systems.

- ACME
- ADS (Attack Detection System)
- AIMS (Automated Intrusion Monitoring System)
- ALVA (Audit Log Viewer and Analyzer)
- APA (Automated Penetration Analysis tool)
- ASAX (Advanced Security audit trail Analyzer on UNIX)
- ASIM (Automated Security Incident Measurement)

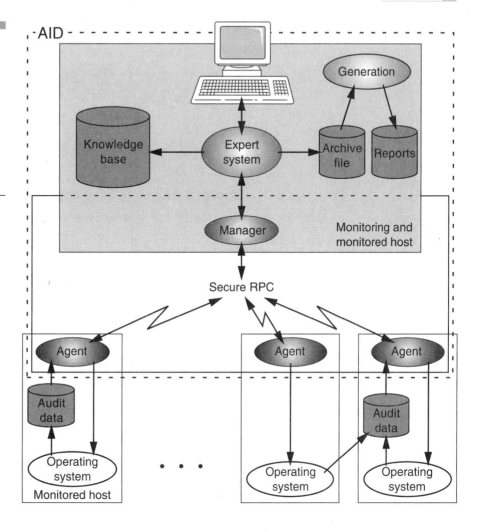

Figure 18-6
Adaptive Intrusion
Detection (AID)
system. (Source:
Michael Sobirey's
Intrusion Detection
Systems page,
*http://www.
rnks.informatik.
tu-cottbus.de/
~sobirey/ids.html*)

- AudES (Audit-based Expert System)
- Autonomous Agents
- Bro
- CMDS (Computer Misuse Detection System)
- ComputerWatch
- CSM (Cooperating Security Manager)
- CyberCop
- DECinspect Intrusion Detector
- DIDS (Distributed Intrusion Detection System)

- Discovery
- DPEM (Distributed Program Execution Monitor)
- DRISC (Detect and Recover Intrusion using System Critically)
- EMERALD (Event Monitoring Enabling Responses to Anomalous Live Disturbances)
- ESSENSE
- GASSATA (Genetic Algorithm for Simplified Security Audit Trail Analysis)
- GrIDS (Graph-based Intrusion Detection System)
- Haystack
- Hyperview
- DA (Intrusion Detection Alert)
- IDA (Intrusion Detection and Avoidance system)
- IDEAS (Intrusion Detection and Alerting System)
- IDES (Intrusion Detection Expert System)
- IDIOT (Intrusion Detection In Our Time (-IDS))
- ID-Trak
- Inspect
- INTOUCH INSA Network Security Agent
- ISM (Internetwork Security Monitor)
- ISOA (Information Security Officer's Assistant)
- ITA (OmniGuard/Intruder Alert)
- KSM (Kane Security Monitor)
- MIDAS (Multics Intrusion Detection and Alerting System)
- MIDS (Master Intrusion Detection System)
- NADIR (Network Anomaly Detector and Intrusion Reporter)
- NAURS (Network Auditing Usage Reporting System)
- NetRanger
- NetStalker
- NetSTAT (Network-based State Transition Analysis Tool)
- NID (Network Intrusion Detector)
- NIDES (Next-generation Intrusion Detection Expert System)
- NIDX (Network Intrusion Detection eXpert system)

- NSM (Network Security Monitor)
- PDAT (Protocol Data Analysis Tool)
- POLYCENTER Security Intrusion Detector
- RealSecure
- RETISS (REal-TIme expert Security System)
- RecureNet PRO
- SecureSwitch
- SIDS (Statistical Intrusion Detection System)
- Stake Out
- Stalker
- TIM (Time-based Inductive Machine) based IDS
- TRW-IDS (system name unknown)
- UNICORN (Unicos Realtime NADIR)
- USTAT (Unix State Transition Analysis Tool)
- WebStalker
- W&S (Wisdom & Sense)

Limiting Intrusion

In any organization, a certain number of intrusions occur because of badly written code, configuration errors, and not using the latest patch/revision levels that are available from the manufacturer. Your organization may not be willing, or have the necessary resources, to install intrusion detection systems. In that case, there are steps that you can take to reduce your vulnerability exposure in any environment, including:

- *Log files.* Periodic review of log files is critical for any computer environment. The problem arises in that there are just so many computer log files that can be viewed. Each host, server, router, and switch all have the ability to create logs; however, they cannot monitor them. You will need some centralized station to take these log files and do some necessary analysis on them. Remember, an attacker can attack anywhere; however, there is usually one way in: through a firewall (unless you have two firewalls and are doing load balancing). Therefore, given the amount of logs you have, you need to set up some kind of priority on the data from the log files.

- *Shut off services.*   Make sure only services that are absolutely necessary are allowed to be turned on on a network device. For instance, the UNIX standard service daemons, like FTP and telnet, generally do not need to be turned on. In particular, if this server is at the Internet access point, make sure standard services are turned off. If you have a need for an FTP server, use a box by itself for FTP service. The same thing applies to NFS; there is no reason a UNIX box at the Internet's connection point should be running NFS.

- *Check system binaries.*   You can easily obtain a freeware cryptographic tool, such as **md5check**. During an initial install, you can easily write a script to run an **md5check** on systems files and use that as a baseline. You can then set up a CRON job to periodically check those files against this baseline. If there is a difference between any two matches, the script could email, page, or send an SMTP trap to warn a system administrator about the difference.

- *NT user configuration settings.*   A number of settings in NT could point to a vulnerability that could be exploited by an attacker. Some of them include guest account enabled, no password aging or syntax checking, weak passwords, or no failed login thresholds.

- *Isolate public devices from private devices.*   Any server or device that is made available to the public should be isolated as much as possible from the private network. You obviously cannot move these devices to a separate physical network; you eventually need the data that may be sent to you. However, treat these devices as you would any other device on the Internet—with caution. Attackers try to hack into these devices and then use them as a jumping-off point into your network. Therefore, treat any data coming in from these servers as you would any other data coming in from the Internet.

- *Setuid scripts.*   An attacker usually leaves script around with the setuid bit set, when **root** runs the script, the attacker usually programs a backdoor into the system. These setuid scripts are placed on a script that **root** may eventually run.

- *Check system files.*   Attackers target specific system files so that later they can regain entry. Potential targets include system files such as the password file, .rhosts, and hosts.equiv. They also scan files for the + symbol, as this symbol usually means no restrictions.

- *Monitor performance.*   You can easily set up scripts that will monitor the performance of the box with system utilities. Most attacks that occur on the box begin to increase the resources required by the box. You can easily run a script for a month and use that as a baseline. Then you can use this baseline and a threshold to continue to monitor the box.

- *Monitor traffic.*   Some attacks increase the data that is on the network going to the server. With standard utilities, you can set up scripts that monitor the traffic, and by using the baseline and threshold mentioned above, you can set the system to signal on abnormal traffic.

- *Configure the mail server correctly.*   Some attacks are not so much an attack as an opportunity. Mail servers are vulnerable to these opportunities. The attacker is not attacking your mail server, but he or she is using your mail server to send spam to others. The result is your mail server crashes due to the load. Configure the mail correctly, shut off relay, and shut off administrative commands originating from a telnet session. In other words, telnet to your mail server on Port 25; if you see an administrative menu, you can issue commands to your mail server, but so could anyone else.

Scanners

A scanner is some piece of software that detects potential security weaknesses on a host, either remotely or locally. There are different types of scanners. Most scanners are the TCP-type port scanners. These scanners look at and attack TCP ports such as telnet and SMTP. Other types of scanners are more like information-gathering scanners; they look at a remote host to see if certain services may be running. These are actually utilities rather than scanners, although at times the distinction is not readily apparent. The commands that are available on a UNIX platform, such as **host, rusers,** and **traceroute,** can all give information that may be exploited by attackers. In fact, through their use, you could assume that the attacker used these utilities to scan a potential victim. Scanners typically check for the following:

- *Exploits.*   Programs that are known to have bugs. For example an attacker telnets to Port 25 of your SMTP server and discovers the version of sendmail you are running is an older one. The attacker therefore tries well-known attacks against it in the chance you have not patched your version.

- *Default configuration*   We discussed earlier how when systems are first installed, they have a default configuration, e.g., guest account on NT and inetd services running on a UNIX server.

These could make you vulnerable to an attack.

- *Administration errors.*   Administrations errors such as the .rhost files and the **xhost +** commands can leave the system open to attacks.

- *Less resource-intensive than IDS.*   Scanners, since they are not monitoring in real-time, take fewer resources to complete their task. Since scanners only use resources when they are active, they can be set to run at times when the system will not be heavily utilized. In contrast, either in heavy or light operating modes, IDS will continue to take system resources.

- *Weaknesses.*   IDSs are more concerned with catching intrusions or checking system files based on a baseline (e.g., an MD5 checksum of the files). Scanners check for vulnerabilities in servers and configuration files, such as inetd files.

Scanners can operate in either local or network mode. In local mode, scanning software running on a particular machine is examining itself; in network mode, it is running on one machine while checking the vulnerabilities of a remote host or network.

Local Scanners

Local scanners operate on the system level—that is, they can go through every file, or a subset of files, to look for configuration errors. Intrusion detection systems can identify if a file has been changed, but a scanner can point to what changes have been made. Scanners can look at more than files; they can check permissions, setuid scripts, user and group settings, and so on. Scanners can also tell if a service can be started up and can test for revision and patch levels. In addition, scanners have the ability to work from the inside. By running as a trusted host on a trusted machine, a local scanner can attempt password modifications and group settings. Some scanners can also test buffer overflow problems.

Remote Scanners

Remote scanners are the complement of local scanners; they scan a remote host to check for vulnerabilities. Remote scanning includes port scans for TCP open ports, anonymous FTP logins, and other remotely started services that may give an attacker an edge. Remote scanners check for buffer overflow problems in services, such as teardrop, ping of death, and syn flooding. Local scanners cannot accomplish this task.

Remote scanners can also check your firewall, Web server, and any public device you have connected to the Internet. They also check for vulnerabilities with authentication services. Many hosts use NIS, .rhosts, and .rhost.equiv for host authentication, and a remote scanner can try to gain access by spoofing its address and fooling the target machine to make it appear that it is a trusted host.

Scanners are available on all platforms. Although they originally were designed for the UNIX operating system, more scanners are being developed for the NT market. Whatever platform you choose, you need a platform that has the CPU and memory resources to implement scans. In addition, scanners are available in both the freeware and commercial markets.

SECURITY NOTE If you download a scanner and decide to scan a remote host or network, be careful; you may end up facing legal action, since some types of scanning are considered illegal.

Whereas pattern (or misuse) intrusion detection systems check against a known set of baseline objects, such as the MD5 cryptographic hash function of system files, scanners check against a baseline of well-known vulnerabilities, such as portmapper and NFE vulnerabilities. In addition, intrusion detection systems try to detect attacks in real time as they are occurring, or if they are the misuse/pattern type, attacks that may have already occurred (e.g., two MD5 hash values don't match). Scanners, on the other hand, attempt to point out where vulnerabilities lie and where an attack could occur later.

Specific Scanners

Network Security Scanner (NSS) Written in Perl, this scanner is not compiled, as other scanners are. NSS is available from many Web and FTP sites across the Internet, and since it is written in Perl, it is available on a number of different platforms. Because Perl is not compiled, a user can make changes to the programming rather quickly.

Some of the vulnerabilities that NSS will reveal are sendmail exploits, anonymous FTP access, and NFS export sets.

Strobe   Short for Super Optimized TCP Port Surveyor. Strobe checks the TCP ports on a given target and reveals which ones are open. By querying the ports that are open, Strobe can tell what services are running on a target. Instead of an actual output, Strobe gives more of an information overview about what is or is not running.

SATAN   Developed by Dan Farmer and Weitse Venema, SATAN is a set of tools that gives an administrator an easy way to scan for vulnerabilities. It contains a complete HTML GUI interface, with predefined forms. SATAN scans for vulnerabilities including NFS, NIS, X-windowing system, FTP vulnerabilities, and most other known vulnerabilities.

Jakal   Jakal falls into the category of stealth scanners and is designed to scan an environment without leaving any trace of being there. Jakal accomplishes this by not completing the full scan process. For a scan to take place, the normal TCP communications apply, but if the scan is not finished, the server or firewall would just drop the packet and not log it as a scanning.

ISS SAFEsuite   Developed by Chris Klaus, ISS is a proactive UNIX network scanner, although there is a version for NT available. SAFEsuite scans a network for vulnerabilities, and when it finds them, it offers suggestions to correct these violations.

Conclusion

In this chapter we went through some of the security mechanisms that a company can put in place to supplement its existing security. Intrusion detection systems (IDS) are not meant to replace security or to act as a single security system for an organization, but rather to add to an existing security policy.

We've noticed that even if a company has a firewall in place, attackers can still penetrate the site by using DNS queries. And even if the DNS is not a point of vulnerability in the system, other areas may be problematic. Mail, Web, and FTP servers are all potential targets for attackers, so there exists a need for additional security functionality. If you cannot stop these attacks, you can at least alert someone when they are occurring to minimize the damage.

Intrusion detection systems are meant to fill that role. By using an IDS set up in a anomaly mode, a rule-based inferential engine is used to monitor traffic and detect irregular patterns in various protocols and services occurring on the network. Misuse, or pattern, intrusion detection systems can tell the administrator that something is wrong; whether or not the anomaly was caused by an intrusion is left up to the administrator. In any case, the administrator would be warned that the specifications from a known baseline have changed.

We've discussed some of the characteristics that make up a good intrusion detection system and some of the limitations of these systems. We saw that in today's network environment with switches and routers, the placement of intrusion detection systems is critical. Network IDS must be placed where they could do the most good and capture the most network data for analysis.

We also saw how network IDS can miss network packets; in a token ring network for instance, where a network IDS could actually miss an attack going on. Intrusion detection systems also suffer from the same type of errors as the biometric scanners we saw back in Chapter 15. There are the false positive errors, false negative errors, and the subversion errors. While the false positive errors are inconveniences, the false negative errors are potentially damaging, since an intrusion is actually going on and the system has failed to indicate that. Subversion errors are when the intrusion detection system has been compromised, and therefore, no data from it can be trusted.

The intrusion footprint is an indication that something has happened. This is also referred to as a signature. A footprint, or signature, is what is left behind to indicate something. It doesn't indicate what kind of attack it is or when it occurred, It merely informs an administrator that "something" went on.

We also saw that there are some serious limitations to intrusion detection systems, namely, their inability to positively identify the attacker. Intrusion detection systems cannot tell you any identifying information about the attacker. To be fair to IDS however, there is no device that can tell you that. The very nature of the Internet allows an attacker across the planet to conduct a series of attacks against a company using multiple routes along multiple ISP backbones.

Scanners are a form of intrusion detection, but instead of replacing IDS, they complement IDS. Scanners try to point out where vulnerabilities lie in your system that may be used in the future by attackers. Scanners also differ in the kind of mechanism they use to scan. IDS will attempt to check in real time, or against some predetermined baseline. Scanners can check the configuration files themselves for exploits; something IDS don't do.

19

Emerging
Technologies for
VPNs

Chapter 19 brings a close to this book on Virtual Private Networks. As technology evolves and matures, so does the impact it will have on VPNs. The Internet will still continue to grow, and along with that, new services, new products, and new ways of doing things will appear. This chapter will cover the things that are out there that will have an impact on VPNs and on the Internet overall.

This book has tried to provide a basis for security—the security of your network, and the security of your VPN. By now, you can easily tell how much security changes, and why you have to keep abreast of the changes around you. Security issues encompass not just whether an attacker is trying to hack into a system; they also concern governmental regulations, which, ironically, often make it easier for attackers to gain advantage. New technology should also be looked at with security in mind. Any new way of doing things that may give an advantage should be examined in its proper context.

As I have said throughout this book, VPNs are a function of security, and varying that amount of security affects the safety of your VPN. Unfortunately, many time issues are overblown. The technology media churns out dire predictions of attacks, and the financial consequences that will ensue. In addition, many articles on security state that "employees are your number one threat." In that case, why worry about outside attackers and governmental regulations? If internal employees are your number-one threat, don't have any. Okay, I'm exaggerating here, but in reality, what can you do? Not every employee is bad; not every employee is stealing corporate data. It's just the few who are that are making it miserable for the rest of the hard-working employees. There has to be security with flexibility; employees are not enemies, and their rights should be respected.

Introduction to Emerging Technologies

This chapter is an exciting topic to write about. Not only does this chapter detail what is under development, but it brings with it the awareness that technology is finally about to change. Until now, technology has been getting smaller and faster, but it still is based upon silicon technology. Very soon in the future, we will see computers that are based on photons (the smallest particular of light) and quantums (the building blocks of atoms). We will see how these developments will change the face of technology. I don't mean simple change, but rather massive change: Every device that exists and every algorithm that is written will have to be thought of again and looked at in a different way. The incredible speeds and computing power that will result will be enormous.

Unfortunately, while change can bring good things, there are also those things that just never die. Government regulations will just refuse to go away, and instead of making it easier to use VPNs, they may be making it tougher. While they may have a mindset to protect the public, they are attempting to impose a one-for-all policy that just wouldn't work in the future. Hopefully, before it's too late, they will agree on something that is agreeable to everyone. While governments profess to be pushing for deregulation, in some cases, they are pushing for re-regulation.

Threats and attacks are growing also. It seems that attackers are getting smarter. Instead of a lone ranger attacking a site, we now have groups of attackers attacking sites. Most systems that were designed to prevent against attacks had the one-attacker model in mind. Therefore, new ways of thinking and new systems will need to be developed to address these new threats.

Advances in Computing

One of the safety mechanisms behind Virtual Private Networks is the strength of the cryptographic algorithms that underlies them. Most of the attacks on these cryptographic systems have been hindered by not having the available computing power to break these codes. According to Moore's Law, silicon-based computing speeds will double every 18 months. Even at that rate, these cryptographic systems are still safe. So in order to break these systems, a new way of computing needs to be created. These new computing systems are in development, and it will not be too long before these advanced systems are ready for production (maybe one to two before commercial production). The speeds of these new systems will outperform any computer system currently on the market, or for that matter, any silicon-based computing machine. In this section, we will look at a couple of new computing systems that may be available soon.

Quantum Computing

Quantum computing relies on the behavior of single atoms. When regarding quantums, you no longer think in terms of a singular state. In modern computer technology, the bits are either in the 0 or 1 state at all times. Since quantums are basically the building blocks of atoms, they can exist at both states (1 and 0) simultaneously. This means that an ordinary 8-bit byte used in silicon computing can be replaced by 3 qubits (quantum equivalent to a computer bits). A quantum register consists of n qubits. In quantum computing, instead of either 1 or 0, each qubit will be in a superposition of states (1 and 0). A qubit therefore can be a superposition of the two states. Because of this liner superposition, a phenomenon known as *quantum parallelism* takes place and allows an exponential amount of computations to take place simultaneously, thereby increasing the speed of computation. The way they are utilized will be by external interactions with the qubits. An application known as Shor's Algorithm and developed by Peter Shor of AT&T Bell Labs solves the prime factoring problem used in many computer discrete logarithm's cryptographic systems. Some of the advantages of quantum computing are detailed in the following sections.

Capacity   The capacity of quantum information in a computer is potentially enormous to the superposition of bits. For example, in silicon computing a 3-bit register can represent only eight decimal numbers: 000=0,001=1,010=2,...111=7. A quantum register as described above contains n qubits that can be superimposed, i.e., being both 1 and 0 at the same time; therefore, a quantum can store all eight numbers at once.

GENERAL NOTE   A 3-bit silicon register can store eight numbers, but one at a time. A 3-qubit quantum register can store eight numbers all at once.

Now if we keep increasing the register size, the next size would be 4 bits, which would mean 16 numbers. These numbers would be stored one at a time for silicon computing. In quantum computing, however, they would be stored simultaneously. Therefore, quantum computing has the properties that as you increase the register size, the number of bits go up exponentially:

$$n \text{ qubits equals } 2^n \text{ numbers simultaneously}$$

Speed   Quantum computing yields incredible speeds compared to today's systems. In comparison, a 500-MHz processor, which is considered lightspeed today, is considered too slow for quantum computing.

One of the reasons is due to the superposition of qubits. Once a quantum register is superpositioned, operations can be performed on them. Since qubits are atoms, lasers are used to change the initial superpositions of numbers into different superpositions. During this superposition, each number is affected, and as a result, we generate a massive parallel computation in one piece of quantum equipment.

What this implies is that in one step, we've done an operation on 2^n input numbers (the size of the quantum register). In typical computing systems we have to accomplish 2^n operations or use 2^*n processors working in parallel. So we've just taken a $2n$ computation in silicon computing and replaced it by a singular step. For a small 8-bit binary register (2^8), instead of 256 operations, we have one operation. For a bigger register, say 16-bits, we've just accomplished over 65,000 operations in one operation.

Quantum computers are not as far off as you may believe. Researchers at Yale University have created a "single-electron" transistor, which they believe could lead to the development of supercomputers the size of a thumbtack. They've developed a technique where by resonating the transistor on each electron arrival, they are able to track and forward that electron as it moves through the switch. Apparently, they are able to achieve speeds in excess of 1000 times than any other device known.

Photonic Computing

Photonic computing is another future avenue for conventional computing systems. Photonic systems try to apply laser technology to existing conventional electronic computing. Laser light is used instead of electricity, and holograms are used instead of silicon chips. Photonic computers use photons (the smallest unit of light) instead of electrons.

To understand the way photonic computing works, you need to understand Boolean logic, invented by George Boole in the mid 1800s. Computer systems use Boolean operations to perform logical operations. Boolean logic states that you can use two Boolean operators to perform all other operations. Boolean operations consist of AND, NAND, OR, NOR, NOT, and XOR. Photonic computers use OR and XOR. Two light beams are represented as light beam ON=1, light beam OFF=0. The two light beams are shot through a special photonic transistor hologram. The output is dependent on the type of hologram and the way in which the beams arrived and how they are viewed by a masked mirror on the end.

Photonic logic states emulate the basic computer electronic logic state. In electronic computer logic states, a 2-bit register would produce four numbers; in photonic computing, the two light beams produce four possible photonic states. Depending on how the light beams are shown— both ON, both OFF, one ON, one OFF, etc.—different logic outputs are produced. In each instance, an OR function or an XOR function is produced; with this, all other switching can be accomplished. The produced OR function will tell the photonic switch whether either light beam or both light beams are ON. The XOR function tells the photonic switch that either both were ON or both OFF, and if they were opposite in phase pulse. Photonic switches have the ability to use a pipeline effect; as each pair of light beams (whether ON or OFF) pass the transistors' hologram, a new photonic state is accomplished. With typical electronic computing, each state is singular and must be cleared before a new state can exist.

Photonic computers have several advantages over their electronic counterparts. Some of them are as follows:

- *Speed.* Laser light travels thousands of times faster than electrons in normal computer chips. The speed can also be applied to computational operations, whereby operations are performed thousands of times faster than normal computers. As with quantum computing, even a 500-MHz computer is slow in comparison.

- *Costs.* Today silicon-based computers come from sand. While there is certainly an abundance of sand, the process of converting sand to silicon is costly. Computers that use light can use materials such as plastic and inexpensive glass.

- *Heat.* Photonic computers use light instead of electrons. Electrons produce heat; on many extremely fast machines, you will notice a heat sink attached to the microprocessor. Photons produce no heat; therefore, they can be made smaller, and the components wouldn't fail due to heat problems.

- *Bandwidth.* Here is where photonic computing has an incredible edge over conventional methods. A single digital electronic signal will carry only one signal (one bit, ON or OFF). A single light beam is only restricted to the fundamental properties of light. That is, by just using only one wavelength of the spectrum of light, a single photonic source can carry many billions of bits of data simultaneously.

- *Interoperability.* In many technologies, you have to upgrade to a new infrastructure to take advantage of the technology. Photonic switches can be added to an existing infrastructure without disturbing the topology. Adding photonic switches will convert electrical signals to light signals to increase the rate of communications. When additional bandwidth is needed, the switches can be upgraded to use a new wavelength of the light spectrum. The Synchronous Optical Network (SONET) technology is based upon using photon technology.

Advances in Cryptographic Systems

In September 1997, The U.S. National Institute of Standards and Technology (NIST) sent out a request for proposal for a new encryption cipher—one that would replace the current 56-bit DES and last for 20 to 30 years. Called the Advanced Encryption Standard (AES), this cipher would contain an Advanced Encryption Algorithm (AEA). In 1998 the DES algorithm, developed by IBM, will be 20 years old. The NIST felt there was a need for a new algorithm to take us into the twenty-first century. The submission deadline was June 15, 1998, and candidates were announced in August 1998. The testing would consist of two rounds. After round one the algorithms would be open to public scrutiny. Round two would be a more technical review in order to pick a winner. In March 1998 Miles E. Smid presented a workshop to various vendors outlining what the NIST wanted. From the start, the NIST wanted a public algorithm—one that could be used, tested, and analyzed by the public.

The NIST placed a minimal set of requirements on the proposals:*

1. "The algorithm must implement symmetric (secret) key cryptography.
2. The algorithm must be a block cipher.
3. The candidate algorithm shall be capable of supporting key-block combinations with sizes of 128-128, 192-128, and 256-128 bits. A submitted algorithm may support other key-block sizes and combinations, and such features will be taken into consideration during analysis."

---

*From the NIST Web site, *http://csrc.nist.gov/encryption/aes/aes_home.htm.*

During the first round, which was held in Ventura, California, in August 1998, the NIST performed the following tests:

- "Key-Block Size Combinations: Round 1 testing by NIST will be performed on the 128-bit key and 128-bit block-size combination. (The public, however, is welcome to also focus on other key- and block-size combinations.) Testing of other key-block sizes may be accomplished if time and resources permit.

- Correctness check: The Known Answer Test and Monte Carlo Test values included with the submission will be used to test the correctness of the reference and mathematically optimized implementations, once they are compiled. (It is more likely that NIST will perform this check of the reference code—and possibly the optimized code as well—even before accepting the submission package as "complete and proper.")

- Efficiency testing: Using the submitted mathematically optimized implementations, NIST intends to perform various computational efficiency tests for the 128-128 key-block combination, including the calculation of the time required to perform: Algorithm setup, Key setup, Key change, and Encryption and Decryption. NIST may perform efficiency testing on other platforms.

- Other testing: Other features of the candidate algorithms may be examined by NIST."

At the end of the first round, on August 20,1998, NIST announced 15 AES candidates. They invited the worldwide cryptographic research community to try to break the algorithms, in order to narrow down this field to five or fewer candidates. This period will continue until April 15, 1999. Finalists will be pick in the summer of 1999, and the NIST hopes that one of these 15 algorithms will be adopted as the Advanced Encryption Standard. However, due to the complexity of the algorithms and the technical scrutiny they must undergo, most experts believe it will not be until 2000 or 2001 before an algorithm is chosen. The AES research candidates cover 12 countries; the algorithms included are as follows:

- *CAST-256 Entrust Technologies; Adams, Carlisle; Canada.* CAST-256 is a symmetric cipher that supports key sizes of 128, 160, 192, 224, and 256 bits and a block size of 128 bits, and is several times faster in software than DES. CAST-256 is an extension of the original CAST-128 cipher.

- *CRYPTON Future Systems Inc.; Lim, Chae Hoon, South Korea.* CRYPTON is a 12-round, self-invertible cipher supporting keys sizes up to 256 bits with 128-bit blocks. It has very high speeds in software and has a fast key scheduling.

- *DEAL; Outerbridge, Richard; Knudsen, Lars; Canada and Norway.* DEAL is a cipher based on DES that uses a block size of 128 bits and key sizes of 128, 192, and 256 bits. It is a 128-block cipher and can be used with existing DES software and hardware.

- *DFC Centre National pour la Recherche Scientifique (CNRS); Vaudenay, Serge; France.*

- *E2 Nippon Telegraph and Telephone Corp. (NTT); Kanda, Masayuki; Japan.* E2 is a 12-round Feistel cipher with a 128-bit block cipher with 128-, 192-, and 256-bit key sizes.

- *FROG TecApro Internacional S.A.; Georgoudis, Dianelos; Costa Rica.*

- *HPC (Hasty Pudding Cipher); Schroeppel, Rich; U.S.A.*

- *LOKI97; Brown, Lawrie; Pieprzyk, Josef; Seberry, Jennifer; Australia.*

- *MAGENTA Deutsche Telekom AG; Huber, Klaus; Germany.*

- *MARS IBM Corp.; Zunic, Nevenko; U.S.A.*

- *RC6 RSA Laboratories; Robshaw, Matthew; U.S.A.* RSA's RC6 is an improvement over RC5, with a 128-bit block size, and using four 32-bit registers and key sizes up to 256 bits.

- *Rijndael; Daemen Joan, Rijman, Vincent, Belgium.*

- *SAFER+ Cylink Corp.; Chen, Lily; U.S.A.* SAFER+ is based on the work of earlier SAFER algorithms. It uses 128-bit blocks and 128, 192, 256 key sizes, and has a faster linear transformation.

- *SERPENT; Ross Anderson, Biham; Eli, Knudsen; U.K., Israel, and Norway.*

- *TWOFISH; Schneier, Bruce; Kelsey, John; Whiting, Doug; Wagner, David; Hall, Chris; Ferguson, Niels; U.S.A.* TWOFISH is a 16-round cipher, using 128-bit blocks and 128, 192, and 256 key sizes.

Some of the proposals, such as those from IBM and RSA, use current technology, while others are using completely new technology. This new technology may take longer to evaluate, which is one reason many experts agree it will be until 2000 or 2001 before an algorithm is adopted. IBM, RSA, and Counterpane offer the fastest algorithms. So far, one of the proposals, LOKI97, has developed some weaknesses in the algorithm.

A group called the Candidate AES for Analysis and Reviews (CAE-SAR) has formed to evaluate some of the algorithms for AES consideration, both in technical (security) terms and feasibility (implementation) terms. They also are maintaining an up-to-date status report of the work by others on other algorithms. Their Web page (*http://www.dice.ucl.ac.be/crypto/CAESAR/caesar.html*) is an excellent source of information on the AES algorithms.

While the new proposals are being considered and evaluated, some wonder if it is just a waste of time, and if the NIST will ever be able to implement them. Even though the NIST standards apply to government facilities, commercial use may follow. Some of the concerns are valid:

- *Encryption standard.* One of the measurements of the new encryption algorithm will be its functionality with personal computers. However, considering that this algorithm is designed to last 20 to 30 years, and with the way technology changes, there is some question as to whether encryption algorithm can be judged on a piece of equipment that will probably be outdated in a year.

- *Other countries' encryption policies.* The AES-proposed encryption algorithms come from 12 different countries. If a non-US encryption algorithm is accepted, what will the legal usage policies be? If the encryption algorithm is stronger than Triple-DES, and U.S. policy forbids the exportation of Triple-DES, how can the U.S. policy apply to another country? We would be back to a situation similar to what is happening with PGP, where U.S. manufacturers cannot export technology that already exists overseas.

- *Key recovery.* This is a major concern of freedom groups. The NIST will be accepting an algorithm stronger than DES, with key lengths greater then 128 bits. This kind of algorithm is unbreakable. With that being the case, and the policy of many governments restricting its use, many believe there will be pressure put on the manufacturer of the algorithm to secretly build in a key-recovery feature.

- *New computing technologies.* We saw in the last section how the new technologies, i.e., photonic and quantum computing, can revolutionize computing. If these computing technologies become standard in the marketplace, then any algorithm that is built will be vulnerable due to the sheer power of these potentially new systems.

Elliptic Curve Cryptography

While work is continually being done on the AES encryption algorithms, it's still a long way off. Some current work is being done on a new type of cryptographic algorithm called elliptic curve algorithm. Researchers have been studying these elliptic curve functions as replacements to the standard exponential algorithms used in modern public-key cryptography. These elliptic curve cryptosystems can use smaller key sizes and are less computationally intensive than their counterparts, but they offer the same degree of security as modern cryptosystems. Elliptic curve cryptosystems are a form of public-key cryptosystem. Elliptic curves can factor large numbers, can be used in the Diffie-Hellman protocol, and can be also used for digital signatures, key exchange, and confidentiality. In addition, elliptic curve cryptosystems can use smaller key size—for instance, an elliptic curve key size of 160 bits may be equivalent to RSA 1024-bit key size. These cryptosystems are also suited for low-resource available situations, like smart cards discussed back in Chapter 14.

As with all cryptosystems, elliptic curve cryptosystems have their limitations. While they are faster at signature generation than some algorithms, they are slower at signature verification. These systems are still in development.

Private Doorbell

As an alternative to the key-recovery feature advocated by the Clinton administration, 13 high-tech companies are pushing for a different type of encryption plan called "Private Doorbell." These companies are hoping this will end the stalemates surrounding the government's policy on exportation of encryption products and desire to wiretap encrypted communication. Private Doorbell applies to network encryption. Key-recovery encryption requires users to provide the decryption key to law enforcement (or third parties) on an as-needed basis. In Private Doorbell, the data is secure until law enforcement agencies serve a network operator with a warrant or court order to unlock (decrypt) the information.

Some of the companies involved in Private Doorbell are Cisco Systems, with support from Ascend Communications; Sun; Novell; Bay Networks; 3Com; Intel; HP; Microsoft; Netscape; Network Associates; RedCreek Communications; and Secure Computing.

With this technology, network administrators would be allowed to encrypt messages when they leave a router, and when presented with a warrant, they would decrypt the message when arriving at the end router. This only applies to network encryption, not user encryption. If a user uses an encryption package such as PGP, encrypted data will enter the originating router and get encrypted again. When it arrives at the destination router, it can be decrypted, but that would only reveal the contents of the original PGP-encrypted message. Law enforcement agencies would still need the private key of the recipient to decrypt the message.

While everyone agrees this is not a total solution, it is at least a step in the right direction and satisfies some of their concerns. This may also appease some groups who say if a court order is warranted, then all future communications should be decrypted, as in a telephone wiretap. In contrast, in a key-recovery situation, any communication can be decrypted: past, present, or future.

The U.S. Commerce Department has issued a statement, neither rejecting the proposal nor accepting it. As one Commerce spokesperson has stated:

> We welcome the development as part of the ongoing dialogue the [Clinton] administration is having with industry to find encryption products that reach a balance between national security and law enforcement concerns on the one hand and the needs of electronic commerce and personal privacy on the other. There are serious issues that must be considered in interagency export review, and we will carefully review Cisco's license application.

Privacy groups, on the other hand, are opposed to this proposal; they see this as just another form of privacy intrusion. Yet since market share is being lost due to government restrictions, businesses are becoming increasingly frustrated by government regulations and feel something must be done.

A problem with Private Doorbell is how strong the encryption is at the router. If hackers know this, they will attack the router. Any encryption algorithm is subject to attack, and if a company's policy of clear text is enforced on the LAN to the Internet router anyone who hacks into the router can read the data. Moreover, the security of the router administrator is questionable. If network administrators can decrypt information, what's to stop them from decrypting it whether or not they are presented with a court order? If this will involve an encryption process between routers, then all of the properties associated with encryption come into play: key generation, key management, secret key, and so on.

As far as Private Doorbell is concerned, it is anyone's guess whether these products will be allowed for exportation. The outlook for this is not good, since the encryption plan doesn't do what the FBI or NSA wants it to do. The only way this encryption debate will be settled will be by congressional legislation.

GENERAL NOTE   Since it is only a matter of time before companies set a policy of no encrypted data on networks (for security reasons), then perhaps Private Doorbell will become acceptable to the government.

Steganography

In many countries the use of encryption is illegal. Those governments view anyone using encryption as doing something deceitful. Other governments allow it, but only so long as they hold the decryption keys. As more and more people use the Internet during business hours, companies will restrict the use of encrypted email on their networks. They normally will take the position that if someone does something illegal and it's done during business hours using the company's resources, then that person will be liable.

GENERAL NOTE   As companies become more aware of security and institute more security procedures, the direction of the companies' security policies will be toward allowing no encrypted email on their networks.

Steganography is not cryptography, but it does apply to the secrecy of the message. Instead of encrypting the message as we have seen in earlier chapters, however, it tries to hide the message. The concept of steganography is to make it look like there is no message at all. Steganography does not replace cryptography, but rather it adds a layer of protection to the message. If an attacker can realize that there is a message in a steganographic message, the attacker may uncover the message. However, the message is still encrypted with a cryptographic algorithm that the attacker would still have to break.

Like cryptography, steganography comes from the military. Just as in a cryptographic system, the strength should lie on the secrecy of the algorithm and the difficulty to reverse-engineer it to uncover the data or a key. A steganographic system should take into consideration that the enemy has full knowledge of the way it was designed. A well-designed steganographic system would hide the message so well that anyone coming across the data stream would not even know it's a message.

SECURITY NOTE   Steganography does not replace cryptography, but adds another layer of protection to the data stream, just as IDS and scanners work together.

Steganography tries to ride over hidden channels, or those channels that ride alongside the main carrier. For example, a normal house uses a 120/240 volt electrical signal. The X-10 standard, which is used for home automation, rides on the side of this 120/240 volt signal, without interfering with any appliances on the circuit. Now taking this a step further and applying this to radio frequency: A transmitted message along radio waves is anywhere from 50 to 100 times weaker than any atmospheric noise, thereby making it invisible to anyone looking for a message. You could apply this to computer equipment by selectively modulating specific computer components to hide a message.

The historical design of steganographic systems has been to replace noise with a secret transmission. Software packages are available that try to modify the bit pattern of an encrypted message to make it appear as a random sequence of data packets. However, there has not been as much interest in steganographic systems as there has been in crypto-graphic systems. As of today, much of the research in steganographic systems has been in analog communication systems. In order to reveal a message, the attacker would need to have equipment that could find the message in the noise. In these environments, however, even stegano-graphic systems cannot replace what appears to be truly random noise, and since they are dealing with noise, there has to be a lot of error-cor-rection in these systems.

GENERAL NOTE   As more governments and companies restrict the use of cryptography systems, commercial development will increase in steganographic systems.

Steganography Tools

Many tools are available that use steganography technology. Listed below is just a sample of what's out there. Some of these tools have embedded cryptographic functions, which are then regulated by the U.S. government. Most of the tools available for steganography use a form of JPG, GFI, or BMP image formats and WAV audio file formats in which to hide the original message. The tools listed here are for the Windows environment, although there are other platforms available.

- *BPCS-Steganography.* Developed by Eiji Kawaguchi at Kyushu Institute of Technology in Japan, this tool uses a new steganographic technology that involves taking the original message and using the bit planes of BMP and GIF images.
- *Contraband.* Takes an input file and transforms it to a 24-bit BMP.
- *Encrypt Pic.* A Blowfish encryption algorithm that then hides the message in 24-bit BMP files.
- *Gif-It-Up.* Gif-It-Up takes and hides data in a GIF image; it also offers a data encryption algorithm.
- *Hide and Seek for Win95.* Developed by Colin Moroney, this tool is BMP-based and was the Blowfish cryptographic algorithm.
- *In The Picture.* In The Picture has the helpful feature of using multiple keys; therefore, you can create a message for several recipients. It hides messages in BMP images.
- *JSteg Shel.* Developed by Derek Upham, this is a shell to the DOS version of Jsteg. It hides messages in the JPG format.
- *MP3Stego.* MP3Stego takes a message and hides it in a WAV file that is MP3 formatted.
- *PGPn123.* PGPn123 is a mail application embedded in such mail programs as Eudora and Agent. After the message is encrypted with PGP, it can then be fed into a steganographic program.
- *Scramdisk.* Scramdisk is an encryption program implementing Triple-DES, IDEA, and Blowfish algorithms. After the encryption process, Scramdisk has the option to convert the message into a WAV formatted audio file.
- *Scytale.* Similar to PGPn123. Scytale hides the message in a PCX image and removes the original clear-text file.
- *Steganos for Win95.* Developed by Deus Ex Machina Communications, this tool allows multiple hiding formats such as HTML, WAV, and BMP. Also, once the conversion is done, it will remove the original clear-text file.

- *S-Tools4.* This is a very popular steganographic tool supporting BMP, GIF, and WAV images.
- *wbStego.* Developed by Werner Bailer, wbStego has encryption capabilities and can hide messages in BMP and HTML file formats.

What Are the New Threats?

Traditionally, the attacker has been portrayed as a loner, perhaps some kid in college who has access to computing resources and too much time on his hands. Attackers were always viewed as social misfits working alone against a company, or at most, as one attacker against several networks. That all has changed.

The U.S. Department of Defense Security staff has announced a new form of attack: The coordinated attack. Several government and private sites have each been attacked simultaneously from different addresses around the world. Intrusion detection systems and network alerting mechanisms have not been set up to handle this type of attack, so they will need to be fitted with this attack signature.

So far the attacks have been the same attacks that occur today throughout the Internet; the only difference is the sources. Up until now the attack strategy has been to focus on a particular pattern developing, but today there can be several patterns developing at the same time, and these patterns may be distributed throughout the world.

According to the DoD's report (*http://www.nswc.navy.mil/ISSEC/CID*), there are three main reasons why an attack like this would occur:

1. *Stealth.* By using multiple IP addresses, the attack may go unnoticed. Since each IP phase of the attack is smaller than a traditional attack, the pattern would not easily be recognized. In addition, new probing techniques are making these attacks difficult to detect.

2. *Firepower.* Having more than one IP address attack one or more sites allows the attackers to deliver a greater amount of attacks in a smaller time frame than in traditional attacks. Therefore, conventional means of blocking a particular network will not work. These attacks may also be trial runs for larger attacks in the future.

3. *Additional data.* By using multiple IP addresses, it may be possible to gain more data from a target than in a regular singular

attack. In addition, by using different addresses, it's possible for one IP to fail and another IP to succeed.

Some of the kinds of coordinated attacks that are documented in this report are as follows:

- *Coordinated traceroutes.*   The attackers would coordinate a traceroute against a victim, all within minutes of each other. The use of this attack is to allow the attackers to gather data about the timing of the circuit.

- *Coordinated reset scans.*   These attacks are designed to map future attacks. Some of these attacks were extremely low in number; the report mentions that one attack only used two a day. By sending these sync packets, routers on the network would send back ICMP time exceeded when an end host or network doesn't exist. By knowing what doesn't exist, the attackers can use that information to guess about what does exist.

- *Coordinated exploits.*   While these attacks have not yet resulted in large-scale successes, they may grow in the future. Some of the documented exploits have been the back orifice scan and DNS resets.

- *Probing a firewall.*   This attack occurred by sending a secure shell connection request, followed by NNTP probes and, finally, by packets with malformed TCP packet flags from multiple locations set as urgent.

- *Coordinated DNS scans.*   This attack uses different source IP addresses, apparently from across the globe, attacking the same target. The hope is for the attack to succeed and reveal DNS servers on particular subnets. With this information, it may be possible to then map the target's network.

These attacks are particularly worrisome in that they no longer constitute a singular effort. Up until now, in general, only one individual conducted the attack. Now it appears as if attackers are beginning to join forces and use their talents to conduct coordinated attacks against networks.

Of particular concern is that all defense security mechanisms have been designed to guard against attacks by individuals, looking at one IP and determining whether it was spoofed. Now we must look at multiple streams of data from different IP addresses. This way of looking at attacks has not been formulated in today's security products. Security vendors will have to examine these new forms of attacks and look at features that can be incorporated into their products to guard against them.

Government Regulations

After reading this section, it would seem the biggest threat to your privacy (which includes your VPN) will be the role the U.S. government plays. Unfortunately, the need to stop terrorism, and the need to protect copyright violations, may have a major negative impact on any security item, including all your authentication devices, your encryption algorithms, and your smart cards. Anything that has a security feature is potentially subject to regulation, and you may no longer be able to test and scrutinize that security algorithm. These regulations are laid out in the Wassenaar Arrangement and the World Intellectual Property Organization treaty.

The Wassenaar Arrangement

The Wassenaar Arrangement (WA) is a global multilateral arrangement on the export of munitions and dual-use weapons. It was founded in July 1996 by the following 33 countries:

Argentina	The Netherlands
Australia	New Zealand
Austria	Norway
Belgium	Poland
Bulgaria	Portugal
Canada	The Republic of Korea
The Czech Republic	Romania
Denmark	The Russian Federation
Finland	Slovakia
France	Spain
Germany	Sweden
Greece	Switzerland
Hungary	Turkey

Ireland   Ukraine

Italy   United Kingdom

Japan   United States

Luxembourg

The WA is designed to exchange views among member countries and share information of the responsibility in transferring conventional arms. It tries to stop the proliferation of weapons of mass destruction and delivery systems. Its purpose is to form cooperation among member states in order to stop the spread and acquisition of armaments and dual-use military items for end users. The members, called participating states, seek to ensure this nonproliferation by the use of national security policies. There is a list of munitions, called categories, that members periodically review due to the advance of technological development. One of the purposes for the exchange of views is to make each member aware of the risks associated with transferring these weapons. According to their charter (found at *http://www.wasseneer.org/*):

> The Arrangement is open on a global and non-discriminatory basis to prospective adherents that comply with the agreed criteria. To be admitted, a state must: be a producer/exporter of arms or industrial equipment respectively; maintain non-proliferation policies and appropriate national policies, including adherence to relevant non-proliferation regimes and treaties; and maintain fully effective export controls. Although the Arrangement does not have an observer category, a diverse outreach policy is envisaged in order to inform non-member countries about the WA objectives and activities and to encourage non-members to adopt national policies consistent with the objectives of greater transparency and responsibility in transfers of conventional arms and dual-use goods and technologies, maintain fully effective export controls and adhere to relevant non-proliferation treaties and regimes.

Now why would the WA affect the safety and security of a VPN? The answer to that is found in an another area of the WA:

> Information exchanged in the Arrangement can also include any other matters relevant to the WA goals that individual Participating States wish to bring to the attention of other members.

This implies that if a country has a concern about a possible weapons or munitions issue, they can bring it up to the states to address. On

December 3, a press statement released from the White House basically said that the U.S. has convinced the other major states to impose strict new export controls on the use of encryption under the guise of weapons control.

Up until now, many high-tech companies have repeatedly said that due to the U.S. export restrictions on encryption software, they couldn't compete; it wasn't a level playing field. What this arrangement has done is supposedly level that playing field. Member states are not required to go along with the standards but must generally accept the consensus. Analysts believe that it was the U.S. pushing for this agreement on encryption, since the U.S. has the most stringent controls on encryption policy. The list of encryption policies is listed under Category 5, part 2:

5. A. 2. a. 1. a.   A "symmetric algorithm" employing a key length in excess of 56 bits; or

                b.   An "asymmetric algorithm" where the security of the algorithm is based on any of the following:

                    1.   Factorization of integers in excess of 512 bits (e.g., RSA);

                    2.   Computation of discrete logarithms in a multiplicative group of a finite field of size greater than 512 bits (e.g., Diffie-Hellman over Z/pZ); or

                    3.   Discrete logarithms in a group other than mentioned in 5.A.1.b.2, in excess of 112 bits (e.g., Diffie-Hellman over an elliptic curve);

So, it seems as though these 33 countries will agree on a common export control policy. This group of 33 has produced some of the major cryptographic algorithms developed today.

The World Intellectual Property Organization Treaty

This is the second governmental regulation, in the guise of copyright protection, that will affect any security implementation you may install. The main problem with this treaty is that it would be illegal to reverse-engineer software to expose its security vulnerabilities. Although not designed for it, what the treaty will do is make it illegal for security companies to reverse-engineer a security product to test its security features. For example, say a bank wants to purchase a high-tech security biometirc device for all its employees, and they want to hire a security expert to come in and try and break into the device for security holes before they purchased it and deploy it companywide. This new treaty would make it a crime for a security consultant to come in and do that.

The treaty is designed to stop copyright violation on the Internet. It is supported by the Senate and the President and is currently in the House for consideration. In order for the copyright to be effective, the treaty states that it would be illegal to take a finished application and find a way to circumvent its security without first obtaining the approval of the vendor who manufactured it. While this is intended to stop a forger from reverse-engineering a CD or VCR movie, it is vague enough to apply to all security systems, whether or not they are used in certain industries.

There are those who are concerned with security vendors hiding bad code behind their products and not undergoing testing, which could make the companies liable for any damages, like the German bank example back in Chapter 6. Some say that if a security vendor is going to put their trust in the product, they should be open up to all tests. This, however, can put a financial strain on a company's resources. A particular manufacturer could have hundreds of so-called security experts tear apart their products on behalf of other companies, and the original vendor may have to create hundreds of responses to these supposed security exports reports.

In both cases, the Wassenaar Agreement or the World Intellectual Property Organization Treaty will make it difficult for companies to sell encryption products. Unfortunately, the World Intellectual Property Organization Treaty can undo what existing security safety we already have.

Wireless VPNs

Is it really possible for wireless VPNs to exist? The actual answer is yes, although it is not a new technology developed just for VPNs. Local Multipoint Distribution System (LMDS) is a wireless technology that uses microwave signals (millimeterwave signals) to send data. It uses the 28 GHz spectrum to send voice, video, and data 3 to 10 miles in diameter. LMDS is a similar technology to the cordless phone with overlapping cells. LMDS can provide customers with multichannel video programming, telephony, video, and two-way data services. It is being offered as a replacement for wireless cable installations.

LMDS has the advantages of being two-way communications, the availability of an enormous bandwidth pipe, and a lower cost than traditional services. In addition, since it is a two-way data communications, it doesn't have the problems with existing infrastructure where a separate line is need for uplink communications. The data steams available will be incredible; some indications are for a 1.5 Gbps downstream and up to 200 Mbps upstream.

LMDS is a line-of-sight technology, so the placement of the transmitter and receiver are critical. Weather and are subjects to shadow areas, where big trees can create shadow areas where LMDS signals may not arrive.

LMDS has enormous potential in wireless technology, and vendors will begin rolling it out in 1999. Some of the services that will be offered will be Virtual Network, Internet access, and Virtual Private Network services.

Conclusion

Chapter 19 brought to light serious technological advances on the horizon, as well as serious issues about governmental interference. Virtual Private Networks can be impacted by any change, acceptance, or usage of any of the items discussed in this chapter.

Some of the advances in computing technology, such as quantum and photonic computing will bring about a major change in the way we think of computers and the power they will deliver. All the applications that have been written for the conventional way of doing programming will change. No longer will they be simple state changes; programmers will have to deal with a totally different way of look at computers and the power they will have.

We examined the Advanced Encryption Standard being developed by the NIST, which will supposedly replace DES. This new cipher will take us into the twenty-first century and offer better security than DES offers now. Of course, there is the concern that since DES cannot be exported, how can an AES algorithm be exported? This is an issue even with many different countries working on the design.

Next, we looked at Private Doorbell, with its network encryption model, and the router administrator responsible for decryption/encryption. We learned that this is an attempt on the part of some high-tech companies to reach a compromise with the government. Although Private Doorbell does not meet all of the FBI requirements, there is hope the FBI will bend and meet the high-tech companies halfway. We also looked at steganography, or the art of hiding a message inside of a message. This field may prove interesting. With encryption technology being heavily regulated, perhaps this field will fill a niche until the encryption policy is finally settled.

Then we looked at more governmental regulations, specifically, the Wassenaar Arrangement and the World Intellectual Property Organization Treaty. Either one of these treaties will impact security, by not allowing strong security or by forbidding the testing of security products. Either way, it makes for an interesting future.

APPENDIX A

LINKS AND REFERENCES

This section consists of the various links, RFCs, articles and books available to any person who wants to continue to learn more about Virtual Private Networks and Security. This is not a complete list by any means, just a good starting point to continue your training.

Cryptography and Encryption

http://elvis.rowan.edu/~berman/Classes/Fall96/DCN/Lecture9/index.htm

http://fn2.freenet.edmonton.ab.ca/~jsavard/jscrypt.html

http://microsoft.com/workshop/security/toc.htm

http://saxophone.agora.com/tutorials/bullet_online.html

http://theory.lcs.mit.edu/~rivest/crypto-security.html

http://users.succeed.net/~kill9/crypto/auth/

http://webopedia.internet.com/TERM/P/PPTP.html

http://wserver.physnet.uni-hamburg.de/provos/photuris/howtouse.html

http://world.std.com/~franl/crypto/

http://www.cet.st.com.sg/digisafe.htm

http://www.clark.net/pub/cme/home.html

http://www.cisco.com/public/library/isakmp.html

http://www.counterpane.com/protocols.html

http://www.cryptocard.com/

http://www.cryptography.com/

http://www.cryptonet.it/paolo/crypto-security.html

http://www.cryptosoft.com/html/privacy.htm

http://www.cs.auckland.ac.nz/~pgut001/tutorial/

http://www.cs.caltech.edu/~adam/LOCAL/trust.html

http://www.dcs.ex.ac.uk/~aba/rsa/

http://www.dms.auburn.edu/hac/about/table_of_contents.html

http://www.hack.gr/users/dij/crypto/overview/

http://www.hhs.net/dpec/courses/t11/

http://www.ietf.cnri.reston.va.us/html.charters/ipsec-charter.html

http://www.ii.uib.no/~larsr/

http://www.iie.edu.uy/~mazzara/pgp/howpgp.htm

http://www.inu.net/maverick/

http://www.io.com/~ritter/GLOSSARY.HTM

http://www.ioc.ee/~helger/crypto/

http://www.inu.net/maverick/

http://www.itl.nist.gov/div897/pubs/fip46-2.htm

http://www.mach5.com/crypto/algorithms.html

http://www.masinter.net/~l2tp/

http://www.mit.edu/afs/athena.mit.edu/user/t/y/tytso/www/ipsec/companies.html

http://web.mit.edu/network/isakmp/

http://www.nai.com/default_pgp.asp

http://www.nomodes.com/coincidence.html

http://www.rsa.com/

http://www.rsa.com/rsa/developers/SMIMEPPT/swan/index.htm

http://www.signal9.com/technical/whitepapers/crypto101/crypto101index.html

http://www.skip.org/

http://www.ssh.fi/tech/crypto/

http://www.subject.com/crypto/crypto.html

http://www.sun.com/security/skip

http://www.tis.com/research/crypto/crypt_surv.html

http://www.verisign.com/

http://www.wkmn.com/secure.html

Electronic Commerce

http://ecom.wharton.upenn.edu/ec/

http://ganges.cs.tcd.ie/mepeirce/project.html

http://web.mit.edu/reagle/www/commerce/commerce.html

http://www.baltimore.ie/

http://www.Certco.com/

http://www.ecommerce.gov/internat.htm

http://www.fecrc.com/

http://www.hypercom.com/

Emerging Technology

http://csrc.nist.gov/encryption/aes/aes_9709.htm

http://ds.dial.pipex.com/george.barwood/ec_faq.htm

http://qso.lanl.gov/qc/

http://feynman.stanford.edu/qcomp/

http://iquest.net/~mrmil/stego.html

http://t4.lanl.gov/dfvj/quantumcomp.html

http://www-dse.doc.ic.ac.uk/~nd/surprise_97/journal/vol1/spb3/

*http://www-nt.e-technik.uni-erlangen.de/~hartung/
    watermarkinglinks.html*

http://www.certicom.com/ecc

http://www.cyberdyne-computers.com/photon1.htm

http://www.dice.ucl.ac.be/crypto/CAESAR/caesar.html

http://www.isse.gmu.edu/~njohnson/Steganography

http://www.jjtc.com/stegdoc/sec201.html

http://www.qubit.org/intros/comp/comp.html

http://www.phase-one.com.au/fravia/stego.htm#anchorefs

http://www.wowarea.com/pages/stega.htm

Frequently Asked Questions

http://world.std.com/~franl/crypto/emoney-minifaq.html

http://www.cis.ohio-state.edu/hypertext/faq/usenet/cryptography-faq/top.html

http://www.cyberdyne-computers.com/faq.htm

http://www.faqs.org/faqs/

http://www.iae.nsk.su/pages/CRYPTO/crypfaq.html

http://www.rsa.com/rsalabs/faq/

http://www.skip.org/

http://www.signal9.com/technical/

http://www.w3.org/Security/Faq/www-security-faq.html

http://www4.ncsu.edu/eos/users/w/wsetzer/www/FAQ/

Governmental Information and Laws

http://207.96.11.93/Encryption/Default.htm#WHDocs

http://csrc.ncsl.nist.gov/

http://csrc.nist.gov/

http://cwis.kub.nl/~frw/people/koops/lawsurvy.htm

http://info.acm.org/reports/acm_crypto_study.html

http://www.bxa.doc.gov/

http://www.darpa.mil/

http://www.doc.gov/bureaus/

http://www.gilc.org/crypto/crypto-survey.html

http://www.ilpf.org/work/ca/exec.htm

http://www.nist.gov/

Privacy Information

http://users.aol.com/jpeschel/contests.htm

http://www.cdt.org/ http://www.crypto.com

http://www.computerprivacy.org/

http://www.eff.org/

http://www.epic.org

http://www.privacy.org/ipc

http://www.vortex.com/privacy.html

Security

http://csrc.nist.gov/isptg/html/

http://guardian.sparc.spb.su/jjb/Security/links.html

http://gue-tech.asee.org/darkgrue/classwork/cs229/index.html

http://ipsec-wit.antd.nist.gov/

http://kumite.com/myths/

http://netsecurity.miningco.com/

http://www.l0pht.com/index.html

http://www.codexdatasystems.com/

http://www.cpio.net/archive/

http://www.alw.nih.gov/Security/security.html

http://www.drsolomon.com/vircen/

http://www.infowar.com/

http://www.internettools.com/

http://www.iss.net/vd/rainbow.html

http://www.iss.net/vd/library.html

http://www.lawandco.com/research/map.htm

http://www.mountainwave.com

http://www.netsurf.com/nsf/v01/01/resource/index.html

http://www.networkguys.com/

http://www.rootshell.com/beta/news.html

http://www.telstra.com.au/info/security.html

http://www.tscm.com/

http://www.tezcat.com/web/security/security_top_level.html

http://www.x.org

http://www.yahoo.com/Computers_and_Internet/Software/Operating_Systems

Security Response Teams/Information

http://www.axent.com/support/secres/default.htm#emerg

http://csrc.nist.gov/

http://www.cert.org/

http://www.fbi.gov/programs/compcrim.htm

http://www.first.org/

http://www.gocsi.com/

http://www.icsa.net/

http://www.iss.net/vd/mail.html

http://www.search.org/

http://www.ncsa.com/

VPN Information and Vendors

http://datafellows.com/

http://freegate.com/products/vpn.html

http://intranetsolutions.3com.com/vpn.faq.html

http://laurent.osgroup.com/showcase/

http://techweb.cmp.com/internetwk/VPN/

http://www.abhiweb.com/

http://www.ascend.com/2868.html

http://www.assured-digital.com/welcome.htm

http://www.aventail.com/index.phtml/solutions/white_papers/ebusiness.phtml

http://www.baynetworks.com/products/Papers/2746.html

http://www.bbn.com/

http://www.busn.ucok.edu/tips/info_hrd/vpn.htm

http://www.cabletron.com

http://www.celotek.com/

http://www.checkpoint.com/vpn/index.html

http://www.cisco.com/warp/public/779/servpro/solutions/vpn/

http://www.compatible.com/vpn_now/index.html

http://www.concentric.net/index1.html

http://www.corp.cwcom.co.uk/prodserv/

http://www.counterpane.com/

http://www.cyberguard.com/

http://www.digital.com/info/software-catalogue/altavista-tunnel.html

http://www.e-lock.com/white-p/whitemain.htm

http://www.entrust.com/

http://www.epm.ornl.gov/~dunigan/vpn.html

http://www.extendsys.com/

http://www.fortresstech.com/vpn1.html

http://www.frontiertech.com/

http://www.garrison.com/

http://www.ibm.com

http://www.icon.com/vpn/index.html

http://www.indusriver.com/indusnew/index.htm

http://www.infoexpress.com/

http://www.ipservices.att.com/worldnet/vpns/

http://www.ire.com/

http://www.isolation.com/

http://www.lucent.com

http://www.matrox.com

http://www.microsoft.com

http://www.netlock.de/

http://www.netscreen.com/

http://www.networkcomputing.com/901/901colmoskowitz.html

http://www.newoak.com/

http://www.novell.com/bordermanager/

http://www.nts.com/html/VPN/VPNtnnlMstr.html

http://www.openroute.com/

http://www.radguard.com/

http://www.raptor.com/lib/index.html

http://www.racal.com/rdg/

http://www.redcreek.com/

http://www.securitydynamics.com/

http://www.setsolutions.com/index.html

http://www.shiva.com/

http://www.signal9.com/technical/vpnconfig/configintro.html

http://www.timestep.com/

http://www.tlicworldwide.com/security/contivity.htm

http://www.tlogic.com/

http://www.v-one.com/links.htm

http://www.vpn.com/

http://www.vpnguide.com/

http://www.vpnet.com/

http://www.xedia.com/

http://www.xyplex.com/

RFCs and Drafts

RFC 1701   Generic Routing Encapsulation (GRE)

RFC 1702   Generic Routing Encapsulation over IPv4 networks

RFC 2401   Security Architecture for the Internet Protocol.

RFC 2402   IP Authentication Header.

RFC 2403   The Use of HMAC-MD5-96 within ESP and AH.

RFC 2404   The Use of HMAC-SHA-1-96 within ESP and AH.

RFC 2405   The ESP DES-CBC Cipher Algorithm with Explicit IV.

RFC 2406   IP Encapsulating Security Payload (ESP).

RFC 2407   The Internet IP Security Domain of Interpretation for ISAKMP.

RFC 2408   Internet Security Association and Key Management
             Protocol (ISAKMP).

RFC 2409   The Internet Key Exchange (IKE).

RFC 2410   The NULL Encryption Algorithm and Its Use with
             IPSec.

RFC 2411   IP Security Document Roadmap.

RFC 2412   The OAKLEY Key Determination Protocol.

RFC 2451   The ESP CBC-Mode Cipher Algorithms.

Point-to-Point Tunneling Protocol (PPTP): draft-ietf-pppext-pptp-07.txt

Layer 2 Tunneling Protocol (L2TP): draft-ietf-pppext-l2tp-12.txt

Point-to-Point Encryption (MPPE) Protocol: draft-ietf-pppext-mppe-
    02.txt

Deriving MPPE Keys From MS-CHAP V2 Credentials: draft-ietf-pppext-
    mschapv2-keys-02.txt

PPP CHAP Extensions: draft-ietf-pppext-mschap-v2-02.txt

Securing L2TP using IPSec: draft-ietf-pppext-l2tp-security-02.txt

Implementation of L2TP Compulsory Tunneling via RADIUS: draft-ietf-
    radius-tunnel-imp-04.txt

Lightweight Directory Access Protocol (v3): draft-ietf-asid-ldapv3-
    dynamic-07.txt

References

Alderman Ellen, and Carolyn Kennedy. *The Right To Privacy*. New York:
    Knopf Publishing, 1995.

Anonymous. *Maximum Security: A Hacker's Guide to Protecting your
    Internet Site and Network*. Indianapolis: Sams, 1997.

Aslam, Taimur. "A Taxonomy of Security Faults in the Unix Operating
    System." Department of Computer Sciences, Purdue University;
    Coast TR 95-09; 1995.

Atkins, Derek, et al. *Internet Security: Professional Reference*. Indi-
    anapolis: New Riders, 1996.

Back, Adam. "PGP Timeline." [Online]. Available at *http://www.
    dcs.ex.ac.uk/~aba/timeline/*

Baker, Steward A., and Paul R. Hurst. "The Limits of Trust: Cryptography, Governments, and Electronic Commerce." Cambridge, Mass.: Kluwer Law International, 1998.

Balasubramaniyan, Jai, et al. "An Architecture for Intrusion Detection Using Autonomous Agents." Department of Computer Sciences, Purdue University; Coast TR, 98-05; 1998.

Banerjee, S. K. "High Speed Implementation of DES," *Computers & Security.* Nov. 1982, p. 261.

Bayer, D., S. Haber, W. S. Stornetta, "Improving the Efficiency and Reliability of Digital Time-Stamping." In Proceedings of Sequences II: Methods in Communication, Security, and Computer Science, Springer-Verlag, 1993, pp. 329-334.

Bellovin, S. M. "Security Problems in the TCP/IP Protocol Suite." *Computer Communications Review,* 19(2):32-48, April 1989.

Bellovin, S. M. "Using the Domain Name System for System Break-ins." Paper presented at the Fifth USENIX UNIX Security Symposium, 1995, p. 205.

Bellovin, Steven M., and Michael Merritt. "Encrypted Key Exchange: Password-Based Protocols Secure against Dictionary Attacks." Paper presented at the IEEE Computer Society Symposium on Research in Security and Privacy, Oakland, Ca., May 1992, pp. 72-84.

Berstein v. U.S. Dept. of Justice. "EFF Legal Cases." [Online]. Available at *http://www.eff.org/pub/Privacy/ITAR_export/Berstein_Case.*

Beth, T., M. Frisch, and G. Simmons. "Public Key Cryptography: State of the Art and Future Directions." Lecture Notes in *Computer Science,* no. 578, Springer-Verlag, 1992.

Biham, Eli, and Adi Shamir. "Differential Cryptanalysis of DES-like Cryptosystems." *Journal of Cryptology,* 4(1), 1991, pp. 3-72.

Blaze, M. "Protocol Failure in the Escrowed Encryption Standard." White paper, May 31, 1994.

Bodo, Albert. Method for Producing a Digital Signature with the Aid of a Biometric Feature. German Patent, DE 42 43 908 A1, 1994.

Booth, K. S. "Authentication of Signatures Using Public Key Encryption." *Communications of the ACM,* 24(11), Nov. 1981, p. 772.

Bosworth, Bruce. *Codes, Ciphers, and Computers: An Introduction to Information Security.* Rochelle Park, N.J.: Hayden Books, 1990.

Brickell, D., et al. Skipjack Review, Interim Report, *The Skipjack Algorithm,* July 28, 1993.

Bryn, Dole, Steve Lodin, and Eugene Spafford. "Misplaced Trust: Kerberos 4 Session Keys." Paper presented at the Symposium on Network and Distributed Systems Security, IEEE, 1997.

Cheswick, William R. "An Evening with Berferd, in which a Cracker is Lured, Endured, and Studied." Paper presented at the Winter USENIX Conference, San Francisco, 1992.

Cheswick, William R., and Steven M. Bellovin. *Firewalls and Internet Security: Stalking the Wily Hacker.* Reading, Mass.: Addison-Wesley, 1994.

Cisco Systems. "Thirteen High-Tech Leaders Support Alternative Solution to Network Encryption Stalemate." New Releases. [Online]. Available at *http://www.cisco.com/warp/public/146/july98/3.html.*

Comer, Douglas E. *Internetworking with TCP/IP.* Vol. 1, *Principles, Protocols and Architecture,* 3d ed., Englewood Cliffs, N.J.: Prentice-Hall, 1995.

Computer Security Act of 1987. Public Law 100-235 (H.R. 145), 101 Stat., 1724-1730.

Coppersmith, D. "Another Birthday Attack." H. C. Williams, ed., Lecture Notes in Computer Science, Vol. 218: Advances in Cryptology, CRYPTO '85.

Coppersmith, Don B., and Stephen M. Matyas. "A Proposed Mode for Triple-DES Encryption." *IBM Journal of Research and Development,* 40(2), March 1996, pp. 253-262.

Cray, Andrew. "Encryption: Can the U.S. Government Really Plug the Security Leaks on Global Networks?" [Online]. Available at *http://www.data.com/roundups/encrypt.html.*

Denning, D. E., and G. M. Sacco. "Timestamps in Key Distribution Protocols." *Communications of the ACM,* 24(8), August 1981, p. 533.

Denning, Dorothy E. "An Intrusion-Detection Model." Paper presented at the 1986 IEEE Symposium on Security and Privacy.

Denning, Dorothy E. *Cryptography and Data Security.* Reading, Mass.: Addison-Wesley, 1983.

Diffie, W. "The First Ten Years of Public-Key Cryptography." Paper presented at the IEEE, 76:560-577, 1998.

Diffie, W., and M. Hellman. "New Directions in Cryptography." *IEEE Transactions on Information Theory,* vol. 22, 1976, p. 664.

EFF Press Release. "EFF Builds DES Cracker that proves that Data Encryption Standard Is Insecure." Electronic Frontier Foundation.

[Online]. Available at *http://www.eff.org/descracker.html*, July 17, 1998.

Farmer, Dan, and Eugene H. Spafford. "The COPS Security Checker System." Paper presented at the USENIX Conference, pp. 165-170, Anaheim, Ca., Summer 1990.

Feldmeier, David C. "A High-Speed Software Implementation of DES." Computer Communication Research Group, Bellcore, June 1989.

Freeh, J. Louis, Director FBI. Hearing before the Senate Judiciary Committee, Washington, D.C., July 9, 1997.

Freeh, J. Louis. "The Impact of Encryption on Public Safety." Hearing before the Permanent Select Committee on Intelligence U.S. House of Representatives, Washington D.C., September 9, 1997.

Friedman, William F. *The Index of Coincidence and Its Applications in Cryptography*. Publication 22, The Riverside Publications, Laguna Hills, Ca.: Aegean Park Press, 1979.

Garfinkel, S., and G. Spafford, *Practical UNIX Security*. Sebastopol, Ca: O'Reilly & Assoc., 1991.

Grant, Gail L. *Understanding Digital Signatures: Establishing Trust Over The Internet and Other Networks*. San Francisco: Commerce Net Press.

Heath, Jim. "How Electronic Encryption Works and How It Will Change Your Business." [Online]. Available at *http://www.iinet.net.au/~heath/crypto.html*.

Hellman, M. "The Mathematics of Public Key Cryptography." *Scientific American,* 1979, p. 130.

Hoffman, Lance J. *Building in Big Brother: The Cryptographic Policy Debate*. New York: Springer-Verlag, 1995.

Hoffman, Lance J., et al. "Cryptography Policy." *Communications of the ACM,* 37, 1994, p. 109.

Hudgins-Bonafield, Christine. "The H-Report, Internet Legal Group Directs New World Order." [Online]. Available at *http://www.nwc.com/705/705/hreportb.html*.

Hudgins-Bonafield, Christine. "Will Spies Hold Your Keys?" [Online]. Available at *http://www.nwc.com/704/704f3main.html*.

Information Research Division. "Encryption: Impact on Law Enforcement." Engineering Research Facility, Quantico, Virginia; March 17, 1998.

Information Technology Outlook 1997. U.S. Department of Commerce.

Infoworld. "Test Center Comparison: Network Intrusion-Detection Solutions." *Infoworld* (1998), no. 20(18), p. 88.

International Traffic in Arms Regulations (ITAR), 22 CFR 120-130.

Kaby, Michael. *The NCSA Guide to Enterprise Security: Protecting Information Assets.* New York: McGraw-Hill, 1996.

Kahn, D. *The Codebreakers.* New York, Macmillan Co., 1967.

Kahn, D. *Kahn on Codes: Secrets of the New Cryptology.* New York: Macmillian Co., 1983.

Kim, Gene H., and E. H. Spafford. "Experiences with Tripwire: Using Integrity Checkers for Intrusion Detection." Paper presented at the Systems Administration, Networking and Security Conference III (SANS); Washington, D.C.; Coast TR 94-03; 1994.

Klein, Daniel V. "Foiling the Cracker: A Survey of, and Improvements to, Password Security." Paper presented at the USENIX UNIX Security Workshop, Portland, Oreg., 1990.

Koblitz, N. "Elliptic Curve Cryptosystems," *Mathematics of Computation,* vol. 48, 1987, p. 203.

Konheim, Alan G. *Cryptography: A Primer.* New York: John Wiley, 1981.

Lakshmivarahan, S. "Algorithms for Public-Key Cryptosystems: Theory and Application." *Advances in Computers,* 1983, p. 145.

Lyons, Frank. "A Network Security Review." *Infosecurity,* 8(2), Mar./Apr. 1997.

Machlis, Sharon. "Signs Point to Looser Encryption Rules." *Computerworld.* vol. 32, no. 13, Mar. 30, 1998.

Massey, J. L. "An Introduction to Contemporary Cryptology." Paper presented at the IEEE, 76(5), May 1998, p. 533.

Matsui, M. "Linear Cryptanalysis of DES Cipher." Paper presented at Eurocrypt '93, 1993.

Matyas, S. M., and C. H. Meyer. "Generation, Distribution, and Installation of Cryptographic Keys." *IBM Systems Journal.* 17(2), 1978, p. 126.

Merkle, R. C. "Protocols for Public Key Cryptosystems." *Secure Communications and Asymmetric Cryptosystems,* by G. J. Simmons. Boulder: Westview Press, 1982, p. 73.

Messmer, Ellen. "Navigating the World of Government Encryption Export Rules." *Network World.* May 18, 1998.

Moore, J. H. "Protocol Failures in Cryptosystems." Paper presented at the IEEE, 76(5), May 1988, p. 594.

Nelson, Mathew. "Network Associates Gets Around Export Laws." *InfoWorld.* vol. 20, no. 13, Mar. 30, p. 58.

Nichols, Randall K. *ISCA Guide to Cryptography.* San Francisco: McGraw-Hill, 1999.

NIST. "Data Encryption Standard (DES)." Federal Information Processing Standards Publication 46-2, Dec. 30, 1993.

Parker, Timothy. *Teach Yourself TCP/IP in 14 Days.* Indianapolis: Sams Publishing.

Price, W., and D. Davies. *Security for Computer Networks.* New York: John Wiley, 1984.

Ptacek, Thomas H., and Timothy N. Newsham. "Insertion, Evasion, and Denial of Service: Eluding Network Intrusion Detection." [Online]. Available at *http://www.secure.com*, 1998.

Rapoza, J. "Sentry CA Cross-Checks Certificates." *PC Week,* April 14, 1997.

Rivest, R. L., A. Shamir, and L. M. Adleman. "A Method for Obtaining Digital Signatures and Public-Key Cryptosystems." *Communications of the ACM.* 21(2): 120-126, Feb. 1978.

Schiller, Jeffrey. "Encryption and Global Commerce." The Encryption Revolution. [Online]. Available at *http://www.nwc.com/704/704f3schiller.html.*

Schneier, Bruce. *Applied Cryptography,* 2d ed., New York: John Wiley, 1993.

Schuba, Christoph L., et al. "Analysis of a Denial of Service Attack on TCP." Paper presented at IEEE Symposium on Security and Privacy; Oakland, Ca.; Coast TR 97-06; May 1997.

Schwartau, W. *Information Warfare.* 2d ed., New York: Thunders Mouth Press, 1997.

Smith, Michael, P. C. Van Oorschot, and M. Willett. "Cryptographic Information Recovery Using Key Recovery." White paper, Key Recovery Alliance, June 17, 1997.

Smith, Richard E. *Internet Cryptography.* New York: Addison-Wesley, 1997.

Spafford, E. H. "The Internet Worm Program: An Analysis." *ACM Computer Communication Review,* 19(1), Jan., pp. 17-57.

Stallings, W. *Network and Internetwork Security: Principles and Practice.* Englewood Cliffs, N.J.: Prentice Hall, 1995.

Stoianov, Alex, Colin Soutar, and Al Graham. "High-Speed Fingerprint Verification Using an Optical Correlator." *Proc. SPIE,* vol. 3386, 1998, p. 242.

Tsudik, Gene. "Message Authentication with One-Way Hash Functions." Paper presented at IEEE Infocom, 1992.

U.S. Industry & Trade Outlook. Libraries of the University of Missouri-St. Louis, 1994. [Online]. Available at *gopher://gopher.umsl.edu:70/11/library/govdocs/usio94.*

Vacca, John. *Internet Security Secrets.* New York: IDG Books, 1996.

VanderLugt, A. *Optical Signal Processing.* New York: John Wiley, 1992.

Wiener, M. "Efficient DES Key Search: An Update," *RSA Laboratories Cryptobytes,* Autumn 1997.

William, Murray. "The Encryption Revolution." An interview with Christine Hudgins-Bonafield. [Online]. Available at *http://www.nwc.com/704/704f3murray.html.*

Zimmermann, Phil. Testimony of Philip R. Zimmermann to the Subcommittee on Science, Technology and Space of the U.S. Senate on Commerce, Science and Transportation, June 26, 1996.

GLOSSARY

A

access control   A property used in authentication systems that ensures that individuals with certain rights can only perform operations based on those rights.

active attack   An attack where an attacker must modify or create some new information.

Address Resolution Protocol (ARP)   A protocol used in TCP/IP to determine the 48-bit hardware MAC address given a particular 32-bit IP address.

Advanced Encryption Standard (AES)   An encryption algorithm yet to be decided that will be used to replace the aging DES encryption algorithm and that the NIST hopes will last for the next 20 to 30 years.

aggressive mode   This is the first phase of the Oakley protocol in establishing a security association using three data packets.

anti-replay protection   A process where a system can identify already authenticated packets arriving again in the same communication session.

Asymmetric Key Cryptography System   See *public-key cryptography*.

authentication   The process of positively identifying the entity requiring access. This authentication is usually done by the means of a cryptographic function.

Authentication Header (AH)   One of IPSec standards that allows for data integrity of data packets.

Authentication Key Exchange Protocol (AKEP)   A key transport protocol for symmetric encryption systems where a secret key could be shared.

automatic rekeying   An automated key exchange where keys are updated without user intervention.

Automotive Network Exchange (ANX)   The forerunner of today's IPSec standard.

B

bastion host An area on an untrusted network where a machine or set of machines offer services to the public community.

biometric Biometric authentication is the process of using human characteristics to identify an individual, for instance, fingerprint or retina scan.

birthday attack A form of attack where it is easier to guess pairs of ciphertexts and their corresponding plaintext, than rather one at a time.

blink signature The process of signing a document without knowing its content.

block Usually referred to as a group of bits on which a cipher operates—for instance, 40-, 64-, 128-, 512-, and 1024-bit blocks.

block cipher A cryptographic algorithm that performs the encryption process on blocks of data at a time.

blowfish A cipher developed by Bruce Schneier that uses a 64-bit block cipher with a variable-length key size. Blowfish is found in many freeware encryption products.

BRI Basic Rate Interface to ISDN that allows remote users to connect to the Internet at up to 128 KBPS.

brute-force attack A type of attack on a cryptosystem where all the possible keys are tried.

bucket brigade Also known as the man-in-the-middle attack.

bypass attack An attack where the attacker takes advantage of a weakness in cryptographic systems where plaintext is allowed to leak out.

C

Capstone A U.S. government project for the development of a set of standards for public-key cryptography. Capstone recommends Skip-Jack, which was used in the Clipper Chip key-recovery algorithm.

certificate A digital document that is signed by a certificate authority and attached to a message sent by an individual. The certificate assures the receiver that the sender is indeed who they claim to be.

certificate authority A trusted third party that vouches for the identity of a user and their public key.

Certificate Revocation List (CRL) A list that contain the names and permissions of individuals or machines whose certificates are no longer valid.

chaining A cipher block with feedback; a method of encrypting the already-produced encryption again.

Challenge Handshake Authentication Protocol (CHAP) CHAP uses a one-way hashing function to provide for the authentication of users; some PPTP implementations use CHAP.

challenge response An authentication mechanism where the user is challenged for a value after the user attempts to gain access.

cipher block chaining (CBC) A cryptographic process of combining past block of cipher texts with future blocks of plain text.

ciphertext Text that has undergone the encryption process.

clear text Human readable characters; also called plaintext.

Clipper Chip A hardware-protected chip that contained the Skipjack algorithm and key-recovery feature.

compression The process of making a packet smaller than the original size. Data compression is useful in the IPSec standard, where in the tunneling mode, the packet size is made larger by the encryption and authentication protocols.

compulsory tunnel VPN tunnels created between the ISP's FEP (PPTP) or LAC (L2TP) to servers on the corporation's boundary; no client software is needed.

confidentiality The process that assures that no one coming across the encryption stream of data can read that data.

CRAB A block hashing cipher, similar to MD5, that operates on a 1024-byte block.

Cross-Certification Public-Key Infrastructure (PKIX) A process where a certificate authority certifies the signing of another certificate authority; used in chaining certificates authorities.

cryptanalysis The science of converting a cipher text back into its original plain text without the use of the encrypting key.

CRYPTOKI (Pronounced "crypto-key"); A cryptographic token interface standard that is technology-independent; used with devices such as smart cards and PCMCIA cards. See also *public-key cryptography* (PKCS #11).

cryptoperiod The amount of data encrypted with a certain key.

cryptography   The science of encryption and decryption.

cryptosystem   The hardware and software that allows for the encryption/decryption process.

D

Data Encryption Standard (DES)   The Data Encryption Standard developed by IBM in 1977 is a 64-bit block encryption block cipher using a 56-bit key.

data integrity   The process of ensuring the data has not been modified in transit.

data key   The encryption key that is used only for data encryption.

decryption   The process of reversing the encryption process, making nonreadable text into readable text.

dictionary attack   A brute-force type of attack using very common words.

Diffie-Hellman (DH)   A public-key algorithm developed by Diffie and Hellman in 1976. It allows for the transfer of secret keys over an insecure medium, such as the Internet.

digital cash   A means of electronic payment used in electronic commerce.

digital certificate   An electronic certificate that identifies a user to a public cryptographic key.

digital signature   A digital signature is equivalent to a handwritten signature, where a user signs his or her public key with a hash value to ensure nonrepudiation.

Digital Signature Algorithm (DSA)   An algorithm based upon the El Gamal algorithm; being pushed by the NIST as the next digital signature standard.

Digital Signature Standard (DSS)   A federal standard digital signature mechanism adopted by the National Institute of Standards and Technology for authenticating electronic documents.

Domain Name System (DNS)   The Internet standard protocol for mapping between names and IP addresses.

Domain of Interpretation   An IPSec term that applies to a set of protocols and parameters that is used for the negotiation of a security association.

E

Electronic Data Interchange (EDI)   A mechanism that ensures the safety and security of shipping documents between end parties. Usually used in business for transferring such things as invoices, shipping notices, and bills electronically.

elliptic curve cryptography   A way to provide for public-key encryption by using the points on an elliptical curve.

El Gamal cryptosystem   A cryptosystem used for digital signatures and encryption.

Encapsulating Security Payload (ESP)   One of the IPSec standards that provides for the confidentiality of data packets.

encapsulation   The process of placing a datagram inside the data packet of another network data packet; can be used with the same or different protocols.

encryption   The process of taking some readable text and converting into non-readable formats by means of a cryptographic function.

end-to-end encryption   A technique for using host-to-host end encryption where the data is completely encrypted on the entire network path; PPTP can be used in end-to-end encryption.

entropy   A mathematical measurement that measures the amount of randomness.

export laws   The U.S. government's laws on exportation of cryptographic systems.

extranet   An Internet server that is used by external customers, suppliers, and so forth.

F

FEAL   A Japan-developed cryptosystem, with a 64-bit block cipher and a 64-bit key.

Federal Information Protection Standard (FIPS 140)   FIPS 140 is a government standard for key recovery that is implemented in hardware. Financial institutions, banks, and the U.S. federal government use FIPS 140.

firewall   A machine connecting the perimeter of a company's trusted network to an untrusted network. It provides protection from attacks using port-filtering, address translation, and stateful inspection technologies, and can perform proxying for internal requests.

Fortezza   A PCMCIA card used in the Capstone project.

frequency (frequency distribution)   When applied to cryptography, a count of the same patterns throughout a plain or cipher text.

G

general solution   A solution on a cryptosystem that is dependent on the weaknesses of that cryptosystem.

Government Access to Keys (GAK)   A procedure where the government has access to individuals keys.

H

hash value   A unique set of digits produced by a given input data stream; if the receiver computes a different hash value on the same input steam, the receiver knows the data has been tampered with.

hardware encryption   The encryption process is done by hardware only.

hardware token   See *token.*

hijacking   An attack where an attacker takes over an already-established connection.

HMAC-MD5   A cryptographic hash function using MD5 that operates on 64-byte blocks, outputs a 128-bit authentication value (hash value), and uses a shared secret key.

HMAC-SHA-1   A cryptographic hash function using SHA-1 that operates on 64-byte blocks, outputs a 160-bit authentication value (hash value), and uses a shared secret key.

Hypertext Transfer Protocol (HTTP)   The protocol used between a Web browser and Web servers; used to access Web pages.

I

ICMP   Internet Control Message Protocol; used for monitoring and diagnostics in a network.

Index of Coincidence (IC) The IC is a ratio of observed number of coincidences in a body of text to the number of coincidences expected, also known as *kappa*.

initialization vector (IV) A string that is used in cryptographic operations; its purpose is to ensure that no two identical plaintext messages have the same ciphertext outputs when encrypted with the same key.

International Data Encryption Algorithm (IDEA) A cryptographic function using a 128-bit key for encryption; used in the popular PGP package.

Internet Assigned Number Authority (IANA) The agency responsible for assigning Internet IP addresses, protocol numbers, and TCP/UDP port numbers.

Internet Engineering Task Force (IETF) An organization that uses working groups and that develops new technologies and standards for the Internet.

Internet Key Exchange (IKE) The key-management protocol used with IPSec; currently defined as ISAKMP.

Internet Network Information Center (InterNIC) Private companies, with the permission of the National Science Foundation (NSF), assign second-level domain names.

Internet Protocol (IP) Internet Protocol is the standard protocol for sending data over the Internet.

Internet service provider (ISP) A commercial company that provides Internet access.

interoperability The mechanism where different systems can communicate effectively with one another.

intranet A server or set of servers connected inside a company's network.

intrusion Access to a resource against a company's established security policy that attempts to compromise the integrity, confidentiality, or availability of that resource.

Intrusion Detection System (IDS) A system that is designed to detect the abnormal use of a computer system or network. Two common approaches are by using statistical data or by a ruled-based inferential engine.

IPSec The Internet security protocol that specifies a network layer model of encryption and authentication of IP data packets. The standard includes the Authentication Header (AH) and the Encapsulated

Security Payload (ESP) for authentication and confidentiality of TCP/IP packets.

ISAKMP   Usually referred to as the Internet Security Association and Key Management Protocol. It provides the framework for key management and is currently defined as the key management protocol for IPSec.

ISDN   Integrated Service Digital Network. An international communications standard and network that has evolved from existing telephone services.

International Traffic in Arms Regulations (ITAR)   A governing body that sets policy for munitions.

J

jitter   A distortion of a signal as it passes through a medium or network where it loses its original reference timing.

K

Kappa   See *Index of Coincidence (IC)*.

Kerberos   A trusted third-party authentication process developed at MIT.

key   A string of digits that is used in a cryptographic function to produce ciphertext.

Key Distribution Centers (KDC)   A third party where secrets are stored for use by other parties.

key encrypting key   An encryption key that is used to encrypt session and data keys, not the actual data itself.

key escrow   The process of depositing the decryption key with a third party.

key exchange   The process of two parties exchanging the session key.

key length   The number of bits in a cryptographic key.

key management   The process of generation, transport, and revocation of public keys.

key recovery   The process of obtaining a decryption key to convert a ciphertext stream into its plaintext counterpart, pushed for by governmental agencies.

Knapsack Algorithm Generally believed to be the first public-key encryption algorithm.

L

LAN-to-LAN tunnel Used in VPN terminology, defines a set of communications endpoints that are engaged in passing encrypted data between each other.

latency The time that lapses between the actual request and the time the response is received. Latency is a stumbling block in VPNs.

Layer 2 Forwarding (L2F) A protocol developed by Cisco Systems that provides for tunneling of high-level protocols, such as IPX, IP, and SNA, into IP packets and provides a means for protecting those IP datagrams by encryption; used in Virtual Private Networks.

Layer 2 Tunneling Protocol (L2TP) A combination of the Point-to-Point and Layer 2 Protocols that permits tunneling of high-level protocols such as IPX, IP, and SNA and provides encryption to those data streams, used in Virtual Private Networks.

leased lines A point-to-point communications line that is set up between two end points.

Lightweight Directory Access Protocol (LDAP) An Internet standard defining the protocol for accessing online directory services defined as X.500 over the TCP/IP protocol suite.

Lucifer An IBM-developed private-key encryption system.

M

main mode This is another first phase of the Oakley protocol in establishing a security association, but instead of using three packets like in aggressive mode, it uses six packets.

Management Information Base (MIB) A database that is accessed by a network management protocol, such as SNMP, to query or set objects on the device.

Man-in-the-middle attack An attack where an attacker substitutes his or her own public key for the key requested; also known as the bucket brigade attack.

masquerade A technique that attackers use where they take the identity of another individual.

MD4, MD5   MD4 and MD5 are common message digest algorithms that produce a 128-bit message digest from an arbitrary length input, developed by Ron Rivest.

Message Authentication Code (MAC)   A key-dependent one-way hash function, used by a receiver key to identify the hash value.

message digest   An output of data (hash value) that is derived by using a cryptographic algorithm on a set of input data. Common hash functions are MD2, MD4, MD5, and SHA-1.

mode   Ways to apply a block cipher to a data stream; available modes are CBC, CFB and OFB.

modulus arithmetic   Used in public-key cryptosystems, modulus arithmetic uses operations in which the result is the remainder of the division.

multipoint tunneling   A tunnel created in VPN technology that allows for multiple sessions inside the tunnel.

munitions   Any item that is useful in wars; regulated by governments.

N

National Institute of Standards and Technology (NIST)   A U.S. government agency that establishes standards.

National Science Foundation (NSF)   A U.S. agency that sponsors scientific research.

National Security Agency (NSA)   A U.S. agency responsible for international intelligence gathering.

NetBEUI   An extended user interface with an enhanced version of NetBIOS.

network access point (NAP)   One of the main Internet backbone points where ISPs transfer data between networks.

network address translation (NAT)   The process of converting one IP address space into another IP address space; available NATs are one-to-one, many-to-many, and many-to-one.

Network Basic Input/Output (NetBios)   A network protocol commonly used in PC LANs providing session and transport layer services.

network encryption   A term applied to encryption that is above the data-link layer but below the application layer.

nonce   A random value sometimes sent between communicating parties to detect replay attacks.

nonrepudiation   The process of positively identifying senders, ensuring that they cannot later deny they sent the message used in an electronic transmission.

O

Oakley   The Oakley Key Determination Protocol provides a way to establish session keys on Internet hosts; also uses a hybrid Diffie-Hellman technique to provide for perfect forward secrecy; currently the standard used with the IPSec ISAKMP protocol.

one-time pad   A Vernam cipher process where keys are generated from a random seed value and only used once in a data stream.

one-way hash functions   A cryptographic function that takes an arbitrary length of data and converts it into a fixed length of data called a message digest. A one-way is a hash function that cannot be done in reverse to reveal the plaintext contents.

output feedback mode   A block cipher mode where the cipher is used to generate the key stream.

P

packet assembler/disassembler (PAD)   A device that assembles and disassembles character strings into blocks of data for transport and then disassembles them at the receiving end.

packet-based network   A network that divides the data stream into small blocks of data.

passive attack   An attack where the data is read but not modified.

password, passcode   Basic security measures for providing user authentication; either the user uses a common one-word password or uses some combination of separate words as a passcode.

Password Authentication Protocol (PAP)   An authentication protocol that uses clear-text passwords and a two-way handshake.

perfect forward secrecy (PFS)   A cryptographic mechanism, where the compromise of a key will only reveal that data stream.

permanent virtual circuit (PVC)   A virtual connection set up between two end points that is established and left up permanently.

personal identification number (PIN)   A unique number assigned to an individual to allow access to machines and network services.

plaintext   See *cleartext*.

Point-of-Presence (POP)   A facility that is located on an ISP's premise that provides for Internet accesses.

Point-to-Point Protocol (PPP)   A protocol that allows for the establishment of the TCP/IP protocol over serial dial-up telephones lines and dedicated lines like ISDN.

Point-to-Point Tunneling Protocol (PPTP)   A protocol developed by Microsoft and others that is a framework for providing encryption of data packets over a network; used in Virtual Private Networks.

Pretty Good Privacy (PGP)   A program developed by Phillip Zimmermann that allows the encryption of documents and email, and allows for the use of digital signatures using RSA and IDEA.

Primary Rate Interface (PRI)   An ISDN service consisting of twenty-three 64 Kbps B channels and one 64 Kbps D channel.

private key   One of two keys that are used in an asymmetric or public-key cryptography system. It is used by the receiver to decrypt a message encrypted with the receiver's public key. Both keys are mathematically related. The public key is well known, the private key is only held by the receiver.

private-key cryptosystem   A cryptographic system that uses a single key for encryption and decryption. Also called a *symmetric cryptosystem*.

proxy server   A machine that caches previously requested items to increase future access speed; can also be used as a firewall with packet filtering and store and forward capabilities.

pseudorandom number generator (PRNG)   A device, either software or hardware, that will attempt to generate a totally random sequence of numbers.

public key   One of two keys that are used in an asymmetric or public-key cryptography system. It is used by the sender to encrypt a file for the destination (receiver). The receiver then decrypts the message with his or her private key. The public key is widely available, and it is mathematically related to the private key.

public-key cryptography   Defines the mechanism for encrypting and signing data using RSA (PKCS #1); defines the process for a Diffie-

Hellman key-exchange protocol (PKCS #3); defines the process of using a secret key derived from a password to encrypt a message (PKCS #5); defines a programming interface (Cryptoki) that is technology-independent and used for such things as smart cards (PKCS #11); defines the mechanism for encryption and signing of data using the elliptic curve cryptosystem (PKCS #13).

public-key cryptosystem   A cryptographic system that uses two keys: a public key and a private key. The public key is used for encryption; the private key is used for decryption. Used for key exchange and digital signatures. Also called an *asymmetric cryptosystem*.

public-key infrastructure   A distributed network of computers and users that are used to verify the identity of an individual with the use of public keys.

Q

Quality of Service (QoS)   A set of parameters that define the how the attributes of a particular network circuit will be.

Quick Mode   In Oakley, the process that is used after the initial security association has been set up for detailing how future communications will occur, e.g., how the session keys will be exchanged.

R

RADIUS   Remote Authentication Dial In User Service; a protocol for the management and authentication of remote users. It is a defined standard in the Internet Engineering Task Force.

random number   A number whose value cannot be predicted; randomness is often produced in nature.

RC2   A variable-key-size block cipher with a block size of 64 bits.

RC4   A variable-key-size stream cipher with byte-oriented operations.

Remote Reservation Protocol (RSVP)   A protocol that was defined that allowed routers to offer quality of service between endpoints.

replay   An attack where a user attempts to use an already-authenticated packet.

RSA   A public-key cryptosystem for encryption and authentication; developed in 1977 by Ron Rivest, Adi Shamir, and Leonard Adleman.

S

salt   A string that is added to a password prior to being operated on by a hashing function; used to protect against dictionary attacks.

Secure and Fast Encryption Routine (SAFER)   A block cipher (64bits), developed by Massey and freely available.

Secure Electronic Payment Protocol (SEPP)   A protocol that specifies band transactions.

Secure Electronic Transmission (SET)   A protocol that specifies the safe exchange of credit card numbers over the Internet.

Secure Hypertext Transfer Protocol (SHTTP)   Designed as an alternative to SSL, it provides for security in Web transactions.

secure messaging   Various protocols, e.g., S/MIME, PGP, and MIME, that enable two parties to exchange messages, emails, etc. between each other.

Secure/Multipurpose Internet Mail Extensions (S/MIME)   A protocol that adds encryption to Internet mail, along with the availability of digital signatures.

Security and Freedom through Encryption (SAFE)   A congressional act to ease export controls.

Security Parameter Index (SPI)   An unstructured index, used with the destination IP address to identify a particular security association.

Secure Sockets Layer (SSL)   Netscape's open standard for providing encryption and authentication services to upper-layer applications, such as HTTP, FTP, and Telnet, using the RSA public-key encryption algorithm.

Secure Sockets Layer LDAP (LDAPS)   This is a secure LDAP (Lightweight Directory Access Protocol) that is implemented over SSL; used for authentication of servers.

security association   A unique communication setting used in IPSec that two end points use to define what parameters they are going to use, e.g., encryption protocols and authentication protocols.

security association bundle (SA bundle)   A sequence of SAs.

security policy   A set of guidelines and policies that define the company's security specifications; it defines what you are trying to protect and what access is allowed.

seed A value often used to generate passwords, or used with a PRNG (pseudorandom number generator) as inputs to generate random numbers.

Secure Transaction Technology (STT) A secure payment protocol developed by Microsoft.

Serial Line Internet Protocol (SLIP) A protocol for using the TCP/IP protocol over an asynchronous serial line.

service level agreement (SLA) A contract between a customer and ISP that offers a level of network performance characteristics, and usually offers some redemption of premium to the customer if the ISP fails to live up to those characteristics.

session encryption A particular instance of communications where data is passed back and forth between two parties and encrypted with a session key that is changed the next time data is passed between the two hosts.

session key The particular cryptographic key that is used in session encryption.

SHA-1 The Secure Hash Algorithm-1. A message-digest hash algorithm that takes a message less than 264 bits and produces a 160-bit digest.

shim A software stack that is loaded between layers of the OSI stack; VPNs make use of shims between the data-link and network layers.

Simple Key Interchange Protocol (SKIP) A public-key management scheme developed by Sun Microsystems for the exchange of cryptographic keys; SKIP is a standard that IPSec supports.

Simple Mail Transfer Protocol (SMTP) Protocol used on the Internet for transferring email between clients and servers.

Simple Network Management Protocol (SNMP) Protocol used to manage network devices from a central monitoring station.

Simple Network Management Protocol Trap (SNMP Trap) An alert message sent from a managed network device to a management server when certain exceptions occur, e.g., restart, shutdown, failed login attempts.

smart card A hardware-based authentication mechanism, consisting of a small credit card sized device which contains a microprocessor chip and algorithm.

SOCKS An Internet-based standard that defines a protocol that runs at the TCP layer and provides for the confidentiality of applications, such as Web browsers.

software encryption   Encryption that is accomplished in software.

Software Optimized Encryption Algorithm (SEAL)   Stream cipher that works on 32-bit machines.

software token   See *token.*

splitting   A process whereby the cryptographic key is split into two halves, so if attackers intercept one key, they cannot intercept the ciphertext.

spoofing   A process where senders forge their original data to make it appear as if the packet were coming from somewhere else; also called address spoofing.

stream cipher   A cipher that operates on a continuous stream of data, instead of blocks of data as in block ciphers.

store-and-forward   Services that receive data from one server, store this data and eventually forward this data to another server or service.

symmetric key cryptography system   See *private-key cryptosystem.*

T

TCP/IP   Transmission Control Protocol/Internet Protocol; a data communication network protocol that provides for reliable delivery of data packets; the Internet is based on TCP/IP.

Terminal Access Controller Access Control System (TACACS)   An authentication system used in the client-server model for remotely administering user access.

three-factor authentication   The process of identifying a user by the use of three items, usually a personal identification code, a token, and a personal aspect of the user, such as a fingerprint.

timestamping   A process that binds a document to its creation or last modification time. It is used to stop a timestamp attack, where an attacker backdates an invalid certificate to a time when it was valid.

token   A hardware- or software-based device that produces a periodic value, usually six to eight numbers, that is often used for user authentication.

topology   The arrangement of network nodes and media within an enterprise.

transport mode   In IPSec, transport mode used in either AH or ESP modes; leaves the original IP header in tact.

Triple-DES (3DES)   The DES function, performed three times with either two or three cryptographic keys.

Trojan Horse   A program that has a hidden purpose, that compromises system integrity.

trusted third party (TTP)   A third party who is used by other parties for verification services.

tunnel mode   In IPSec, tunnel mode used in either AH or ESP modes; encrypts the whole IP packet with a new IP packet.

tunneling   A process where a logical connection is created between two end points. Tunnels are usually described in Virtual Private Networks, where two end points are communicating via encapsulation of various protocols.

two-factor authentication   The process of identifying a user by the use of two items, usually a personal identification code and a token.

U

UDP   User Datagram Protocol; a connectionless transport protocol that runs on top of the IP protocol; it provides for fast but sometimes unreliable delivery of data packets.

V

Vernam cipher   A cipher that was used on teletype traffic.

Virtual Private Network (VPN)   A method of communicating securely between parties.

virus   A small program attached to a legitimate program; when the legitimate program is run, the virus invades the system.

voluntary tunnel   VPN tunnels created between clients on the Internet to servers on the corporation's boundary; client software is needed.

W

wide area network (WAN)   A network consisting of two or more LANs connected by a communication infrastructure, e.g., ATM, Frame, ISDN, etc.

World Wide Web (WWW)   An Internet service that enables a browser to view various data via the HTTP protocol.

worm   An Internet attack that keeps copying itself across computer systems and affected thousands of computer systems in 1998.

wrapper agents   Software programs that act like front ends to legacy systems. They are used in the PKI infrastructure to provide certificates, session encryption, digital signatures, etc.

X

X.25   A protocol that specifies packet switching.

X.400   A protocol that specifies email services.

X.500   Protocol standard that defines a distributed global directory, offering decentralized management, single namespace, and structured naming conventions.

X.509   A standard that defines the format for public-key certificates and certificates revocation lists; currently X.509v3 is the working standard.

XOR   A Boolean operation (exclusive-OR) used in many cryptographic systems.

Z

zeroing   A safety procedure used in cryptographic systems in which the memory contents where the key is located is erased.

INDEX

About the Author

Steven Brown is a prominent knowledgeable professional in the field of Virtual Private Networks, firewalls, and Internet security. He currently works with Cable & Wireless USA, in Research Triangle Park, NC, as part of Cable & Wireless's Internet Security Team. Prior to his engagement with C&W, Mr. Brown has had over 18 years in the client-server networking arena and has worked on well over a thousand networks, ranging from banks and brokerage house trading room computer systems on New York City's Wall Street, to universities, businesses, governmental and international projects. His extensive experience has allowed him to assist in the design of a sensitive governmental computer system which was designed to manage in excess of 400,000 nodes, and on an international telecommunications cellular phone system for Germany.

Thus far in his technical career, Mr. Brown has obtained a Certified Novell Engineer (CNE) status, a Certified Sun Microsystems Engineer (CSA), a Certified Checkpoint Systems Administrator (CCSA), and a Certified Checkpoint Systems Engineer (CCSE).

Mr. Brown has also held many supervisory roles in the forms of technical director, project manager, technical lead, pre/post sales, technical consultant, etc., and is the author of "Web-Based Network Monitoring, A Free Add-On to HP-Openview," Sys-Admin, September 1997, and is listed in the *International Who's Who of Information Technology* and the *Lexicon Who's Who*.

In addition to his extensive technical abilities, Mr. Brown is also an academic and enjoys teaching. He holds a Bachelor's of Electrical Engineering (B.S.E.E.) from City University of New York, a Master's of Business Administration (M.B.A.) from Pace University, and is currently nearing the completion of his Doctorate in Business Administration from Nova Southeastern University, where his main interests are in information technology diffusion studies and the diffusion of the Internet on marketing theories.

Steven lives with his wife, Dina Ann in Moncure, NC, and can be reached at *ids@vnet.net, ids@pobox.com*, and at *itdiffusions.com, http://users.vnet.net/ids*.